CONSUMING MODERNITY

•
•
•

EDITED BY
CHERYL KRASNICK WARSH
AND DAN MALLECK

Consuming Modernity :

Gendered Behaviour and Consumerism before the Baby Boom

UBCPress · Vancouver · Toronto

Library and Archives Canada Cataloguing in Publication

Consuming modernity : gendered behaviour and consumerism before the baby boom / edited by Cheryl Krasnick Warsh and Dan Malleck.

Includes bibliographical references and index.
Issued also in electronic formats.
ISBN 978-0-7748-2468-2

1. Consumption (Economics) – Sex differences – History – 20th century. 2. Consumption (Economics) – Political aspects – History – 20th century. 3. Consumption (Economics) – Political aspects – Canada – History – 20th century. 4. Consumer behavior – Sex differences – History – 20th century. 5. Women consumers – History – 20th century. 6. Women in advertising – History – 20th century. I. Warsh, Cheryl Lynn Krasnick II. Malleck, Dan

HC79.C6C65 2013   306.309'041   C2012-906979-5

Canadä

UBC Press gratefully acknowledges the financial support for our publishing program of the Government of Canada (through the Canada Book Fund), the Canada Council for the Arts, and the British Columbia Arts Council.

This book has been published with the help of a grant from the Canadian Federation for the Humanities and Social Sciences, through the Awards to Scholarly Publications Program, using funds provided by the Social Sciences and Humanities Research Council of Canada.

Printed and bound in Canada by Friesens
Set in COM4 Fine, Castle and Minion by Artegraphica Design Co. Ltd.
Copy editor: Deborah Kerr
Proofreader: Lana Okerlund

UBC Press
The University of British Columbia
2029 West Mall
Vancouver, BC V6T 1Z2
www.ubcpress.ca

Contents

•

•

•

Figures and Table

•
•
•

Figures

Table

CONSUMING MODERNITY

·
·
·

Introduction: Consuming Modernity

Dan Malleck and Cheryl Krasnick Warsh •

Between 1919 and 1945, residents of Western countries faced tremendous cultural, social, economic, and political change. The economic expansion of the post-war period was combined with new techniques in advertising, and a concomitant growth of a new culture of consumption, which had begun well before 1914, gained speed in the 1920s and then faced significant modification during the Great Depression. Along with this accelerating consumerism, the mobilization of citizenry during the Great War forced a reconsideration of gendered social roles, with the result that, in the interwar period, ideas of womanhood (and manhood) challenged a status quo that was already in flux. The intersection of the changes in gender roles and the growth of mass consumption presented new challenges and opportunities. Images of the New Woman infiltrated and at times drove advertising strategies. Ideas of the importance of the consumer, and the need to nurture both male and female buying habits, expanded the reach and altered the assumptions of advertisers.[1] At the same time, the image of the female body became even more clearly contested terrain.[2] Progressive reformers and everyday people resisted what they saw as a damaging and socially corruptive sexualization of the female form. But to little avail: by the end of this interwar period, it is fair to say that their world had, in the words of W.B. Yeats, "all changed, changed utterly." And (to extend the quotation), in some ways "a terrible beauty was born."

The essays in this collection examine key themes in the intersection of modernity and gender, framed by the expansion of consumer culture in the decades bookmarked by the two world wars. The book itself emerges from a session titled "Between Fantasy and Reality: Changing Gendered Behaviours and Consumerism in North America and Britain, 1920s-1940s" at the American Historical Association Pacific Coast Branch annual meeting, held in 2007 at the University of Hawai'i at Manoa. The editors, as well as the co-chair of the panel, Penny Tinkler of Manchester University, have researched the impact of marketing and regulation on alcohol and tobacco consumption in Canada, the United States, and Great Britain. The interwar years proved pivotal in naturalizing those behaviours across gender and class. Our call for papers for the panel produced an exceptionally varied host of subjects, many of which are presented in this collection.

Although consumption was not new in the twentieth century, and people in every era have probably called themselves "modern," the interwar period was arguably a time of significant social, political, and cultural change. The growth of the professional advertising industry, fuelled by the priorities of expanding market capitalism, harnessed archetypes and stereotypes of idealized consumers to push the agendas of clients.[3] Some of the most common images were gendered, usually female. The modern woman, representing a new independence and non-traditional lifestyle, captured the imagination of both advertising executives and consumers alike. This process was roughly coincidental with the rise of mass consumer culture, with the need for more, new, and technologically advanced products, leading to a changed relationship between the citizen and the capitalist market.[4] Seduced by the images and the possibilities, citizenship was about consumption, and the important role of the consumer her- or himself affected the way in which politicians defined key issues during Depression-era election campaigns. This was not simply something foisted on the people by free-market capitalism. Within this changing market, governments and regulators sought to harness or control the way that citizens consumed for broader nationally significant ends (indeed, the need to "get out there and spend" as a form of nationalistic imperative was reiterated after the 11 September 2001 terrorist attacks and in subsequent economic crises).

This work contributes to a growing literature on the histories of consumption, gender, and ideas of modernity. Consumer culture and gender have been the focus of several important collections, with essays spanning several centuries.[5] Although it is not specifically concerned with consumption, the collection *The Modern Girl around the World* (2008) by the research group of the same name, includes numerous essays that suggest an inevitable intersection of consumerism with gender and modernity in the twentieth century. Covering roughly the same period as this current collection, a special issue of *NWSA Journal* ("Gender and Modernism between the Wars, 1918-1939") presents essays that consider the literary representations of gender in several countries and diverse political contexts between the two world wars. Here the emphasis is on presentation and re-presentation of gender in often tumultuous and transformative political situations, resulting in shifting discourses and revised self-identities.[6] The "sense of the self" has become intricately intertwined with consumerism, and the power of consumerism to define self-identity has been explored in detail by Gary Cross. Though not focusing specifically on gendered identities, Cross illustrates how modern capitalism materially and discursively restructured the individual's sense of self-worth. Demonstrating that modernity did not lead to more leisure, he shows that consumer culture emerged from a prioritization of consumption of goods, rather than from "wasting" time with leisure.[7] As Jennifer Scanlon notes in her introduction to *The Gender and Consumer Culture Reader,* researchers have viewed consumer culture from the perspective that it represented the "insidious victimization" of individuals but have also claimed that consumer culture "can be liberating."[8] In the examinations of gender and modernity, and consumerism and modernity, this rearrangement of identities in the expansion of consumer culture is a central concern.

We can learn much from studies that look beyond the traditional Anglo-American nexus. *Consuming Modernity* is the first collection to combine a Canadian focus with an international perspective that illuminates the similarities as well as differences of early twentieth-century modernization across continents, languages, and political structures. Except for Chapter 1, all of the chapters focus on consumerism and gender. That exception (Bettina Liverant's study of the mid-Depression federal election) looks at the centrality of consumerism in the rhetoric of national politics, underlying how consumerism had become such a dominant discourse, shaping identities and justifying actions, in modern society. In many ways, the exceptions to some of the dominant patterns help us prove the rule. So, the multinational narratives and analyses presented by essays from countries outside Britain, Canada, and the United States provide some valuable contrasts, allowing us to see how the lure of "Western" culture was consumed, rejected, or modulated to fit national and/or cultural contexts. After all, that culture was decidedly white, middle class, and English speaking. Even within Canada, such a cultural behemoth could be complicated by cultural and linguistic differences.

The international perspective also encourages us to reflect on the concept of modernity itself, since it has been used to define various aspects of twentieth-century life. As several authors have noted, some research on "modernity" often end up equating the term with "Western," "developed," or "ahead" (versus "catching up").[9] This perspective contains an inherent hierarchical and ethnocentric bias. This issue becomes more complicated when one begins to look at mass consumer culture, where the notion of a "developed" world stands in stark contrast to the less-, under-, or undeveloped countries in which the economic situation does not facilitate such blatant consumer cultures. Moreover, considering gender in modernity leads in potentially contradictory directions; as Rita Felski observes in *The Gender of Modernity,* modernity may be presented as "a purposefully striving masculinity" or a "fetishized, libidinized and commodified femininity."[10] In her introduction to the *NWSA Journal* special issue on gender and modernism between the wars, Margaret McFadden presents her idea of "the modern" as political – "the modern of socialist politics and Depression economics." Elsewhere she acknowledges that the terms "modern" and "modernity" often change depending on disciplinary traditions.[11] Harvie Ferguson has argued that the best way to understand modernity is to see it as a mindset in which genuine experience replaces experience that is mediated by "extra-empirical reality." In premodern times, then, all experience was given meaning through the interpretation of the church or other elite institution. According to Ferguson, "For the modern world, there is no higher authority than experience."[12]

These definitions of modernity demonstrate the range of meanings for, and the complex nature of, the term. If we assume that "modern" is just a trope for "developed," we could argue that not only is our perspective of modernism ethnocentric, but also that "modern consumer culture" is potentially redundant. Could consumer culture exist in an "undeveloped" society? Similarly, if we apply Ferguson's definition of modernity, consumerism may be considered the quintessential modern activity, since consumption is a real, almost visceral, experience. At the same time, however, given that consumerism is mediated by advertising, which gives meaning to consumption, we could argue that modern consumer culture replaces one form of mediated experience (such as that facilitated by the church, for example) with another (consumerism given meaning by advertising). Due to the wide range of ideas around modernity, the editors of this collection have imposed no restrictions on its meaning apart from the chronological positioning of the chapters themselves. The essays in this collection explore the various "modernities" that consumed and were consumed in the interwar period. Here modernity cannot be distilled to one definition. The "modern" held diverse cultural, economic, and political meanings in each of the contexts under examination.

Although the modern consumer culture examined by all the chapters in this book was harnessed by the capitalist market, we would be mistaken in imagining that the stories of consumerism and modernity are all about capitalism dominating the individual; the influences were multi-directional. Capitalism certainly may be considered the most powerful catalyst of this change, and individuals were drawn to the self- and lifestyle-improving arguments of product advertisements, but a more nuanced consumption was going on. As noted earlier, consumer culture could be liberating. Advertisements themselves were consumed, when the targets of their fantastic promises, such as the characters of Mary Quayle Innis's short stories, consumed the dream, even though they could rarely afford the products. Governments and regulators sought to push back or embrace the expansive appeal of mass culture. Consumerism became intertwined with national identity. In some places, such as Weimar Germany, fears of the consumption of foreign, corrupt culture led citizen regulators to clamp down. In Argentina and Mexico, the consumerist modernity became a fundamental part of national identity. Reconfiguring gender identity and the modern consuming citizen created a multi-faceted gem, or a many-headed beast, however one chose to view it.

The expansion of mass-market capitalism altered the relationship between citizens and consumption, a link that was forged and refined by the art of advertising.[13] Here was an industry that developed – perhaps transmogrified might be a better word – into the art of convincing the individual not only of a need for a product's material utility, but of its importance to the consumer's self-perception. In Chapters 3 and 4, Kristin Hall and Denyse Baillargeon each explore how advertising to women drew on their anxieties as mothers. Lysol Disinfectant would ensure a healthy family; medical advertising more broadly reinscribed gendered discourses of a woman's dependence and simultaneously her responsibility for the health of her family. In Chapter 2, Tracy Penny Light illustrates how medical authority was sought to reiterate this influential discourse, using science to convince women to buy products that would best protect the home.

The power of the consumerist discourse is demonstrated well in the Canadian federal election of 1935, when each political party (some newly formed) sought to assert its interpretation of how best to encourage consumption. As Bettina Liverant illustrates in Chapter 1, politicians argued that the Depression was not a problem of production, but one of consumption. It was up to the political leadership to ignite the will to spend, and the ability to do so. Most economic solutions, then as now, involved convincing citizens to do their patriotic duty: spend money to support national capitalistic enterprise. Liverant's description of the power of consumerism as an economic ideal on which each political party could imprint its own strategic vision, and a discursive reconstruction of what it meant to be a modern citizen, helps to inform the perspectives of other chapters. She shows us that consumerism was not just something pushed on individuals by the private capitalist market; it pervaded many if not all aspects of "modern" life.

In many advertisements and even entire marketing campaigns, the female body became a central discursive trope. The women who were used to sell products were not just traditional mothers or housewives, who might have some influence in the purchasing of the product. Rather, women's bodies became metaphorically consumed by the gaze of the potential purchaser. In Chapter 9, Jane Nicholas demonstrates that advertising allowed for a "re-enchantment" of consumer goods that was reflexive; women looked at images of the idealized woman and scrutinized their non-ideal selves. The power of ads expanded far beyond the market for their products; in Chapter 13, Donica Belisle illustrates how consumerism fuelled fantasies for poor women during the 1920s and 1930s, who dreamt of living the fabulous lifestyles advertised as a way of escaping, however temporarily, the reality of their own lives.

This process of consumption was not simply a paternalistic imposition of male values on women. As several authors demonstrate, women were asserting their new roles and visibility in society, opening themselves up, often willingly, to the new public role. The "modern woman" was perceived as independent, intelligent, and socially active. Characterized in the stereotype of the flapper, with her bobbed hair, short skirts, and androgynous physical form, this modern woman defied social expectations, asserting her independence against traditional roles that would push her back into the home and motherhood. Referring to Marshall Berman's *All That Is Solid Melts into Air*, Rita Felski shows that modernity can be considered a masculine drive and push for expansion, contrasted with a traditionalism and conservatism that is gendered female. Felski discusses how the feminist critique of this characterization of modernity as male "carries with it the seeds of domination ... and ... fear of subjugation."[14] As essays in this collection reveal, modernity combined with consumerism could be liberating to women, who had been repressed by a male-centred traditionalism. Nevertheless, as several critics have shown, and as several authors in this collection also note, the stereotype of the modern woman (or "modern girl") is problematic, bourgeois, and not universal.[15]

The modern woman had her male counterpart – the damaged man – and both stereotypes were seen as threats to traditional society. Whereas the modern woman was newly independent, the damaged man, most often associated with the psychologically compromised returned soldier, represented an equally socially troublesome stereotype. The former was strong, independent, and resilient; she challenged traditional values and norms, and she was unwilling to be shoehorned into the role of wife and mother. The latter was weak, dependent, and broken, unable to fulfill his role as husband and breadwinner.

Unsurprisingly, then, it was the modern woman whose body graced the pages of print advertising across the Western world. She was both consumed and a consumer: living the good life, driving the best car, wearing the best clothes. As an idealized image, manipulated by the increasingly professionalized advertising industry, the modern woman became a type to which actual women had to conform. Female athletes, as both Fiona Skillen and Marilyn Morgan demonstrate in Chapters 6 and 7, were consumed, constrained, and eroticized under the gaze of the market. Thus, the female athlete was adulated as long as she behaved herself; the strong female swimmers, some of whom bested men at their sport, fuelled an expanded swimsuit industry and, ironically, led to the swimsuit phase of beauty pageants. Independence and self-actualization became just two more forms of dependence and submission, as real women found themselves craving that lifestyle. Similarly, Devon Atchison's Chapter 8 study of suntanning, a new fashion statement in the 1920s, explores the expansion of the cosmetic industry, the swimsuit industry, and the consumption of the exposed female form. In the arena of mass-market capitalism, the modern woman's lifestyle was usually unrealizable to most women, but it was not inaccessible. The power of the mass market was its ability to keep these dreams alive, just out of reach, to drive the market forward.

The modern woman was not solely a white Anglo-American construct. In Chapter 5, De Anna J. Reese examines the career of African American entrepreneur Annie Turnbo Malone, for whom consumerism facilitated entrepreneurial success and a redefinition of the "new black woman." As Susanne Eineigel and Cecilia Tossounian show in Chapters 10 and 11, Latin American women also sought to challenge traditional values, and in doing so, they pushed against a monolithic cultural resistance. This opposition, though partly resting in the power of the Catholic Church, was also nationalistic; American movies and culture were perceived as fundamentally corrosive and damaging to the nation. This resistance in non-Anglo-American societies to the corrupt images of mass media is also shown by Kara Ritzheimer, who argues in Chapter 12 that movie censorship in the German city of Heidelberg sought to restrict the types of images and themes that were perceived as violations of decency and as potentially undermining the foundations of stable social life.

Several common themes run throughout this book: the role of advertising in driving the mass market; how the images of women as successful, desirable, and virtuous were increasingly shaped by advertising and mass media; and the evolving role of women as consumers and consumed. Obviously, there remained the contradictions between the expansion of the market, which sold dreams of independence, and the ongoing inability of the financially and socially margin-alized to realize those dreams. This bait and switch, of course, is fundamental to advertising, whose promise of permanent physical or emotional satisfaction is ephemeral and unattainable. Yet its impact, along with that of mass media, has been to provide universally recognized, and constantly changing, parameters to a modernity, or various modernities, that can never be obtained yet need constantly to be consumed.

Notes

1   See Roland Marchand, *Advertising the American Dream: Making Way for Modernity, 1920-1940* (Berkeley: University of California Press, 1986); T.J. Jackson Lears, *Fables of Abundance: A Cultural History of Advertising in America* (New York: Basic Books, 1994).

2   Victoria de Grazia with Ellen Furlough, eds., *The Sex of Things: Gender and Consumption in Historical Perspective* (Berkeley: University of California Press, 1996); Alys Eve Weinbaum et al., eds., *The Modern Girl around the World: Consumption, Modernity, and Globalization* (Durham, NC: Duke University Press, 2008).

3   Marchand, *Advertising the American Dream*; Lears, *Fables of Abundance*; Gary S. Cross, *Time and Money: The Making of Consumer Culture* (New York: Routledge, 1993).

4   Cross, *Time and Money*; Gary S. Cross, *An All-Consuming Century: Why Commercialism Won in Modern America* (New York: Columbia University Press, 2000).

5   De Grazia, *The Sex of Things*; Lawrence Glickman, *Consumer Society in American History: A Reader* (Ithaca: Cornell University Press, 1999); Jennifer Scanlon, ed., *The Gender and Consumer Culture Reader* (New York: New York University Press, 2000); Maggie Andrews and Mary M. Talbot, eds., *All the World and Her Husband: Women in Twentieth-Century Consumer Culture* (London: Cassell, 2000).

6   "Special Issue: Gender and Modernism between the Wars, 1918-1939," *NWSA Journal* 15, 3 (Fall 2003).

7   Cross, *An All-Consuming Century*.

8   Scanlon, "Introduction," in Scanlon, *The Gender and Consumer Culture Reader*, 7.

9   Alys Weinbaum et al., "The Modern Girl as Heuristic Device: Collaboration, Connective Comparison, Multidirectional Citation," in Weinbaum et al., *Modern Girl around the World*, 7-8.

10 Rita Felski, *The Gender of Modernity* (Cambridge, MA: Harvard University Press, 1995), 3, 5.

11 Margaret H. McFadden, "Introduction: Making the Modern," in "Special Issue: Gender and Modernism between the Wars, 1918-1939," *NWSA Journal* 15, 3 (Fall 2003): ix-xiii.

12 Harvie Ferguson, *Modernity and Subjectivity: Body, Soul, Spirit* (Charlottesville: University Press of Virginia, 2000), 2-3. Ferguson's consideration of the meaning of modernity ranges beyond the interwar scope of our collection, but his work is valuable for conceptually situating our studies and informing our understanding of how modernity can be interpreted.

13 For advertising in America, see Marchand, *Advertising the American Dream*; Lears, *Fables of Abundance*; Daniel Delis Hill, *Advertising to the American Woman, 1900-1999* (Columbus: Ohio State University Press, 2002). For Canada, see Russell Johnston, *Selling Themselves: The Emergence of Canadian Advertising* (Toronto: University of Toronto Press, 2001), though this study ends around 1930.

14 Felski, *Gender of Modernity*, 2.

15 An extensive analysis of the meaning of the "modern woman" and the contrast with the "modern girl" can be found in the introduction to Weinbaum et al., *Modern Girl around the World*.

Part 1 CONSUMERISM AS POLITICS, PRACTICE, AND IDEOLOGY

•
•
•

1

Canada's Consumer Election (1935)

Bettina Liverant

Although times of widespread poverty are not conventionally associated with increased consumerism, it was during the Great Depression that the consumer emerged as an identifiable political category in Canada. Adequate consumption by every Canadian – man, woman, and child – was discussed as a marker of democratic citizenship. Politicians appealed to Canadians as consumers in their efforts to win votes, convinced that consumption could mobilize civic engagement. As election day neared, the universal language of rights was augmented by appeals to wives and mothers, who were responsible for stretching the family dollar.

As other chapters in this collection demonstrate, consumption opportunities had expanded rapidly in the decades leading up to the Depression. As spending increased, many social observers regarded middle- and working-class consumers with suspicion, fearful that the temptations of commercialized mass consumption would subvert the morals of the nation.[1] With the arrival of hard times, the politics of consumerism contracted around the necessities of life.[2] The Depression made clear the extent to which ordinary Canadians had come to depend on buying their food, clothing, and shelter.

From a high point in 1929, the economy spiralled rapidly downward. At the depth of the Depression in 1933, 28 percent of the labour force was out of work and one-fifth of the population dependent on government assistance. Worst hit were workers in primary industries, farmers in Western Canada whose misery was compounded by drought, blue-collar workers laid off as factories closed, and young people unable to enter the workforce. Recovery was slow and halting.

In the lead up to the federal election of 1935, the consumer became one of the common reference points in political platforms and voter appeals.

On the surface, the election changed little. After five years in Opposition, the Liberal Party returned to power on the basis of a platform that made few concrete promises. However, the study of party platforms and promises reveals the emergence of consumption and the consumer in Canadian political discourse. Rather than seeing the election as a reaffirmation of the status quo by an anxious populace, we should recognize it as the locus of an extended discussion that assigned a new importance to consumption. Political rhetoric, including frequent statements that the state had a duty to provide Canadians with basic necessities, helped to forge a link between citizenship and consumption.

The Promise of Abundance

R.B. Bennett swept to power in 1930, placing the Conservative Party in office during the early years of the Depression. Canadians knew that some time before 1935, they would again go to the polls.[3] The campaign to influence the outcome began with little fanfare in 1932, when J.S. Woodsworth, a leading figure in Canadian Progressivism, stood in the House of Commons and called for the establishment of a cooperative commonwealth. Introducing his motion, Woodsworth acknowledged that capitalism had "a great many achievements to its credit" and "conceded that under this system the problem of production is very largely solved ... Undoubtedly the general standard of living has been substantially raised."[4] Although our collective memories of the Depression years are haunted by images of extreme poverty, contemporaries perceived the Depression as a crisis, not of scarcity, but of surplus, where the principal challenges were related to the distribution and consumption rather than the production of goods. Woodsworth, like many Progressives, believed that the origins of the Depression lay in the inherent defects of a system that required expanding markets to dispose of surplus products and new investment opportunities for surplus capital. The challenges Canada faced were both moral and economic: excess savings by the wealthy were linked to insufficient spending by working-class Canadians. Now, as Woodsworth explained, having "reached the stage where the great mass of the people do not seem to be in a position to buy back what has been produced," the system had "stalled."[5] Calling for production to be geared to consumption rather than profit, he proposed that Canada become "a co-operative commonwealth in which all natural resources and the socially necessary machinery of production would be used in the interests of the people."[6]

Although the House adjourned without voting on Woodsworth's motion, his vision of a cooperative commonwealth provided the basis for compromise when representatives of the farm and labour parties gathered with supporters in Calgary that summer. The decision to consolidate reform forces under the banner of the Co-operative Commonwealth Federation (CCF) was largely pragmatic, but delegates were committed to changing a system that all agreed was no longer working for ordinary Canadians. The next February (1933), when Woodsworth re-presented his resolution to the House, the formation of a new political party with potentially widespread appeal guaranteed that his motion would attract attention.

Woodsworth's motion was taken up by a succession of CCF speakers and supporters. Consumer themes were prominent in the discussion. Agnes Macphail, representing the United Farmers of Ontario, rose to second the motion: "We have now solved the problem of production but not that of distribution ... In order to distribute goods and services the purchasing power of the masses of the people must be increased ... We must," she insisted, "pass at once from an economy of production to an economy of consumption and we must continue to address ourselves to that problem until the consumption of goods equals the production, and continue even further, until the amount of goods consumed is equal in volume to the amount of goods which all our plant and equipment is capable of producing."[7] Speaking for the Labour Party, Abraham Heaps celebrated the ingenuity of man: "With the advent of the machine in industry our capacity to produce the essentials and even the luxuries of life has reached a capacity undreamt of by our forebears. Productive capacity has increased to such an enormous extent that it is a generally accepted fact that there is practically no limit to it." However, Heaps continued, while this had been taking place, "the question of consumption and distribution has been left to take care of itself ... The greater our production and accumulation of wealth, the more poverty ... do we find in our midst."[8] Former clergyman and social reformer G.C. Coote similarly described Canada as a land of plenty where people lived lives in hunger and anxiety: "We have goods and services of all kinds in abundance ... but the people are not in a position to obtain anything like a sufficient quantity of these things. There is no scarcity of anything ... except a scarcity of money."[9] Long-time Progressive E.J. Garland spoke for all when he stated that "the only problem is to discover how best to consume the wealth of goods which we are so capable of producing."[10] Although some called for changes in the system of taxation and others for new monetary policies to improve the availability of cash and credit, each speaker agreed that increased consumption of goods by ordinary Canadians should be substituted for profit as the goal of the economic system.

With each new voice, a consumerist orientation was being formulated as an alternative to capitalism. The "cornerstone of the co-operative common-wealth," CCF co-founder William Irvine told the House, was laid "on the bed-rock fact of abundance."[11] Calling for a managed economy rather than class warfare, the leaders of Canada's reform movements spoke of the need for greater purchasing power and the right to basic goods and services. The consumer was the representative of all those who were denied access to basic necessities by an economic system that made its profits by restricting production. Increased purchasing power was the starting point for a more equitable distribution of wealth that would enable all Canadians to reach their potential. Expanding consumption opportunities were associated with the moral and social progress of society.

The Liberal Response

The effort to consolidate energies for political reform under the banner of the CCF represented a clear threat to the Opposition Liberal Party, pressuring a reluctant William Lyon Mackenzie King to move beyond generalized expres-sions of social concern and prepare a statement of policies that would define the party's position on major issues.[12] When King addressed the Woodsworth resolution late in February, he agreed with the CCF leader that the "great ques-tion" of the day was "the problem of how masses of people are to live."[13] The Liberal Party, he insisted, shared the CCF's sympathy for humanitarian reform. However, King rejected the call to expand the state, on grounds of both efficacy and liberty. In marked contrast to the CCF, he insisted that the existence of plenty was the direct result of capitalism and the incentives and direction pro-vided by the opportunity for profit: "Fortunately the problem of production in a large measure has been solved under the so-called and much berated capitalist system. To-day there is plenty ... So far as industry is concerned with production that part of the problem presents little in the way of difficulty. That part has already been largely solved."[14]

The system of socialism advocated by the CCF, King argued, would almost certainly reverse the pattern of progress by reducing production. The practical challenges of government management of the economy were insurmountable. As for the Depression, King asserted, far from being the result of the breakdown of the system, the current economic crisis was "man-made" by those who re-fused to share their prosperity.[15] Poverty was a social problem rather than an economic one, requiring a change of heart but not a change in the structure of the economy.[16]

The CCF resolution had been presented to the House in the spring of 1933. Both the Liberals and the CCF prepared campaign materials based on these debates. William Irvine, writing for the CCF, used the opportunity to reassure party members and prospective voters that the principle of socialization applied only to the means of production and to the nation's natural resources. A cooperative commonwealth, he promised, "does not mean taking private property from the people, but adding a great deal more to what they have ... What we really want is to see every individual have more private property ... Our motto might well be stated as 'More private property to all and no public property for any individual.'"[17]

King's address was reprinted with its key points itemized to form an election platform.[18] Whereas the CCF promised government intervention in the service of a consumption-oriented economy, the Liberal Party remained committed to capitalism. The profit motive and the exploitation of natural resources continued to be seen as the best ways to increase the long-term supply of goods and services. The well-being of Canadians, King insisted, would follow from the success of business. Industrialists and consumers shared a mutual interest in abundant consumption: what was good for business was good for the consumer and vice versa. Both the Liberals and the CCF agreed that social justice should be measured by access to goods and services.

Investigating Price Spreads

Early in 1934, an event occurred that would alter the dynamic of Canadian politics heading into the election cycle. When attending a speaking engagement at the behest of the prime minister, the Conservative trade and commerce minister H.H. (Harry) Stevens launched an aggressive and widely publicized attack on big business. Present hardships, Stevens charged, were the result of monopolies of production and distribution that disadvantaged small businessmen, farmers, fishermen, and industrial workers in both their producer and their consumer roles. Drugstores used loss leaders to drive neighbourhood stores out of business. Department stores exploited dressmakers to keep prices low. Describing big business practices as "a canker" threatening the economic life of the nation, Stevens contended that the "unscrupulous and cold-blooded" leaders of industry prospered at the expense of ordinary Canadians.

Some dismissed Stevens's accusations as a "witch hunt," but his remarks received wide publicity nonetheless. In the face of rising public indignation, a parliamentary committee was appointed with a broad mandate to investigate the spread between the prices paid by producers and the prices paid by consumers, and the impact of mass buying on Canadian commerce. The committee, chaired by Stevens, began hearings almost immediately. The public nature of the inquiry ensured ample press coverage. When Parliament was prorogued in July, an Order-in-Council transformed the inquiry into the Royal Commission on Price Spreads and Mass Buying. Political battles waged within the Conservative Party held the public's attention through the summer months, accentuating differences between Stevens (the champion of "inarticulate sufferers") and the interests of big business (embodied by Prime Minister Bennett).[19] Although hearings resumed in October under a new chair, Stevens continued to play a prominent role, and indeed the inquiry was often referred to as the Stevens Commission. Sessions were held regularly until January 1935, when the commission withdrew to prepare a report that was presented to the House in April.[20]

For over a year, Canadians were captivated and scandalized by revelations of corporate practices that kept profits and prices high and wages low. Evidence was published daily in newspapers throughout the country and considered closely by experts writing lengthier articles in serious journals. Although a key public event of the Depression period, the Price Spreads Inquiry seldom considered economic themes. Instead, Stevens's aggressive questioning of witnesses highlighted the ethics of business practices that pitted the large against the small and the organized against the unorganized, giving the Price Spreads Inquiry the tone of a moral crusade. Testimony exposed an intense struggle under way between large corporations and chains that relied on the advantages of size, standardized goods, high turnover, and low prices, and earlier forms of commerce rooted in community, family, and a mutually understood sense of value. Consumers, already struggling to stretch low wages, were shown to be further exploited by misleading advertising and packaging, adulterated goods, inferior substitutes, short-weighted scales, and a host of other deceptions. Confronted on the one hand by fiercely competitive practices that erased profit margins and drove down wages, and on the other by misleading commercial practices that further eroded purchasing power, ordinary Canadians, the testimony revealed, were often unable to afford the goods they helped produce.

The Report of the Royal Commission on Price Spreads and Mass Buying presented to the House in April differed in tone from that of the hearings themselves, arguing that abuses originated in economic realities rather than moral failings. A lengthy introduction explained that modern business methods had concentrated economic power, setting the stage for predatory practices encouraged by extreme

competition in a difficult economy. Exploitation was the inevitable consequence of structural change. Because these changes were unlikely to be corrected
by the "automatic forces" of the marketplace, the report called for the creation
of a Federal Trade and Industry Commission with broad powers to supervise
and regulate industrial and commercial activity. Specific recommendations were
devised with the dual object of assuring small enterprises, workers, and primary
producers a larger return for their labour and protecting consumers and small
investors against profiteering, whether by the sale of inferior goods, the manipulation of markets, or the use of deceptive sales practices.

Whereas the Price Spreads Inquiry had an aspect of public theatre, the report
was prepared by the professional civil service. As such, it presented administrative solutions to technical problems in the name of the common good.[21] A full
chapter was devoted to the consumer, discussed as an economic category with
interests and rights distinct from both labour and business. As the authors
explained, it

> is now a commonplace of economic thought that the significance of the wage-
> earner is not confined to his activities as a producer. Production cannot
> continue without profitable markets; business activity of every sort ceases
> without prosperous buyers. Despite the importance of certain export markets,
> our own workers constitute the biggest market for Canadian products. On the
> stability of their income and purchasing power depend the profits of business
> enterprise. On their standards of living rests the possibility of commercial
> prosperity.[22]

Calling for the creation of an agency mandated to protect consumer rights, the
report proposed to incorporate consumer concerns into the workings of government. The language of exploitation and victimization that had dominated
the hearings gave way to the language of rights. Because shoppers of all genders
and classes were affected by unfair business practices, defending the consumer
interest was a matter of common public interest.

Although the report began to advance a larger vision of the role of consumption in the workings of the Canadian economy, it did not recommend measures
to directly stimulate domestic spending akin to those being proposed by Keynes
in England or in America's New Deal legislation. Despite strong rhetorical support for the role of the consumer, the majority of recommendations were designed to help small producers by restraining competition, standardizing
working conditions, and supporting prices.

Objecting to this pattern of emphasis, three of the four Liberal members on the commission signed the report but added a memorandum of reservations, arguing that problems of marketing methods had been overemphasized while the more basic need for markets had been neglected. Noting a tendency "to think of the various subdivisions of society entirely in the capacity of producers," the Liberal members insisted that consumers were alike in a way that producers were not. It was, they proposed, the consumer who constituted "the main general interest, as distinguished from particular interests."[23] Because lower prices would best serve Canadian consumers, efforts to intensify competition and stimulate trade were preferable to increases in government regulation.

The case for the consumer was made even more strongly in a well-publicized dissenting report submitted by Manitoba Liberal Edward J. Young. Indeed, Young, known for his anti-tariff views, insisted that his protest was motivated solely by the commission's inadequate defence of consumer interests. Young argued that the problem with the Canadian economy was not monopoly and mass buying, but the collapse of commodity prices and the subsequent loss of purchasing power. As for regulation, Young insisted that government intervention would serve only to protect the obsolete. It was up to the consumer, "exercising his right not to buy," to force the readjustment between supply and demand that industry had prevented. It was the consumer, "unorganized and voiceless, the victim of special interests who conspired on every hand to extract more from him," who stood against the organized corporation.[24] Instead of competing to serve, business was holding the consumer hostage. In a vigorous summation, Young declared that

> the only common ground upon which we all stand is as consumers. The only legislation that can be just to all is legislation in the interests of the consumer ... The only interest that is not a class interest is the consumer interest. In seeking the remedy for our economic ills, we should always keep the consumer's interest uppermost in our minds for "the consumer's interest is the interest of the human race."[25]

It should be noted, however, that Young's advocacy of the consumer interest continued to emphasize the need to eliminate tariffs and restore international trade rather than stressing policies to increase domestic spending. The role of the consumer was to regulate supply and demand, not to stimulate growth.

In the course of the Price Spreads Inquiry and particularly in its report, the consumer emerged as a new type of citizen, representative of the entire community, with needs for protection that legitimized government intervention in the economy. Accuracy in packaging and labelling, and standardized weights and measures would provide consumers with the tools required to make rational decisions in the marketplace. With shoppers empowered by information and protected from fraudulent practices, domestic spending would automatically grow.

The Election

For over a year, the mechanics of the modern economy had been under the spotlight, often centre stage in Canadian political life. The sustained impact of the lengthy investigation altered the dynamic of Canadian politics, creating heroes and villains and opening the door to new political parties and tactical opportunities.[26] Both the release of the commission's report, calling for unprecedented levels of government intervention in the economy, and the Liberal dissent on behalf of lower tariffs and the consumer were front-page news. Members of the House left for a summer recess knowing that an election would have to be called before the fall. The misery of the Depression, the rise of the CCF, the questions raised by the Price Spreads Inquiry, and the recommendations set out in its report provided the backdrop for the coming campaign. The lengthy investigation, with exhaustive testimony and numerous special reports, supplied details of business practices, both questionable and routine, for politicians to draw on.

In the months ahead, the consumer would assume an increasingly prominent place in Canadian politics. Every party addressed the Canadian voter as a consumer and pledged to defend consumer interests in the marketplace. The government, all agreed, had a responsibility to protect consumers from fraudulent and misleading commercial practices. Competing to articulate a compelling vision of the consumer interest, politicians began to advance a concept of positive rights, expanding the understanding of political freedom to include the right to an adequate return for one's efforts, with government responsible for providing a basic, although always unspecified, level of material welfare.[27]

There was, however, considerably less consensus around the means by which purchasing power could be increased and the importance of private consumption as a force in the Canadian economy. The campaigns of the CCF and the Social Credit Party hinged on the promise of government intervention but differed dramatically on the role that aggregate consumption might play in the economy. Whereas the CCF emphasized the public provisioning of many goods and services, the Social Credit Party favoured individual consumers making choices in the market. The Reconstruction Party recognized the appeal of increased consumption as part of its commitment to national renewal but continued to privilege the need for jobs and opportunity. The Liberals successfully linked traditional policies of low tariffs to a new consumer-oriented agenda. The Conservative Party, meanwhile, seldom wavered in the belief that increases in consumption had to follow from increases in profits. The right to low prices was not absolute. Bennett, for example, insisted that high tariffs were necessary to maintain wages and profits.

Seeking broad appeal, most speakers ignored differences of income, gender, and region, and addressed their remarks to a homogenized "Canadian" consumer. However, as election day neared, women were often addressed as a group with specific interests in consumption. Purchasing power was an inherently contested category, involving negotiation between wages, prices, and profits.[28] Growing attention to purchasing power and consumer interests did not replace traditional commitments to production but added new themes and inflected ongoing patterns of emphasis in a new direction.

The Co-operative Commonwealth Federation

From the time of the CCF's founding, its policy statements had distinguished between production (which was to be socialized and centrally planned), distribution (which was to be equalized), and consumption (which could remain private). Whereas the Liberal and Conservative Parties insisted that national prosperity depended on the restoration of international trade, the CCF proposed to operate the Canadian economy as much as possible as a self-contained unit, with a sustainable balance in producing and consumer power. By shifting the economy away from the making of profits and toward the making of goods and services, the CCF promised a consumption-oriented economy with production geared to people's needs and increased economic stability. Arguing that Canada's efforts to compete in world markets meant lowering "living standards to those of the peasant, the fellah, the peon, and the coolie," Woodsworth proposed that socially useful public works should replace exports as the driver of the economy.[29] He explained that the CCF welcomed the productivity of modern industry and remained committed to the system of mass production, advanced mechanization, and expert management that had emerged under capitalism. Economic and political seclusion went hand-in-hand: turning inward would allow for better control of Canada's destiny.

Heading into the election, Woodsworth reaffirmed the commitments made at the party's founding, emphasizing that "in this age of potential plenty" socialization of the means of production would offer economic security for everyone at a reasonably high standard. "Political liberty without economic liberty is a sham," he proclaimed, calling on Canadians to embrace a "new brand of social democracy."[30] Campaign addresses often drew on the revelations of the Price Spreads Inquiry to analyze the costs of common items. In a CBC Radio talk, for example, Woodsworth joked, "I fancy there would be greater interest taken in politics" if a smoker were to "count out the coppers" paid for each package of cigarettes, noting the pennies directed to taxes, manufacturers, and retailers, with only a single cent left for the grower.[31] Woodsworth often repeated earlier promises that the CCF had no objection to private property. The party, he insisted, supported the efforts of ordinary Canadians to obtain "those things which we can personally use and enjoy. It hopes that people will have more of these things."[32] Indeed, once production was managed with greater efficiency and according to need rather than profit, the CCF implied that Canadians might expect to see modest increases in the availability of some goods and services.

Although the party addressed pocketbook concerns, it did not endorse unlimited consumption. Indeed, most CCF leaders, including Woodsworth, were uncomfortable with the idea of growth driven by indiscriminate mass expenditures.[33] Instead, the CCF called on the ordinary citizens of Canada to reject the parties of the status quo, choosing the party that stood for "things as they ought to be" with a program of social justice measured by improved access to consumer goods.[34]

The Reconstruction Party

It was perhaps inevitable that Harry Stevens would find the government's response to the recommendations of the royal commission unequal to the crusade he had waged. In July 1935, he made a final break with the Tories, announcing the formation of the Reconstruction Party. Although the election date had yet to be set, the new party issued a fifteen-point platform pledging "to open up avenues of opportunity for all who are willing to work ... to enable them to retain their self-respect and earn a moderate living."[35] Observing that the "boundary between politics and economics had dissolved," Stevens asserted that it was "now as much the duty of the State to ensure for its people the elementary needs of food, clothing and shelter on a civilized scale as to protect them and their property from molestation."[36] The party promised that the recommendations made in the royal commission report would be fully enacted. Freed from the tyranny of concentrated power, material well-being would flow to all.

Presenting Reconstruction policies to *Maclean's* magazine, Stevens described Canada as "a country of homes" and the family as "the unit and basis of society."[37] Job creation and restraint of big business were the first priorities; however, Stevens cited the inability of farmers and industrial workers to buy goods as evidence that the system was unhealthy.[38] It was, he insisted, "absolutely essential to the welfare and happiness of Canadians that there should be a wider enjoyment of those things that make for a happy Canadian livelihood."[39] Stevens told voters that the Reconstruction Party would ensure "in every way possible" that exploitation of the public through unwarranted profits would be vigorously restricted. Although the party's primary commitment was to the well-being of the independent producer, support for the consumer was regarded as the natural counterpart to support for the producer: restricting cut-throat competition would allow wages to rise, and eliminating fraud would assure value for money. Recognizing that "the responsibility of making the consumer's dollar go as far as possible rests largely with the women," the party embraced a broadened understanding of the household.[40] Shopping was not an indulgence but an act of production; one of the tools for reconstructing the Canadian family.

The Arrival of Social Credit

It was the Social Credit Party that presented the clearest vision of a nation of citizen consumers in which everyone was not only entitled to, but indeed had a responsibility to consume the products of industry and agriculture. Canada's reform leaders had discussed social credit theory since the twenties. In the summer of 1935, William Aberhart, a school principal and fundamentalist radio evangelist, swept to victory in the Alberta provincial election by offering voters a simplified version of social credit theory and the promise of a twenty-five-dollar dividend for every bona fide citizen. The election of the Social Credit Party electrified the nation.[41] Full slates of Social Credit candidates immediately entered the field in Alberta and Saskatchewan; a scattering of contenders also campaigned in British Columbia and Manitoba. Social Credit might not have the same appeal in a federal election that it had demonstrated in Alberta, but no one was certain what would happen. Aberhart was unique, but every province had been affected by the Depression.[42]

The most sensational aspect of the party's platform was the promise of a social credit to be paid every man, woman, and child regardless of whether they were employed or not, and regardless of their personal wealth. As described by Aberhart, the dividend was both a social program designed to ameliorate poverty and an economic measure intended to stimulate job creation. The underlying principle was set out in the party's *Social Credit Manual:* it is "the duty of the State through its Government to organize its economic structure in such a way that no bona fide citizen, man, woman, or child, shall be allowed to suffer for lack of bare necessities of food, clothing, and shelter, in the midst of plenty or abundance."[43] Every individual had the right to economic security and a share in the common cultural heritage and resource wealth of the nation. Dividends would never have to be paid back, but they would have to be spent. Indeed, as credits expired at the end of each year, they existed only to be spent. From the economic perspective, credits worked in conjunction with a fixed "Just Price" and increased government spending to offset the lack of purchasing power that plagued the modern economy. With the economy driven by the power of aggregate consumer spending, the productive capacity of the industrial system would be utilized and developed to the fullest. From an ethical perspective, credits would end dependency. (It is interesting that Aberhart felt obliged to reassure male constituents that the credit, by ending the vulnerability of women, would ultimately make for "happier homes.")[44] Mainstream politicians and economists ridiculed social credit theory, but the appeal of a national economy built on spending and consumption rather than savings and investment could not be ignored.

The Conservative Campaign

In spite of the electorate's desire for change, the Conservative campaign held true to Bennett's vision of a nation made great by hard work, self-discipline, and the development of abundant natural resources. In 1930, Bennett and the Conservative Party had won power by promising to "blast" Canada's way into the world's markets and restore prosperity and jobs. The policies that followed were those traditionally adopted in times of economic recession: tariffs were raised to protect domestic manufacturers, preferences were negotiated to increase foreign trade, and efforts were made to control the budget deficit and to preserve a sound currency. As the Depression deepened, the government – finding itself largely unable to increase demand – moved to manage supply by collaborating in international efforts to limit production of silver and wheat, and by encouraging the formation of monopolies among Canadian agricultural producers in order to reduce competition, fix prices, and restore profitability. A "Buy Canada" campaign was announced, but increasing domestic spending in the face of collapsing export markets was difficult.[45] Proposals advanced by the CCF to improve mass purchasing power through government intervention were condemned as evidence of class warfare and communism.

Although the grip of the Depression had begun to loosen by 1934, Conservative Party prospects remained grim. The price spreads investigation had been tremendously popular, but the schisms created within the Tories bolstered Stevens's image as the people's hero while confirming Bennett's reputation as a champion of capitalism.[46] With an election looming, Bennett moved to regain the initiative in January of 1935. Speaking to the nation in a series of five radio broadcasts, Bennett announced that the "old order is gone."[47] Calling for government intervention to restore industrial equilibrium, he accepted that the benefits of modern technology should be broadly available, with security provided to all who were "willing to work as a member of our economic society."[48] Although increases in private consumption were desirable, government programs, including public works, were aimed at restoring the profitability of private enterprise rather than reorienting the economy toward private consumption. When jobs appeared, workers – a category that included both the men and women of Canada – would be able to buy what they needed.

When Bennett fell ill in the spring of 1935, the energy generated by his "New Deal" broadcasts dissipated. During the election campaign, little mention was made of social reform measures. Bennett pointed instead to the government's efforts to maintain living standards by supporting price levels and restoring trade.[49] "I did my best for the producers and exporters in this country," he often declared. Constant in his praise of capitalism, Bennett drew no distinction between producer and consumer interests. Failing to acknowledge the political potential of consumerism, he persistently associated the promise of improved lives with the rewards of hard work.

The Liberal Party

Of all the parties involved in the election, the Liberals were the least concerned with the fate of capitalism as an economic institution. King consistently argued that financial mismanagement rather than fundamental flaws was responsible for the ongoing economic crisis. Rejecting extreme government intervention, the Liberal Party promised to balance "the pull of tradition and the urge of innovation ... to make possible a more abundant life for all members of the community."[50] Campaign literature drew from the address King had made to the House in February 1933 and frequently concluded with the nonspecific, vaguely consumerist pledge he had made at that time:

> The Liberal party recognizes that the problem of distribution has become more
> important than that of production, and believes that personality is more sacred

than property. It will devote itself to find ways and means of effecting a fair and just distribution of wealth with increasing regard to human needs, to the furtherance of social justice, and to the promotion of the common good.[51]

Recognizing the trend away from laissez-faire liberalism and toward intervention, but seeing only limited consensus between young and long-time Liberals, King steered the party cautiously, loathe to open discussions that might lead to dissension.[52] Instead, efforts were undertaken to publicize King's record as a social reformer and the party's historic commitment to progressive social action.[53] A campaign biography presented King and Canadian liberalism responding to the challenges of the age, fighting to give "freedom a larger social content."[54] Economic insecurity, especially fear of poverty and unemployment, was described as the "negation of freedom" and "subversive of human personality."[55]

The involvement of Liberal members in the Price Spreads Inquiry created challenges as well as opportunities for the party. In the face of tremendous public interest, it was imperative that the Liberals both support the process and develop an independent position. The Liberals adopted a two-part strategy, seeking to widen divisions within the Conservative Party while casting doubt on Stevens's sincerity as a crusader for social justice and claiming that proposed legislation was potentially unconstitutional while simultaneously insisting that Conservative efforts did not go far enough to help ordinary Canadians. King met regularly with the Liberal members of the commission to discuss tactics; together they agreed that the memorandum of reservations would be the basis of Liberal policy in the coming campaign.[56]

The Forgotten Consumer Crusade

While the Liberal leader sought to balance interests within both the nation and the party, consumer issues took on heightened visibility in the weeks leading up to election day (Figure 1.1). Liberal activists seized on the consumer issues raised by the Liberal members of the Price Spreads Inquiry to launch a "Forgotten Consumer Crusade." Radio addresses, newspaper advertisements, and prominent speakers at campaign rallies urged Canadians to "Vote Liberal and lower the cost of living." The centrepiece of the crusade was a series of price comparisons conducted by Mrs. Charles Thorburn, a prominent Liberal involved in many Ottawa welfare institutions. Listing the prices of fifty products ranging from matchboxes to mayonnaise, Thorburn demonstrated that Canadians were paying more than Americans for identical products. In the last three weeks of

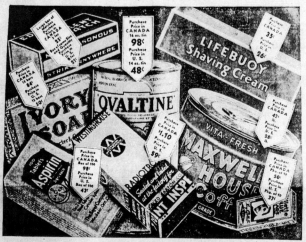

Figure 1.1 Appeals to the consumer interest were a feature of Canada's 1935 federal election. Here the Liberal Party promises to restore to the housewife the rights of which she has been robbed by Conservative tariff policies. "Women of Vancouver!" *Source: Vancouver Sun*, 12 October 1935, 5. *Courtesy of* the *Vancouver Sun*.

the campaign, she spoke to groups in Ontario, Manitoba, and M
Although her addresses were often presented at Women's Association Meetings, they received front-page attention in the daily press. Thorburn was also a key-note speaker at the Liberal Party's closing campaign rally, usually remembered as the occasion of coordinated radio greetings from the eight Liberal provincial premiers.[57]

The Forgotten Consumer Crusade operated on two levels. Speeches by Thorburn as well as those by the Liberal members of the recent Price Spreads Inquiry developed the theme of a consumer interest as a socially unifying force able to bridge conflicts between different producer interests. A circular, begin-ning with a phrase from Young's dissenting report ("the consumers' interest is the interest of the human race"), was distributed at rallies and reprinted in the *Toronto Star*.[58] Used in this way, the consumer was a general category with the potential to transcend party loyalties.[59]

But the message was also crafted to appeal to women in their role as house-hold managers. Mrs. Thorburn, newspaper reports often noted, demonstrated that American wives could give their husbands two cups of coffee for the price that Canadian women could serve one. "We can't compete with that handicap," she concluded. Thorburn encouraged Canadian women to consider questions of politics and economics from the standpoint of the pantry shelf when marking their ballots. Through the requirements of the home, women could gain insight into the economic needs of the country as a whole. "Let us acquire the habit of regarding ourselves as consumers, a wider term than housewives," Thorburn urged. Although consumption was an issue of concern to all voters, it was particularly seen as a motivating consideration for women, with the potential to recruit voters to the Liberal cause – especially newer voters whose party loyal-ties might not be firmly established. Because price comparisons highlighted the taxes paid by Canadian shoppers, the message was also intended to focus consumer frustrations on Tory policies.

Whereas Thorburn often spoke specifically to women, other appeals to consumers in the final week of the campaign were directed to male voters. "Mr. Consumer's Dollar: Where Does It Go?" asked *Saturday Night* in a front-page feature on 5 October 1935.[60] The article, politically neutral but prepared by Liberal and Reconstruction Party sympathizers, presented an analysis of the price of four items selected as representative of a typical farmer's wardrobe (a worsted suit, a tweed suit, work boots, and a pair of shoes) purchased in a medium-sized Ontario town. The purpose of the study was to shed light on the relative influence of the primary producer, manufacturer, retailer, tariff, and

taxes in the final price of goods. The authors avoided determining the characteristics of a "fair price" but did note that consumers received greater cost savings
from mass production than from mass distribution.

Appealing to voters as citizen-consumers, these speeches and articles effectively bridged traditional producer ethics (thrift, work, discipline) and
modern spending practices.[61] Shopping, like voting, was characterized as an
informed practice of skilful decision making. Indeed, the citizen and the shop-
per shared similar political characteristics: exercising freedom of choice, formal
equality, and entitlement to the protection of the state.

The Election Results

Interest in the election was high; record crowds had turned out to hear the
leaders, and 75 percent of the eligible voters went to the polls. The results largely
reaffirmed Canada's commitment to a free-market economy. The Liberals were
elected with an overwhelming majority. Parties advocating extreme roles for
the state, whether on the left or the right, failed to win power.[62] Considered
solely as competing efforts to win power, the campaigns changed little. It is possible, however, to evaluate the effects of election campaigns differently, not as a
race between winners and losers, but as an extended discussion in which ideas
were advanced and debated by politicians attempting to persuade voters of the
importance of particular causes. The election reaffirmed the existing social
order, but the campaign recognized new claims and changed circumstances.

During the campaign, consumers became an identified political constitu-
ency. Material security rather than property ownership was discussed as the
basis of an orderly society. Although few Canadian economists endorsed the
power of mass consumption to revitalize the economy, politicians recognized
the power of the consumer as voter.[63] Measures to protect consumers from
exploitation were endorsed by every leader and identified with the promotion
of the public good. Similarly, every party committed itself to ensuring the economic security of individual Canadians and a decent standard of living. The
details of what this standard would be were scanty, but assurances that every
Canadian would have basic necessities of food, clothing, and shelter were now
fundamental. The responsibility to provide an adequate standard of living was
recognized as part of good government. Most importantly, the understanding
of freedom was being modified to include economic as well as political rights.

Historically, citizen and consumer are often understood as opposites. In
spite of recent challenges to long-standing stereotypes, there is a persistent
tendency to represent the citizen as politically engaged, rational, self-sufficient,

and often male. The consumer, by comparison, is associated with private life, domesticity, irrationality, and self-indulgence, and is often gendered female. In Canadian politics during the thirties, these distinctions were not firmly drawn. The inherent tension between the universal citizen-consumer and gendered appeals to shoppers was not so much resolved as put on hold by the extraordinary circumstances of the Depression.

The politics of the grocery aisle did not displace the politics of the factory floor and the farmer's field, but joined them. The consumerism of 1935 was not the ever-expanding materialism of the post-war period; however, consumption was no longer peripheral to politics. As they sought to mobilize consumers to win votes, politicians made consumption a legitimate public concern and a political rather than a private matter.

Notes

1 For Canada, see Bettina Liverant, "Buying Happiness: English Canadian Intellectuals and the Development of Canadian Consumer Culture, 1895-1965" (PhD diss., University of Alberta, 2008), 35-55, 168-98; Donica Belisle, "Greedy and Gullible: Canadian Representations of Shopping Women" (paper presented at "Inventing and Reinventing the Gendered Consumer from the Early Modern to Postmodern Periods," University of Limerick, Ireland, 21 May 2010). For America, see Daniel Horowitz, *The Morality of Spending: Attitudes toward the Consumer Society in America, 1875-1940* (Baltimore: Johns Hopkins University Press, 1985). On Germany, see Chapter 12 in this volume.

2 See Patricia Maclachlan and Frank Trentmann, "Civilizing Markets: Traditions of Consumer Politics in Twentieth-Century Britain, Japan and the United States," in *Markets in Historical Contexts: Ideas and Politics in the Modern World,* ed. Mark Bevir and Frank Trentmann (Cambridge: Cambridge University Press, 2004), 170-201, for a very useful discussion of parallel circumstances in other nations. On "politics contracting around the essentials," see ibid., 177.

3 In the 1930s, Canadian federal election dates were not fixed but called at the request of the prime minister. Parliament has a maximum term limit of five years, dating from the return of the writs of the last election.

4 *House of Commons Debates* (2 March 1932), 727.

5 Ibid., 728.

6 Ibid., 739.

7 Ibid. (1 February 1933), 1697.

8 Ibid., 1706.

9 Ibid., 1698.

10 Ibid. (2 February 1933), 1710.

11 Ibid., 1743. Although the CCF used the fact of abundance as the basis for political claims, David Laycock argues that an emphasis on abundance paired with technocratic solutions to inequality is fundamentally depoliticizing. David Laycock, *Populism and Democratic Thought in the Canadian Prairies, 1910-1940* (Toronto: University of Toronto Press, 1990), 199.

12 H. Blair Neatby, *William Lyon Mackenzie King, 1932-1939: The Prism of Unity* (Toronto: University of Toronto Press, 1976), 28-30.

13 *House of Commons Debates* (27 February 1933), 2505.

14 Ibid., 2501, 2505.

15 Ibid., 2502.

16 Ibid., 2501-3, 2512.

17 William Irvine, *Political Servants of Capitalism; Answering Lawson and Mackenzie King* (Ottawa: Labour Publishing, 1935), 80-81. The speeches given in the House in support of Woodsworth's motion were also collected and circulated in pamphlet form.

18 Neatby notes that King was convinced "that he had struck the necessary balance. In future, when correspondents criticized the party for having no clear statement of its policies, King merely mailed them a copy." Neatby, *William Lyon Mackenzie King*, 38. In January 1935, King reread his address from Hansard of 1933 back into the record as the policies on which the general election would be fought. "The Debate on the Address," *Canadian Annual Review*, 1935-36, 14-15.

19 Stevens quoted in "Stevens Gives Lie to Bennett in Row," *New York Times*, 31 October 1934, 5.

20 A brief note of explanation will help to clarify the course of the inquiry and its changing identity. A Special Select Committee of the House of Commons was appointed in February 1934 to investigate Stevens's accusations. Normally the powers of parliamentary committees cease when the House is prorogued; however, given the importance of the topic, the committee was reorganized as the Royal Commission on Price Spreads and Mass Buying. The eleven original members, representing three political parties and various regions of Canada, were appointed as royal commissioners. Stevens was the chair of both the committee and the royal commission until his falling out with Bennett in the summer of 1934. When the royal commission resumed sittings in October of 1934, W.W. Kennedy, MP for Winnipeg, was the chair. The same group of appointees met for sixty sessions as a committee and for sixty-five sessions as a royal commission. *The Report of the Royal Commission on Price Spreads and Mass Buying* was formally signed on 9 April 1935. The press used a variety of terms when discussing these events, including the "Stevens Committee," the "Stevens Inquiry," and the "Price Spreads Commission." In this study, "Price Spreads Inquiry" denotes the entire period of investigation, stretching from February 1934 to April 1935.

21 *The Report of the Royal Commission on Price Spreads and Mass Buying* stretched to five hundred pages and included a memorandum of reservations contributed by the three Liberal members of the commission (who also signed the main report) and a vigorous dissenting report by E.J. Young (who declined to sign the main report). Credit for imposing a coherent structure on the extensive testimony and for producing recommendations in spite of party differences was given to future prime minister Lester B. Pearson, the commission's secretary, and to his staff, which included economists V.W. Bladen and C.A. Curtis. Pearson was later awarded the O.B.E. for his work on the Royal Commission on Price Spreads and Mass Buying and became Canada's 14th prime minister in 1963.

22 *The Report of the Royal Commission on Price Spreads and Mass Buying* (Ottawa: King's Printer, 1937), 106.

23 Ibid., 277-78. The Liberal members of the commission were Samuel "Sam" Factor, J.L. Ilsley, O. Boulanger, and E.J. Young.

24 Ibid., 293. See also E.J. Young, "A Western Farmer Looks at Business," in *Addresses of the Canadian Club of Toronto, 1935-1936* (Toronto: Warwick Bros. and Rutter, 1936).

25 *Royal Commission on Price Spreads and Mass Buying*, 293, 307.

26 On this theme, see H.A. Innis, "For the People," *University of Toronto Quarterly* 5, 2 (January 1936): 279.

27 D. McArthur, "Public Affairs," *Queen's Quarterly* 41 (Summer 1934): 256.

28 Meg Jacobs, *Pocketbook Politics: Economic Citizenship in Twentieth-Century America* (Princeton: Princeton University Press, 2007), 146.

29 J.S. Woodsworth, "The Issues as I See Them," *Maclean's Magazine*, 15 September 1935, 11, 31.

30 Ibid., 11; J.S. Woodsworth, "A New Brand of Canadian Social Democracy," *The CBC Digital Archives*, Canadian Broadcasting Corporation. (The archives list the date of the broadcast as 1 January 1935, but Woodsworth refers to events that occurred in April 1935.)
31 Woodsworth, "A New Brand."
32 Woodsworth, "The Issues as I See Them," 32.
33 This was particularly evident in the text of *Social Planning for Canada*, released by a group of academics closely associated with the CCF one month prior to the election. Its authors insisted that everyone should enjoy the material benefits of the modern age, but they strongly condemned the materialism of society. The privileged were dismissed for their interest in "things" and for the "vulgar display of houses and lands." The working classes, "rendered unfit by fatigue" and barren of inner resources, occupied themselves "in the vicarious excitement of commercialized sports and amusements." While declaring that the "ultimate end of all productive activity is the satisfaction of the wants of consumers," the authors left readers with the clear sense that some forms of consumption were regarded as better than others. League for Social Reconstruction, Research Committee, *Social Planning for Canada* (Toronto: T. Nelson, 1935), 36-37, 195, 425.
34 Woodsworth, "A New Brand."
35 Reconstruction Platform of 1935, *Ottawa Journal*, 12 July 1935, quoted in D.O. Carrigan, *Canadian Party Platforms, 1867-1968* (Toronto: Copp Clark, 1968), 130.
36 "Text of Stevens Manifesto," *Toronto Globe*, 13 July 1935, 3; H.H. Stevens, "The Issues as I See Them," *Maclean's Magazine*, 15 September 1935, 11.
37 Stevens, "The Issues as I See Them," 11.
38 "Text of Stevens Manifesto," 3.
39 Quoted in Carrigan, *Canadian Party Platforms*, 133.
40 Ibid.
41 John Herd Thompson and Allen Seager, *Canada, 1922-1939: Decades of Discord* (Toronto: McClelland and Stewart, 1985), 235.
42 Neatby, *William Lyon Mackenzie King*, 114.
43 *The Social Credit Manual*, excerpted in William Aberhart and David Elliott, *Aberhart: Outpourings and Replies* (Calgary: Alberta Records Publication Board, Historical Society of Alberta, 1991), 129.
44 William Aberhart, "An Exposition of Social Credit," *Edmonton Journal*, 27 December 1934, quoted in *William Aberhart and Social Credit in Alberta*, ed. L.H. Thomas (Toronto: Copp Clark, 1977), 69; and *The Social Credit Manual*, Questions and Answers, 29.
45 "The Canada First Policy Is a Consumer Last Policy," *Canadian Forum* 11, 123 (December 1930): 84.
46 Larry Glassford, *Reaction and Reform: The Politics of the Conservative Party under R.B. Bennett, 1927-1938* (Toronto: University of Toronto Press, 1992), 153.
47 *The Premier Speaks to the People, the Prime Minister's January Radio Broadcasts Issued in Book Form, the First Address* (Ottawa: Dominion Conservative Headquarters, 1935), 9.
48 Ibid., *The Second Address*, 15-16.
49 "Bennett Defends Gov't Record at Big Rally in City," *Calgary Herald*, 20 September 1935, 1, 12-13.
50 Norman Rogers, *Mackenzie King* (Toronto: T. Nelson and Sons, 1935), 192.
51 See, for example, W.L. Mackenzie King, "The Issues as I See Them," *Maclean's Magazine*, 15 September 1935, 31; and Mackenzie King, "The Liberal Party's Position," National Liberal Federation of Canada, Ottawa, cited in Carrigan, *Canadian Party Platforms*, 130.
52 Although Liberal traditionalists supported laissez-faire economics, speakers at the Liberal summer school in 1933 insisted on the right to a minimum standard of living to be achieved through a planned economy. Vincent Massey, chair of the conference and president of the

National Liberal Federation, set the tone, suggesting that the ultimate objective of the civilized state was the "happiness of the individual. If civilization means anything, men and women must have the assurance of security against those material evils from which the State can protect them; and they must enjoy the guarantee of minimum standards of life." Vincent Massey, "The Approach to the Problem," in *The Liberal Way, a Record of Opinion on Canadian Problems as Expressed and Discussed at the First Liberal Summer Conference, Port Hope, September, 1933* (Toronto: J.M. Dent and Sons, 1933), 4.

53   These included a new abridged version of King's *Industry and Humanity,* a campaign biography of King prepared by Norman Rogers, and a series of articles drawing favourable comparisons between *Industry and Humanity* and Franklin Delano Roosevelt's National Recovery Administration. See Reginald Whitaker, *The Government Party: Organizing and Financing the Liberal Party of Canada, 1930-58* (Toronto: University of Toronto Press, 1977), 81-83; Neatby, *William Lyon Mackenzie King,* 97-98; and Bernard Rose, *Industry and Humanity: An Outstanding Contribution to the Understanding of Industrial Relations and the Need for Economic Justice, Analysis and Re-Valuation* (Montreal: Labour World, 1934).

54   Rogers, *Mackenzie King,* 201. On the preparation of the campaign biography, see Mark Mohr, "The 'Biography' in Politics: Mackenzie King in 1935," *Canadian Historical Review* 55, 2 (June 1974): 239-48.

55   Rogers, *Mackenzie King,* 193.

56   Neatby, *William Lyon Mackenzie King,* 102-3; D.F. Forster, "The Politics of Combines Policy: Liberals and the Stevens Commission," *Canadian Journal of Economics and Political Science* 28, 4 (November 1962): 515, 519.

57   Both the forms and the content of political campaigning were being affected by burgeoning consumerism. Social Credit policies were presented in a booklet illustrated with and partially paid for by the advertisements of Alberta businesses. The *Temiskaming Speaker* refused to provide detailed election coverage and instead told local candidates to purchase advertising at regular rates. "Politicians in the Limelight," *Temiskaming Speaker,* 26 September 1935. King believed that his biography would be a profitable financial venture for the party as well as a useful political tool. Mohr, "The 'Biography' in Politics: Mackenzie King in 1935," 244.

58   "50 Household Articles Higher Here than in U.S. Mrs. Thorburn Reveals," *Toronto Star,* 20 September 1935, front page.

59   "The Forgotten Consumer," *Toronto Globe and Mail,* 10 October 1935, 4; "'I, Not Bennett, Drew Up U.K. Pacts,' Says Stevens," *Toronto Star,* 10 October 1935, 3. Of course, Liberal recognition of the consumer had the added benefit of reinforcing perceptions that Prime Minister Bennett lacked sympathy for ordinary Canadians.

60   "Mr. Consumer's Dollar: Where Does It Go? Answer Is Not Where Most People Think," *Saturday Night,* 5 October 1935, 17 19, 21.

61   The term "citizen consumer" was made popular by Lizabeth Cohen, *A Consumers' Republic: The Politics of Mass Consumption in Postwar America* (New York: Alfred A. Knopf, 2003). For a recent discussion, see Frank Trentmann, "Citizenship and Consumption," *Journal of Consumer Culture* 7, 2 (2007): 147-58.

62   As commentators have noted then and since, the magnitude of the Liberal victory and the Conservative loss was exaggerated by the structure of Canada's electoral system. Although the Liberals won control of the House, the difference between the two parties in the popular vote was less decisive. Over half of the voters preferred other parties. One in five Canadians voted for parties that had not even existed at the time of the last election in 1930. The election results were as follows: Liberals (173 seats, 44.8 percent popular vote); Conservatives (40 seats, 29.6 percent popular vote); CCF (7 seats, 8.8 percent popular vote); Reconstruction (1 seat, 8.7 percent popular vote); Social Credit (17 seats, 4.1 percent popular vote); other (7 seats,

3.9 percent popular vote). In at least forty-five constituencies, the combined Conservative and Reconstruction vote would have won the seat. Thirty-six of these constituencies had been Conservative in the last Parliament. Jack Granatstein, *The Politics of Survival: The Conservative Party of Canada, 1939-1945* (Toronto: University of Toronto Press, 1967), 8. Election analyses are available in J. Murray Beck, *Pendulum of Power; Canada's Federal Elections* (Scarborough: Prentice-Hall, 1968), 206-22; Escott Reid, "The Canadian Election of 1935 – and After," *American Political Science Review* 30, 1 (February 1936): 111-21; and Thompson and Seager, *Canada, 1922-1939*, 274-76.

63   For the views of economists, see H.A. Innis and A.F.W. Plumptre, eds., *The Canadian Economy and Its Problems* (Toronto: Canadian Institute of International Affairs, 1934); and *Canadian Problems as Seen by Twenty Outstanding Men of Canada* (Toronto: Oxford University Press, 1933). For a general discussion, see Liverant, "Buying Happiness," 206-10.

2

Consumer Culture and the Medicalization of Women's Roles in Canada, 1919-39

Tracy Penny Light

A Post's Bran Flakes advertisement in a 1924 issue of *Ladies' Home Journal* summed up the role of Canadian women in building a "strong and healthy nation."[1] It asked, "Health is your family's greatest treasure – Do you guard it well?"[2] Similarly, a 1934 editorial in the *Canadian Public Health Journal* noted that "motherhood is not only the physical source of a people but one of the foundations upon which nation is built."[3] These messages, which reinforced the importance of rebuilding the nation after the losses of the Great War, also prescribed the proper and acceptable roles for girls and women – they were to be wives and mothers. But they also point to an increasing connection, in the interwar period, between health and modernity, of which women as wives and mothers needed to be aware. Although the prescriptions that promoted and shaped gender roles were found in a variety of discourses, perhaps the two most important were that of the growing consumer culture and that of the medical profession (science).[4] As both Kristin Hall and Denyse Baillargeon state in Chapters 3 and 4 of this volume, advertising rhetoric of this period stressed the maternal responsibilities of women, a view shared by the medical profession. Products marketed to women capitalized on this convergence of views that women's roles were inextricably linked to reproduction.[5] Indeed, my survey of the expert advice found in magazine advertisements indicates that it was intentionally "scientific," as advertisers capitalized on the authority of the modern medical profession and used medical science to market their products to women. Increasingly, the authority of marketing found in popular literature – here I am particularly interested in ads that appeared in *Chatelaine* and the *Ladies' Home*

Journal – led the charge in promoting and reinforcing "proper" roles for girls and women.[6]

This chapter explores how the authority found in the public and professional spheres, reflected in the ads of popular women's magazines and the medical discourse in professional medical journals, constructed femininity.[7] The modern feminine identity (women as wives and mothers) that emerged in the interwar era was tied to consumption. Although historians have examined femininity and consumption, they have not explored how advertisements, which sold and reinforced the feminine ideal during this period, used science, and how the consumer and medical discourses reinforced or contradicted one another.[8] Yet it is clear that manufacturers, advertisers, and publishers appropriated scientific discourse to sell their products to women, promising to make them beautiful, clean, and knowledgeable mothers.[9] It is perhaps not surprising that consumer discourse capitalized on medical authority as Canadians increasingly recognized the medical profession as expert on the body due to its scientific roots.[10] In the early twentieth century, doctors worked to maintain their status as experts on the body as they monitored the health of the nation by promoting new scientific approaches. This was primarily evident in the emerging public health movement.[11] For instance, a 1926 editorial in the *Canadian Medical Association Journal* *(CMAJ)* noted that "the desirability of educating the general public regarding all important facts in connection with both personal and public hygiene is unquestionable."[12] In other words, physicians cared for the health of society as much as for their patients' health. Although consumer messaging that promoted women's role as wife and mother initially converged with the medical profession's advice to women, by the 1930s, some doctors began to shift their discourse to address a specific interest in women's health and welfare, particularly evident in their discussions of abortion. The problem of abortion forced doctors to acknowledge that some women did not conform to the prescriptions found in popular (consumer) culture. They acknowledged the ideal of women as mothers, but the high mortality rate associated with abortion indicated that some mothers needed to limit their family sizes for medical reasons or, in the worst cases, to escape the trouble of illicit pregnancy. Their divergence from the prescriptions found in consumer discourse is significant and raises the question of how public authority (that of consumer culture) came to be seen, and understood, as synonymous with professional authority, an issue present in contemporary culture.[13] I explore how consumer culture appropriated medicine to sell products in the past, where the convergences of those discourses occurred, and perhaps more importantly, where public authority did not map to professional authority. This has important implications for how we understand consumer messaging and suggests that we need to question the advertisements that cite the endorsement of science or experts, even today. It is my hope that by interrogating the legitimacy of public authority, we will be forced to consider how we understand gender, the role of consumer culture in dictating how gender should be performed in various periods (in other words, what is considered normal), and how medical science is used to ensure that we buy in to the prescriptions. Such interrogation is necessary if we are to question the "patriarchal construction of the female body" and find ways to revision our bodies by critiquing the authoritative messages that are inscribed on them daily.[14]

Selling the Feminine Ideal: Consumer Culture, the Modern Woman, and Science

In her exploration of prescriptions for girls in British magazines, Penny Tinkler points out that the "treatment of the female body and sexuality reveals the complex, and often insidious, workings of magazine representations of femininity."[15] The same can be said with respect to the representations of femininity in magazines read by Canadian women. In the Canadian context, women's roles during the interwar period as seen in consumer culture are most fascinating due to the fact that, at least on the surface, they were not complex at all. There was only one goal – marriage and motherhood. This goal clearly delineated the proper role that girls and women were to achieve (that goal denoted normalcy), and as Canada became modern and more women were visible in the public sphere, few openly performed anything other than traditional maternal and spousal femininity.[16]

The rise of "Mrs. Consumer" as a specific identity for women helped to reinforce the private/public dichotomy of women as mothers in the domestic sphere and men as breadwinners in the public sphere.[17] In the early twentieth century, women became identified with consumerism as purchasing was linked to their ability to effectively accomplish their domestic duties. This promoted a growing sense that consumption was not only about purchasing goods but was, in fact, a part of life.[18] Mass marketing and magazines reinforced traditional ideas of heterosexuality, marriage, and motherhood for women while, at the same time, encouraging them to engage in consumptive practice that was increasingly seen as a leisure activity associated with modernity. Another key feature of modernity was, of course, the infusion of medical science into daily life, and advertisements increasingly used scientific experts to sell products.[19] Two areas in particular were targeted to assist women in fulfilling their modern roles. First, their appearance, which included a focus on their health and hygiene, was highlighted, in order to help them find and keep a husband. Advertisements for products ranging from cosmetics to food and even appliances were pitched to help women maintain their looks (including their body shape) and their scent. Second, in order to cast mothers as guardians of their families' health, a variety of products from antiseptics to foodstuffs were marketed to women.

Performing Gender: Scientific Prescriptions for "Proper" Women

Beauty was the most important factor in the quest for a husband (the first step in pursuit of the ideal), and many products claimed that they helped women look good. In consumer culture, though, a total package was required if a woman expected to find (and keep) a man. This included proper skin care and overall good health and hygiene. Manufacturers advertised goods with endorsements from health professionals to sell women on the efficacy of their products. For instance, a 1932 ad for Ivory Soap claimed that "physicians who have studied the care of the skin say that simple cleanliness is the one most important aid to the health and beauty of your complexion."[20] The company that made Calay Soap declared that "73 Dermatologists approve[d]" its product, and Woodbury's asserted that its facial powder was prepared by "skin scientists" who used "a new blending process."[21] These statements legitimized the products, but what were they intended to do for the women who purchased them? The claims of manufacturers moved beyond simple avowals regarding their effectiveness to play into the prescriptions for women by purporting that the health and beauty advantages conferred by their products would ensure success in finding a marriage partner (Figure 2.1). As Calay pointed out, men admired natural-looking women, and these were the girls they wanted to marry.[22]

A number of products specifically addressed the connection between health and beauty. For instance, advertisements for Fleischmann's Yeast, which appeared in *Chatelaine* magazine throughout the late 1920s and 1930s, emphasized this relationship.[23] These ads promoted living life to its fullest, a goal that could be attained by consuming Fleischmann's Yeast three times a day. For instance, a 1928 ad noted that, as the result of eating Fleischmann's yeast, "Dorothy's health was proverbial. She was one of those lucky people who 'never had a day's illness!' She was simply everlastingly full of the happiness and energy that come from perfect health."[24] It was important for potential wives to be healthy as well as beautiful. In a 1932 ad, Fleischmann's focused on the advantages to the complexion of taking yeast. A "Dr. Singer" of Vienna, purportedly a "famous" doctor, explained to readers that "it's remarkable how quickly such skin eruptions

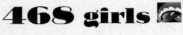

disappear" as a result of consuming yeast. The implications for female readers were obvious – if they let their skin become "sallow-looking," they would have difficulties in finding, and possibly keeping, a husband.[25] These yeast advertisements continued throughout the interwar period and targeted a host of health issues, all of which could be solved by ingesting three cakes a day (Figure 2.2).[26]

Other products pitched their campaigns at women by promoting the positive effects of their goods for feminine appearance. For instance, women who did not use Forhan's Toothpaste risked losing their beauty to the ravages of pyorrhea. A July 1932 Forhan's ad, titled "She was a beautiful woman before her teeth ... went bad," opened with a brief scenario in which a woman has lost her looks due to the disease. As her friends "brood mournfully over the glories that have passed," the ad repeats "She was – she *was* – a beautiful woman."[27] Advertisers attributed marital problems to a loss of beauty, and as Hinds suggested, dry skin could make a woman "resentful," which could contribute to marital discord. Similarly, an ad for Lux Soap claimed that dishpan hands led to problems in marriage.[28] The ads advocated that if women were to succeed in their "natural" role, they needed to purchase consumer products to combat the variety of problems that could hamper their ability to look their best.

Of course, women were expected not only to look good but also to smell good. Ads for a variety of products to combat the smell from "bodily secretions," such as Odorono, were available to women in this period. The Odorono company declared in 1932 that by using its product, a woman was better able to find a partner: "She knew that underarm perspiration was death to smart dresses and lasting friendships. So, before she dressed for the party she used Odorono. Her lovely new dress stayed fresh and sweet. And she attracted the nicest man there. Clever girl – to rely on Odorono for perfect protection against unsightly perspiration stains and offensive underarm odor."[29] An earlier ad had established the scientific nature of Odorono. Not only was it effective and used by "hundreds of women," but it was a "scientific and safe way of avoiding the constant anxiety over underarm perspiration."[30] Other deodorant ads noted that perspiration odour was especially offensive and could lead to serious losses. One company claimed that by failing to use its product, a woman could cheat "herself out of good times, good friends, good jobs – perhaps even out of good marriage."[31] The message relayed to women by consumer products was that they needed scientific ways to look and smell good if they hoped to find a husband and keep him.

Health and its link to beauty were important for consumer goods, but even more significant was the emphasis on beauty and hygiene. The connection between looking good and being hygienic was particularly strong in the advertisement of feminine hygiene aids such as Kotex Sanitary Napkins. Early campaigns noted that a modern woman must be "charming, immaculate, exquisite under all circumstances." She needed to shine every day, even on days marred by that "serious problem."[32] The problem, of course, was menstruation, which previous generations had managed with washable cotton rags. The beautiful, hygienic, and modern woman, however, could not have her life interrupted by her period, because her days were "filled with social and business activities."[33] For women who were out and about, the logistics of dealing with soiled rags were problematic. The ad implied that only an unsophisticated hick, uninformed regarding personal hygiene, would favour the washable rags that could not be disposed of easily. The modern woman was worldly; informed about the latest advancements, even in hygienic products, she was therefore in the know about Kotex disposable sanitary napkins.

Later campaigns also created ads to mirror earlier ones that focused primarily on cleanliness. For instance, a 1929 Kotex ad emphasized both the hygienic and scientific aspects of the product. "Women, every day are learning of this new hygienic need," it proclaimed, and it reinforced that this was "why doctors urge its use."[34] Similarly, a 1926 Kotex ad claimed that "throwing the light of scientific frankness on woman's greatest problem has changed, in this way, the hygienic habits of millions."[35] This pairing of consumer discourse and medical science was commonplace (Figure 2.3). The manufacturers outlined for women why it was important to use the product:

> For Kotex is outstandingly different from anything of the sort you have ever known. To call it a sanitary napkin does not fully describe it. Doctors call it a hygienic service to women. Kotex, they say, definitely proves its value in improved health. It brings you poise and peace-of-mind, assurance, and, above all else, physical comfort. Home-made napkins, doctors say, often caused ill-health ... Each Kotex napkin is shaped scientifically to be form-fitting – to be non-detectable when worn. The softest material is used. And the absorbency of Cellucotton absorbent wadding is more satisfactory than any like product. Important, too, is the deodorizing feature of Kotex. No fear from this source need mar your composure. Kotex deodorizes, effectively, safely, thoroughly.[36]

Not only were Kotex pads more sanitary and able to prevent odour, they were "scientifically" designed to fit.[37] This was important because a proper fit meant that "no telltale lines or wrinkles" would show through "that close fitting gown." The new Phantom Kotex promised in 1932 not to allow the monthly problem to spoil the look of those dresses designed along the "most extreme modern lines."[38] Thanks to Kotex, women could look good, even while menstruating.

Advertisers' use of medical science and innovation to sell feminine hygiene products was nothing new. Alia Al-Khalidi has demonstrated that the first patented sanitary towels, produced by Southalls in Britain, were not accepted by the general public until medical journals featured them as "new inventions and novelties" that medical professionals endorsed.[39] For instance, the *British Medical Journal* noted in 1884 that the new pads were "in the highest degree cleanly, and diminish materially the risks of septic infection."[40] Infection was a major concern for physicians in the late nineteenth century, before standardized antiseptic practices.[41] These early endorsements that emphasized the importance of hygiene from the medical perspective continued to be used by advertisers to

Figure 2.3 Kotex
Sanitary Napkins ad.
Source: Maclean's, 15
August 1931, 41.

At such times take care...

you need the *purity* of Kotex

Kotex is too closely related to health to risk doubtful substitutes

SANITARY protection is too closely related to your health . . . your personal ideals of cleanliness . . . to risk methods of whose hygienic safety you are uncertain.

Consider for a moment the infinite care with which Kotex is made. Hospital standards of cleanliness prevail, in every step of manufacture. Modern machinery makes Kotex from start to finish.

Hospitals use Kotex

And so Kotex comes to you immaculate, pure, clean through and through. Last year, millions of pads were used by hospitals alone. Kotex fully meets their requirements.

No sanitary protection of lower standards should ever be used. True, substitutes may cost a few cents less —but remember that your health is involved.

Before accepting a substitute for Kotex, consider these questions: "What do I know of this sanitary protection? What assurance have I

KOTEX IS SOFT

1. *Kotex is soft* . . . laminated layers absorb scientifically, away from the surface.
2. The gauze is specially treated to make it amazingly soft.
3. *Can be worn on either side* with equal comfort. No embarrassment.
4. *The Kotex absorbent* is the identical material used by surgeons in Canada's leading hospitals.
5. *Disposable,* instantly, completely.

that it's fit for such intimate, personal use?"

In addition to health protection, Kotex offers every refinement of comfort. Skillful shaping—soft, and remains soft because laminated layers distribute moisture scientifically. In addition, Kotex gauze is specially treated to make it amazingly soft. Kotex is readily adjusted to individual needs. It is treated to deodorize. Buy Kotex at any drug, dry goods or department store.

KOTEX
MADE IN CANADA

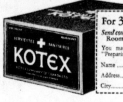

For 3 FREE KOTEX Samples

Send coupon to:—Moyra Monk, R.N., Dept. 7-8-1 Room 1103, 330 Bay St., Toronto, Ont.

You may send 3 Samples of Kotex and book, "Preparing for Womanhood," in plain envelope.

Name

Address

City   Prov.

promote their products and to reinforce the "domestic purity" of their users. Indeed, Al-Khalidi notes that "medical certification [of such products] became an established strategy in advertising copy and in illustration."[42] Science was an important marketing strategy, and its use continued throughout the period.

Although the connection between science and feminine products was often tenuous at best, certain products could realistically claim a link with health and hygiene. The importance of guarding against germs was well understood by the interwar epoch, and a number of products were marketed in this regard.[43] Listerine is one of the most famous, but other products such as Pepsodent Antiseptic, Zonite, and Lysol also came into their own.[44] All focused on killing troublesome germs. Listerine in particular made the connection between a girl's chances at marriage and her bad breath (halitosis). In an ad from 1923, the company noted that this insidious problem could prevent an engagement:

> She possessed a world of personal charm. Most men called her beautiful. Her circumstances enabled her to enhance her beauty with just the kind of clothes that were most becoming. She was well-educated. She knew her French and her bridge and played the piano well. Yet the marriage goal – the thing every girl and woman wants most to attain – remained to her an elusive thing. All of her friends were becoming engaged. And as her years crept closer and closer to that uncomfortable thirty-mark, the empty third finger of her left hand became almost a tragedy in her life.[45]

The message was clear: bad breath meant that a woman would not fulfill her natural role. Advertisers also promoted Listerine as a deodorant, a dandruff treatment, and a remedy for sore throats and colds, which could all prevent a young woman from performing her proper function.[46]

Other antiseptics followed the same logic, pointing to the science of germ fighting that was so important for a woman's health and for that of her family. As Lysol stated in 1937, if its product was good enough to safeguard the health of the Dionne quintuplets, it was a necessity for the average family: "This example of scientific care holds a pointed suggestion to housewives and mothers. Surely you want to give your family the same protection science gives the Dionne babies." The company even offered to send a booklet, which explained how the Dionnes were protected with Lysol, so that other mothers could emulate the example.[47] Clearly, women were expected to have children and raise them scientifically.

Other products followed Lysol's lead in stressing the need for women to employ science in protecting the health of their families. This was particularly the case for food and food-related items. From Post's Bran Flakes to kitchen appliances, women were expected to adhere to modern, scientific approaches. An ad for Grape-Nuts Cereal, for instance, listed the "danger signals of malnutrition" that "every mother should know." Following an already well-trodden track, the ad cited a scientific expert: the danger signs of malnutrition had been identified by a "certain famous American doctor" who had devoted his life to studying child malnutrition. Similarly, Heinz Strained Foods were "just what the doctor ordered." Women were expected to follow the advice from medical professionals. The ad stated that "conscientious mothers" were responsible for carrying out doctors' orders.[48] Modern women were expected to know and to follow the medical, scientific prescriptions.

Magazines, and advertisements generally, straddled a line between promoting (and reinforcing) the modern image of women in the interwar period in "attractive and appealing" ways, while at the same time adhering to patriarchal representations of femininity.[49] The modern woman was held up to traditional definitions of the feminine, but what had changed from previous generations, which advocated similar definitions, was increasingly easy access to these consumer products – there was no excuse (according to the advertisements) for women not to know how to improve their appearance and manage their families scientifically. Although there is no question that consumer values represented the norms of a modernizing Canadian society, it is clear that not all women bought into the prescriptions being sold in consumer culture.[50] Some women actively subverted the ideals by looking for ways to control their family size or even to avoid having children. In public, they worked to ensure that they appeared normal, but behind closed doors they used the information in consumer ads to avoid becoming wives and mothers.

Made to Be Mothers? Women and Doctors Question the Feminine Ideal

A number of ads stressed the importance of "internal" cleanliness, which Andrea Tone posits was actually a birth control method. "Manufacturers," she notes, "sold a wide array of items, including vaginal jellies, douche powders and liquids, suppositories, and foaming tablets as 'feminine hygiene,' an innocuous-sounding term coined by advertisers in the 1920s."[51] Tone focuses on the United States, but advertisements for the same products appeared in Canada. For instance, Lysol ran a series of ads labelled as "frank talks by eminent women physicians" for women in the 1930s. Dr. George Fabre, a "prominent gynecologist in France," outlined the "facts" about "feminine antisepsis." She noted,

It is important that a personal antiseptic should have real germicidal value, while still serving as a soothing lubricant to delicate tissue. Many of the so-called feminine hygiene solutions fall short in one or the other of these respects. Either they irritate and harden tender membranes, or they become ineffective in contact with organic manner ... Lysol disinfectant [is the] most effective for feminine hygiene. "Lysol" does not lose its germicidal action in the presence of organic matter. With its low-surface tension, it searches out and destroys undesirable germ-life lurking in hidden crevices which other antiseptics fail to reach.[52]

As Tone suggests, female consumers were able to "deconstruct" advertising text to discern their "real purpose."[53] As in this ad, words such as "destroy" and "organic matter" were subtle signals to women about how the products could be used. It was precisely the alternative uses of certain products that concerned physicians and caused the medical discourse to diverge from the prescriptions found in advertisements.[54]

Early in the nineteenth century, physicians had used their ability to uphold women's roles as wives and mothers as a way to regulate their own profession. Arguing that "women were made to be mothers," they embedded their scientific stance in the moral imperative for women to be mothers.[55] But by the interwar period, doctors had become recognized as professionals, so they no longer focused on the morality of women's roles. Instead, they were interested in women's health as it assisted them in their role of wife and mother. They promoted scientific methods for successful pregnancies and for raising children. Yet despite the authority invested in medical science and the various products aimed at preserving the health of women and their families, doctors were concerned with high maternal mortality rates during the interwar period. Obviously, these death rates reflected negatively on the ability of science to protect the body, but they also prevented women from fulfilling their "natural" role. In their investigations into maternal mortality statistics across the country, doctors increasingly realized that the overall rate included deaths that were not directly linked to childbirth but rather, to some women's desire not to give birth. For instance, a study of 334 maternal deaths that occurred in Ontario during 1934 showed that almost 18 percent of them were due to abortion.[56] Further, the greatest cause of death was puerperal sepsis at 23 percent. These two figures, representing about 41 percent of all maternal deaths, were significant, and doctors were convinced that even more maternal deaths reported as resulting from sepsis were, in fact, due to abortions.[57] As *CMAJ* reported in December 1936,

"Mortality from abortion is due chiefly to sepsis following illegal interference with pregnancy."[58]

The concern that women were having abortions – in some cases, repeated abortions – to control their fertility was linked to the hazards of the practice. Although women would certainly have opted for dependable birth control rather than resorting to dangerous abortions, the reliability of many products advertised in this period was often questionable.[59] Indeed, we know that women typically chose abortion only when other birth control methods had failed.[60] Thus, many women pursued the option of abortion in their attempts to subvert the ideal and assert agency over their own reproductive functions. A number of cases reported in 1930 in *CMAJ* highlighted women's desperate attempts to terminate their pregnancies:

> Case 1
> A case I saw in the out-patient's department was an abortion self-induced with stove-pipe wire. The woman had aborted three weeks previously ... Death occurred a few hours after admission.

> Case 2
> I was called in consultation, to give a prognosis in a case of insanity (puerperal). There was a history of self-induced abortion twenty-two days previously ... Death occurred eight hours after consultation.

> Case 3
> I was called to the medical wards to see a recent admission; the medical diagnosis was suspected ectopic gestation. Elicited the history of an induced abortion one month previously ... Death followed a few hours after admission.[61]

Such cases showed that despite the illegality of abortion, women were seeking to terminate their pregnancies and that they were aware of ways to do so. Indeed, as Dr. J. Wyllie, a professor of preventative medicine at Queen's University in Kingston, Ontario, stated in a 1933 *Canadian Public Health Journal* article, "The part played by abortion in maternal mortality is at present evoking serious consideration and there is reason to believe that the practice of self-induced abortion is greatly on the increase."[62] Although doctors perceived that abortion deaths were on the rise, the trend was difficult to quantify. This was problematic for the profession because it questioned, doctors believed, their ability to prevent maternal deaths.

The main thrust of doctors' discussions of abortion was that they should not be held accountable for maternal deaths associated with illegal operations.

Frustrated at being unable to help women who arrived in septic states, they were also concerned that the high death rate led to questions about their authority. Their discussions indicate a need to find someone to blame, and increasingly, it was "obvious" to them that the women themselves – who were too enthralled with their public lives and not interested enough in their proper role as mothers – were at fault. Like so many other members of the middle class, doctors believed that the aftermath of the Great War should focus on "rebuilding the race" and that women played a central role in this enterprise. "Motherhood is not only the physical source of a people," commented a 1934 editorial in the *Canadian Public Health Journal*, "but one of the foundations on which the nation is built."[63] The foundation that women were supposed to create with their reproductive activity was believed to be weakening as increasing numbers of them took on new roles in the public sphere. However, though many women in the 1920s and 1930s held paid employment at some point in their lives, and some women may have delayed childbearing for a few years to work, the majority did not remain employed after marriage. For the most part, their incomes were not large enough to permit financial independence, so it was uncommon for women not to pursue the ideal of marriage and motherhood.[64]

Despite the desire of many medical professionals to reinforce the ideal feminine role, there was some recognition that the preference of doctors generally was to avoid having to deal with the consequences of women taking their fertility into their own hands. Because of its illegality, few physicians were willing (or able, at least publicly) to provide birth control information, but many believed that it would excuse both women and doctors from having to make a moral decision regarding abortion. The public unavailability of information about contraception meant that women arrived at hospitals in trouble, and doctors tried to save them. This disturbed them, not just because it negatively affected the maternal mortality statistics, but because they were concerned for their patients' well-being. "From the standpoint of maternal welfare, apart from any moral or legal objections," argued prominent public health advocate Dr. Helen MacMurchy, "abortion must be regarded as associated with considerable danger to health, mainly on account of sepsis which not seldom accompanies it, and also because of the unhealthy condition of the pelvic organs which may be one of its sequelae."[65]

Not only did abortion risk women's health and raise questions about doctors' status as professionals, physicians also recognized that women who were left to the risky option of abortion might be incapacitated by it and unable to have children in the future. For these reasons, doctors increasingly emphasized the health of mothers. To some degree, this was a pragmatic approach by the profession, one intended to achieve two goals. First, doctors wanted to maintain their professional status. Abortions were a perceived factor in the maternal mortality rate, which called into question their ability to prevent maternal deaths. Second, their increased interest in maternal welfare was also a regulatory measure as they endorsed that the maintenance of healthy mothers meant that women could fulfill their duty to the state through reproduction.[66]

Reinforcing Patriarchal Ideals Scientifically: Some Conclusions

This shift in the medical profession's view of femininity as it related to abortion is interesting because it represents a departure from the patterns found in the consumer advertising. Yet the modern feminine identity that viewed women as wives and mothers continued to be promoted. Women were expected to be beautiful, clean, and scientifically knowledgeable mothers, and consumer discourse reinforced that this was the natural and normal role for them to play, particularly after the war. Increasingly, public authority was derived from a growing use of medical science to claim legitimacy for products ranging from cosmetics to foodstuffs. This judicious employment of science implied to consumers, who were mainly women, that medical professionals were aligned with the manufacturers who sold products to improve beauty, health, and the family. In reality, doctors were shifting their discourse to address the importance of maintaining women's welfare. Indeed, by the end of the interwar period, their definition of health had changed significantly.[67] This would open up the possibility for doctors to, legitimately and legally, provide access to both birth control and therapeutic abortions for women who needed to limit their fertility. Despite physicians' changing view of women and doubts about the legitimacy of some advertising that made scientific claims, advertisers continued to use medical science to sell their products. Indeed, doctors' concerns in 1934 that the public was often "uncritical," which meant that "a lucrative field for exploitation is always available" for advertisers, remain in force today.[68] The public authority masquerading as professional authority can still be found in consumer culture and indicates the power that society has invested (sometimes uncritically) in science as an influential discourse.

This initial exploration of the ways that professional authority was employed to sell products that reinforced patriarchal ideals suggests that we need to more fully interrogate the social construction of women's bodies as found in a variety of sources. In particular, the use of medical science as a means of reinforcing these roles needs to be more fully investigated as this study and Chapters 3 and 4 in this volume indicate. In addition, this study demonstrates that, despite the rules defining their behaviour, women did not always perform in ways that adhered to the "norm." Indeed, some women sought to avoid the prescriptions and were active agents as they attempted to control their own fertility. Finally, it suggests the need for a fuller critique of authoritative messages found in advertising. Despite what the ads suggested, doctors were not always in agreement with the values they championed. To take at face value consumer messaging that attempts to sell us goods endorsed by "experts" is problematic at best. To understand our bodies in terms of these prescriptions seems dangerous at worst – an interesting conundrum given the length to which advertisers have gone to make us scientifically minded! By critically questioning the legitimacy of the public authority of consumerism, we might begin to re-vision our bodies in a manner that helps us move toward performing gender in non-traditional ways.

Notes

1 Cynthia Comacchio, *Nations Are Built of Babies: Saving Ontario's Mothers and Children, 1900-1940* (Montreal and Kingston: McGill-Queen's University Press, 1993).

2 Post's Bran Flakes advertisement, *Ladies' Home Journal,* September 1924, 91.

3 Editorial, "Puerperal Mortality: Success or Failure?" *Canadian Public Health Journal* 25, 12 (December 1934): 600.

4 My interchangeable use of "medicine" and "science" is intentional. I argue that in this period of modernization, these two discourses were seen to be synonymous.

5 Mary Lynn Stewart outlines how ideals of feminine beauty in France were evident in both scientific and cultural discourses. See Mary Lynn Stewart, *For Health and Beauty: Physical Culture for Frenchwomen, 1880s-1930s* (Baltimore: Johns Hopkins University Press, 2001).

6 *Chatelaine* is distinctly Canadian but did not begin publishing until into the period under discussion. Prior to that time, the *Ladies' Home Journal* was distributed and read by middle- and upper-class women in Canada. Although it came from the United States, its prescriptions for women were essentially the same as those of *Chatelaine.* Comparisons of Canadian and American advertising may be possible, but I have chosen not to do that here. Like popular literature, the medical journals of both the USA and Britain were read by Canadian physicians, and articles in the medical press from those countries were routinely reprinted in the *Canadian Medical Association Journal.* I am interested in how the discourses of popular literature promoted a specific role for girls and women, but, of course, they also sent messages to men about the roles they were expected to play.

7 Ads that reinforced prescriptions of both femininity and masculinity did not only appear in women's magazines, of course. Similar prescriptions can be found in other magazines in this period such as *Maclean's.* High quality images of the ads from *Chatelaine* and the *Ladies' Home Journal* described here were unavailable but similar ads from *Maclean's* have been included here as examples. This reinforces my argument that the discourses found in popular culture that promoted specific roles for women (and men) were ubiquitous throughout this period.

8 For instance, see Alia Al-Khalidi, "'The Greatest Invention of the Century': Menstruation in Visual and Material Culture," in *All the World and Her Husband: Women in Twentieth-Century Consumer Culture,* ed. Maggie Andrews and Mary M. Talbot (London: Cassell, 2000), 65-81; Kathy Peiss, "American Women and the Making of Modern Consumer Culture" (lecture delivered at the University at Albany, State University of New York, 26 March 1998, recorded for the *Journal for MultiMedia History* 1, 1 [Fall 1998], http://www.albany.edu/); Kathy Peiss, *Hope*

in a Jar: The Making of America's Beauty Culture (New York: Henry Holt, 1998); Shelley M. Park, "From Sanitation to Liberation? The Modern and Postmodern Marketing of Menstrual Products," *Journal of Popular Culture* 30, 2 (Fall 1996): 149-68; William R. Leach, "Transformations in a Culture of Consumption: Women and Department Stores, 1890-1925," *Journal of American History* 71, 2 (September 1984): 319-42; Gretchen Papazian, "'Feed My Poor Famished Heart': Constructing Womanhood through Consumer Practices," *American Transcendental Quarterly* 21, 2 (June 2007): 127-45; Nancy Tomes, "Merchants of Health: Medicine and Consumer Culture in the United States, 1900-1940," *Journal of American History* 88, 2 (September 2001): 519-47; Lori Loeb, "Doctors and Patent Medicines in Modern Britain: Professionalism and Consumerism," *Albion: A Quarterly Journal Concerned with British Studies* 33, 3 (Autumn 2001): 404-25; and Andrea Tone, "Contraceptive Consumers: Gender and the Political Economy of Birth Control in the 1930s," *Journal of Social History* 29, 3 (Spring 1996): 486. Heather Molyneaux has explored the ways that advertisements of the 1950s and 1960s reveal "cultural anxieties about women's sexuality, gender roles and health by containing deviant representations of women within definitions of illness." What this points to is a need for a study of advertisements over the course of the twentieth century to trace the changes (or not) in depictions of women's roles in ads that appropriate medical science. See Heather Molyneaux, "In Sickness and in Health: Representations of Women in Pharmaceutical Advertisements in the *Canadian Medical Association Journal,* 1950-1970" (PhD diss., University of New Brunswick, 2009), 275; and Heather Molyneaux, "Controlling Conception: Images of Women, Safety, Sexuality and the Pill in the Sixties," in *Gender, Health and Popular Culture: Historical Perspectives,* ed. Cheryl Krasnick Warsh (Waterloo: Wilfrid Laurier University Press, 2011), 65-88.

9   Other historians have documented the construction of motherhood in this period. For instance, see Comacchio, *Nations Are Built of Babies;* and Katherine Arnup, *Education for Motherhood: Advice for Mothers in Twentieth-Century Canada* (Toronto: University of Toronto Press, 1994).

10   By the twentieth century, the "regular" medical professionals, those doctors trained in the scientific method, were established as experts on the body and had beat out competition from "irregulars" – homeopaths, naturopaths, and midwives. For details on earlier competition between regulars and irregulars, see S.E.D. Shortt, "Physicians, Science, and Status: Issues in the Professionalization of Anglo-American Medicine in the Nineteenth Century," *Medical History* 27 (1983): 51-68; and R.D. Gidney and W.P.J. Millar, "The Origins of Organized Medicine in Ontario, 1850-1869," in *Health, Disease and Medicine: Essays in Canadian History,* ed. Charles G. Roland (Toronto: Hannah Institute for the History of Medicine, 1984), 64-95.

11   Cynthia Comacchio discusses public health in relation to motherhood in *Nations Are Built of Babies.* See also Heather MacDougall, *Activists and Advocates: Toronto's Health Department, 1883-1983* (Toronto: Dundurn Press, 1990). Closely connected and intertwined with the public health movement was the larger social reform movement in Canada. See Mariana Valverde, *The Age of Light, Soap and Water: Moral Reform in English Canada, 1885-1925* (Toronto: University of Toronto Press, 2008); and Angus McLaren, *Our Own Master Race: Eugenics in Canada, 1885-1945* (Toronto: Oxford University Press, 1990).

12   Editorial, "Publicity in Medicine," *CMAJ* 16, 11 (November 1926): 1377. See also "Necessity for Education of the Public in the Details of Personal Hygiene," *CMAJ* 14, 12 (December 1924): 1228; and "Publicity and Health Education," *CMAJ* 18, 3 (March 1928): 820.

13   The use of medical science to legitimize consumer products remains a pervasive issue. The marketing of Viagra is perhaps the best-known example, but medicine is used to reinforce the effectiveness of many other products, from toothpaste to cosmetics and food.

14   Sandra Lee Bartky, "Foucault, Femininity, and the Modernization of Patriarchal Power," in *Feminism and Foucault: Reflections on Resistance,* ed. Irene Diamond and Lee Quimby (Boston: Northeastern University Press, 1988), 109.

15 Penny Tinkler, *Constructing Girlhood: Popular Magazines for Girls Growing Up in England, 1920-1950* (London: Taylor and Francis, 1995), 152.
16 On gender as performance, see Judith Butler, *Gender Trouble: Feminism and the Subversion of Identity* (New York: Routledge, 1990). Those women who performed outside the norm were perceived as problems. See Carolyn Strange, *Toronto's Girl Problem: The Perils and Pleasures of the City, 1800-1930* (Toronto: University of Toronto Press, 1995); and Regina Kunzel, *Fallen Women, Problem Girls: Unmarried Mothers and the Professionalization of Social Work, 1890-1945* (New Haven, CT: Yale University Press, 1993).
17 Peiss, "American Women," 2. See also Christine Frederick, *Selling Mrs. Consumer* (New York: Business Bourse, 1929).
18 Peiss, "American Women," 2.
19 For an extended discussion of this, see Kristin Hall, "Prescriptions for Modern Womanhood: Advertising Lysol in Interwar North America" (master's thesis, Laurentian University, 2008).
20 Ivory Soap advertisement, *Ladies' Home Journal*, January 1923, 2.
21 Calay Soap advertisement, *Chatelaine*, September 1931, 33; Woodbury's Facial Powder advertisement, *Chatelaine*, May 1936, 35.
22 In her discussion of feminine beauty in France, Mary Lynn Stewart states that "in Europe, as in other patriarchal civilizations, beauty ideals are defined primarily for men's pleasure and are camouflaged as 'natural.'" Advertisements in Canada for beauty products such as Calay certainly seem to support this assertion. See Stewart, *For Health and Beauty*, 10.
23 A similar product was advertised in the *Ladies' Home Journal*. See Yeast Foam advertisement, *Ladies' Home Journal*, March 1921, 119.
24 Fleischmann's Yeast advertisement, *Chatelaine*, March 1928, 2.
25 Fleischmann's Yeast advertisement, *Chatelaine*, February 1932, 25.
26 Fleischmann's claimed that yeast could assist with constipation, a form of "intestinal poisoning" that it claimed led to "headaches, dreary dragging lassitude, lack of appetite, mental Depression, heartburn, [and] skin eruptions." See *Chatelaine*, July 1928, 2; February 1931, 2; October 1931, 27; January 1932, 27; February 1932, 25; March 1933, 25; January 1934, 19; February 1935, 29; and November 1935, 23.
27 Pyorrhea is an inflammation of the gums and tooth sockets, which can lead to tooth loss. Forhan's Toothpaste advertisement, *Chatelaine*, July 1932, 1 (emphasis in original).
28 The Lux ad pointed to "the ? in marriage," which was whether dishwashing needed to make a woman's hands "ugly." It also provided statistical evidence of the issue, noting that "nearly 2000 young brides in 11 cities told us how they plan to meet this vexing problem." Advertisement, Lux Soap, *Chatelaine*, September 1931, 54.
29 Advertisement, Odorono, *Chatelaine*, May 1932, 53. See also Advertisement, Odorono, *Chatelaine*, August 1935, 30. This particular ad suggested, "Ask your doctor and he will tell you that Odorono is entirely safe for you to use." See also Listerine advertisement, *Ladies' Home Journal*, August 1925, 68.
30 Odorono advertisement, *Chatelaine*, March 1928, 31.
31 Mum Deodorant advertisement, *Chatelaine*, August 1935, 30. Advertisements for laundry soap also reinforced that odour was a "deal-breaker" for budding relationships. For instance, see Lux Soap advertisement, *Chatelaine*, July 1933, 39.
32 Kotex Sanitary Napkins advertisement, *Ladies' Home Journal*, February 1924, 126. This ad was attributed to Ellen J. Buckland, "Graduate Nurse," implying its authenticity as a medical document.
33 Ibid.
34 Kotex Sanitary Napkins advertisement, *Chatelaine*, January 1929, 31.
35 Kotex Sanitary Napkins advertisement, *Ladies' Home Journal*, December 1926, 107.
36 Kotex advertisement, *Chatelaine*, January 1929, 31.

37 An advertisement in *Maclean's* in 1931 noted that "Kotex is too closely related to health to risk doubtful substitutes" to reinforce the connection between the product and scientific approaches to hygiene that women were to employ in this period. August 15, 1931, 41.

38 Kotex Phantom Napkins advertisement, *Chatelaine*, July 1932, 29. Several other versions of the sanitary pad emerged during the interwar period, including the Equalizer and the Wondersoft. By the mid-1930s, tampons had also entered the scene as Tampax began to market its product. In a 1939 ad, the company reinforced that Tampax were "preferred by a doctor." Tampax advertisement, *Chatelaine*, August 1939, 20.

39 Al-Khalidi, "'The Greatest Invention,'" 70-71.

40 *British Medical Journal*, 15 November 1884, 969, quoted in ibid., 71.

41 See Wendy Mitchinson, *The Nature of Their Bodies: Women and Their Doctors in Victorian Canada* (Toronto: University of Toronto Press, 1991), 180-82.

42 Al-Khalidi, "'The Greatest Invention,'" 73.

43 Lister's late-nineteenth-century discovery of air-borne bacteria was widely known by the early twentieth century. Mitchinson describes how antiseptic practice altered childbirth but was also relevant to general surgical procedures. See Mitchinson, *The Nature of Their Bodies*; and Wendy Mitchinson, *Giving Birth in Canada, 1900-1950* (Toronto: University of Toronto Press, 2002). Doctors were particularly concerned with sepsis as the result of botched attempts at abortion. See Tracy Penny Light, "Shifting Interests: The Medical Discourse on Abortion in English Canada, 1850-1969" (PhD diss., University of Waterloo, 2003).

44 See Pepsodent Antiseptic advertisement, *Chatelaine*, March 1933, 33; Zonite advertisement, *Chatelaine*, November 1933, 41; and Lysol advertisement, *Chatelaine*, May 1932, 29.

45 Listerine advertisement, *Ladies' Home Journal*, August 1923, 56.

46 See also Roland Marchand, *Advertising the American Dream: Making Way for Modernity, 1920-1940* (Berkeley: University of California Press, 1985).

47 Lysol advertisement, *Chatelaine*, January 1937, 37. This type of ad, which suggested that women were at fault if they did not use certain products, was not uncommon. For instance, see Pepsodent New-Day Dentifrice advertisement, *Ladies' Home Journal*, January 1922, 61; Grape-Nuts advertisement, *Ladies' Home Journal*, May 1926, 64, and December 1926, 53; and Hygeia Nursing Bottles advertisement, *Ladies' Home Journal*, October 1921, 34, and December 1926, 41. A number of historians have discussed the movement to raise children scientifically in this period. See Comacchio, *Nations Are Built of Babies*; and Arnup, *Education for Motherhood*. On Lysol specifically, see Hall, "Prescriptions for Modern Womanhood."

48 Grape-Nuts advertisement, *Ladies' Home Journal*, May 1926, 64; Heinz Strained Foods advertisement, *Chatelaine*, April 1937, 76.

49 Peiss, "American Women," 2. See also Peiss, *Hope in a Jar*.

50 See Veronica Strong-Boag, *The New Day Recalled: Lives of Girls and Women in English Canada, 1919-1939*, 2nd ed. (Toronto: Copp Clark Pitman, 1993).

51 Tone, "Contraceptive Consumers," 486.

52 Lysol Disinfectant advertisement, *Chatelaine*, May 1932, 29. See also Hall, "Prescriptions for Modern Womanhood."

53 Tone, "Contraceptive Consumers," 486.

54 In her work on feminine hygiene products, Rebecca Ginsburg writes that "goods can serve as aids that complete the self-portraits that people carry around in their heads." In this line of thinking, the purchase by women of consumer goods that reinforce what is "normal" is particularly significant in light of evidence that, behind closed doors, some women were attempting to avoid the ideal. See Rebecca Ginsburg, "'Don't Tell, Dear': The Material Culture of Tampons and Napkins," *Journal of Material Culture* 1, 3 (1996): 366.

55 Whereas biological determinism permeated the medicalization of the body during the nineteenth century, it was increasingly less evident as the twentieth century progressed. The best

discussion of doctors' construction of femaleness in Canada is Mitchinson, *The Nature of Their Bodies;* and Mitchinson, *Giving Birth in Canada.*

56 J.T. Phair and A.H. Sellars, "A Study of Maternal Deaths in the Province of Ontario," *Canadian Public Health Journal* 25, 12 (December 1934): 566.

57 A study conducted in Manitoba from 1928 to 1932 provided similar conclusions. See F.W. Jackson, R.D. Defries, and A.H. Sellars, "A Five-Year Survey of Maternal Mortality in Manitoba, 1928-1932," *Canadian Public Health Journal* 25, 3 (March 1934): 103-19. For a discussion of both this and the Ontario report, see Angus McLaren and Arlene Tigar McLaren, "Discoveries and Dissimulations: The Impact of Abortion Deaths on Maternal Mortality in British Columbia," *BC Studies* 64 (Winter 1984-85): 3-26.

58 "Topics of Current Interest: A Clinical Study of Abortion," *CMAJ* 35 (December 1936): 692.

59 For a further discussion of birth control methods, see Angus McLaren and Arlene Tigar McLaren, *The Bedroom and the State: The Changing Practices and Politics of Contraception and Abortion in Canada, 1880-1996,* 2nd ed. (Toronto: Oxford University Press, 1996). In the United States, see Janet Farell Brodie, *Contraception and Abortion in 19th Century America* (Ithaca: Cornell University Press, 1994). Tone notes that, though they claimed scientific advances, many manufacturers were not producing effective birth control products. She suggests that more conventional forms of birth control would have been more successful in many cases. However, manufacturers successfully promoted the idea that their products were technologically advanced, and therefore necessary for the modern woman, even if the products were not always effective. Tone, "Consuming Contraceptives," 488.

60 Angus McLaren, "Birth Control and Abortion in Canada, 1870-1920," *Canadian Historical Review* 59 (1978): 319-40; Tracy Penny, "'Getting Rid of My Trouble': A Social History of Abortion in Ontario, 1880-1929" (master's thesis, Laurentian University, 1995).

61 Dr. James Goodall, "Puerperal Infections: An Extramural Lecture," *CMAJ* 22, 5 (May 1930): 694. Obviously, as implied by reports such as this one, doctors viewed self-induced abortions as quite dangerous. For an extended discussion, see Penny Light, "Shifting Interests."

62 J. Wyllie, "Sex Differences in the Mortalities of Childhood and Adult Life," *Canadian Public Health Journal* 24, 11 (November 1933): 535. Several accounts of women's demise due to abortion exist in the medical literature from this period. See William Bethune, "Inversion of the Uterus," *CMAJ* 29, 6 (December 1933): 631; W.B. Hendry, "The Problem of Hemmorhage in Obstetrical Practice," *CMAJ* 30, 6 (June 1934): 629; D.F. MacDonald, "Missed Ectopic," *Nova Scotia Medical Bulletin* 16, 4 (April 1937): 208; J.H. Duncan, "Maternal Mortality in Country Practice," *CMAJ* 38, 6 (June 1938): 551; J. Ross Vant, "Report of the Committee on Maternal Mortality," *Alberta Medical Bulletin* 3, 4 (October 1938): 16; and B.K. Cody, "Case Reports," *Dalhousie Medical Journal* 4, 1 (February 1939): 43.

63 Editorial, "Puerperal Mortality: Success or Failure?" 600. See also H.W. Hill, "Prenatal Negligence and Loss of Population," *CMAJ* 11, 9 (September 1921): 615-19; W.B. Hendry, "Maternal Mortality," *CMAJ* 13, 4 (April 1923): 252-54; Ross Mitchell, "The Prevention of Maternal Mortality in Manitoba," *CMAJ* 19, 9 (September 1928): 292-96; Adelaide M. Plumptre, "A Mother's Duty to the State," *Public Health Journal* 18, 4 (April 1927): 178-81; and Annah L. Prichard, "Maternity," *Public Health Journal* 14, 7 (July 1923): 322-24.

64 Statistics indicate that female labour force participation was on the rise. In 1921, 17.7 percent of women worked, and by 1941, that figure had increased to 22.9 percent. See Strong-Boag, *The New Day Recalled,* 43. Strong-Boag also notes that women's wages were still only about 60 percent of those of men and that women in the interwar years typically worked in female job ghettoes, undertaking traditional female occupations such as domestic work, teaching, clerical jobs, and the service industry. See ibid., Chapter 2, "Working for Pay." Despite this, the prescriptions for traditional femininity abounded. For instance, though *Chatelaine* acknowledged that women did work, it gave the definite sense that this was temporary. In a

series of articles written by Annabelle Lee for *Chatelaine* about women's fitness and weight reduction, one outlined how women could slim down while working around the house. "There are all sorts of household tasks that are exercises in themselves," Lee wrote. "The woman who does her own housework has her reducing studio right in her home." Annabelle Lee, "Work-A-Day-Beauty," *Chatelaine,* November 1933, 32-33.

65 Helen MacMurchy, "Report on the Committee on Maternal Welfare," *Nova Scotia Medical Bulletin* 11, 4 (April 1932): 462.

66 For instance, in a 1929 *Manitoba Medical Bulletin* article, E.W. Montgomery remarked that "the general health of the mother before and during pregnancy has been found to directly influence the mortality rate, the death rates being just double in that group which comprised individuals who were designated as having 'unsatisfactory' general health." E.W. Montgomery, "Maternal Mortality," *Manitoba Medical Bulletin* (1929): 4. The health of mothers and the campaign to promote prenatal education were very prominent at this time. For example, see K.C. McIlwraith, "Obstetrics and the State," *CMAJ* 10, 4 (April 1920): 305-13; R.E. Wodehouse, "Maternal Deaths," *CMAJ* 34, 5 (May 1936): 525-27; H.E. Young and J.T. Phair, "Maternal Mortality in Canada," *Public Health Journal* 19, 3 (March 1928): 135-36; and Ethel Cryderman, "Significant Facts," *Public Health Journal* 19, 4 (April 1928): 191-92.

67 Initially, the medical profession defined upholding health as dealing with anything that threatened a woman's physical health. Only severe contraindications to pregnancy could justify the performance of an illegal operation. However, a 1938 British legal case called this stance into question. The precedent set in the *Bourne* case enabled physicians to argue that health was defined as both physical and mental wellness. The judge in the case ruled that "no line can be drawn between danger to life and danger to health: that no doctor knows whether life is in danger until the patient is dead; and that if on reasonable grounds, based on adequate knowledge, after consultation with colleagues, a doctor forms the opinion that the probable consequences of the continuance of pregnancy would make the woman a physical or mental wreck, then he is not only entitled, but it is his duty, to perform an abortion." This ruling paved the way for future discussions about therapeutic abortion in Canada. "Topics of Current Interest: Therapeutic Abortion and the Law," *CMAJ* 39, 4 (October 1938): 402.

68 A.G.N., "The Ethics and Psychology of Advertising," *CMAJ* 30, 2 (February 1934): 187.

3

Selling Lysol as a Household Disinfectant in Interwar North America

Kristin Hall

By the second decade of the twentieth century, Lysol Disinfectant was being sold across the United States and Canada as both a household cleaner and a feminine hygiene product. To market Lysol, manufacturers Lehn and Fink launched a massive advertising campaign in North American women's magazines such as the *Canadian Home Journal, Chatelaine,* and the *Ladies' Home Journal,* directing it at white English-speaking middle-class female consumers. Household cleaning and feminine hygiene advertisements were mutually exclusive, however, and of the 197 interwar Lysol advertisements collected for this study from the three aforementioned periodicals, 136 highlighted Lysol's use as a household cleaner. This chapter examines Lysol's interwar household cleaning campaign and analyzes the methods advertisers employed to target white middle-class housewives and mothers with the intention of prompting consumptive change in relation to their cleaning practices.[1]

In examining Lysol's ad campaign, this chapter parallels the essays of Tracy Penny Light and Denyse Baillargeon (Chapters 2 and 4 in this volume), for, like them, it investigates the ideological underpinnings of interwar modernity and the ways in which these ideologies translated into new prescriptive responsibilities for women in the realms of familial health and childrearing. But whereas Penny Light reveals gendered prescriptions in the medicalized and scientific nature of ads from the interwar years, and Baillargeon explores modern ideologies such as the links between health and happiness in representations of women's bodies in medicine ads, this chapter is based on an analysis of the ad campaign for a single product. The purpose of this product-centred analysis is to discern how a single consumer good was marketed, using the prescriptive rhetoric of interwar modernity, and to situate Lysol's campaign within prescriptive modern advertising trends, such as those skilfully revealed by Penny Light and Baillargeon.

This approach allows Lysol's campaign to be situated within the larger thematic advertising trends of the period. It also allows for a detailed analysis of how notions of modernity and modern advertising techniques were employed, given the nature of Lysol's intended use as a cleaning product, and how specific socio-cultural trends were used to connect Lysol to female consumers. In investigating Lysol ads, the advertising techniques employed to create them, and the target market and its contextual milieus, this level of analysis allows for a greater understanding of what historians John Staudenmaier and Pamela Walker Lurito Laird have termed the historical "causal influences" of advertising. According to them, uncovering the historical causal influences of advertising includes an examination of advertising content, technique, target market, and historical context, which are considered in conjunction with one another to determine how and why specific ad campaigns would have affected the target audience. Given the rise of modern advertising techniques in the 1920s, which were designed to produce strong emotional reactions among audiences, the interrogation of causal influences is especially pertinent to gain an understanding of why certain campaigns may have resonated with their intended audiences on an emotional level.[2]

In applying this product-centred approach, this chapter argues that Lysol advertisers employed modern negative emotional appeal techniques by juxtaposing women's conventional pre-war cleaning and mothering practices with the new concepts of household management and scientific motherhood as they conveyed that housewives risked their families' health (and lives) if they did not use Lysol to practise modern housekeeping and mothering techniques. Additionally, in constructing their campaign, Lysol advertisers exploited historically specific concepts such as the germ theory of disease and emphasized the ever-present risk of infant mortality and childhood illness, which were prevalent during the interwar period.[3]

Significantly, during the First World War and for a time afterward, it was not overly apparent that North American women would have responded to advertising campaigns such as Lysol's, which focused solely on domesticity and women's roles in the home. During the war, women had participated in the paid workforce, and female citizens over the age of twenty-one had also attained the federal suffrage in Canada in 1918 and the United States in 1920. These changes caused a great deal of uncertainty regarding the social, cultural, and economic roles women would play in the post-war world.[4]

The perception that women's social function was shifting from that of housewife and mother to paid worker and enfranchised citizen led to a profound sense of crisis over the future of North American family life. Combined with the social disruption caused by increased urbanization, industrialization, and immigration as well as revelations about the poor physical health of army recruits and the death toll of numerous potential fathers (which fed into pre-existing fears about race suicide and the destruction of the patriarchal family), the concern over women's gender roles caused widespread fears that the North American family would fall apart. Because the family was considered the principal social unit in both countries, contemporaries firmly believed that its destruction would lead to the disintegration of society as a whole.[5]

Government officials, social reformers, and scientific experts such as doctors and home economists, however, were convinced that the social fabric could be saved. Paradoxically, these authorities insisted that although women were considered a main cause of familial degeneration, they alone could be its cure. Officials believed that the crisis could be averted if women would embrace their traditional domestic roles, return to the home, and restore the family. This was not an unreasonable expectation, for, despite the supposed advances they had made during and after the war, the majority of North American middle-class women still expected to marry, have children, and lead primarily domestic lives. Though increasing numbers of middle-class women were working for wages prior to marriage, they assumed that once they became wives, they would leave the paid workforce and concentrate on the home.[6]

The popularization of home economics and home management during the period also ensured that women would embrace domesticity. Advocated by those same authorities who longed to see women return to the home and restore the family, the home economics movement was essentially a means of professionalizing and modernizing housework, thereby making domesticity into a modern career choice for women. The home economics movement predated the interwar period, as Catherine Beecher first expounded the value of training women in the scientific study of the home during the mid-nineteenth century. By the interwar era, however, household economists such as Christine Frederick believed that new advances in the areas of sanitation, medicine, nutrition, and technology could be combined with the new principles of scientific time management to improve the field. Scientific management was an industrial response to the desire for increased production; it advocated that tasks be timed, analyzed, and planned to ensure that they were carried out as efficiently as possible. Experts such as Frederick believed that the combination of home economics and scientific management would ensure that women would become professional, proficient, and efficient home managers.[7]

Home management was the result of this fusion, and it appealed to women, for during the interwar period, science was extolled as modern, and only those who partook in "scientific practices" in one way or another could consider themselves modern as well. As historian Rima D. Apple has succinctly noted, home economics and household management were "the only science(s) gendered female," and women enthusiastically adopted their principles.[8] Therefore, this combination would not only promote the allure of housewifery as a profession, but women's applied knowledge and proficiency in the home would rebuild and uphold the traditional North American family.[9] Through the proliferation of advice manuals, magazine articles, and home economics classes, home economists were able to disseminate their ideas to the masses. The overarching message women received from these sources was that they were expected to use modern science and technological principles, applying them to the care of their homes and families.[10]

Although household management taught women about all aspects of caring for the home, experts believed that some aspects of domestic life, such as family health, needed more attention than others. Basing their approach on the germ theory of disease, which dictated that illness was caused by the invasion of living organisms otherwise known as germs, home economists and other experts taught women that the only way to guard their family's health was through cleanliness.[11] Scientific housekeeping emphasized that cleaning must move beyond mere dusting and tidying to a "sanitary crusade" against the dangerous disease-causing germs that lurked in every North American home.[12] Women would probably have responded enthusiastically to this directive, for, as historian Nancy Tomes has argued, during the early twentieth century, Americans became increasingly anxious regarding the dangers posed by germs.[13]

Due to the growing emphasis on domesticity in the post-war years, and because many women associated their personal fulfillment with familial well-being, the threat posed by germs was especially distressing during the 1920s and 1930s. If women failed to protect their families, not only would they feel intense guilt, they would also be deemed inefficient housewives for being unable to stop supposedly preventable diseases from harming their families. This was a devastating castigation for any woman who prided herself on her ability to care for her family with the new, modern, scientific methods.[14]

Because women no longer produced the goods they used for domestic chores (and because the goods used in the past would have been considered obsolete), housewives were encouraged to turn to the mass market for the products needed to scientifically manage their homes. Due to the heavy emphasis home experts placed on science, health, and cleanliness, Lysol was in an ideal position to take advantage of the popularization of household management. In addition, because women were also expected to internalize the scientific principles of housewifery and to base their self-worth on their success in attaining the ideals of health and wellness for their beloved families, advertisers had the emotive foundation they needed to exploit the developing principles of emotionally based modern advertising.[15]

Indeed, by the early 1920s, the methods used in the advertising industry underwent a significant shift as advertisers began to appeal to consumers' emotions rather than their sense of reason, as had previously been the case. Lysol advertisers adopted modern methodology, but they initially blended the traditional informational approach with the emotive method. This tactic was not unusual, for although historians and theorists such as Daniel Hill have depicted advertisements from the 1920s and 1930s as differing significantly from those of earlier in the century, which focused on product features, price, and availability, such was not always the case.[16] Instead, as historian Roland Marchand suggests, advertising practices transformed gradually, mixing the conventional information-based "factory viewpoint" copy with the new "emotive" style, especially in the early 1920s.[17]

Despite this blending of techniques, early interwar Lysol advertisements succeeded, through emotional appeals, in conveying that women needed to eschew their traditional cleaning methods if they were to guard their homes and families against germs. This is clearly displayed in a May 1920 Lysol ad from the *Ladies' Home Journal* (Figure 3.1). A Lysol bottle, the visual focal point, is placed on its side, and the disinfectant is dripping out. Four images appear between the falling drops of Lysol, including a bathroom, a windowsill, a garbage pail, and a bucket of water. As the text suggests, these are the "danger zones" where women should use Lysol to "rid the house of all germ life."[18]

The ad mentions the price of the product and where it can be purchased, but it is designed so that this information appears to be of secondary importance. The text is divided into two sections, the first placed below the Lysol bottle and above a large image of the Lysol brand name. The second portion of text is beneath the large Lysol emblem, and it is here that the product information is placed.[19] The primary textual component of this ad highlights the benefits

Figure 3.1 "Every Drop a Powerful Weapon against Contagious Disease," Lysol advertisement. *Source: Ladies' Home Journal*, May 1920, 167.

of using Lysol and suggests what the repercussions would be for family members if housewives continued to rely on traditional cleaning methods. The advertisement insists that "each drop of Lysol Disinfectant contains sufficient strength to kill instantly thousands of deadly disease germs. And if you accept the following suggestions you may feel assured that through proper disinfection you are making it practically impossible for contagious disease to attack your family."[20]

The text of this ad is an early example of what Marchand has described as "scare copy," which was increasingly used in Lysol ads throughout the period. Scare copy was intended to jolt consumers into new purchasing practices by frightening them. As interwar advertising theorist and psychologist Albert Poffenberger suggests, this approach was also known as creating a negative appeal.[21] By using language that would generate a negative emotional response among women, emphasizing the sheer number of germs in the home and implying that these germs were simply waiting to attack the family, advertisers endeavoured to frighten consumers into purchasing Lysol. Not only was scare copy used in this manner, but advertisers, like doctors and home economists, also clearly intimated that women alone were responsible for preventing family illness, which could be deflected only if they accepted expert advice and modern practices. If housewives chose to ignore Lysol's suggestions, they alone would be guilty of the disastrous consequences of such neglect.

Hybrid-style Lysol ads remained prevalent for the first two years of the decade, but by 1922, advertisers began to incorporate even more emotionally provocative content. As a July 1922 ad demonstrates, this was done through text and imagery (Figure 3.2). A large Lysol bottle occupies centre stage, as in previous ads, but the background is no longer empty. Instead, it features a middle-class brick house with a white door, decorative railing, and neat white curtains in the window.[22] In the middle of the door hangs a sign that reads "Contagious Disease – Board of Health," indicating that the family has contracted a communicable illness. The text reads "Keep this sign from your door ... If proper precautions were taken, many cases of serious sickness could be prevented ... In the absence of disinfection, disease germs breed by the million ... And contagious disease is a logical result."[23] By suggesting that the use of Lysol simply equates with taking proper precautions, the ad conveys that it should be considered both necessary and commonplace, and that women should know that they must apply the product to kill dangerous germs. Should they fail to do so, the inevitable outcome would be disease. And, of course, it was completely their own fault for not modernizing their cleaning practices.[24]

The image demonstrates that the consequences of not using the supposedly obvious "proper precaution" might be more than familial illness, as the sign

Keep this sign from your door

CONTAGIOUS
·DISEASE
BOARD OF HEALTH

Lysol Disinfectant
Reg. U.S. Pat. Off.

Kills Germs

If proper precautions were taken, many cases of serious sickness could be prevented. By "proper precaution," we mean regular disinfection. Disinfection kills germs. In the absence of disinfection, disease germs breed by the millions on floors, in toilet bowls, sinks, dark corners, garbage pails, from which they constantly assail your health. And contagious sickness is a logical result.

Sprinkle all such places in your house with "Lysol" Disin-fectant mixed with water. Do that at least twice a week. It takes only a few moments of your time and may prevent dangerous illness.

On cleaning days add a few drops of "Lysol" Disinfectant to the cleaning water. Being a soapy substance, it helps to clean while it disinfects.

A 50c bottle makes 5 gallons of germ-killing solution. A 25c bottle makes 2 gallons.

"Lysol" Disinfectant is also invaluable for personal hygiene.

Send for free samples of other Lysol products

You can purchase a 25c bottle of "Lysol" Disinfectant for trial purposes at any drug store. We shall be glad to mail you free samples of the other Lysol products.

Shall we send a sample of "Lysol" Shaving Cream for the men folks? Protects the health of the skin. Renders small cuts aseptically clean. We will also include a sample of "Lysol" Toilet Soap. Refreshingly soothing, healing, and helpful for improving the skin.

Send name and address on a postcard.

Manufactured only by LYSOL, Inc.
LEHN & FINK, Inc., Sole Distributors
635 Greenwich Street, New York

Makers of Pebeco Tooth Paste
Canadian Agents: Harold F. Ritchie & Company, Limited, 10 McCaul Street, Toronto

Figure 3.2 "Keep This Sign from Your Door," Lysol advertisement.
Source: Ladies' Home Journal, July 1922, 66.

indicates that medical authorities have deemed the home and its inhabitants to be a danger to public health. This would have suggested that women needed to adopt Lysol for the sake of family health as well as to avoid external judgment and public humiliation. As historian Ruth Schwartz Cowan asserts, during this period, women often compared their housewifery skills to those of female kin and neighbours to determine how successful they were in managing their own homes.[25] It would seem, then, that this advertisement would certainly have stirred a negative emotional reaction, as having one's home categorized as unhealthy would have been mortifying for such a housewife. Cowan also concludes that due to increased public emphasis on the importance of domesticity, "housework was to be thought of no longer as a chore but, rather, as an expression of the housewife's personality and her affection for her family."[26] Therefore, the Board of Health's sign signalled much more than the simple presence of illness, for contemporaries would have viewed it as a public declaration of a housewife's neglect and lack of devotion to her family.

Into the late 1920s and the 1930s, Lysol advertisers became increasingly blatant in their efforts to garner sales through negative appeal. As Poffenberger suggests, due to the ever-increasing number of ads vying for consumers' attention, advertisers were forced to do whatever they deemed necessary to ensure that their ads stood out from the rest, including shocking or frightening potential customers.[27] Lysol took this approach, bombarding its target market with fearsome headlines such as "The Deadly Doorknob," "Domestic Warfare," "Even Your Broom May Be a Jungle of Germs," and "Germs Lurk Everywhere."[28]

Yet Lysol's most overt use of scare copy, which contrasted traditional practices with modern cleaning methods, came in 1931. In a series of six ads that appeared in the *Ladies' Home Journal,* the *Canadian Home Journal,* and *Chatelaine,* the company sought to demonstrate the value of Lysol to modern life by recounting various European "historical" instances in which many people had died due to improper disinfection (or a complete lack thereof). Examples of plagues and wartime infection-related tragedies from Germany, England, France, and Russia were used to demonstrate the need for proper household disinfection with Lysol. Indeed, the September 1931 ad that focused on an unidentified Russian plague read, "Death stalked the streets of Russia. Peasants were dropping like flies ... Doctors were helpless, remedies useless. Everything was tried, nothing availed against the scourge – not even such ancient charms as hitching four widows to a plow in the dead of night, and drawing a furrow around the village."[29] This ad underscores the unsophisticated and unscientific state of the Russian people by highlighting the fact that, unlike modern North Americans, they did not know the cause of disease and believed that an epidemic could be halted through "superstitious" practices such as hitching widows to a plow. Explaining that "thanks to modern methods of antisepsis and sanitation," disease can be controlled, the ad stresses that women have the power to do so by using Lysol, "properly diluted wherever germs are apt to lurk – on wounds, cuts and human tissue; in the household, on telephones, doorknobs, woodwork, nursery furniture, baby's toys, and utensils."[30] Fear inducing though it is, this ad also assured Depression-ravaged consumers that buying Lysol was an intelligent decision, for they would be protecting their families while saving money by purchasing "the most economical disinfectant in the world."[31]

The Lysol company may have had another reason to believe that this series of ads would appeal to consumers. As Suellen Hoy suggests, during the interwar years, the North American preoccupation with cleanliness was highly racialized. Cleanliness was considered the civilized world's greatest virtue, and for Canadians and Americans, only those who were native-born, white-skinned, and English speaking could truly be considered inherently civilized.[32] Prior to and during the 1920s and 1930s, domestic science experts and the general public began to fear the unsanitary threat posed by "uncivilized" immigrants who, supposedly without any appreciation of proper sanitation, arrived in North America. Although programs were developed to teach them the value of cleanliness, Hoy insists that most found North American standards both onerous and confusing. This generated a great deal of fear among the native-born population, as many believed that newcomers carried disease caused by their unclean practices.[33] The September 1931 Lysol ad, with its references to plague in Russia, may therefore be read as an indirect attempt to capitalize on this concern in the hope that female consumers who feared the sanitary habits of immigrants would purchase more Lysol to protect themselves and their families.

Housewifery was a major component of most women's lives, but Lysol advertisers recognized that mothering, too, could be capitalized on to sell their product. Although ads such as those mentioned above, which perpetuated the importance of scientific household management, remained a crucial part of the campaign throughout the interwar era, by 1926 the company began to incorporate the concept of scientific motherhood into its ads. In fact, by the end of the period, 58 (42.6 percent) of Lysol's 136 household cleaning ads focused on women's roles as mothers and their responsibility for the health of their children.

As Poffenberger and historians such as Hill, Marchand, and Ewen have asserted, invoking women's roles as mothers alongside imagery of babies and children was common in ads during the interwar years.[34] Poffenberger assumes that advertisers merely wanted to capitalize on women's instinctive inclination to nurture and protect the young.[35] An examination of Lysol ads in conjunction with secondary literature pertaining to advertising and the social construction of childhood and motherhood, however, suggests that the use of infants and children in advertising was not as ahistorical as Poffenberger believes. In fact, in the case of Lysol, it appears that advertisers were very much in tune with specific shifts in the conceptions and concerns of motherhood and childhood. This was especially apparent as Lysol ads included the historically specific concept of "scientific motherhood" and the related social concern over infant mortality and childhood disease.

Since the turn of the century, experts had grown increasingly alarmed regarding North American infant mortality rates and the society-wide belief that nothing could be done to remedy the problem. By 1915, 10 percent of all North American infants died before their first birthday. This number improved somewhat during the interwar years, with 64.8 per 1,000 American and 76.9 per 1,000 Canadian babies dying on average each year between 1920 and 1939, but doctors and social activists remained anxious.[36]

Outside the medical community, many merely comforted themselves with the belief that it was God's will that infants died so early in life; however, doctors argued that infant mortality had a distinctly human dimension. They insisted that contaminated food and unsanitary environments caused disease and death among babies. Due to rapidly developing public health bureaucracies in both Canada and the United States, doctors, nurses, reform workers, and scientists possessed the means to disseminate their message of prevention and to provide education to avert disease.[37] Of course, this message was directed at mothers, as experts emphasized that they were responsible for protecting infants from disease and death. Mothers were told that they must follow the dictates of "scientific motherhood," meaning that they must seek out and apply expert scientific and medical advice to raise their children healthfully. According to experts, doing anything less was simply negligence.[38]

Astute Lysol advertisers quickly picked up on the concern over infant mortality and experts' subsequent insistence on prevention and household cleanliness, incorporating these social trends into their interwar campaign. This movement provided an important opportunity for Lysol, especially given that the company's ads were based on the germ theory of disease. The concern over infant mortality due to uncleanliness fit perfectly with Lysol's existing campaign, and the focus on infants, the most vulnerable members of North American families, provided advertisers with additional emotional ammunition to attract the attention of female consumers.

Much like the ads based on scientific household management, those focusing on preventing infant mortality through cleanliness utilized the method of negative appeal that was designed to frighten mothers into altering their conventional cleaning practices by adopting Lysol. Although these advertisements combined text and imagery, initially only text was employed to inculcate fear. This is reflected in an August 1926 Lysol ad in the *Ladies' Home Journal* (Figure 3.3). The top two-thirds of the ad features an image of a healthy looking infant in a playpen. A German shepherd dog stands beside the child, presumably to protect her, and a large bottle of Lysol appears in the background. It is raised above the child and the dog, a positioning that implies it, too, is watching over the baby. The text suggests this as well, as the headline indicates that Lysol is "On Guard" against germs when used in the home.

The remainder of the ad is less reassuring, however. It reads, "'Baby's Safe,' you tell yourself as she plays about in her pen. But Baby is *not* safe. On the surfaces that her little hands touch, in the corners to which she crawls, lurk millions of virulent germs – source of the very diseases you dread most."[39] The intent of this ad is clear: to frighten new mothers by convincing them that their homes are a breeding ground for potentially lethal germs that threaten the health and safety of their children.

Once the ad has established the danger of germs, it presents the concept of scientific motherhood as the only means of nullifying the peril. Mere soap and water are not enough, for they cannot destroy germs; only a modern disinfectant such as Lysol can properly protect children from disease. Since scientific mother-hood was grounded in the belief that mothers should always heed the advice of experts, advertisers attempted to capitalize on women's uncritical acceptance of medico-scientific instruction. Thus, this ad underscores the point: "Health authorities say that only a true disinfectant in your cleaning water will make your home a safe home. And the disinfectant they use in hospitals and in their own homes is 'Lysol.'"[40] The ad does not specify which health authorities are meant, no doubt because there is no evidence that any particular authority advocated the use of Lysol, but mothers who were accustomed to and welcomed expert advice would probably have responded positively to this claim.[41]

Lysol also incorporated the concept of maternal neglect into its campaign. Its ads emphasized that women who did not use Lysol knew they were putting their children at risk of disease and death, and were therefore negligent mothers. This tactic would probably have been especially effective as it paralleled con-temporary experts' opinions (and reprimands) regarding mothers whose infants became ill because they themselves did not follow the advice provided to them.[42]

This tendency is clearly displayed in a June 1927 Lysol ad from the *Ladies' Home Journal*. Beside the prominent image of an infant's empty shoes is a small illustration of a soundly sleeping, healthy looking child, which suggests that he or she has not been affected by germs. Nevertheless, the text implies that this child, too, is in danger, especially if Mother does not adopt Lysol. The text asks

Figure 3.3 "'On Guard,'" Lysol advertisement. *Source: Ladies' Home Journal,* August 1926, 87.

women, "Have you done your best? Will you ever have anything to reproach yourself with when you look down at his empty shoes?"[43] This hypothetical question probably caused women to wonder about their mothering and house-cleaning practices, for the bombardment of expert advice during the period had already caused a degree of disempowerment among women, who no longer trusted their own judgment within the home.[44]

The ad goes on to stress that mothers who use soap and water to clean their homes have not done their best, as this can be achieved only through the use of Lysol. It reminds women that they should always "use this same reliable disinfectant in your home. Be sure – whatever happens – that you have really done your best to protect your family from germ life."[45] Not only does the ad suggest that women need Lysol to "do their best," it also insists that failing to use the product was careless. Germs cannot be killed with soap, yet "it is so easy to kill them" with Lysol.[46]

Maternal negligence, or "mother blame," continued to be a prevalent theme throughout the period, alongside the use of the fear-evoking spectre of infant mortality. Just as the advertisements invoking the concept of household management became increasingly blatant in their use of scare copy, so too did the infant mortality ads. The headlines alone, including "Infection ... the Most Dangerous Kidnapper in the World," "The Watch-Dog Never Barked yet the Most Dangerous Criminal in the World Threatened This Sleeping Youngster," and "Madam, You Are to Blame!" were far more likely to arouse maternal anxiety than those in earlier examples ("On Guard" and "His Empty Shoes").[47] Also, unlike the earlier advertisements, later ads did not portray happy, healthy babies. Instead, they conveyed that infants were in immediate danger due to their mother's negligent, backward cleaning practices.

The December 1935 advertisement from the *Canadian Home Journal* entitled "The Watch-Dog Never Barked" insists that infection is the "most dangerous criminal in the world" and claims that no matter how diligent mothers believe they may be, their children are in danger unless they use Lysol (Figure 3.4).[48] The ad depicts a sleeping infant in a crib, with a large dog sleeping on the floor beside her. Looming behind the child is the massive shadow of a stern-looking man, who wears a coat and hat. The word "infection" is written across his chest, indicating that he personifies a disease that is invading the home from outside. The text confirms this, noting that "no matter how careful you think you are, germs come into your home unknown to you."[49] The startling imagery is accompanied by mother blame, as the text reminds women who do not heed its recommendations to use Lysol that, "neglected, infection spreads causing sickness or even more serious tragedies."[50]

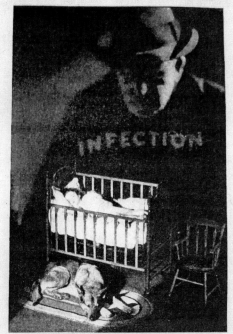

Figure 3.4 "'The Watch-Dog Never Barked Yet the Most Dangerous Criminal in the World Threatened This Sleeping Youngster,'" Lysol advertisement. *Source: Canadian Home Journal*, December 1935, 63.

This ad was published in a Canadian magazine, but the same tactics were implemented in the *Ladies' Home Journal* as is demonstrated by a May 1936 Lysol ad.[51] In it, a small child sleeps in her crib; her brow is furrowed and her blankets appear dishevelled, as if she has been restless. It is apparent that she is ill, and her concerned mother looks on with her hand across her chest as if she were in despair. Beside the mother is the family doctor, who tells her, "Madam, you are to blame!"[52]

The remainder of the copy suggests that though this mother "would have given her right hand" to keep her baby well, she herself is at fault for the child's illness. "Careless about cleanliness," she had failed to ensure that her home was "hospital clean" by using Lysol as recommended, with the result that she had allowed germs to enter the house and infect her child. The ad also enlists the medical profession in its effort to sell product. Any woman who might ask her physician what disinfectant would enable her to avoid the catastrophe of child-hood illness, as the culture of scientific motherhood dictates she should, would find that her "own doctor will tell [her] that using a reliable disinfectant like 'Lysol' ... is an important part of the constant war against infection."[53] Because the ad insists that both doctors and hospitals trust Lysol, women may simply have taken this assertion as medical advice in itself, buying the product without actually consulting a physician.

Lysol's modern advertising tactics, an astute combination in which guilt and fear were accompanied by appeals to reason within the contextual framework of scientific motherhood, would probably have enticed women to purchase the product. By the mid-thirties, however, the company added yet another persua-sive element to its campaign by offering consumers proof of Lysol's effectiveness. This came about largely by chance, with the birth of the Dionne quintuplets near the small rural town of Callander, Ontario, on 28 May 1934. Dr. Allan Roy Dafoe delivered the five premature babies and was credited with saving their lives, as they were not expected to survive. As the first surviving set of quintuplets in recorded medical history, the Dionnes became instant celebrities across North America as did Dr. Dafoe.[54] Significantly, Dafoe claimed that he and his nurses had used Lysol at the quints' delivery, and he credited the product with keeping their environment clean throughout their infancy.[55]

The company quickly capitalized on the quints' celebrity status and Dafoe's avowed use of Lysol. Indeed, although the world viewed the girls as "miracle babies," Lysol ads informed consumers that their survival was no miracle at all, but was due to modern methods of childrearing, using Lysol. Advertisements insisted that the girls survived because they were "given every modern advantage, carefully guarded ... every standard of modern, scientific childrearing being observed. Foremost among these modern standards is Disinfection – and for this purpose 'Lysol' Disinfectant is being used as it has been ever since the birth of the Dionne Quintuplets."[56] In essence, the Dionne quintuplets became living proof of Lysol's efficacy.

From 1935 to 1939, the Dionnes appeared as happy, healthy children in fifteen North American Lysol advertisements.[57] Though these ads seem to represent a complete shift in Lysol's tactics, this was not entirely the case. The use of the quints as evidence of Lysol's effectiveness as a modern disinfectant and Dafoe's expert "celebrity endorsement" constituted a change from previous ads, but the company also managed to include some fear-inducing rhetoric. Once the ad copy had stated that Lysol succeeded in saving the quints, mothers were told that they should give their own babies "the same scrupulous care the little Dionnes get." The ads also emphasized that if women used Lysol in conjunction with the practices of scientific motherhood, it would "save [them] the heartache of vain regrets," because not using the product could lead to the infection and death of infants.[58]

We cannot know exactly how women reacted to Lysol advertisements, but the concern shown by Dr. Harold H. Mitchell, medical director of the American Child Health Association, suggests that they had expressed confidence in Lysol as a modern means of preventing infant and childhood disease. In 1927, Mitchell asserted that, despite its claims, Lysol alone could not protect children from infectious illnesses and insisted that its campaign was "questionable from the public education standpoint."[59] Mitchell believed that the company's ads, with their emphasis on the threat of germs and childhood illness, could provoke mental distress in mothers, who could become "over-anxious about such dangers." He also felt that using Lysol may have given mothers "a false sense of security."[60] The American Medical Association agreed, stating that the ads were "obviously written by some bright copywriter of an advertising agency, whose sole purpose is to 'sell' Lysol to the reading public."[61]

Regardless of these criticisms, women across North America purchased huge amounts of Lysol during the interwar years.[62] Playing on their sense of responsibility, fear, and guilt, as well as their belief in modernity and reliance on expert advice, the company conveyed that doing anything less than using Lysol was backward and negligent. Its success suggests that these tactics did have a significant impact on female consumers in terms of their purchasing patterns and their conceptions of their domestic gender roles.

It is perhaps difficult to comprehend that advertisements could have affected women so strongly that they would be willing to alter both their consumption and cleaning habits. However, North Americans today are experiencing a similar shift in their conceptions of responsible consumer and cleaning practices. An understanding of this trend, which in some ways parallels the changes that took place in interwar North America, makes women's adoption of Lysol much more understandable. Prompted by an ever-growing sense of environmental responsibility and fears regarding the toxicity of indoor air, the "green cleaning" movement has caused many to give up long-trusted anti-bacterial disinfectants for supposedly safer, natural "green" cleaning products.[63] As was the case in the interwar years, many doctors and experts endorse the use of these products. In stark contrast to interwar experts, however, doctors and scientists now suggest that North Americans have become overly and even compulsively hygienic. Some insist that this obsession has led to repercussions beyond environmental damage, as studies have demonstrated that the indoor air pollution caused by harsh chemical cleaners has (ironically) been making children ill. The increased prevalence of childhood respiratory illnesses such as asthma has been linked to the use of household cleansers.[64]

Advertisers have been quick to seize on this contextually specific trend. By invoking women's continued responsibility as familial health providers and employing scientific evidence, they (along with experts) now insist that a safe home is one bereft of dangerous chemical fumes and residues.[65] Such rhetoric has not only proved convincing for consumers, it has become commonsensical to some, as evidenced by the ever-increasing market share of green cleaners. Therefore, like their interwar counterparts, countless present-day consumers have been persuaded to change their buying and cleaning habits due to concerns in their milieu and the way in which a mix of doctors, environmental experts, and advertisers have come together to promote the importance of this socio-cultural consumerist shift.[66]

This contemporary example emphasizes that, as in the present, interwar female consumers found themselves in the midst of an extremely credible contextual web that made using Lysol seem completely logical in the face of domestic germ- and disease-related issues. As is the case today, during the interwar years, advertisers played on medical and social concerns, especially in relation to children's health and safety. Clearly, then, Lysol ads did not resonate so compellingly with consumers because women were simply gullible or over-emotional, but because they were both caught within and expected to play a part in their historical context. Indeed, interwar modernity proved to be a pervasive force that shaped the world in which North Americans lived and influenced their purchasing decisions, even in relation to which household disinfectant they chose (or chose not) to buy. It is no wonder that women were convinced to purchase Lysol, as they wanted to clean their homes and protect their families, all the while abiding by the dictates of household management and scientific motherhood. Lysol promised to make these socially prescribed expectations attainable; all female consumers had to do was modernize by altering their cleaning and purchasing practices.

Acknowledgments

I would like to thank the editors of this collection as well as Linda Ambrose, Stephen Azzi, Sara Burke, and Wendy Mitchinson for their comments on earlier versions of this essay. I would also like to gratefully acknowledge the financial assistance of the Social Sciences and Humanities Research Council of Canada.

Notes

1 For further discussion of how Lysol was marketed as a feminine hygiene product, see Kristin Hall, "Prescriptions for Modern Womanhood: Advertising Lysol in Interwar North America" (master's thesis, Laurentian University, 2008).

2 John Staudenmaier and Pamela Walker Luríto Laird, "Advertising History," *Technology and Culture* 30, 4 (1989): 1035.

3 For more on child illness, infant mortality, and advertising, see Cheryl Krasnick Warsh, "Vim, Vigour and Vitality: 'Power Foods' for Kids in Canadian Popular Magazines, 1914-1954," in *Edible Histories/Cultural Politics: Towards a Canadian Food History*, ed. Franca Iacovetta, Valerie J. Korinek, and Marlene Epp (Toronto: University of Toronto Press, 2012), 387-408.

4 Veronica Strong-Boag, *The New Day Recalled: Lives of Girls and Women in English Canada, 1919-1939*, rev. ed. (Toronto: Copp Clark Pitman, 1993), 1; Carol Lee Bacchi, *Liberation Deferred? The Ideas of the English-Canadian Suffragists, 1877-1918* (Toronto: University of Toronto Press, 1983), 141; Steven Mintz and Susan Kellogg, *Domestic Revolutions: A Social History of American Family Life* (New York: Free Press, 1988), 112-13.

5 Rima D. Apple, "Constructing Mothers: Scientific Motherhood in the Nineteenth and Twentieth Century," in *Mothers and Motherhood: Readings in American History*, ed. Rima D. Apple and Janet Golden (Columbus: Ohio State University Press, 1997), 98; Cynthia Comacchio, "'A Postscript for Father': Defining a New Fatherhood in Interwar Canada," *Canadian Historical Review* 78, 3 (1997): 388-89; Cynthia Comacchio, *The Infinite Bonds of Family: Domesticity in Canada, 1850-1940* (Toronto: University of Toronto Press, 1999), 65-75; Mintz and Kellogg, *Domestic Revolutions*, 112-13.

6 Anngret S. Ogden, *The Great American Housewife: From Helpmate to Wage Earner, 1776-1986* (Westport, CT: Greenwood Press, 1986), 139; Ruth Schwartz Cowan, *More Work for Mother: The Ironies of Household Technology from the Open Hearth to the Microwave* (New York: Basic Books, 1983), 151-91; Strong-Boag, *The New Day Recalled*, 81, 113, 145.

7 Janice Williams Rutherford, *Selling Mrs. Consumer: Christine Frederick and the Rise of Household Efficiency* (Athens: University of Georgia Press, 2003), 43-45; Strong-Boag, *The New Day Recalled*, 126-27.

8 Apple, "Constructing Mothers," 104.

9 Rutherford, *Selling Mrs. Consumer*, 36-45; Ogden, *The Great American Housewife*, 139; Apple, "Constructing Mothers," 98.

10 Helen MacMurchy, *How to Take Care of the Father and the Family* (Ottawa: F.A. Acland, 1923), 1-32; Helen MacMurchy, *How to Manage Housework in Canada* (Ottawa: F.A. Acland, 1926), 1-48; Dianne Dodd, "Advice to Parents: The Blue Books, Helen MacMurchy, M.D., and the Federal Department of Health, 1920-34," *Canadian Bulletin of Medical History* 8 (1991): 204,

210-14; Sarah A. Leavitt, *From Catherine Beecher to Martha Stewart: A Cultural History of Domestic Advice* (Chapel Hill: University of North Carolina Press, 2002), 49-51; Nancy Tomes, *The Gospel of Germs: Men, Women, and the Microbe in American Life* (Cambridge, MA: Harvard University Press, 1998), 135-36; Rutherford, *Selling Mrs. Consumer,* 44.

11   Jacalyn Duffin, *History of Medicine: A Scandalously Short Introduction* (Toronto: University of Toronto Press, 1999), 80-82.

12   Barbara Ehrenreich and Deirdre English, *For Her Own Good: 150 Years of the Experts' Advice to Women* (Garden City, NY: Anchor Press, 1978), 158.

13   Tomes, *The Gospel of Germs,* 157-82.

14   Cynthia Comacchio, *Nations Are Built of Babies: Saving Ontario's Mothers and Children, 1900-1940* (Montreal and Kingston: McGill-Queen's University Press, 1993), 9.

15   Ibid.

16   Daniel Delis Hill, *Advertising to the American Woman, 1900-1999* (Columbus: Ohio State University Press, 2002), 8.

17   Roland Marchand, *Advertising the American Dream: Making Way for Modernity, 1920-1940* (Berkeley: University of California Press, 1985), 9.

18   "'Every Drop a Powerful Weapon against Contagious Disease,'" Lysol advertisement, *Ladies' Home Journal,* May 1920, 167.

19   Ibid.; "'Lysol Disinfectant Used in Cleaning Protects Your Home from Disease,'" Lysol advertisement, *Ladies' Home Journal,* March 1920, 167.

20   "'Every Drop a Powerful Weapon,'" 167.

21   Albert Theodore Poffenberger, *Psychology in Advertising* (New York: McGraw-Hill, 1925), 28; Marchand, *Advertising the American Dream,* 14.

22   "'Keep This Sign from Your Door,'" Lysol advertisement, *Ladies' Home Journal,* July 1922, 66.

23   Ibid.

24   Ibid. This 1922 ad may also be intended to invoke fearful memories of actual outbreaks such as the 1918-20 influenza pandemic that ravaged the United States and Canada, killing 725,000 North Americans. Niall P.A.S. Johnson and Juergen Mueller, "Notes and Comments: Updating the Accounts: Global Mortality of the 1918-1920 'Spanish' Influenza Pandemic," *Bulletin of Medical History* 76 (2002): 111. As Esyllt W. Jones suggests in the case of Winnipeg, care was often home-based, and some households were quarantined. Infected homes were monitored through placarding, meaning that the Lysol advertisement would probably have resonated with women who remembered this aspect of the outbreak. Esyllt W. Jones, "'Co-operation in All Human Endeavour': Disease Vectors in the 1918-1919 Influenza Pandemic in Winnipeg," *Canadian Bulletin of Medical History* 22, 1 (2005): 68, 72.

25   Cowan, *More Work for Mother,* 152.

26   Ibid., 177.

27   Poffenberger, *Psychology in Advertising,* 165.

28   "'The Deadly Doorknob,'" Lysol advertisement, *Ladies' Home Journal,* May 1923, 100; "'Domestic Warfare,'" Lysol advertisement, *Ladies' Home Journal,* August 1923, 38; "'Even Your Broom May Be a Jungle of Germs,'" Lysol advertisement, *Ladies' Home Journal,* April 1936, 125; "'Germs Lurk Everywhere,'" Lysol advertisement, *Chatelaine,* March 1937, 48.

29   "'Hitch Four Widows to a Plow in the Dead of Night,'" Lysol advertisement, *Canadian Home Journal,* September 1931, 83; "'Hitch Four Widows to a Plow in the Dead of Night,'" Lysol advertisement, *Chatelaine,* September 1931, 29.

30   Ibid.

31   Ibid.

32   Suellen Hoy, *Chasing Dirt: The American Pursuit of Cleanliness* (New York: Oxford University Press, 1995), 88. In *Imperial Leather: Race, Gender and Sexuality in the Colonial Contest* (New York: Routledge, 1995), historian Anne McClintock notes that such racialized preoccupations

concerning cleanliness were also a central component in Victorian soap advertising. As is the case with Lysol during the interwar era, Pears Soap ads in particular implied that those who used Pears were both socially and racially superior to those who did not. In both contexts, advertisers for Pears and Lysol created racially based hierarchies that cast white English-speaking consumers as modern and superior to those of other races and ethnicities. For further discussion on the Pears case study in Britain during the Victorian era, see McClintock, *Imperial Leather*, 207-31.

33 Hoy, *Chasing Dirt*, 114.

34 Stuart Ewen, *Captains of Consciousness: Advertising and the Social Roots of the Consumer Culture* (New York: McGraw-Hill, 1976), 139-49; Poffenberger, *Psychology in Advertising*, 65-67; Hill, *Advertising to the American Woman*, 77-78; Marchand, *Advertising the American Dream*, 191-92.

35 Poffenberger, *Psychology in Advertising*, 65-67.

36 Richard A. Meckel, *Save the Babies: American Public Health Reform and the Prevention of Infant Mortality, 1850-1929* (Baltimore: Johns Hopkins University Press, 1990), 238; *The Canada Year Book 1922-23: The Official Statistical Annual of the Resources, History, Institutions, and Social and Economic Conditions of the Dominion* (Ottawa: F.A. Acland, 1923), 200; *The Canada Year Book 1931: The Official Statistical Annual of the Resources, History, Institutions, and Social and Economic Conditions of the Dominion* (Ottawa: F.A. Acland, 1931), 164; *The Canada Year Book 1941: The Official Statistical Annual of the Resources, History, Institutions, and Social and Economic Conditions of the Dominion* (Ottawa: Edmond Cloutier, King's Printer, 1941), 97.

37 Rima D. Apple, "Educating Mothers: The Wisconsin Bureau of Maternal and Child Health," *Women's History Review* 12, 4 (2003): 560; Katherine Arnup, "Educating Mothers: Government Advice for Women in the Inter-War Years," in *Delivering Motherhood: Maternal Ideologies and Practices in the 19th and 20th Centuries*, ed. Katherine Arnup, Andree Levesque, and Ruth Roach Pierson (London: Routledge, 1990), 191.

38 Apple, "Constructing Mothers," 90; Rima D. Apple, *Perfect Motherhood: Science and Child-rearing in America* (New Brunswick, NJ: Rutgers University Press, 2006), 37; Comacchio, *Nations Are Built of Babies*, 9-10, 40.

39 "On Guard," Lysol advertisement, *Ladies' Home Journal*, August 1926, 87 (emphasis in original).

40 Ibid.

41 Molly Ladd-Taylor, *Raising a Baby the Government Way: Mothers' Letters to the Children's Bureau, 1915-1932* (New Brunswick, NJ: Rutgers University Press, 1986), 99, 111-12; Apple, "Constructing Mothers," 104; Arnup, *Education for Motherhood*, 124-28.

42 Comacchio, *Nations Are Built of Babies*, 9-10, 40; Apple, *Perfect Motherhood*, 37.

43 "His Empty Shoes," Lysol advertisement, *Ladies' Home Journal*, June 1927, 67.

44 Apple, *Perfect Motherhood*, 87.

45 "His Empty Shoes," 67.

46 Ibid.

47 "Infection ... the Most Dangerous Kidnapper in the World," Lysol advertisement, *Chatelaine*, June 1934, 49; "The Watch-Dog Never Barked yet the Most Dangerous Criminal in the World Threatened This Sleeping Youngster," Lysol advertisement, *Canadian Home Journal*, December 1935, 63; "Madam, You Are to Blame!" Lysol advertisement, *Ladies' Home Journal*, May 1936, 131.

48 "The Watch-Dog Never Barked," 63.

49 Ibid.

50 Ibid.

51 "Madam, You Are to Blame!" 131.

52 Ibid.

53 Ibid.

54 A.G.N., "Editorial Comments: Dr. Allan Roy Dafoe," *Canadian Medical Association Journal* 34 (January 1936): 73; Kari Dehli, "Fictions of the Scientific Imagination: Researching the Dionne Quintuplets," *Journal of Canadian Studies* 29 (1994): 86.

55 Peter Morell, *Poisons, Potions, and Profits: The Antidote to Radio Advertising* (New York: Knight, 1937), 69-75.

56 "'Precious Babies!'" Lysol advertisement, *Chatelaine*, November 1935, 54.

57 "'Lysol Protects the Dionne Quintuplets from Infection,'" Lysol advertisement, *Canadian Home Journal*, April 1935, 75; "'Lysol Protects the Dionne Quintuplets from Infection,'" Lysol advertisement, *Chatelaine*, April 1935, 62; "'Precious Babies! Dionne Quintuplets,'" Lysol advertisement, *Canadian Home Journal*, November 1935, 53; "'Precious Babies!'" Lysol advertisement, *Chatelaine*, November 1935, 54; "'Change for Five ... Laundered with Lysol,'" Lysol advertisement, *Canadian Home Journal*, January 1936, 40; "'Five New Movie Queens ... Their Future Protected by Lysol,'" Lysol advertisement, *Canadian Home Journal*, March 1936, 41; "'Change for Five ... Laundered with Lysol,'" Lysol advertisement, *Chatelaine*, January 1936, 37; "'Five Past Two,'" Lysol advertisement, *Chatelaine*, June 1936, 30; "'Change for Five ... Laundered with Lysol,'" Lysol advertisement, *Ladies' Home Journal*, March 1936, 121; "'Five ... Going on Three,'" Lysol advertisement, *Ladies' Home Journal*, July 1936, 83; "'Infection: Lysol Protects the Quints from This Hidden Danger,'" Lysol advertisement, *Chatelaine*, October 1936, 48; "'Five Reasons Why Lysol Is Used in Thousands of Homes,'" Lysol advertisement, *Canadian Home Journal*, January 1937, 56; "'Five Reasons Why Lysol Is Used in Thousands of Homes,'" Lysol advertisement, *Chatelaine*, January 1937, 37; "'It's Their Birthday ... but Your Gift!'" Lysol advertisement, *Chatelaine*, June 1937, 41; "'It's Their Birthday ... but Your Gift!'" Lysol advertisement, *Ladies' Home Journal*, June 1937, 71.

58 "'Change for Five,'" *Canadian Home Journal*, 40; "'Five New Movie Queens,'" 41; "'Change for Five,'" *Chatelaine*, 37; "'Five Past Two,'" 30; "'Change for Five,'" *Ladies' Home Journal*, 121.

59 Dr. Harold H. Mitchell Medical Director of the ACHA to the AMA, 17 November 1927, box 483, folder 3, American Medical Association Historical Health Fraud Archives (AMA), Chicago.

60 Ibid.

61 The AMA to Dr. Harold H. Mitchell, 22 November 1927, box 483, folder 3, AMA.

62 "Lehn and Fink Sales Higher," *Barron's*, 17 June 1929, 26; "Lehn and Fink Attractive?" *Barron's*, 16 September 1929, 19; "Lysol Appropriation Increased," *New York Times*, 21 January 1937, 41.

63 Catherine Lawson, "Mr. Green vs. Mr. Clean," *CanWest News*, July 2008, 3; Beth Greer, *Super Natural Home: Improve Your Health, Home, and Planet—One Room at a Time* (New York: Rodale Books, 2009), 146.

64 Adria Vasil, *Ecoholic: Your Guide to the Most Environmentally Friendly Information, Products, and Services in Canada* (Toronto: Vintage Canada, 2007), 181; Greer, *Super Natural Home*, 146.

65 Nancy Hajeski, David R. Goucher, and Philip J. Schmidt, *The Earth Friendly Home: Save Energy, Reduce Consumption, Shrink Your Carbon Footprint* (Irvington, NY: Hylas, 2009), 107; Greer, *Super Natural Home*, 146; Vasil, *Ecoholic*, 181. For products that present themselves as green, see the Clorox Company's website for Green Works at http://www.greenworkscleaners.com/.

66 Elizabeth Blackwell, "Catalogue Critic: Clean Goes Green," *Wall Street Journal*, 4 November 2005, W.3; Emily Gravelle, "Easy Being Green," *Canadian Grocer* 123, 2 (2009): 34.

4

Medicine Advertising, Women's Work, and Women's Bodies in Montreal Newspapers, 1919-39

Denyse Baillargeon
Translated by Zoé Blowen-Ledoux

Considered a feature of mass consumer societies, advertising in the written media is a nearly inexhaustible source of representation of femininity and masculinity, and as a result, it has been the object of many studies devoted to the construction of gender.[1] However, though these studies have examined various types of items, including household appliances, vehicles, cigarettes, alcohol, and beauty and personal hygiene products, they have less frequently investigated medicine from a similar gendered perspective.[2] Yet many researchers have shown that advertising campaigns for patent medicines were among the first to reach a national and even international scale, thus contributing, according to Jackson Lears, to the creation of "a modern advertising industry" that financed the development of mass media and gave rise to the modern concept of consumer rights, all characteristics testifying to their importance.[3] Fascinated by the often fraudulent nature of nineteenth- and early-twentieth-century ads, specialists in advertising and medical history have focused on this period, pointing out the exaggerated claims of the ads, their confusing rhetoric that aimed at being "scientific," and their exploitation of the fears and gullibility of the targeted clientele, particularly the urban working class. However, except for Quebec historian Denis Goulet, very few have lingered over the ads' representation of gender.[4] In his book *Le commerce des maladies: la publicité des remèdes au début du siècle,* Goulet concludes that between 1900 and 1910, advertising for patent medicine reflected the medical discourse that had been building since the nineteenth century, which represented women as weaklings, totally dominated by their reproductive system, and plagued by physical ailments and mental derangement from puberty to menopause. But, as Goulet also illustrates, though advertisements for miraculous pills and other sensational medicines attributed women's morbidity to their "nature," they also played up women's domestic responsibilities and numerous household tasks with the intent of convincing them to buy the advertised products. As Goulet also points out, the advertising rhetoric that promoted patent medicines during the first decade of the twentieth century took its reference from an instrumental vision of the body – that is, a body conceived as a machine to be maintained in good repair – and from an ethic of hard work and duty. Though building on and reinforcing the ideology of separate spheres and endorsing a purely utilitarian concept of the body, the ads were nonetheless a form of public recognition regarding women's contribution to the family economy since their tasks seemed to be sufficiently physically demanding to necessitate good health.[5] Ads illustrated in Goulet's *Le commerce des maladies* show women as mature homemakers, with well-built bodies.

This chapter will address the following questions: How did medicine advertisements evolve in Quebec during the interwar years, and especially, how did they represent women, their bodies, and their work? Indeed, the many changes that occurred during the 1920s and 1930s suggest that these years are particularly conducive to such a study. Now primarily urban, Quebec and Canadian societies increasingly felt the influence of American consumer culture, which took the form both of the mass distribution of goods manufactured either in the United States or in Canada by American companies, and the publication of advertising to sell these products in daily newspapers and magazines across Canada and Quebec.[6] Associated with a period of prosperity and then of economic depression, these two decades witnessed major transformations in women's lives. Just after the First World War, women gained suffrage in federal elections and in all provinces except Quebec.[7] And during the 1920s, increasing numbers of young women found employment in the expanding clerical sector. Furthermore, the new ideal of the companionate marriage promoted marital relationships based on a more egalitarian vision, and couples from a broader range of the population increasingly used contraception. Finally, women also enjoyed the liberalization of fashion and feminine behaviour, including sexual behaviour.[8] Of course, a vast majority of women, whether in the United States, Canada, or Quebec, never fit the image of the flapper, and a large proportion of them participated only marginally in consumer culture, even in the 1920s. Nonetheless, the interwar period marks a break with the traditional feminine model, even if the latest embodiment of the "modern" woman left the gender hierarchies intact.[9]

Corresponding to the new, mostly urban lifestyle, the increased presence of women in the public sphere, and the new values and concepts surrounding male-female relationships, a novel feminine corporeal ideal was spread by the movies and the printed press. Young, svelte, freed from the constraints of out-dated clothing and the moral tethers of Puritanism, this well-cared-for body, exuding health and complete with makeup and styled hair, seemed designed for action, seduction, and pleasure.[10] According to several historians, these decades also marked a major turning point in the development of the advertising industry, particularly in the United States, which, as we have already mentioned, produced a good proportion of the ads appearing in daily newspapers and magazines in Canada and Quebec. The growing professionalization of the advertising sector, the creation or consolidation of national agencies to better cover the domestic and international markets, the increasingly systematic use of psychology and market studies to develop striking brand images and powerful messages, and the utilization of new techniques, such as photography, contributed to transforming the face of publicity as it became, if not more convincing, at least more seductive.[11]

Measuring the impact of these transformations on medicine ads is one of the main objectives pursued here. The analysis is based on the perusal of four French-language Quebec publications: three magazines, *La Canadienne, Mon Magazine,* and *La Revue Moderne,* and one weekly newspaper, *Le Petit Journal.* The three magazines were systematically examined for each year they were in publication, and the first issue of each month of *Le Petit Journal* was scrutinized between 1926 (the year of its inception) and 1939. *La Canadienne* and *Mon Magazine,* published from 1920 to 1923 and from 1926 to 1932 respectively, were ostensibly intended for a family audience, but many columns (on beauty, child care, sewing, cooking, and domestic arts) were clearly pitched to a female readership. On the other hand, *La Revue Moderne,* published from 1919 to 1959, set itself to compete with the American women's magazines circulating among the French Canadian elite, in hopes of preventing their Americanization.[12] With their long articles and serialized stories, the three magazines visibly targeted an educated readership, most likely of the urban middle classes, whereas *Le Petit Journal,* in tabloid format and amply illustrated, sought primarily to attract working-class consumers fascinated with trivia, scandals, sports, and the movies and their stars, especially from Hollywood.[13]

Targeting different audiences, these four publications reserved considerable space for advertisements, a necessary source of funding, many of them selling medicine. During the period under study, ads for patent remedies, some of which dated from the nineteenth century, coexisted with ads for new medicines resulting from developments in the pharmaceutical industry, which was undergoing a period of expansion in the early twentieth century. Next to ads for Lydia Pinkham's Vegetable Compound, Gin Pills, Dodd's or Red Pills, Lambert and Fellows' Syrup, Fruitatives, Tiger Balm, Vin St-Michel, and Dr. Chase's Nerve Food, to name but a few, readers would find ads for Aspirin, Vicks VapoRub, and Phillips' Milk of Magnesia. In fact, the research revealed that the emergence of modern pharmacology and, starting in 1908, the adoption of laws regulating the medicine market, did not immediately disqualify the older concoctions, which continued to be advertised until the Second World War.[14] With the intent of making this plethora manageable, the study focused on three products: Lydia Pinkham's Vegetable Compound, Dr. Chase's Nerve Food and his other remedies (ointment and Paradol), and Aspirin tablets. For each of these, all the ads for the same product, but presenting substantial differences in the texts or illustrations, and intended for women, were retained. For comparison, a few ads that displayed men (other than doctors) or that were addressed to men were also included in the sample. The choice of these medicines was in large part guided by the style of the ads and length of the advertising campaigns.[15] In other words, the three products were selected because the textual message in their ads was long enough for content analysis, and because they were the object of sustained campaigns over the entire period, thus making it possible to trace the evolution of the representation of women's work and bodies. In all, the sample contains 156 ads, including 85 for Dr. Chase's Nerve Food, three-quarters of which appeared in the 1920s, 47 for Aspirin, of which the majority (37) were published in the 1930s, and 24 for Lydia Pinkham's Vegetable Compound, all of which date from the 1920s.[16] Of these 156 ads, about 15 targeted men: 3 promoted Aspirin and a dozen sold Dr. Chase's products.[17]

The three medicines have fairly well-known origins and histories. Invented in the United States in 1875 by a reformer and abolitionist, Lydia E. Pinkham's Vegetable Compound (which ironically contained a good dose of alcohol) was sold across North America for more than a hundred years to ease "women's pains," using an overabundance of extreme advertising that was typical for patent medicine.[18] Employing the same publicity strategies, the Alwin Wood Chase Medicine Company was founded by an Ann Arbor physician who was trained before the first school of medicine was opened in Michigan and who published a recipe book in 1865, prior to moving into the production and mail order sale of his medicinal preparations.[19] The German manufacturer of Aspirin, Bayer and Company, expanded into the United States in 1900, where it was able to obtain the exclusive right to manufacture and sell acetylsalicylic acid, the main component of Aspirin, at least between 1900 and 1917, thus assuring the basis of its fortune.[20]

Lydia Pinkham's and Dr. Chase's companies offered home remedies concocted from the traditional pharmacopeia, but Bayer sold a drug that was produced by synthetic chemistry, a fact that was quickly reflected in its marketing, which was much more impersonal than that of Pinkham or Chase. Indeed, the manufacturers of Lydia Pinkham's Vegetable Compound and Dr. Chase's Nerve Food did not hesitate to use the image of their inventors in their efforts to convince consumers of their seriousness. A Dr. Chase ad published in *La Canadienne* in 1923 states, "This liniment, to which Dr. Chase lends his name, is the result of the creator's patient research and many years of experience in medical practice."[21] "After two attacks of rheumatism three years apart, I was cured," continues the ad, using the famous doctor's own testimony.[22] "Lydia Pinkham would now be 109 if she were still alive," declares another ad published in the *La Revue Moderne* in 1928. "Her descendants continue to produce her famous Vegetable Compound and this product is backed by the integrity of four generations."[23] By alluding to the family nature of the business or the personal experience of the founder, these ads sought to reassure potential buyers of the remedy's efficacy by appealing to their emotions. They also skilfully used "real-life" stories of "ordinary" people who claimed to have been cured by the medicine. As historians have noted, this strategy sought to lead consumers to identify with the person quoted and, like him or her, to procure the remedy in question.[24] Expressed in language understood by the working class to whom these ads were especially directed, the invented or authentic stories were indeed sales arguments.

Bayer never introduced Aspirin's creator to its consumers: Felix Hoffmann remained forever unknown to the public. Rather than resorting to testimonies, Aspirin ads emphasized the "unique manufacturing process" of the tablet, the "instant relief" it provided even for "big headaches," and its lack of effect on the heart. Facing fierce competition after the 1917 expiration of its patent, the company also repeatedly stressed its product's exclusive nature: for example, a 1934 ad insists, "When you buy some, don't be talked into accepting imitations. If you want the quick relief that Aspirin provides, make sure the Bayer cross is embossed on each tablet."[25] Listing the properties of Aspirin, Bayer relied on the rationality, rather than the sentiment, of the consumer, and thus certainly projected a much more scientific image. Ads for Lydia Pinkham's Vegetable Compound and Dr. Chase's Nerve Food pretended to heal a wide variety of often vague and unconnected afflictions (including weakness, fatigue, anxiety, thin blood, anaemia, insomnia, indigestion, and irregularity), attributing them to equally nebulous causes that prominently included "women's ailments."[26] By contrast, the advertising pitch for Aspirin listed the few conditions (headache and sore throat, neuralgia, nephritis, rheumatism) for which the product had proven to be effective. The choice of a more precise taxonomy would indicate that the company, at least in the beginning, sought wealthier clients who were better equipped to describe their symptoms and ailments.[27] In the 1920s, Aspirin ads often mentioned that "doctors prescribe Aspirin; it is not bad for the heart," and many ads showed practitioners or nurses, sometimes even both.[28] This desire for medical approval and the use of individuals who incarnated modern medicine support the hypothesis that Bayer presented Aspirin in a manner that would appeal to the middle class, which was inclined to seek care and trust health professionals.[29]

Beyond these general characteristics, how did the advertising represent women, their work, and their bodies? In the 1920s, Lydia Pinkham's and Dr. Chase's ads continually allude to the problems and pains felt by women during their reproductive life (most often via testimonies): "I began suffering from cramps and belly aches when I was 11. I became so anxious, I could not stay in bed, and I cried from the pain," said a certain Mrs. Nelson Yott, from Eberts, Ontario, in a 1923 Pinkham's ad.[30] Another Pinkham's testimonial ad from the same year praised the vegetable compound for its amelioration of menopausal woes: "During my change of life, I took your remedy, which had a marvellous effect. I had hot flashes; I was so nervous and weak that everything became black, like I had been blinded. I had crying fits for no reason."[31] A third commented, "I was in a very weakened state, exhausted and nervous, constantly tired, from the time I woke up until I went to bed."[32] Two others from 1921 and 1928 claimed, "I was nervous, irritable, unable to sleep," and "I was a nervous wreck."[33] We could indefinitely multiply the examples of testimonies that portray women as overwhelmed and mentally traumatized beings. Clearly, the advertising rhetoric of the 1920s still widely echoed the medical discourse that, since the nineteenth century, had reduced the female body to its genitalia. As several feminist historians have shown, women's bodies seemed intrinsically pathological in the eyes of doctors who, governed by gender prejudices, considered the male body to be the norm.[34] According to this rhetoric, women were necessarily unwell, weak, and nervous, especially when they passed through a new stage in their reproductive cycle. Echoing this rather dreadful discourse, one ad for Lydia Pinkham's Vegetable Compound maintained, "There are three painful stages in a woman's life: when she becomes a woman, at the birth of her first child and when she reaches middle age."[35]

The pattern discussed by Goulet for the first decade of the twentieth century – of women's ineptitude in accomplishing their household tasks prior to taking the miracle medication – appears in 1920s advertising for Lydia Pinkham's Vegetable Compound and Dr. Chase's Nerve Food. As a Pinkham's testimonial explains,

> I was always tired and the smallest amount of overexertion wore me out for the next day or two. I had a dull pain above my eyes, pain in the nape of my neck and when I leaned over, I could not get up without help because my back was so sore. I did not sleep well and I jumped at the slightest noise. I'm a homemaker, but I was so tired that I could neither sweep nor wash the dishes without having to lie down afterwards. A friend told me how the Vegetable Compound had helped her, and so I started taking it. I felt stronger right from the first bottle and could wash the dishes and sweep without having to rest. Afterwards, my menstrual periods became regular again.[36]

A Dr. Chase's Nerve Food ad points out that

> housework is dull and tiring. Always doing the same things over again, day after day, is what breaks down the nervous system. Housework is hard work. Take ironing, for example: a day of work in itself, notwithstanding the cooking, caring for the children and the thousand other little things that must be done during the day. With time, this monotonous routine frays the nerves. You suffer insomnia, frequent migraines, indigestion and bouts of irritation and Depression. Under such conditions, there is nothing like Dr. Chase's Nerve Food to chase away the clouds and soothe the nervous system.[37]

As Goulet states so well, "There was absolutely no doubt in the minds of these advertisers that housewives bore a huge burden."[38] Of course, the emphasis on housewives' workload was intended to sell remedies, but the strategy was also based on the widespread perception of the uses of the body during this period, especially in the less fortunate classes. For the working class – the main target of the ads – the body, whether female or male, was indeed conceived, represented, and even experienced as an instrument, a work tool that should be kept in good order to accomplish the tasks that the family and society expected of it.[39] To increase sales, the ads built on both this widely accepted instrumental vision of the body and on the poor health of the working classes, which fed their fears of being unable to perform the work that enabled the family to survive. But in doing so, the ads explicitly acknowledged women's contribution to the family economy and gave them high visibility, not only in the texts but, in the case of Dr. Chase's, also in the illustrations.

Indeed, whereas Lydia Pinkham's advertising generally took the form of writing topped with a catchy title that was sometimes accompanied by a simple portrait of a woman, Dr. Chase's ads in the 1920s frequently included detailed drawings, many of which show housewives in full action or at least in a domestic setting.[40] Women hang the wash (Figure 4.1), sew, mend clothes, cook, or stand before their pantries.[41] Entrenched in settings to remind readers of their own multiple and onerous responsibilities, women are prostrate on chairs, collapsed over kitchen tables, or beleaguered by children.[42] With only a few exceptions, these women clearly come from modest backgrounds, belong to the working class, and are labourers' or even farmers' wives, such as the woman in Figure 4.1, who do their own housework.[43] Middle-aged, they pose in simple, unadorned dresses and sometimes wear an apron. Their long hair – despite the fashion of the 1920s, which tended toward shorter styles – is gathered in a bun, and they wear no jewellery. Although their bodies are not heavy-set, they are not sleek either and do not project an air of refinement or extreme fragility, despite all the disorders that affect them.[44] These bodies seem perfectly adapted to the demands of housework and child care, which require, if not physical strength, at least endurance. This image of the homemaker is obviously reinforced by the text, which tells the story of a long ordeal and subsequent miraculous healing thanks to the pills or decoctions that have made it possible to resume housework with renewed vigour.

During the 1920s, two advertisements for Dr. Chase's Nerve Food show women who are clearly very old: grandmothers busily sewing. In both cases, they are pictured with younger women (Figure 4.2). This ad, which contends that sewing can lead to a nervous breakdown because it causes visual tension, especially when done for long hours in "artificial light," implies that even old ladies can be obliged to carry out strenuous tasks. Obviously, domestic work spares no woman, old age not yet being a synonym for non-work.[45]

Focusing on the other end of the age spectrum, three ads show young office workers. Published in 1928, when Chase first used photography, one ad shows a young woman preparing to type a document (Figure 4.3). In all three cases, the advertising copy highlights the anxiety and irritability that clerical work can cause, especially when combined with other activities.[46] Titled "The type-writer is getting on my nerves," one ad also explains a young woman's exhaustion

Le Travail est un Plaisir
Quand la Santé est Bonne

Avec une abondance de sang riche et rouge circulant dans les veines et les artères pour maintenir la vigueur des nerfs et la force des muscles, la vie est une jouissance et le travail un plaisir.

Si l'on ressent une fatigue passagère, un sommeil naturel et bienfaisant restaure l'énergie dépensée et l'on se sent avec plaisir en état d'accomplir de la besogne—de faire bien et complètement le travail que l'on a à faire.

Ce n'est que lorsque le sang est pauvre, que le système est ébranlé, que les nerfs sont épuisés et appauvris, que le travail vous pèse, que vous manquez de coeur et de courage. Dans un pareil état, vous ne reposez plus, vous ne dormez pas bien et, le matin, vous vous levez fatigué et effrayé de la journée de travail que vous avez devant vous.

C'est dans de pareils cas que le Dr Chase's Nerve Food peut vous être d'un secours incalculable.

En fournissant au sang les éléments dont est formé le sang neuf, le Dr Chase's Nerve Food rebâtit le système épuisé de la façon la plus naturelle et la plus rationnelle imaginable.

Dans le sang il fat circuler une nouvelle énergie; il infuse une vigueur nouvelle dans le système nerveux, et répand un bien-être dans tout l'individu.

Les organes vitaux reprennent leurs fonctions, la digestion est meilleure; vous dormez, vous reposez naturellement, et vous regagnez graduellement et avec certitude la vigueur et l'énergie de la santé.

En employant le Dr Chase's Nerve Food, vous pouvez être, en quelque sorte le maître de votre propre santé.

La boîte, 50 cents, chez tous les marchands ou chez Edmanson, Bates & Co., Ltd., Toronto. Sur chaque boîte de la véritable préparation vous trouverez le portrait et la signature de A. W. Chase, M.D., l'auteur fameux du Livre de Recettes.

Figure 4.1 A woman in a rural area hangs her washing. "Le travail est un plaisir quand la santé est bonne [Work is a pleasure when health is good]," Dr. Chase's Nerve Food ad. *Source: La Canadienne,* July 1920, 45. *Courtesy of* Stella Pharmaceutical Canada Inc.

Une Cause Fréquente de la Dépression Nerveuse

RIEN ne déprime autant le système nerveux que la tension continue de la vue.

Vous pouvez croire que coudre est un travail léger et cependant vous vous demandez pourquoi il vous fatigue.

La tension du regard en est la cause.

Le contrôle de la vue constitue le labeur le plus délicat du système nerveux et lorsque ce travail se porte surtout sur la vue cela veut dire une dépense considérable de l'énergie nerveuse.

Il arrive souvent, cependant, qu'il vous est absolument nécessaire de persister à ce travail pendant de longues heures et de coudre à la lumière artificielle, mais il pourrait en résulter pour vous une dépression nerveuse.

Il est alors bon de connaître le Dr. Chase Nerve Food comme le moyen de restaurer votre système nerveux.

Quelle que puisse être la cause de la dépression dont vous souffrez, il a été démontré dans des milliers de cas qu'il n'y a rien comme le Dr. Chase Nerve Food pour les nerfs épuisés.

Les maux de tête, les sensations de fatigue, le manque de sommeil, l'indigestion, le manque d'énergie et d'appétit constituent quelques-uns des signes caractéristiques de l'épuisement des nerfs.

Votre système digestif ne fournit pas au sang et aux nerfs une nutrition suffisante et il devient alors nécessaire d'employer un reconstituant comme le Dr. Chase Nerve Food.

Le repos aidera; une nourriture nutritive bénéficiera au malade. Le recouvrement de la santé sera cependant hâté considérablement et assuré par l'emploi du Dr. Chase Nerve Food.

La boîte, 50 cts., chez tous les marchands ou chez Edmanson, Bates & Co., Ltd., Toronto. Sur chaque boîte de la véritable préparation vous trouverez le portrait et la signature de A. W. Chase, M. D., l'auteur fameux du Livre de Recettes.

Figure 4.2   As shown in this ad for Dr. Chase's Nerve Food, old age does not prevent women from working in the home. "Une cause fréquente de la dépression nerveuse [A frequent cause of nervous breakdown]." *Source: La Canadienne,* May 1920, 47. *Courtesy of* Stella Pharmaceutical Canada Inc.

by explicitly referring to the additional help that she must give her mother, who is sick.[47] The other alludes to frequent outings and ensuing lack of sleep that sap the energy needed by the employee to do her work well. In the ad shown here, the state of exhaustion is attributed to "the burden of so many business worries," leading the reader to believe that young typists share the weighty responsibilities of their employers. Whatever the leverage used to convince women to take Dr. Chase's Nerve Food, the fact is that the ads portray not middle-aged women, but rather elegant, well-coiffed young-looking women, who are therefore presumably single. Thus, the ads reflect and reinforce the idea that paid work is the exclusive domain of unmarried women.[48] Beyond this hardly surprising realization, we noted that, like their mothers or grandmothers, these young women are shown working or at least in their workplace. Though the young typists in these ads depict a new reality – the growth of this kind of employment during the 1920s – the corporeal practices represented are first and foremost associated with the necessity of ensuring one's survival, just as they were for married women.

When targeted to men, Dr. Chase's advertisements more frequently emphasize the consequences of nervous health disorders on their responsibilities as providers or, inversely, the impact of these responsibilities on their health. An April 1929 ad published in *Le Petit Journal* represents a good example of the rhetoric of the male breadwinner. Associating the "sudden death of so many businessmen and professionals" with a defective nervous system, the text ends with a plea: "For the love of those who depend on you, do not wait to use this treatment [regular consumption of Dr. Chase's Nerve Food], do not wait until you become a physical wreck and almost desperate to get back to your life responsibilities."[49] Capped with a photograph showing a man daydreaming of his wife and three children in a particularly touching family scene and titled "Everything depends on my health," this text leaves no doubt as to the heavy financial responsibilities men must assume. The setting in which the woman and children can be seen and also the father's suit, which associate him with a white-collar management job as a professional or businessman, clearly imply that this family belongs to the middle class. However, this man, who sits in an easy chair and holds a book, is not necessarily working. At the very least, the photo leaves room for interpretation on this issue. In fact, except for a drawing of a man standing near a teletypewriter, the men in Dr. Chase's ads are not shown working; surprisingly, they are more likely to appear in a domestic setting, perhaps studying their reflection in the mirror, which reveals the devastation inflicted by nervous disease, or lying sleepless in bed, prey to insomnia.[50] Another ad depicts two men sitting in easy chairs, one of the two clearly

Vous sentez=vous parfois fatiguée?

OUTRE la dépense d'énergie mentale et physique, durant le jour, la sténographe porte souvent le fardeau de bien des soucis d'affaires.

C'est ce souci qui épuise le système nerveux, qui vous vole votre sommeil et votre repos, et vous rend fatiguée et épuisée au matin.

Le souci est le plus grand destructeur de l'énergie nerveuse. Vous pouvez restaurer les nerfs épuisés en vous servant de l'aliment pour les nerfs du Dr Chase. Tant de milliers de gens fatigués et nerveux ont été aidés par ce traitement vivifiant que vous pouvez l'utiliser avec la certitude qu'il en fera autant pour vous.

Mais ne vous laissez pas épuiser mentalement ou physiquement. Il est beaucoup plus facile de prévenir que de surmonter une telle condition.

L'Aliment pour les Nerfs du Dr Chase

Le plus grand des restaurateurs pour les nerfs.

Figure 4.3 This ad for Dr. Chase's Nerve Food is directed at young female clerical employees. "Vous sentez-vous parfois fatiguée? [Do you sometimes feel tired?]." *Source: Mon Magazine,* November 1928, 33. *Courtesy of* Stella Pharmaceutical Canada Inc.

weakened by illness, the other visiting the first to convince him to take Dr. Chase's Nerve Food, as the text explains.[51] Of the two old men shown in the ads, one painfully climbs a staircase, helped by a middle-aged woman, surely his daughter, to better illustrate the extreme exhaustion that is overwhelming him.[52] The other sits surrounded by his grandchildren, with the caption "The reason grandfather is so popular."[53] Thus, unlike women, these men are not seen in industrious activities, even if the advertising rhetoric associated with them very explicitly connects their disorders to their role as provider. In their case, the ads focus on depicting the exhaustion or anxiety that plagues them or, as with the grandfather who plays with his grandchildren, the positive effects of Dr. Chase's Nerve Food on their personal lives.

Except for the ads promoting Lydia Pinkham's Vegetable Compound, which remained unchanged, those from the late 1920s and 1930s for both Dr. Chase's and Aspirin used new characters set in new surroundings. The image of the housewife going about her household tasks disappears completely from Dr. Chase's ads. When focusing on married women, the ads now show them as mothers. However, they are no longer surrounded by children who clamour for their attention when they themselves are obviously unwell; nor are they confronted by both their offspring and the housework yet to be done.[54] Instead, the advertising rhetoric seeks to exploit the image of a mother who is entirely focused on her children's needs. Bolstered by Dr. Chase's Nerve Food, she devotes herself completely to them, taking the time, for example, to read them a story. According to a 1929 Dr. Chase's ad, children are a source of joy for their mother when she is in good health, but they are "an irritation ... for the weak, nervous and excitable mother" (Figure 4.4). With her pretty dress, her stylishly bobbed hair, and her attractive necklace, this mother has a young and refined look that associates her with the middle class, an impression that is confirmed by her surroundings. In particular, her smile indicates that she is truly taking pleasure in reading to her two little ones. Far from being a weighty responsibility or a burden, her children bring her gratification – or at least, that is the message the photo hopes to transmit.

In another ad, a mother obviously wearing a bathing suit under her sundress holds a magazine on her lap while watching her child play beside her in the sand. Entitled "Mother's vacation" this ad asserts, "There's nothing like a change of scenery and routine to rest tired and over-stimulated nerves. And who needs more rest than a mother of young children."[55] Although one might suggest that a mother caring for her child is not exactly on holiday (a fact that does not seem to have crossed the advertiser's mind), the very idea of a vacation constitutes a radical break with the notion of work that, until then, permeated all the ads

LORSQUE LES NERFS DE LA MÈRE SONT EN SANTÉ

Quelle joie sont les enfants à la mère en santé!

Quelle irritation ils sont pour la mère faible, nerveuse et excitable!

Tant de milliers de femmes ont recouvré la santé et le bonheur en utilisant l'aliment des nerfs du Dr Chase, pour restaurer le système nerveux épuisé, qu'on ne discute plus l'efficacité de ce traitement.

Graduellement et naturellement, les qualités nutritives du sang sont augmentées et les nerfs épuisés reviennent à la santé et à la vigueur.

Bientôt vous reposez et dormez bien, vous appréciez vos repas et réalisez une fois de plus la joie de la santé vivifiante.

L'ALIMENT DES NERFS DU DR CHASE
Le plus grand des restaurateurs des nerfs.

Figure 4.4 A mother reads to her children. "Lorsque les nerfs de la mère sont en santé [When mother's nerves are healthy]," Dr. Chase's Nerve Food ad. *Source: Mon Magazine,* March 1929, 25. *Courtesy of* Stella Pharmaceutical Canada Inc.

directed at women. As in the previous example, this ad shows a young and modern mother, which is highlighted by the fact that she wears a bathing suit, a piece of clothing still highly objectionable in Quebec during the interwar years.[56] She, too, is financially comfortable, as is indicated by her family's presence at a resort community. Here again, it is the image of the mother who is devoted to her child and rejoicing in their mutual delight that this ad attempts to make obvious. Though they seem more relaxed and less concentrated on specific tasks, these new advertising images nonetheless reflect another facet of the medical rhetoric that, in the early twentieth century, began to stress women's maternal responsibilities.[57] Endorsing this discourse, which started to focus on children's psychological development during the interwar period, advertising for Dr. Chase's presented the image of the ideal mother who prioritized her children at the expense of household tasks.

The couple also emerged as a new advertising feature in the 1930s. For example, without directly alluding to vacations, one ad for Dr. Chase's shows a young man and woman wearing bathing suits and holding hands, clearly very happy (Figure 4.5). More than any other ad by this company, this one brings the body and recreational corporeal practices to the fore. Indeed, its text does not even allude to work or the obligation of recharging one's batteries so as to return refreshed to household, maternal, or professional obligations. The only mention is the necessity of taking Dr. Chase's Nerve Food to ensure that enough vitamin B is consumed to keep illness at bay. Even if it remains implicit, the text and image suggest that the benefit of good health is especially that of enjoying pleasant physical activities and fully relishing life – which is also a novelty. In the 1920s, advertising tended to show men and women separately, surely because the health problems of each gender supposedly sprang from different causes, but also because advertising rhetoric made a direct link between work and a return to health, a sphere that men and women rarely shared. In the 1930s, the emergence of a new perception of marriage, emphasizing the couple's harmony and shared activities, made it possible to bring husband and wife into the same ad, especially if leisure activities or outings were promoted. In cartoon form (a type of publicity that was very popular during the 1930s), some ads for Aspirin tell the story of a woman who initially refuses to accompany her husband to an evening event because of a terrible headache or nephritis, before, of course, being cured by the fantastic tablets.[58]

The association between health, vacation, leisure, and outings that began to appear during the late 1920s is also very visible in ads that feature women alone. A 1929 ad for Dr. Chase's Nerve Food shows a woman driving a sports car and asks, "Isn't it marvellous to feel good in the springtime, to be able to go out in

Figure 4.5 A healthy young couple on holiday. "Manquant les vitamines et minéraux essentiels, la race humaine devra périr [Without vitamins and essential minerals, the human race would perish]," Dr. Chase's Nerve Food ad. *Source: Le Petit Journal,* 8 January 1939, 12. *Courtesy of* Stella Pharmaceutical Canada Inc.

the sun and the fresh air when nature is being renewed?"[59] Hardly an isolated example, the representation of women as young athletes was very popular at the dawn of the 1930s, as shown in a series of 1931-32 ads for Dow Brewery, which portrayed "Miss Dow" in various sporting activities (skating, skiing, water skiing, horseback riding, and diving). According to these ads, the enzymes in beer stimulated good health, itself a source of pleasure.[60] The exploits of female athletes in the 1920s – a particularly prolific decade for women's sports – surely inspired these ads, which also make a direct connection between health and the use of one's body for leisure activities.[61]

Ads in the 1930s also focused on the social life single women could lead thanks to the relief supplied by the advertised medicines. "Always have Aspirin on hand and accept all the invitations you receive," urges an ad titled "Migraines" that shows a woman sitting in an easy chair, head thrown back, and hand behind the neck in a somewhat theatrical pose.[62] "Before taking Dr. Chase's Paradol, I was racked by nearly unbearable pain every month, which forced me to cancel all my engagements. I have never before used such an effective treatment ... Paradol freed me from the dreadful pain," says another ad dating from 1937.[63]

As these examples illustrate, advertising from the 1930s projected the image of young, modern women who, married or not, seem absorbed by their personal lives and even dare to undertake unconventional activities – in other words, liberated women. Far from emphasizing the notions of constraint, duty, and work, the ads constantly allude to the medications' abilities to restore joie de vivre and to encourage enjoying life's pleasures to the fullest. In the ads of the 1930s, physical well-being, a guarantee of psychic well-being, becomes the prerequisite for pleasant, satisfying, or entertaining activities, not for assuming household or professional responsibilities, as was the case in the 1920s. In shifting their emphasis to preserving health in order to enjoy life, these ads were promoting a new way of conceiving the body, what can be called a new somatic culture, which located leisure and self-realization, not work and duties, at the centre of the pursuit of life. In this perspective, ads were also eager to convince their audience that suffering was pointless. Rather than publishing testimonies from women who had endured years of countless miseries before finally taking a medication that gradually ended their ordeal, the ads now more readily emphasized the futility of waiting before seeking treatment and its quick results. Thus, hoping to change the submissive and resigned attitude of women when they experienced pain, Aspirin ads relentlessly attempted to convince female consumers to take Aspirin at the first sign of symptoms. According to these ads, women, more than men, tended to endure suffering needlessly, when they could obtain immediate relief, thanks to Aspirin: as the ad in Figure 4.6 states, "Most men take the tablets as soon as pain or suffering threatens their comfort. Do it too ... These tablets relieve symptoms almost as soon as they have been swallowed." From a hedonistic perspective, the advertising rhetoric advised readers to avoid distress and to seek relief to better enjoy life, which Aspirin promised to accomplish in just a few seconds.

Unlike housework, which disappeared from the advertising radar during the 1930s, office employees continued to be pictured in certain ads, especially those for Aspirin. However, as Figure 4.6 shows, these ads depend on photographic compositions that arouse viewers' doubts about the employees' dedication to their job.[64] Perching on a stool that is much too high for her desk, the young woman poses languidly and turns her back on her work. This, combined with the rather distant way she holds the documents and the fact that she has

POURQUOI quelques femmes ont-elles tant de patience avec la douleur? Allant dans les magasins quand leur tête est douloureuse. Travaillant quand tout le corps souffre. Quelque fois il se passe des heures avant qu'elles ne prennent de l'Aspirine et qu'elles soient soulagées! La plupart des hommes prennent ces tablettes dès qu'une douleur ou une souffrance quelconque menace leur confort. Faites-le vous aussi! La véritable Aspirine est parfaitement inoffensive; elle ne peut pas déprimer le coeur. La tablette portant le nom Bayer est toujours la véritable Aspirine; toujours la même, toujours sûre. Il n'est pas raisonnable de souffrir d'un mal de tête, d'un rhume, de douleurs névralgiques, ou de quoi que ce soit, que ces tablettes soulagent presqu'aussitôt qu'elles sont avalées. Achetez-en une bouteille, c'est une économie. Toutes les pharmacies vendent la bouteille économique de 100 tablettes.

Figure 4.6 A young woman at work in the early 1930s. "La douleur est si facilement soulagée! [Pain is easily relieved]" Aspirin ad. *Source: Le Petit Journal,* 3 August 1930, 14. *Courtesy of* Bayer Canada Inc.

not removed her hat, suggests that she is hardly absorbed in her task, and not solely because she is unwell. Indeed, her posture, gestures, and appearance indicate refinement and, at the same time, indifference to the necessity of earning a salary. In fact, the text that accompanies the image alludes not only to work but also to shopping: "Why are some women so patient when it comes to pain? Going shopping when they have a headache, working when their body hurts." In comparison, a man in another 1930 ad appears to be truly suffering as he holds his head in his hand.[65] The text encourages him to take Aspirin solely to work better, comparing the male brain to a mechanism that must be maintained, an argument that surely seemed convincing when applied to men.

Conclusion

This study of how women's bodies and work were presented in advertisements during the interwar period shows – at least in the ads analyzed here – that housework and the housewives themselves were practically eclipsed, starting in the late 1920s, by images of women enjoying themselves without constraint. This is not to say that the housewife, wearing an apron and doing the dishes, the laundry, or the cooking, completely disappeared from the publicity world: thousands of ads for soap, household appliances, and other products exist to prove the contrary. Chapters 2 and 3 in this volume also demonstrate that publicity for various products, from cereal to disinfectant, targeted women as mothers and homemakers, capitalizing on the medical discourse that stressed the importance of diet and cleanliness to preserve the health of their families. However, in the case of medicine per se, there is no doubt that publicity firms had other goals in mind. In part perhaps because increasing numbers of women were indeed beginning to benefit from products and technology claiming to do the work for them, advertising for medications – except that for Lydia Pinkham – switched its focus from the homemaker to the young mother, the young wife, and the young single woman.

Youth is the very essence of advertising in the 1930s. From the start of that decade and onward, grandmothers are no longer shown, at least in our compilation, and even mature women are practically non-existent.[66] Young in body, the women in the ads seem just as young in spirit, free of the heavy obligations that overwhelmed their peers during the 1920s. Even the mothers seem to be enjoying themselves. Far from being a burden, or a worrying responsibility, children are portrayed as a source of satisfaction, as proven by their wide grins. For their part, wives appear by their husbands' side, elegant and wearing makeup, ready to go on an outing, not darning socks, hanging the wash, or cleaning the house.

But even more often, the ads focus on young, single women who worry about their social life. As office employees who are barely interested in their jobs, they seem especially attracted to shopping, excursions, or sports. Svelte, elegant, even sophisticated, these women, who are easily identified with the middle rather than the working class, seem made for happiness, not work. A hedonistic vision thus emerges from the publicity of the 1930s, with physical comfort and psychological well-being depicted as the foundations of an agreeable existence, the source of all the pleasures that none but a foolish person would refuse to enjoy. Thus, the instrumental vision of the body, which insists on the capacity and necessity of working to earn one's living, gives way to a new conception where the body is perceived as a tool made to experience pleasure. This transition signals the emergence of a modern somatic culture centred on preserving health in order to better enjoy life – an attitude that advertising helped to spread. In this new understanding of the body, the homemaker, unlike the wife and the mother, was obviously left out in the cold as she was irremediably associated with work and duty.

Notes

1   Bonnie Fox, "Selling the Mechanized Household: 70 Years of Ads in the *Ladies' Home Journal*," *Gender and Society* 4 (1990): 25-40; Kathy Peiss, *Hope in a Jar: The Making of America's Beauty Culture* (New York: Henry Holt, 1998); Tani E. Barlow et al., "The Modern Girl around the World: A Research Agenda and Preliminary Findings," *Gender and History* 17, 2 (August 2005): 245-94. Feminist scholars have been particularly interested in ads for household technologies and cosmetics, automobiles, alcohol, and cigarettes. See Laura L. Behling, "'The Woman at the Wheel': Marketing Ideal Womanhood, 1915-1934," *Journal of American Culture* 20, 3 (1997): 13-30; Emily S. Rosenberg, "Consuming Women: Images of Americanization in the 'American Century,'" *Diplomatic History* 23 (1999): 479-97; Penny Tinkler, "Red Tips for Hot Lips; Advertising Cigarettes for Young Women in Britain, 1920-1970," *Women's History Review* 10 (2001): 249-72; Penny Tinkler, "Refinement and Respectable Consumption: The Acceptable Face of Women's Smoking in Britain, 1918-1970," *Gender and History* 15 (2003): 342-60; Penny Tinkler, *Smoke Signals: Women, Smoking and Visual Culture in Britain* (Oxford: Berg, 2006); Cheryl Krasnick Warsh, "Smoke and Mirrors: Gender Representation in North American Tobacco and Alcohol Advertisements before 1950," *Histoire sociale/Social History* 31, 62 (1998): 183-222; and Cheryl Krasnick Warsh and Penny Tinkler, "In Vogue: North American and British Representations of Women Smokers in *Vogue*, 1920s-1960s," *Canadian Bulletin of Medical History/Bulletin canadien d'histoire de la médecine* 24, 1 (2007): 9-47.

2   One exception is Kim Chuppa-Cornell, "Filling a Vacuum: Women's Health Information in *Good Housekeeping*'s Articles and Advertisements, 1920-1965," *Historian* 67, 3 (2005): 454-73. In *Female Complaints: Lydia Pinkham and the Business of Women's Medicine* (New York: W.W. Norton, 1979), Sarah Stage investigates the growth, development, and marketing techniques of the Lydia Pinkham Company, founded in 1875. See also Chapters 2 and 3 in this volume.

3   T.J. Jackson Lears, *Fables of Abundance: A Cultural History of Advertising in America* (New York: Basic Books, 1994); Nancy Tomes, "The Great American Medicine Show Revisited," *Bulletin of the History of Medicine* 79 (2005): 627-63.

4   According to Nancy Tomes, James Harvey Young's *The Toadstool Millionaires: A Social History of Patent Medicines in America before Federal Regulation* (Princeton: Princeton University Press, 1961), is still the best history of the nineteenth-century American proprietary medicine industry. Tomes, "The Great American Medicine Show," 636. See also James Harvey Young, *The Medical Messiahs: A Social History of Health Quackery in Twentieth-Century America* (Princeton: Princeton University Press, 1967). For other contexts, see F.B. Smith, *The People's Health, 1830-1910* (London: Croom Helm, 1979); Marc Martin, *Trois siècles de publicités en France* (Paris: Éditions Odile Jacob, 1992); Thomas P. Kelley Jr., *The Fabulous Kelley: Canada's King of the Medicine Men* (Don Mills: General Publishers, 1974); Joseph E. Wilder, *Lotions, Potions, and Liniments Cure: A Look at the Drug Trade in Winnipeg in the 1900s* (Winnipeg: Prairie Publishing, 1992). For a semiotic analysis of the ads published in Quebec between 1900 and 1930, see Guildo Rousseau, "La santé par correspondance: un mode de mise en marché des médicaments brevetés au début du siècle," *Histoire sociale/Social History* 28, 55 (1995): 1-25.

5   Denis Goulet, *Le commerce des maladies: la publicité des remèdes au début du siècle* (Quebec, QC: Institut québécois de recherche sur la culture, Coll. Edmond-de-Nevers No. 6, 1987), 99.

6   It should be noted that in English Canada, mass media, especially women's magazines such as the *Ladies' Home Journal,* were widely circulated and read. American films also predominated in Canadian theatres – even in Quebec, where 80 percent of the population was French speaking. Radio stations broadcasted mainly American advertisements, especially in English Canada. For a history of the interwar years in Canada, see John Herd Thompson and Allen Seager, *Canada, 1922-1939: Decades of Discord* (Toronto: McClelland and Stewart, 1985). On media and advertisements, see Mary Vipond, "Canadian Nationalism and the Plight of Canadian Magazines in the 1920s," *Canadian Historical Review* 58 (1977): 43-65; Michel Filion, "La publicité américaine à la radio canadienne: le cas du réseau français de Radio-Canada, 1938-1958," *Revue d'histoire de l'Amérique française* 51 (1997): 71-92; and H.E. Stephenson and Carlton McNaught, *The Story of Advertising in Canada: A Chronicle of Fifty Years* (Toronto: Ryerson Press, 1950).

7   In Quebec, women finally won the vote in 1940. On women's struggle for suffrage in Canada, see Catherine Cleverdon, *The Women Suffrage Movement in Canada* (1947; repr., Toronto: University of Toronto Press, 1974).

8   On the history of women in Canada and Quebec, see Alison Prentice et al., *Canadian Women: A History,* 2nd ed. (Toronto: Harcourt Brace Canada, 1996); and Clio Collective, *Quebec Women: A History* (Toronto: Canadian Scholars' Press, 1990). On office work, see Kate Boyer, "Re-Working Respectability: The Feminization of Clerical Work and the Politics of Public Virtue in Early Twentieth-Century Montreal," in *Power, Place and Identity: Historical Studies of Social and Legal Regulation in Quebec,* ed. Tamara Myers et al. (Montreal: Montreal History Group, 1998), 151-69. On marriage, sexuality, and contraception in Canada, see Cynthia Comacchio, *The Infinite Bonds of Family: Domesticity in Canada, 1850-1940* (Toronto: University of Toronto Press, 1999); Angus McLaren and Arlene Tigar McLaren, *The Bedroom and the State: The Changing Practices and Politics of Contraception and Abortion in Canada, 1880-1980* (Toronto: McClelland and Stewart, 1986). On fertility in Quebec, see Danielle Gauvreau, Peter Gossage, and Diane Gervais, *La fécondité des Québécoises, 1870-1970: d'une exception à l'autre* (Montreal: Boréal, 2007). On fashion, see Suzanne Marchand, *Rouge à lèvres et pantalons: des pratiques esthétiques féminines controversées au Québec, 1920-1939* (Lasalle: Hurtubise HMH, 1997).

9   Comacchio, *The Infinite Bonds;* Denyse Baillargeon, *Making Do: Women, Family and Home in Montreal during the Great Depression* (Waterloo: Wilfrid Laurier University Press, 1999).

10 On the history of the body, see Alain Corbin, Jean-Jacques Courtine, and Georges Vigarello, *Histoire du corps,* vol. 3, *Les mutations du regard: Le XXe siècle* (Paris: Seuil, 2006).

11 Roland Marchand, *Advertising the American Dream: Making Way for Modernity, 1920-1940* (Berkeley: University of California Press, 1985); Stephen Fox, *The Mirror Makers: A History of American Advertising and Its Creators* (New York: William Marrow, 1984), esp. 78-171; Lears, *Fables of Abundance*; Stephenson and McNaught, *The Story of Advertising in Canada*. In *Advertising the American Dream*, 286-88, Marchand contends that the Depression did not have a clearly discernible impact on advertising, an observation that my analysis confirms.

12 Marchand, *Rouge à lèvres et pantalons*, 47-48.

13 Around 1935, *Le Petit Journal* sold seventy thousand copies per week throughout the province. André Beaulieu and Jean Hamelin, *La Presse québécoise des origines à nos jours*, vol. 6, *1920-1934* (Quebec, QC: Presses de l'Université Laval, 1984), 12-14.

14 On regulation of patent medicines in Canada, see Stephenson and McNaught, *The Story of Advertising in Canada*, 237.

15 In the sample created by Luc Côté and Jean-Guy Daigle for their study on ads in Quebec daily newspapers between 1920 and 1960, Lydia Pinkham's Vegetable Compound ranked sixth of the most frequently advertised products, whereas Dr. Chase's came in tenth and Aspirin fourteenth out of 92. Only Dodd's Pills appeared more frequently than these three products, coming in third. Luc Côté and Jean-Guy Daigle, *Publicité de masse et masse publicitaire: le marché québécois des années 1920 aux années 1960* (Ottawa: Presses de l'Université d'Ottawa, 1999), 100-1.

16 In fact, Lydia Pinkham's Vegetable Compound continued to be advertised during the 1930s, but no new or different ads were issued.

17 In all likelihood, the ads were translations from English originals that appeared in other magazines and newspapers in English Canada or the United States. For example, ads for Lydia Pinkham's Vegetable Compound generally offer testimonies from women living in small towns in Ontario or even the United States.

18 Stage, *Female Complaints*.

19 Marsha Ackerman, *A Man, a Book, a Building, or, the History of Dr. Chase's Steam Printing House* (Ann Arbor: Dobson-McOmber Agency, 1994), cited in *Feeding America: The Historic American Cookbook Project*, http://digital.lib.msu.edu/.

20 Jan R. McTavish, "What's in a Name? Aspirin and the American Medical Association," *Bulletin of the History of Medicine* 61 (1987): 343-66.

21 All subsequent quotations are translated by Zoé Blowen-Ledoux.

22 Dr. Chase's Liniment advertisement, *La Canadienne*, February 1923, 29.

23 Lydia E. Pinkham's Vegetable Compound advertisement, *La Revue Moderne*, July 1928, 28.

24 Goulet, *Le commerce des maladies*, 92.

25 Aspirin advertisement, *Le Petit Journal*, 4 February 1934, 11.

26 Goulet, *Le commerce des maladies*, 47-50.

27 Luc Boltanski, "Les usages sociaux du corps," *Annales E.S.C.* 26, 1 (1971): 205-33.

28 Aspirin advertisement, *Le Petit Journal*, 3 March 1929, 25; Aspirin advertisement, *La Revue Moderne*, December 1928, 15. For an example of an ad featuring medical staff, see Aspirin advertisement, *La Revue Moderne*, February 1929, 19.

29 However, ads for the two other medications sometimes used stories from doctors, most frequently foreign, lauding their efficacy.

30 Lydia E. Pinkham's Vegetable Compound advertisements, *La Revue Moderne*, May 1923, 39, May 1924, 63, and July 1924, 40.

31 Lydia E. Pinkham's Vegetable Compound advertisement, *La Revue Moderne*, July 1923, 41.

32 Lydia E. Pinkham's Vegetable Compound advertisements, *La Revue Moderne*, June 1923, 39, and June 1924, 42.

33 Dr. Chase's Nerve Food advertisement, *La Canadienne*, May 1921, 38; Lydia E. Pinkham's Vegetable Compound advertisement, *La Revue Moderne*, May 1928, 43.

34 On medical discourse in nineteenth-century Canada, see Wendy Mitchinson, *The Nature of Their Bodies: Women and Their Doctors in Victorian Canada* (Toronto: University of Toronto Press, 1991).
35 Lydia E. Pinkham's Vegetable Compound advertisement, *La Revue Moderne*, July 1929, 46.
36 Lydia E. Pinkham's Vegetable Compound advertisement, *La Revue Moderne*, September 1923, 39.
37 Dr. Chase's Nerve Food advertisements, *La Revue Moderne*, March 1927, 31, and May 1927, 6.
38 Goulet, *Le commerce des maladies*, 99.
39 Ibid., 98; Boltanski, "Les usages sociaux du corps."
40 For an example of a Pinkham's ad, see *La Revue Moderne*, October 1927, 26.
41 Dr. Chase's Nerve Food advertisements, *La Canadienne*, May 1920, 47, November 1920, 50, and June 1921, 9; Dr. Chase's Nerve Food advertisement, *La Revue Moderne*, July 1922, 52.
42 Dr. Chase's Nerve Food advertisements, *La Revue Moderne*, October 1926, 55; *La Canadienne*, June 1921, 28; *La Revue Moderne*, July 1922, 52, November 1923, 36, and October 1924, 31; *La Canadienne*, June 1922, 35; *La Revue Moderne*, July 1923, 32, and January 1922, 32. See also *La Revue Moderne*, March 1927, 31, and May 1927, 6.
43 Only three ads in our sample depict domestic servants.
44 According to Penny Tinkler, "Refinement required attention to the finer details of appearance and depended on careful maintenance and control/containment of the female body. Aside from appearance, refinement also required a certain posture (elegant and contained) and behaviour (polite, not coarse)." Tinkler, "Refinement and Respectable Consumption," 343.
45 Aline Charles, *Quand devient-on vieille? Femmes, âge et travail au Québec, 1940-1980* (Quebec, QC: Presses de l'Université Laval et Institut québécois de recherche sur la culture, 2007).
46 Dr. Chase's Nerve Food advertisements, *La Canadienne*, January 1921, 30, and December 1922, 32; Dr. Chase's Nerve Food advertisements, *Mon Magazine*, November 1928, 33.
47 Dr. Chase's Nerve Food advertisement, *La Canadienne*, December 1922, 32.
48 According to some estimates, less than 5 percent of married women worked outside the home in Quebec during the 1920s. Although it is impossible to pinpoint the exact proportion, we know that many more women performed paid work inside their homes (mostly sewing). For examples drawn from oral testimonies, see Baillargeon, *Making Do*, 96-102.
49 Dr. Chase's Nerve Food advertisement, *Le Petit Journal*, April 1929, 32.
50 Dr. Chase's Nerve Food advertisements, *La Revue Moderne*, April 1923, 32, and June 1924, 56.
51 Dr. Chase's Nerve Food advertisement, *La Revue Moderne*, March 1927, 18.
52 Dr. Chase's Nerve Food advertisement, *La Revue Moderne*, May 1923, 32.
53 Dr. Chase's Nerve Food advertisement, *La Revue Moderne*, November 1922, 36.
54 See Dr. Chase's Nerve Food advertisements, *La Revue Moderne*, January 1922, 32, and May 1927, 6.
55 Dr. Chase's Nerve Food advertisement, *Mon Magazine*, August 1928, 2.
56 Marchand, *Rouge à lèvres et pantalons*.
57 Denyse Baillargeon, *Un Québec en mal d'enfants: la médicalisation de la maternité, 1910-1970* (Montreal: Remue-Ménage, 2004); Cynthia Comacchio, *Nations Are Built of Babies: Saving Ontario's Mothers and Children, 1900-1940* (Montreal and Kingston: McGill-Queen's University Press, 1993).
58 Aspirin advertisements, *La Revue Moderne*, March 1934, 19, May 1934, 15, and October 1934, 25.
59 Dr. Chase's Nerve Food advertisement, *Mon Magazine*, June 1929, 33.
60 See, for example, Dow Brewery advertisement, *La Revue Moderne*, June 1933, 47. At the end of the 1930s, Dr. Chase's Paradol was also advertised as a remedy for the maladies of female athletes. See Dr. Chase's Paradol advertisement, *Le Petit Journal*, 1 November 1936, 41.

61 Margaret Ann Hall, *The Girl and the Game: The History of Women's Sport in Canada* (Peterborough: Broadview Press, 2002).
62 Aspirin advertisements, *La Revue Moderne,* November 1931, 7, and April 1934, 17. See also Aspirin advertisement, *La Revue Moderne,* December 1931, 18.
63 Dr. Chase's Paradol advertisement, *Le Petit Journal,* 7 November 1937, 8.
64 See also Aspirin advertisement, *Le Petit Journal,* 2 February 1930, 38.
65 Aspirin advertisement, *Le Petit Journal,* 2 November 1930, 30.
66 The last grandmother appears in 1930 in an ad for Dr. Chase's Nerve Food. Only her face can be seen. Instead of working, she smiles and waves goodbye to her family through the window. The text asserts that young children no longer make her nervous since she started taking Dr. Chase's medicine. See Dr. Chase's Nerve Food advertisement, *Mon Magazine,* March 1930, 25.

5

Annie Turnbo Malone and African American Beauty Culture in the American West

De Anna J. Reese

The rise of consumer culture and the expansion of a mass market for cosmetics made the early twentieth century an especially significant period for African American beauty entrepreneurs. Although hairstyling and makeup had become affordable indulgences for American women across class by 1930, commercial beauty culture moved black and white women in different directions. Both groups shared a belief in the promotion of women's economic independence and the social significance of appearance, but the "ethnic market" created by African Americans involved separate distribution networks, advertising strategies, and professional methods that were culturally and politically distinct from those of the dominant culture.[1]

Part of a small cadre of self-made female millionaires, Annie Minerva Turnbo Malone was among the founders of black beauty culture in America. Malone was the creator and president of Poro College in St. Louis, Missouri, and though her pioneering contributions to black beauty culture have often been eclipsed by the fame of her former student and business rival Madam C.J. Walker, both were responsible for redefining beauty and femininity for African American women in the twentieth century. For Malone, this was done through operating a chain of beauty schools from which she broadened "acceptable" public presentations of working-class black women outside of the domestic sphere. During an era in which white businesses and advertisers refused to acknowledge the purchasing power of African Americans, Malone created a vision of feminine beauty that increased both the visibility and respectability of women of colour.[2]

Although the significance of Malone and her business, the Poro Company, in the development of black beauty culture has been well documented, few studies explore the arenas in which Malone's leadership, business activity, and philanthropy existed outside the main St. Louis and Chicago headquarters of her company. Addressing themes of work, racial uplift, and respectability, this chapter examines the social and business networks of Annie Malone in Los Angeles and how each informed and expanded the concept of the "new black woman." With striking similarities to the New Woman of the early twentieth century, the new black woman shared in the new status granted white American women as citizens, consumers, and pleasure seekers. Yet she was not a newcomer to the labour market; nor was she able to take full advantage of the new lines of work available to other middle-class women. Inspired by the rise of racial solidarity found in the New Negro and Marcus Garvey movements, the new black woman exerted a heightened self-confidence in which beauty culture and appearance played a pivotal role.

These roles have been acknowledged by historians such as Kathy Peiss, who argues that beauty culture was an integral part of how black women navigated the changing landscape of modernity. Despite the ongoing effects of Jim Crow, black women carved out new visions of economic independence and social participation. In this context, commercial beauty culture involved something more than isolated acts of consumption or vanity. Rather, it assumed an economic and aesthetic significance that spoke to black women's collective experience and aspirations.[3]

At the heart of this experience was finding more manageable ways to style and care for their hair. In *Hair Raising: Beauty, Culture, and African American Women,* cultural theorist Noliwe Rooks comments that definitions of black beauty took on political significance long before the feminist movement. Having served as a site of African American women's efforts to define their identity, hair was part of an intergenerational struggle that exposed both the tensions and contradictions in black families as they grappled with issues of respectability, racial pride, and mainstream definitions of beauty.[4]

Recognizing the vast potential of black consumers, Malone achieved success in the beauty industry, not only for the quality of her product, but for her creativity in reaching women of colour in various markets through newspapers, door-to-door demonstrations, lecture tours, a state-of-the-art training college, and a series of national beauty school franchises. These distribution methods and institutions provided new options for black women, whose physical appearance assumed greater importance within an urban, industrial, consumer-driven society. With the use of Poro products, black women adopted better grooming and hygiene standards that allowed them entry into wider social circles. It also provided them the chance to reshape ideals of beauty and modernity into opportunities for collective progress, economic advancement, and self-respect.

Examining racialized representations of femininity beyond the Jim Crow era, sociologist Maxine Leeds Craig underscores the importance of beauty in the struggle to win respect for African American women. In her book *Ain't I a Beauty Queen? Black Women, Beauty and the Politics of Race,* Craig argues that African Americans contested and revised the social meaning of black identity through spectacle, protest, and daily acts of self-preservation.[5] Under the drudgery of low-paying jobs, black women found the means to present themselves whenever they could with as much propriety as they could afford. Donning decorative hats, wearing fashionable dresses, and carefully styling their hair enabled black women to display their dignity and convey racial pride.[6] Such behaviours were ones that Malone and her products aptly reflected, encouraging black women to reclaim their womanhood, even if it meant rejecting the rural lifestyles and aesthetic categories to which they had grown accustomed.

African American Beauty Culture in Post-War Los Angeles

Among the nation's largest metropolitan cities, Los Angeles experienced dramatic change prior to the Second World War. Streetcars, electric lighting, commercial business, and a steady influx of Latino, Asian, and African American migrants made Los Angeles a symbol of diversity and modernity.[7] Constituting nearly half of the state's black residents by 1930, African American women sought refuge from the sexual abuse and discrimination of the Jim Crow South.[8] Newspapers such as the *California Eagle,* the city's largest black weekly, heralded the state as one of the best places for African Americans: "Everything that can be produced anywhere else can be produced in this great State, and as we pass from county to county, city to city, taking in villages and hamlets, we are greatly convinced that this is the ideal location for the dark Americans."[9] However, this optimism was tempered during a time in which skin colour barred African Americans from all but a few hundred feet of Southern California's beaches, from employment in white-owned businesses, and from access to hotels. Such policies were often challenged by community members who denounced City officials for "turning their backs on the progressive interests of blacks in the city" after the Los Angeles suburb of Santa Monica established special zoning legislation to block the development of a bathhouse "for the benefit of colored people." Though race was not specified as a reason for rejecting the proposal, community assumptions of blacks as an inferior, undifferentiated group made many hostile to their presence near oceanfront property.[10]

Limited economic options left African American women concentrated within the city's lowest-paid personal service jobs. Rigidly excluded from the trade, transportation, manufacturing, and business sectors, 87 percent of employed black women and 40 percent of employed black men in Los Angeles worked as household servants by 1930.[11] Such conditions led many to seek new employment opportunities in the beauty industry. One of few professions offering a level of economic independence and skill at minimal cost, beauty culture provided steady employment, better wages, and the possibility for upward mobility – making it one of the most popular and respected lines of work for black women in urban areas.[12]

The tenth of eleven children, Annie Minerva Tue was born on 9 August 1869 in Metropolis, Illinois. After losing both parents as a child, Malone went to live with an older sister. Once in high school, she began to experiment with chemical solutions to straighten and enhance the texture of black hair. During the early years of product development, Malone, dissatisfied with the hair-care remedies and styling techniques available to black women, introduced a product she claimed would make thin, dull, and sparse hair grow. Adopting the name "Poro," which was of West African origin, Malone advertised her beauty system as one that improved both the physical and spiritual well-being of her customers.[13]

After years of perfecting her signature product, known as the Wonderful Hair Grower, Malone moved her business across the Mississippi to St. Louis, where its immediate success marked the beginning of her entrance into the hair-care industry. After years of hard work and the investment of her life savings, Malone began a business empire with the building of St. Louis's largest black-owned and -controlled institution, Poro College, in 1918. Throughout the 1920s, Malone and other beauty entrepreneurs struggled to define a more diverse beauty ideal for black women and to expand the range of economic options available in a segregated labour market. Mass advertising, a burgeoning entertainment industry, and greater accessibility to store-bought goods made Los Angeles an ideal location for beauty entrepreneurs to advertise their product lines and expertise. For thousands of migrant women, attractive hair became a symbol of social respectability and urban living. This was especially true for black women who, on moving to the city, recognized the importance of fashionable hair and clothing for acceptance into middle-class circles.[14]

Among the practices black women used to symbolize this transition was hair straightening. As Maxine Leeds Craig notes, the social and political meanings attached to hair developed in the context of poverty, demeaning work, and vulnerability to the sexual victimization that characterized black women's lives.[15] An overwhelmingly black female practice in the 1920s and 1930s, hair straightening was part of a gendered discourse on race and respectability. Representing pride, modernity, and good grooming, straightened hair was perceived as a personal action that one could take to win respect; but it was also controversial. By the early decades of the twentieth century, African American women were bombarded by advertisements that promoted light skin and straight or wavy hair as the desirable beauty standard. Many in the black community condemned this ideal, accusing those who used these products and methods of denying their African heritage and wanting to look white.

Malone and other beauty culturists contested these claims. As historian Susannah Walker reminds us, African American beauty culture was never entirely about creating glamour and beauty. Malone and others insisted that their products and methods were not about accepting a white beauty ideal, but about treating damaged hair, healing scalp disease, and helping hair grow. They straightened hair, too, but they portrayed the practice of straightening as part of a modern, healthy, and progressive way for black women to care for their hair. Some even viewed it as a route to racial uplift, using one's appearance to help raise the individual or collective fortunes of black people.[16]

On the other hand, neither Malone nor her contemporaries challenged the prevailing notions of beauty during the time. Instead, they sought to create safe, affordable products that would give all classes of black women a means of achieving this straight-haired ideal. Such critiques, however, must be considered within their historical context. Malone did not create the idea that black hair must be straight to be presentable. Many factors, including the culture's disparagement of black bodies and exclusion of black women from the dominant beauty ideal, were based on physical difference. As biographer A'Lelia Bundles explains, the goals of beauty entrepreneurs such as Madam C.J. Walker and Annie Malone entailed more than merely selling their products: they intended to make black women feel good about how they looked.[17]

This new emphasis on appearance and consumption was evident in the black press, beauty pageants, local fashion shows, and dances. The annual springtime Silver Fox Dance was one occasion that brought out hundreds of young women, all looking to demonstrate their unique sense of style or showcase a new hairstyling trend. Sponsored by the Silver Fox Club, a popular young men's organization, the dance's most notable feature was the "beautiful hair contest." In 1926, nearly a thousand people arrived at Blanchard Hall "to see who has the most beautiful head of hair in Los Angeles."[18] According to the *California Eagle*, this was twice the number who had attended previous dances. After examining hundreds of hairstyles, the judges awarded first prize to Genevie Clay, whose hairdresser, Miss Marcia Pruitt, worked at the Poro substation on Hooper Avenue.

Located on one of the busiest corners for black businesses in Los Angeles, the Poro substation was known for producing some of the best hairdressers of the city, including Pruitt, who was described as an "expert marcellist." After completing courses in beauty culture at Jefferson High School, Pruitt moved to St. Louis, where she earned a certificate in beauty culture from Poro College.[19] It was there that she perfected the technique of marcel waving, first popularized by white hairdressers. In a discussion of the tools used by black hairdressers, historian Julia Kirk Blackwelder describes the marcel iron as similar to today's electric curling iron. However, marcelled hair was creased between blades rather than being wound around a heated rod. The finished look consisted of a series of cascading waves formed by lateral crimps over wide locks of hair.[20]

Made popular by models and celebrities, the marcel wave was one of many techniques for which the Poro Beauty School in Los Angeles was known. In one advertisement, potential students were advised to train at Poro to master the skills needed to become both efficient and well-paid operators. In addition, the Poro School offered individual instruction, living models, and teachers with years of experience. As a specialist in marcelling and wig making, the Poro School guaranteed that its graduates would become competent in all areas of hair and skin care treatment.[21] To keep up with competitors, Poro also taught classes in hair cutting, hair dyeing, bleaching, and finger waving. This repertoire of techniques became a staple for American beauty schools, black and white, from the 1920s into the 1950s. Many salons also included facial, scalp, and upper-body massages as part of the hairdressing experience.[22]

The popularity of Poro College and the success of its products resonated with black women from across the country, especially in Los Angeles, where many discovered a city that offered a climate of possibility for economic advancement, homeownership, and social freedom.[23] Yet, anticipation of such benefits did not halt the spread of racial discrimination in employment and housing, both of which led African Americans to develop their own business and residential neighbourhoods along Central Avenue.

Whereas residential segregation divided the city along race and class lines, it also demonstrated the strong presence of African Americans in specific neighbourhoods, such as South Central Los Angeles. In this predominantly white district with large numbers of ethnic immigrants, African Americans had a major impact on the culture and spirit of the community. Though small in number, black Angelenos bought homes and created a host of churches, nightclubs, restaurants, and shops that soon made Central Avenue the heart of a vibrant nightlife and thriving business community. The Westside, an area that included lands west and north of Main Street, housed upwardly mobile or wealthy whites. Eastside neighbourhood, which included Central Avenue in between Main Street and Alameda Avenue, was home to mostly poor and working-class residents. The hub of black community life, Central Avenue, with its convenient streetcar lines and theatres, also became the centre of the beauty culture trade.[24]

Among the neighbourhood businesses that promoted financial freedom and social solidarity, the Bookertee Investment Company urged black residents to buy rather than rent homes in the city. Offering hundreds of desirable lots and free auto rides to new homesites, the company viewed home buying as a means to increase one's social and economic standing. This idea was supported by the California Realty Board, whose president, Sidney Doans, lauded the city's warm climate, scenic mountain views, and "lovely residential districts" as key factors in attracting African American homebuyers, who were believed to be more numerous than in other cities.[25]

Real estate investment and homeownership were also among the goals promoted by the Poro Company during the 1920s. Although they were a minority among those blacks who were able to purchase homes, beauty culture agents, especially those with years of service to the company, received additional incentives from Malone, who awarded employees with cash and jewellery for buying property for either themselves or their families. Malone's recognition of these endeavours reflected her belief that saving money and purchasing a home were significant to securing true wealth for African American women.

In a speech made before Poro graduates, Malone emphasized the connection between good grooming and material prosperity: "Before black women began to cultivate beauty, we were called 'aunty,' 'mammy' ... and 'Jane.' Now we are Miss and Mrs. as we assume dignity, poise, and grace. This physical appearance leads to modesty, thrift, culture, and the acquiring of homes –healthful and attractive."[26] For Malone, black women's low status as domestic workers could be overcame with the proper grooming methods. In turn, self-confidence was vital to building the habits necessary to acquire material prosperity.

These values were ones that Malone readily shared with other young women across the country when she spoke on national tours of Poro schools. In a speech to members of Zeta Phi Beta Sorority, of which Malone was an honorary member, she underscored the importance of independence, altruism, and the planning and execution of one's goals: "No dream, no matter how beautiful, meant [anything] ... unless realized; no plan no matter how ambitious and rife with benefit to humanity meant [anything] unless executed."[27] Malone's career was a testament to these sentiments as she managed her business and provided generous financial support to projects for women through networks inside women's clubs, churches, schools, and civic organizations. Having carved out a place among her peers, Malone spared neither her fortune nor her time in assisting those who were closest to her.

This generosity began with her siblings, one of whom received a twelve-room mansion and a separate three-room apartment purchased with cash. Praised as "one of the most handsome properties in [the] residence district," the house was described as "strictly modern and exquisite in taste."[28] One of many extravagant gifts Malone bought for family, it was a testament to her new millionaire status and the depth of her gratitude for the support and assistance given by her sister, Mrs. N. Cooper. Malone also used her sister's new mansion as a "hotel" during numerous visits to Los Angeles for both herself and her guests.

Within months of this purchase, Malone sponsored a "Poro Club" outing at Bruces Beach, named for Charles and Willa Bruce, who built a black beach resort in what is now Manhattan Beach, California. One of few beaches in Southern California during the early twentieth century that was not off-limits to African Americans, it offered the best available facilities, including a bathhouse and dining club.[29] With over 1,100 guests in attendance, the "gala affair" was one of contests, games, and educational programs. After awarding prizes and toasting the success of Poro agents in the West, Annie Malone and her husband, Aaron, supervised a sumptuous dinner for everyone on the beach. Enjoying a "menu fit for a king" and service "handled in perfect order" with no restrictions, guests dined in style before posing with the Malones for a group photo that included friends from San Diego.[30] Such events made the beauty pioneer a well-known and respected figure among the locals, who celebrated her commitment to improving the lives of African American women and welcomed her willingness to share the fruits of her success with the larger community.

Among the multitude of well-wishers at Bruces Beach was *California Eagle* managing editor, Charlotta Spears Bass. A relative newcomer to the city, she had come to Los Angeles in 1910, where she discovered a black community undergoing steady growth. After the death of the *Eagle's* founder, John Neimore, Bass became its owner, editor, and publisher. In 1914, she agreed to jointly run the paper with new husband Joe Bass. The two shared similar views about the purpose of running a black or "race paper," which they believed was an important vehicle in helping to safeguard and expand black civil rights during the tenuous period of Jim Crow.[31] Their mission to focus on issues of social justice and the achievements of African Americans made Malone and the Poro Company, with its emphasis on racial uplift, a popular feature covered by the *California Eagle* during the 1920s.

As a black female editor in a profession that was very much a "man's world," Bass intimately understood the difficulties facing other successful black women and made every effort to regularly assign space on the front pages of the *Eagle* to cover women's clubs, organizations, performances, and individuals. With long-time support from the black press, Malone received tremendous backing from Bass and the paper during troubling times as well. By the end of the decade, Malone faced a public scandal and a bitter divorce when her husband, Aaron, attempted to wrest controlling interest of her company from her. This crisis, followed by the onset of the Great Depression, forced the beauty entrepreneur to slash Poro's advertising budget, change its marketing strategy, and limit personal visits to her beauty schools out west.

Commercial beauty culture has played an important role in the lives of African American women since the turn of the century, but by the 1920s, it had become even more prominent. The growth of urban black communities such as Los Angeles, along with the expansion of mass consumer culture, made beauty a consumer product readily purchased by those who could afford it. Moreover, the experience of black beauty entrepreneurs reveals much about how race, gender, and class affected the ways in which African Americans understood and participated in a culture that was becoming increasingly consumer-based, commercial, and profit-oriented. The politics of appearance was a salient issue for women across racial lines in the twentieth century, but it was unique among African Americans in large part because they confronted popular images of feminine beauty that perpetually celebrated European features as ideal.[32]

Like that of other entrepreneurs of her time, Malone's impact on beauty culture in Los Angeles offers additional clues regarding how both she and her business influenced the social and economic opportunities of African Americans in the city. It also demonstrates the ways in which black beauty culture contributed to supporting notions of racial uplift and progress for the entire community. The growth of industrial America, new job placement and training for women, and the increase in cosmetic purchases wove together women's identities as consumers and workers. In this way, Malone's Poro School in Los Angeles brought hundreds of women into a consumer culture that was previously unknown to them. Given little attention by national advertisers and magazines, Malone's customers, many of them working-class women, gained access to a market that typically excluded them.[33]

Getting one's hair done was not only an act of consumption but also a social activity. Every black woman who applied lipstick, chatted with her neighbour-hood Poro agent, or read an article on blues artist Ma Rainey was acting as a consumer of beauty culture.[34] Moreover, as the demands for Jim Crow legislation in Los Angeles grew louder, beauty entrepreneurs such as Annie Malone found a means to use the race-based restrictions to their advantage. With extensive black media coverage from the *California Eagle,* Malone advertised the benefits of her beauty school to thousands of Afro-Angelenos who became better ac-quainted with her products and generosity through social activities sponsored by either herself or others.

During a period in which American popular culture routinely devalued and demeaned the appearance of people of African descent, beauty culturists at-tempted to refute such claims by introducing products and practices that pro-moted personal grooming, encouraged female economic independence, and supported the improvement of the greater community. Continuing a reputation for the excellence of its products and training, the Poro Beauty School in Los Angeles taught and attracted a clientele that in many ways combined the key elements associated with both the smart, stylish, and sophisticated New Woman, *and* the new Negro woman – respectable, assertive, and proud of her heritage. With these ideas in mind and reminders from her good friend and founder of the first black advertising agency, Claude A. Barnett, Malone set out to re-create the image of modernity for African American women into the 1930s – but not without returning even larger shares of her time, talent, and wealth to the com-munities that she served.

Notes
1 According to historian Kathy Peiss, beauty culture should not only be understood as a type of commerce, but as a system of meaning that helped women navigate the changing conditions of modernity. For more information on the social history of America's beauty industry, see Kathy Peiss, *Hope in a Jar: The Making of America's Beauty Culture* (New York: Henry Holt, 1998), 95.
2 Ibid., 5.
3 Ibid., 7, 95. The term "new Negro woman" refers to the heightened sense of confidence and pride of black women during the early twentieth century. The "new black woman" is my at-tempt to bring together the "new Negro" and the "new woman," both of whom are integral parts of African American beauty culture.
4 Noliwe M. Rooks, *Hair Raising: Beauty, Culture, and African American Women* (New Brunswick, NJ: Rutgers University Press, 1996), 5.
5 Maxine Leeds Craig, *Ain't I a Beauty Queen? Black Women, Beauty and the Politics of Race* (New York: Oxford University Press, 2002), 14.
6 Ibid., 34.

7   Jules Tygiel, "Metropolis in the Making: Los Angeles in the 1920s," in *Metropolis in the Making: Los Angeles in the 1920s,* ed. Tom Sitton and William Deverell (Berkeley: University of California Press, 2001), 2-4.

8   Shirley Ann Wilson Moore, "'Your Life Is Really Not Just Your Own': African American Women in Twentieth Century California," in *Seeking El Dorado: African Americans in California,* ed. Lawrence B. De Graaf, Kevin Mulroy, and Quintard Taylor (Los Angeles: Autry Museum of Western Heritage, 2001), 211, 213.

9   "From Rather Busy Vacation – Some Things Seen and Heard," *California Eagle* (Los Angeles), 1 October 1921, 1.

10 "Blacks Again Feel Iron Fist of Race Prejudice," *California Eagle* (Los Angeles), 1 April 1922, 1.

11 Josh Sides, *L.A. City Limits: African American Los Angeles from the Great Depression to the Present* (Berkeley: University of California Press, 2003), 26.

12 Susannah Walker, *Style and Status: Selling Beauty to African American Women, 1920-1975* (Lexington: University Press of Kentucky, 2007), 2-3.

13 Evelyn Newman Phillips, "Ms. Annie Malone's Poro: Addressing Whiteness and Dressing Black-Bodied Women," *Transforming Anthropology* 11, 2 (2004): 4.

14 Ayana D. Byrd and Lori L. Tharps, *Hair Story: Untangling the Roots of Black Hair in America* (New York: St. Martin's Griffin, 2001), 30-31.

15 Craig, *Ain't I a Beauty Queen?* 30-31.

16 Walker, *Style and Status,* 29.

17 A'Lelia Perry Bundles, *On Her Own Ground: The Life and Times of Madam C.J. Walker* (New York: Scribner, 2001), 69, 91.

18 Byrd and Tharps, *Hair Story,* 37; "Silver Fox Dance Draws Many Beautiful Heads of Hair and Large Crowd," *California Eagle* (Los Angeles), 30 April 1926, 1.

19 "Poro Sub Station Takes First Prize for Efficiency and Beauty," *California Eagle* (Los Angeles), 7 May 1926, 8.

20 Julia Kirk Blackwelder, *Styling Jim Crow: African American Beauty Training during Segregation* (College Station: Texas A & M University Press, 2003), 83.

21 "The Poro School of Marcel Waving," *California Eagle* (Los Angeles), 21 August 1925, 1.

22 Blackwelder, *Styling Jim Crow,* 30.

23 Douglas Flamming, *Bound for Freedom: Black Los Angeles in Jim Crow America* (Berkeley: University of California Press, 2005), 2.

24 Ibid., 92-93, 96.

25 "For the Investor and the Homeseeker," *California Eagle* (Los Angeles), 15 November 1919, 1; "Negro Cities – Los Angeles," *California Eagle* (Los Angeles), 26 December 1924, 1.

26 "New England Pays Tribute to Mrs. Malone and Poro," *California Eagle* (Los Angeles), 24 June 1927, 8.

27 "Founder of Poro College Addresses College Women," *California Eagle* (Los Angeles), 28 January 1926, 1.

28 "Mrs. Malone Presents Sister Beautiful Home Site," *California Eagle* (Los Angeles), 23 June 1923, 1.

29 Flamming, *Bound for Freedom,* 272.

30 "Poro Club Triumphant," *California Eagle* (Los Angeles), 19 October 1923, 1.

31 Flamming, *Bound for Freedom,* 27.

32 Although race was not absent from the selling of beauty to white women, their beauty culture managed to invoke race without specifically referring to African American women. For more information, see Walker, *Style and Status,* 3-8.

33 Peiss, *Hope in a Jar,* 95.

34 Walker, *Style and Status,* 6.

Part 2 CONSUMERISM AND PUBLIC DISPLAY

•
•
•

6

Women, Identity, and Sports Participation in Interwar Britain

Fiona Skillen

The two decades following the end of the First World War were years of severe economic decline and uncertainty, dominated by high levels of unemployment and political unrest across much of Britain. Against this backdrop, it seems unlikely that sports participation should have increased. However, the rapid growth of consumerism, and with it, leisure provision, ensured that, for the first time, many people were gaining access to new activities in Britain.[1] Although participation and spectatorship in a range of sporting activities increased, levels and equality of experience varied by region, sex, and class. Little research has explored in any depth the ways in which women were involved in this new trend. This seems rather surprising, given that gender relations in this period have been the subject of thorough scrutiny by historians. The interwar years are regarded as a pivotal and transitional period during which traditional gender relations were challenged and renegotiated.[2] Yet historians are divided over the nature of these changes.

Recent research has questioned the robustness of the existing historiography and in particular the "backlash," which highlights the media and government's attempts to re-assert the importance of the family unit and women's place within the home. It is easy to understand why many researchers have seen this period as one of containment and re-emphasis of traditional roles for women, for focusing solely on certain aspects of employment and politics does produce a bleak picture.[3] Yet recent contributions to the historiography have questioned the idea that the interwar years were characterized by "domesticity and retreat."[4] Historians have pieced together a narrative that suggests that the period was one in which women self-consciously articulated a new female modernity by drawing "upon real changes in the political, social, economic and sexual position of women."[5] This new body of research stresses the importance of age, class, marital status, and geographical region in influencing women's experience of "modernity" during the interwar years. Such an approach has much to offer to an understanding of the growth of sports participation. Many of these studies have indicated that involvement in the emerging consumerism and leisure markets took on a new significance for many women in the interwar years. Although magazines and newspapers predominantly focused on women's roles in the family unit, the media also dwelt on the "problem" of women's leisure.[6] Sport in particular proved a popular topic for comment. Discussions in the press examined all aspects of women's leisure, from where and when women chose to pursue their interests, to what they should wear and participate in, and with whom. Despite this wealth of material, few studies have explored women's leisure or, more specifically, women's participation in sports.[7]

The modern New Woman of interwar Britain was symbolic of youth and freedom; she embraced life and spent her time in the pursuit of fun and enjoyment. This chapter will explore the place of sport and exercise in her life. It will consider the centrality of sport and exercise to concepts of modernity for women, concepts such as fashion and physical beauty. Ultimately, this chapter seeks to explain the rapid yet complex growth of women's sports participation during the interwar period in the context of the newly emerging ideals of modernity for women.

Context

During the early interwar years, the popular press increasingly turned its attention to the changes brought about by the First World War, welcoming the dawn of an era it christened the "new modernity." The emergence of the modern woman, or flapper, was symbolic of this phase; she epitomized all that was new and different, and she provided a stark contrast with her Victorian and Edwardian sisters.[8] The flapper represented the new fashions and new lifestyles being adopted by young women during this early period. She wore certain styles of dress, acted in particular ways, and even thought about things in a different manner, all of which distinguished her from older generations of women.[9] Even her body had to conform to a new "boyish" shape.[10]

The widespread proliferation of articles concerning "young moderns" in the contemporary press suggests that most young women were fully partaking of this new lifestyle, through fashion and involvement in activities as diverse as dancing, cinema attendance, golf, and motor racing.[11] However, the reality was very different. Gender, age, and class could, and did, play a significant role in the degree to which a woman could immerse herself in this new modernity. Those who benefited most from the growth of consumer culture in this period were young and single female wage earners.[12] This group had both the time and the money to indulge in the new styles and trends, whereas older women with dependants had little of either to spare.[13] Similarly, Horwood has argued that many women were still influenced by traditional discourses concerning respectability, which informed their choices about where they went during their spare time and what they wore.[14] However, the term "modernity" was all-consuming, covering a vast assortment of activities and modes of behaviour, which meant that many women could participate in it, fitting it into their lifestyles. The opportunities to take part in many aspects of the new modernity grew throughout the interwar period. The rapid expansion of mass production methods lowered prices and increased the availability of many consumer goods. Clothing, too, could be produced faster and at a fraction of the price, which made the latest fashions accessible to a wider range of buyers. The boom in commercial leisure after the First World War also ensured that most towns had cinemas, dance halls, and sports grounds to cater to all budgets, thus opening up the availability of a variety of recreational pursuits.

Sport, Modernity, and Emancipation

Sports were often cited alongside a range of other activities by those who discussed young moderns. In a 1923 short story titled "The Perfect Girl," Arnold Bennett listed the qualities of the ideal modern girl, Elvira: "She was brilliantly familiar with literature, tongues, art, history, physics, metaphysics, philosophy and politics ... She could play well at tennis, [field] hockey, golf, and bridge. She exhibited taste and skill on the piano. She danced well and loved dancing. She dressed well and loved nice frocks. She had a low voice. She was a graceful and amusing talker."[15] Although an article titled "Woman and the Sport Fetish" decried just how engrained the idea of women playing sports had become – "Girls have been rushed to the goal posts and wickets, and not to carry a hockey stick or net ball [sic] is regarded as a sign of decadence and eccentricity" – it added that if a woman seemed uninterested in sport, "her hostess will regard her as being almost mentally deficient."[16] Both these examples reveal that, by the end of the 1920s, women were commonly expected to play certain sports.

Recent research into women's sporting participation during the interwar years in Britain has demonstrated a dramatic increase in the number of women taking up sports and playing regularly.[17] This research has indicated that involvement covered a wide range of activities and participation sites, and was not restricted to the upper and middle classes.

Given the central importance of the physical aesthetic, concerning both body image and fashion, to modernity, it is perhaps not surprising that sport and exercise should assume an important place in many women's lives. For some women, their experiences of working during the First World War had improved their fitness, and they had come to appreciate the benefits of keeping their bodies healthy.[18] This, combined with the importance that new modern women placed on body shape, ensured that female sports participation increased greatly during the early 1920s.[19] As one writer in the *London Times* explained, as a result of the war, "the idea of 'training to be fit' became established in the feminine mind ... Physical culture is becoming as widely prevalent among women as among men. More and more it is realized that health and beauty are complementary to one and other and that both can be retained if sufficient care is exercised."[20] Sport could train and tone the body, improve posture, and, it was believed, even enhance beauty. It therefore offered an opportunity to acquire some essential attributes of the young modern woman: a lithe figure, grace of carriage, and a clear complexion. It would seem that sport was a central part of participation in modernity for women.

Sport also assumed an important role in modern lifestyles. Young women enjoyed a variety of leisure pursuits, as "modern girls went out to work and they went out to play."[21] Attendance at the sports field, either as competitor or spectator, provided a new type of arena for social interaction. Oral history interviews conducted by the author between 2004 and 2008 showed that local sports clubs gave women an opportunity to socialize, a fact of particular importance when they were young and single. Certain sports such as tennis and golf embodied "social sensibilities," which were very specific to the middle classes. Thus, participating in these activities at private clubs ensured that young people would mix with others of a similar (acceptable) background and outlook.[22] In addition, the sports clubhouse was often one of "the" local venues at which to be seen.[23] As several interviewees noted, their parents permitted them to go to these local clubs, which they perceived as "respectable" because they themselves or their friends were often members.[24] Greta stated that her parents allowed her to go to dances at her local tennis club because they did not provide alcohol and were attended by other locals.[25] Even those women who played sports at the national level felt that the social aspects of the competition were an important part of their overall experience. Indeed, the records of the ladies' national golf and field hockey associations of Scotland, for example, highlight the prevalence of dances, dinners, and outings arranged alongside national competitions.[26]

In addition to using sport as a way of socializing with their friends and family, many women played sports in the company of their boyfriends and husbands.[27] This practice is clearly mirrored in written and visual representations in the press.[28] As early as 1919, the *London Times* had picked up on this trend:

> It is quite safe to say that domestic happiness had been much increased by the active part taken by ladies in so many sports. It has given husband and wife a very common ground of interest ... Now that both play the same game, at least one reason for marital strife has been withdrawn, sport has brought the sexes together in a remarkable way ... The health and physique of women have also been improved beyond all knowledge. Even doctors, who so seldom agree about anything, admit that games in moderation are excellent for ladies.[29]

These ideas were echoed in both the popular press and women's magazines. *Women's Own* remarked,

> Whether as a social amusement, a form of exercise, or a thrillingly enjoyable game, tennis is unsurpassed. No need to bother making arrangements for large teams. Husband and wife can go out in the evening and have a knock-up on the spur of the moment, and come back to supper with the glow of health and incidentally, the hearty appetite which exercise brings. Being one of the few games which women can play with their menfolk it is naturally immensely popular.[30]

The trend was also mentioned by interviewees, many of whom referred to playing sports with their fiancés; some retained sport as part of their social life once they were married. Both married and single women were playing sports, and they viewed this activity as an important way, not only of becoming fit, but also of socializing.

Despite the growth of female participation in certain sports, opinion regarding this development remained mixed, at least during the early interwar period. Concerns varied from which sports were appropriate for women to where, when, and with whom they should play.[31] Some saw the trend as just another example of regrettable modernity; women's involvement in a wider range of sports was perceived as part of their continued push for equality, which was particularly the case where they demanded a place in traditionally male activities. In doing so, women directly, and more often indirectly, threatened the status quo, challenging long-held notions of what constituted acceptable feminine behaviour, dress, and manners.

The diversity of sports activities taken up by women during the interwar period was obviously seen by some contemporaries as part of their demand for political and social emancipation. Constanzo contends that "popular magazines directly equated women's physical exercise with social emancipation and political activism."[32] Satirical cartoons in contemporary newspapers often focused on women's sport, drawing pointed parallels between political activists and the types of women who played sports.[33] However, many people regarded women's involvement in sport as fundamental to their new independence. As one male commentator put it, "Much of the so-called emancipation of women has been brought about by their active participation in games which were originally looked upon as belonging to men alone."[34] Another contemporary, writing for the *London Times,* stated, "Lawn tennis was the first game of real action in which ladies took part, and may be taken as one of those landmarks of which they are so pleased to call their emancipation."[35]

In her study of women's sport between 1870 and 1914, McCrone found that "the fight for women's sporting rights was more actional than verbal, with the result that there is no great corpus of literature defending women's athletic rights such as exists in the educational, legal and political spheres."[36] To some extent, this is also true of the interwar period. Although there is widespread evidence that sport was becoming a regular aspect of women's lives, there was very little articulation of feminist discourses in connection with the subject. Instances are few in which women unequivocally advocated their right to access sports on equal terms with men, but numerous examples exist in which this is implied. One female cricketer commented,

> These [male] players always say women will never play like men. Which brings me to a point that I think matters enormously ... We do not want, wish, or hanker after games of cricket with men. That suggests that we are averse to men. I would kill that thought immediately. But it is sound and sane to realize from the start that men and women cannot play team games together or against each other. Individual games, yes; but team games, no ... I am not suggesting that the standard of women's games is so far below that of men's that they cannot play together or against each other. I think that the standards are different – just that – different.[37]

This comment contains no explicit statement that cricket contributes to female independence or that women's participation constitutes a challenge to men. Instead, the speaker is at pains to show that female cricketers have no wish to compete with male players, implies that both sexes are equally good at the game, and insists that they play in different ways. Thus, there is an implicit belief that women are different from yet equal to men.[38]

This type of argument appears constantly, where the supporters of sportswomen imply but never fully articulate the importance of sporting participation in women's push for independence and recognition of their abilities. Of course, it may simply reflect the beliefs of some sportswomen that their individual experiences were not important to changing dominant views of women. Hargreaves, for example, has argued that early sportswomen were "keen to get on with their sports, but tended to be conservative about the general politics of women's position in society."[39] None of the sportswomen whom I interviewed directly equated their experiences or decisions regarding how they spent their free time to any concept of political activism or independence.[40] Indeed, none saw their participation in golf, tennis, badminton, or field hockey as challenging the status quo. However, when asked about the abilities of women to play rugby or football (soccer), still very masculine sports in this period, they stated that such games would not have been regarded as "respectable." Thus, we may infer that earlier generations would have perceived almost all sports, including golf and tennis, as male domains, because they had a long tradition of being played by men, and because small groups of women took up these games only in the late nineteenth century. Yet by the mid-interwar years, the interviewees saw their participation in certain sports as normal, believing that only the rougher, aggressive games such as rugby were unsuitable for women. Importantly, however, whether they were aware of it or not, they were functioning within certain socially created and changing limitations because of their sex. This indicates that, as they themselves acknowledged, some activities were still deemed socially unacceptable for women. Their participation in physically demanding and aggressive games was the target of harsh criticism in the press.[41]

Similarly, a medical study that evaluated the suitability of sports for the physical education classes of schoolgirls reported that "football met with less approval than any other game; of the fifty-two schoolmistresses who expressed their views on this game, only two were in favour of it, and among women students, though few approved, many more objected to it on physical or other grounds."[42] Interestingly, football was found objectionable, not only because it could inflict physical damage, but also because it was rough and unfeminine. The study concluded that the game did not damage young women's bodies but could potentially encourage a player to overexert herself. However, the issue of which sports were acceptable and which were not is complex. Simplistically, it seems that physically demanding, aggressive, and competitive activities were the primary focus of concern. Detractors argued that such sports were incompatible with traditional notions of femininity and feared that the associated physical demands and strains would encourage masculine qualities, both physically and mentally.[43] However, field hockey, which was a rough, aggressive game, received relatively little negative publicity. This, too, suggests that the unsuitability of female involvement in sports such as rugby and football was also linked to their traditional designation as male activities. Perhaps, for some, women's participation in these games was too far a step on the road to "regrettable modernity."

This is not to say that some women did not transgress these established notions. Many did pursue so-called masculine activities, such as cricket, mountaineering, and football. It is perhaps unsurprising that they did so out of the public gaze, generally in private sports grounds or private clubs catering to women. However, this was not always possible, and women's sports groups often relied on men for access to facilities. Women's football is a clear example of this. There is evidence that some women did play football in this period.[44] Many had become involved in the game as a result of their war work, and it was common for factory workers to play football during their breaks.[45] In 1920 and 1921, Dick Kerr's famous ladies' football team played several times in Scotland, taking on local teams in games attended by large crowds. However, in 1921, the Football Association withdrew all support for women's football, and the subsequent adoption of this policy by the Scottish Football Association ensured that women's football was severely curtailed in Scotland.[46] This formalized and official disapproval meant that pressure was put on local clubs to withdraw access to pitches and changing facilities, a measure that undermined the ability of many female teams to play. McCaig has argued that the lack of both access and support, brought about in large part by this new policy, retarded the development of women's football in Scotland; many women's clubs did not re-form until the end of the 1930s.[47]

Although not all women seem to have viewed their participation in sport as a political or social statement, those who did may have understood that the price of acceptance in well-established sports and organizations was to refrain from challenging the status quo. Simply being able to play on a golf course, tennis court, or hockey pitch, and thus making themselves visible as sportswomen, may have been enough for some.

Indeed, many women did avail themselves of these opportunities. The records of the Scottish Women's [Field] Hockey Association (SWHA) and the Ladies' Golf Union (LGU) reveal that both organizations experienced dramatic growth. Between 1900 and 1939, the number of clubs affiliated with the SWHA increased from 11 to 101.[48] Gauging exactly how many women this represents is difficult as club sizes varied greatly, but a 1932 estimate indicated that approximately sixty-five thousand British women and girls were members of affiliated clubs.[49] The growth of golf was equally impressive. The number of clubs affiliated with the LGU had increased from 922 in 1925 to 1,417 by 1939. In regional terms, this meant that English LGU-affiliated clubs had grown from 756 to 1,060; in Scotland, the number rose from 97 to 236; Irish figures grew from 13 to 14 and Wales from 56 to 107.[50] The unprecedented growth of these sports is perhaps slightly misleading as they were particularly popular among women. Nevertheless, it does reflect the broader trend in women's participation across a range of sports during this period.

Women continued to face many impediments to their involvement in sports, for the attitudes of male spectators and players were slow to change. As one female golf champion wrote,

> From what I can gather, lady golfers have obtained a more secure position than ever they occupied before the war. The change is distinctly perceptible ... It is less common to see a look of astonishment on the face of the gentleman whose "mixed" partner has pitched over a high mound and laid the ball in the neighbourhood of the hole ... The feeling is steadily gaining ground that women are capable of playing the same kind of golf as the men – naturally on a different level of power – but still a game of the same character and played in much the same way.[51]

Although some may have regarded participation in certain physical activities as the ultimate embodiment of female independence and the personification of modernity, in reality women were rarely equal with men when it came to sports. More often than not, they were forced to play on smaller pitches, with modified equipment, for shorter periods, and with different handicapping systems. In addition, they were often ineligible for full membership in sports clubs. It is also worth noting that, given these obviously inequitable circumstances, British sportswomen rarely demanded equal rights or rules. Nevertheless, especially during the 1920s, public consciousness directly linked sport with women's emancipation and, ultimately, with their increased independence.

Fashion and Sport

Even in the so-called acceptable sports, areas of conflict existed, including when and where women should play and, most crucially, what they should wear while they did. Burman states that women's dress was traditionally associated "with frivolity, helplessness, compliance and inaction."[52] Thus, changes in female attire such as higher hemlines, shorter sleeves, and cleaner lines reflected the new modern woman's attempt to break free of the ideals and notions that had constrained previous generations. By changing the way she looked, she was making a strong visual statement about her intention to be more physically active and independent, and ultimately, to have a new approach to life. Therefore, fashion was an important part of women's involvement in modernity; it was also very significant to sportswomen. Sports clothing changed constantly throughout the interwar years.[53] Indeed, in serials from the period, not only were fashion pages an increasingly common feature of women's magazines, but the outfits worn for the tennis court, swimming pool, and golf course were among the important and regular topics in these pages and in advice columns written for women.[54] If we look, for example, at the "Dear Christine" problem page in *Nash's Pall Mall Magazine,* sports-related matters were popular subjects. The July 1934 issue offers a typical example: after a female reader had asked which swimming costumes were the best in terms of cost and fashion, the magazine responded with an article, which it printed alongside three others, one on perfumes, one explaining how to clean a bathtub, and one featuring destinations for short holidays.[55] The sometimes subtle changes between each season's clothing were discussed at length in these publications, often accompanied by photographs or diagrams. These pages regularly provided a breakdown of an entire outfit, demonstrating the most fashionable and appropriate blouses, jackets, skirts, shoes, hats, and even socks or stockings, as well as how to combine them.[56] In numerous examples, advertisers and editors alike implied that any self-respecting woman would choose to wear the latest sporting fashions, whether playing at her local tennis court or private golf course, or attending Ascot as a spectator.[57] This was particularly evident in the women's "Highway of Fashion" pages that ran in every issue of *Tatler* throughout the interwar years. In this feature, generally anonymous fashion advisors offered suggestions for the forthcoming seasons. Topics varied widely from the colours, cuts, and textiles that were the latest "must haves" to the clothing and accessories that should be worn for various events and activities. Sports fashion was an integral feature of these pages, and valuable advice on appropriate attire, such as which hats and gloves were both practical and fashionable for a specific activity, was regularly provided. Clothing companies ran ads that emphasized the affordability and durability of their products, and many highlighted the versatility of individual garments, often showing how to combine them with other items so that they could be worn on the sports field or in the clubhouse.

It has been argued that because these fashions were accessible to consumers of all backgrounds, dress could no longer be relied on to distinguish working-class women from their middle-class counterparts. This was also the case for sportswomen. Sports garments were designed along the same lines, but, produced by diverse methods and using a range of materials, they could be targeted to differing budgets. One advertiser even claimed that "thanks to [us] you can no longer tell a shop girl from a Duchess."[58] Photos in newspapers and magazines illustrate the similarities between the clothes worn by tennis and golf players on both public sports grounds and private ones. In some of the more middle-class publications, such as *Tatler,* readers were directed to specific shops where they could purchase the latest sporting attire, whereas hints on how to update old styles were more commonplace in working-class serials.[59] Some publications even published dress patterns so that women who could not afford ready-made items could make their own.[60] This example from the "Ladies' Corner" of the *Paisley and Renfrewshire Gazette* combines general playing tips with fashion advice:

Tennis courts are so plentiful nowadays that even the town girl plays tennis almost as a matter of course and for the country girl it is the most popular game of the year. The advantages of tennis are many and its disadvantages are difficult to find. It is a healthy pastime, and gives grace and suppleness of figure if it is not overdone. Very many business houses have their own tennis clubs, and churches and other organizations have clubs too, so that it is generally possible for a girl who is keen to play tennis to secure the opportunity. It is a good plan for the novice to have a few lessons from a good coach before she attempts to play with others. It is rather a disadvantage for a girl who knows little about tennis to play with those who can play well. Generally she is so self-conscious and awkward that she plays even worse than usual and spoils her own enjoyment and that of the others. No girl can feel perfectly happy on the tennis court unless she is properly equipped and nicely dressed. Pale shades are now worn by tennis players and white dresses are trimmed with colour, but it is advisable to have one or two all-white dresses and when in doubt what to wear always choose white for white is never incorrect. There are some clubs which make it a rule that all-white clothes must be worn. A simple washing dress with short sleeves and a skirt wide enough to allow ample freedom of movement is necessary. The dress can be made of linen, crepe, or any cotton material or washing silk. The majority of girls prefer a silk dress as it retains its freshness longer than cotton. Japshan is an ideal material for a tennis frock as it is hard-wearing, good-looking and very easy to "get up." It is also non-transparent, and has enough substance not to appear at all flimsy.[61]

Women's sports clothing had undergone a change, and in many places it was no longer viewed as controversial. As one contemporary noted in an article titled "The Revolution in Dress,"

> It is not many years since hockey-skirts reaching below the knees, with volu-
> minous and ugly bloomers as a second line of defence, were regarded as a little
> risky, though instances when they ungovernably aroused the passions of the
> opposite sex were not easily discovered. Today, you may find yourself, as I did
> recently, talking between events to the woman world's champion of something
> or other in athletics, clad like a boy in singlet, shorts, socks and shoes, without
> the smallest trace of embarrassment on either side.[62]

Of course, not all sports followed fashion; many, such as golf, had strict rules about what could be worn on the course. Although there was arguably some flexibility in its rules, golf experienced far fewer changes in fashion during the period than many other sports. Horwood suggests that this sprang from the difficulties encountered by many women in their attempts to join clubs, maintaining that they dressed conservatively so as not to disrupt the status quo any further. It is certainly true that women's golf clothing was among the most conventional of the period; colours were muted and skirts and sleeves both remained long during a time when, in all other sports, hemlines were rising. That is not to say that golf escaped all attempts to impose new fashions; some efforts were made at modernization, primarily through the promotion of new styles of hats and shoes.[63] One female golfer, however, did attempt to push the boundaries of women's golf fashion. At the English Ladies' Golf Champion-ships in 1933, Gloria Minoprio attempted to play in trousers. This was too radical for the golfing elite, and the LGU acted quickly, noting that it "deplored any departure from the traditional costume of the game" and making it clear that neither its members nor those who wished to participate in its competitions would be allowed to play in trousers.[64]

Despite the attempts of some trail-blazing sportswomen, such as Minoprio and Suzanne Lenglen in tennis, to shake up women's sports dress, women were still trying in the 1930s to negotiate the lines between practicality, modesty, fashion, and notions of femininity. In sports that were traditionally regarded as male activities, they seem to have been particularly keen to emphasize their femininity. Moreover, they stressed a "traditional" femininity, opting for long sleeves and long skirts that covered the legs. Wearing trousers would have made many sports such as golf and cricket easier to play, but women rejected them because of the masculine connotations. In other sports, a newer femininity was

Figure 6.1 "Tennis Pavilion, 1900, St Georges' School Edinburgh."
Courtesy of St George's School Archive.

being displayed; modernity emphasized speed and freedom of movement, and thus ensured that most sportswear became less restrictive and sleeker.[65] This was particularly evident in tennis and swimming. For example, as Morgan discusses in Chapter 7 of this volume, the Victorian costumes worn for swimming differed markedly from their modern equivalents. Similarly, the contrasts between early tennis costumes and the modern fashions of the 1920s and 1930s are very obvious, as Figures 6.1 and 6.2 demonstrate. There is little doubt that these styles were far more practical for the new athletic woman; shorter sleeves and skirts allowed greater freedom to stretch for a wayward ball or play out of a bunker, and the abandonment of restrictive corsets, layers of clothing, and tight-fitting fashions was more conducive to sports as it gave women greater mobility, kept them cooler, and allowed freer breathing.

Figure 6.2 "Tennis Team, 1932, St George's School, Edinburgh."
Courtesy of St George's School Archive.

For much of the period, the main debate around women's sports clothes was one of established notions of decency versus practicality. In many ways, this conflict was merely representative of wider issues surrounding women's increased participation in sport. The clearest example of this is seen in women's cricket. Ideally, trousers were the most practical type of clothing for this sport, but because donning trousers was thought to signify a desire to emulate men in all aspects of the game, women were banned from wearing them. The WCA took pains to point out that, far from wishing to imitate men, it wanted to create a new way of playing cricket that suited women. The impact of negative comments about the sport is evident, with WCA members being actively encouraged to seek out positive publicity for the game:

The word of the year was, however, Publicity. Some players shied at the very mention of it – it was considered bad form, and so to be avoided. But pictures appeared in some papers, so obviously posed, with girls in trousers [the players of the WCA wore skirts at this time], caps, headdresses, and others with bare legs, bathing costumes, all purporting to be "Eves at the wicket," that it became obvious, even to the most rabid on the matter, that good publicity must be found, tolerated, even assisted.[66]

There is little doubt that fashion formed an important part of modernity. Wearing certain styles allowed women to identify themselves as "moderns." Through the growth of cheap ready-made clothing and the proliferation of patterns and advice on updating and making clothing in women's magazines, more women could participate in these trends. This research has revealed what has generally been previously overlooked, that sport had a significant role in the process of modernity for many women, and that the clothes worn for both participation in and spectatorship of sports were carefully developed to mirror fashionable everyday dress.

Sportswomen and Consumerism

Women's entry into the world of sport marked them out as a distinct set of consumers.[67] As highlighted, sport was an intrinsic part of creating a new modern identity for women. Modern women were expected to immerse themselves in sport through playing and watching games, and they were also expected to follow the latest fashions. This involved not only purchasing equipment but also buying or making sports costumes. Indeed, one can argue that the centrality of sport in modern lifestyles is further confirmed by the regular use of its imagery and language in advertising for both non-sports and sports-related products. Contemporary ads illustrate the development of this trend and the increasing recognition among advertisers of women, and more importantly of sportswomen, as consumers.

During the interwar period, women's magazines proliferated, a development that is itself symptomatic of the increase in the number of female consumers.[68] These publications included fashion news, household management tips, advice columns, short stories, and advertising.[69] White has noted that advertising not only provided important income for these magazines, but that demographic considerations were taken into account with respect to ads. For example, a magazine with a feature on cooking might contact beef producers to advertise in an issue focusing on beef recipes. By the 1930s, she argues, it was becoming increasingly common for editors to work in conjunction with advertisers to run special offers, to promote specific products in the main text of the magazine, or even to issue consumer surveys to their readers.[70]

Advertising, which is often a neglected source, can offer an interesting insight into the complex relationship between sport and modernity. Its purpose has traditionally been to instill values and ideas that will ultimately help to perpetuate the existing economic systems of a particular society.[71] However, it has also played a significant social role. Dyer states, "It has become more and more involved in the manipulation of social values and attitudes."[72] The complex interplay between advertisements and social discourses is particularly interesting. It is possible that dominant discourses filtered into ads while at the same time they were being used to instill these notions. In short, ads encouraged, extended, and entrenched multiple, and often conflicting, definitions of women's roles.

An examination of *Tatler* shows that women's growing participation in sport was reflected in its advertising campaigns.[73] Sports-related ads proliferated in *Tatler* between 1925 and 1935, a testament to the general growth in expenditure on leisure during those years.[74] Between 1925 and 1935, the number of pages that *Tatler* devoted to advertising increased by approximately 10 percent.[75] Its ads varied widely, touting clothes, cars, holidays, sports equipment, alcohol, and beauty treatments. Women's increased involvement in sport was represented as well, though the diversity of their actual experience was not, as they were repeatedly presented playing certain sports much more than others, such as skiing, swimming, tennis, riding, racing, hunting, and skating. Table 6.1 shows the number of ads that featured women playing sports as well as the products they were attempting to sell.

A 1925 Wills Gold Flake Cigarette ad that appeared in *Tatler* features the archetypal image of a young flapper and is typical of its period. Depicted in motion, she has short-cropped hair, a lithe figure, and fashionable clothing, and she smokes a cigarette in a long holder. The ad succinctly captures several aspects of modernity; it includes a flapper, and it hints at speed, excitement,

Table 6.1

Tatler ads featuring sportswomen

Year	Product ads		Total per year
	Sports-related	Non-sports-related	
1925	51	9	60
1930	148	33	181
1935	131	36	167
Total	*330*	*78*	*408*

Source: *Tatler* 1925, 1930, and 1935.

and independence. Although smoking is the focus here, the product is set in an exciting situation. As Elliot has demonstrated, cigarette manufacturers were keen to associate their products not only with the everyday aspects of life but also with newly emerging trends in leisure.[76]

By employing sporting images, advertisers could attract the attention of young, fashionable flappers who were keen to take an active part in the leisure scene. Many of these athletic images were used to sell a variety of products, often unrelated to the sport depicted. These included hair preparations, drinks, lawnmowers, confectionary, clothing, and cars. Indeed, somewhat ironically, many of the products, such as cigarettes and alcohol, would now be considered detrimental to health. Nevertheless, the increasing use of both sportsmen and sportswomen to advertise a diverse range of products emphasizes the centrality of sporting participation to concepts of modern living. Thus, whereas these ads may have encouraged women to buy products that were linked to their own leisure activities, they would also have appealed to those who could not participate. Advertisers created aspirational lifestyles in their ads.

The upsurge in *Tatler* advertisements correlates with the findings of Davies, that spending on leisure and luxury goods was growing rapidly throughout this period.[77] Likewise, the high number of ads for clothes, beauty items, and holidays, which were aimed specifically at female consumers, further substantiates the hypothesis that women's spending powers increased during these years.

Conclusion

Women's growing involvement in sport seems to have been symptomatic of the development of modernity. In many ways, the female body was a focus of the new modernity. The way it was dressed, its hairstyle, and even its shape were all intrinsic symbols of a woman's conformity to modernity and its associated ideals. In this lifestyle, sport had an important role to play. It gave women an opportunity to tone and shape their bodies in an effort to conform to the new boyish shape. It also provided new arenas for women to socialize with each other and with the opposite sex. The importance of sport to the new modernity for women is indicated by the rapid growth of distinct sportswear, a development revealing that participation in sports was as important as dancing and working for young modern women. Indeed, this is underscored by advertisers' use of images of sportswomen to sell sports-related items and services, but perhaps more importantly, to sell items that were not connected with sports. Many advertisers, especially those who sold expensive cars and holidays, were keen to promote a certain type of lifestyle in their ads, that of the ultra-modern consumer. In their campaigns, images of sporting women occupied an important position.

It is clear that modernity and women's sporting participation were intricately linked during the interwar years. The idealized modern lifestyle was just that, an ideal: for many women, factors such as income, class, lifestyle stage, and traditional discourses concerning femininity and respectability all influenced the degree to which they could immerse themselves in the ideal.

Acknowledgments
This chapter was developed from research conducted during my PhD, funded by the Economic and Social Research Council. I am grateful to Eleanor Gordon, Annmarie Hughes, and Valerie Wright for their constructive comments on earlier drafts of this essay.

Notes

1 Jennifer Hargreaves, *Sporting Females: Critical Issues in the History and Sociology of Women's Sport* (London: Routledge, 1994), 112; Alun Howkins and John Lowerson, *Trends in Leisure 1919-1939* (London: Sports Council and Social Science Research Council, 1979).

2 See D. Beddoe, *Back to Home and Duty: Women between the Wars 1918-1939* (London: Pandora, 1989); B. Melman, *Women and the Popular Imagination in the Twenties: Flappers and Nymphs* (Basingstoke: Macmillan, 1988); A. Bingham, "'An Era of Domesticity'? Histories of Women and Gender in Interwar Britain," *Cultural and Social History* 1 (2004): 225; S. Kingsley Kent, *Making Peace: The Reconstruction of Gender in Interwar Britain* (Princeton: Princeton University Press, 1993); and M. Pugh, *Women and the Women's Movement in Britain, 1914-1959* (Basingstoke: Macmillan Education, 1992).

3 Bingham, "'An Era of Domesticity?'"

4 S. Alexander, "Becoming a Woman in London in the 1920s and 1930s," in *Becoming a Woman and Other Essays in 19th and 20th Century Feminist History* (New York: New York University Press, 1995), 203-25; C. Langhamer, *Women's Leisure in England 1920-1960* (Manchester: Manchester University Press, 2000); B. Solande, *Becoming Modern: Young Women and the Reconstruction of Womanhood in the 1920s* (Princeton: Princeton University Press, 2000); S. Todd, *Young Women, Work and Family in England 1918-1950* (Oxford: Oxford University Press, 2005); Bingham, "'An Era of Domesticity?'" 232; D. Fowler, "Teenage Consumers? Young Wage-Earners and Leisure in Manchester, 1919-1939," in *Workers' Worlds*, ed. A. Davies and S. Fielding (Manchester: Manchester University Press, 1992), 133-54.

5 Bingham, "'An Era of Domesticity?'" 230.

6 Ibid., 225.

7 The notable exceptions to this are Langhamer, *Women's Leisure in England*, which broadly explores women's leisure; Hargreaves, *Sporting Females*, 119; and M. Huggins, "'And Now, Something for the Ladies': Representations of Women's Sport in Cinema Newsreels 1918-1939," *Women's History Review* 16 (2007): 681-700, both of which are short studies of women's sports involvement in interwar Britain.

8 For an example of contemporary usage of the term "flapper," see G. Frankau, "Four Flappers," *Nash's Magazine*, July 1928, 50-53.

9 See ibid.; and A. Bennett, "The Perfect Girl," *Nash's Pall Mall Magazine*, February 1923, 518-28.

10 Solande, *Becoming Modern*, 47.

11   See T. Hall, "Will the Modern Girl Make as Good a Wife as Her Mother?" *Quiver,* October 1920, 1099-101.
12   See Todd, *Young Women, Work and Family;* and Langhamer, *Women's Leisure.*
13   Between 2004 and 2008, I interviewed twenty women regarding their involvement in sport for a larger study about women's sports participation in interwar Scotland. Several interviewees emphasized this point.
14   Catherine Horwood, *Keeping Up Appearances* (London: Sutton, 2005), 4.
15   Bennett, "The Perfect Girl," 518.
16   M. Seaton, "Woman and the Sport Fetish," *Saturday Review of Politics, Literature, Science and Art,* 26 December 1931, 821.
17   For statistics, see Fiona Skillen, "'When Women Look Their Worst': Women and Sports Participation in Interwar Scotland" (PhD diss., University of Glasgow, 2008); and for general discussion, see Hargreaves, *Sporting Females,* 112; and Howkins and Lowerson, *Trends in Leisure.*
18   "Health Culture for Girls," *London Times,* 3 March 1922, 9; Margaret Hallam, "Physical Exercises," *London Times' Women's Supplement,* October 1920, 60.
19   As we saw earlier, female membership in many sports was increasing throughout this period, and the 2004-8 oral history interviews conducted by the author highlighted that it was common for women to play sports by the end of the 1920s.
20   "Health Culture for Girls," 9.
21   Solande, *Becoming Modern,* 47.
22   C. Brown, "Sport and the Scottish Office in the Twentieth Century," *European Sports History Review* 1 (1999): 166.
23   Skillen, oral history interviews, round-table discussion with six interviewees, 5 October 2005.
24   Ibid. Whereas many interviewees recalled family debates regarding which local cinemas they were permitted to attend, as some were deemed "rougher" than others, no similar disagreements occurred in connection with local tennis and golf clubs.
25   Skillen, oral history interviews, Greta, interviewed 5 October 2005.
26   Skillen, "'When Women Look Their Worst,'" Chapter 2.
27   Skillen, oral history interviews, round-table discussion with six interviewees, 5 October 2005.
28   See Hall, "Will the Modern Girl Make as Good a Wife as Her Mother?" 1099-101; and A. Maill, "Athleticism for Women: Is It Carried Too Far?" *Quiver,* October 1921, 1092-96.
29   "Ladies in Sport," *London Times,* 15 February 1919, 3.
30   "Games Keep You Fit," *Women's Own,* 3 June 1933, 12.
31   Seaton, "Woman and the Sport Fetish," 821.
32   M. Constanzo, "Images of Gender in *Punch* 1901-10," *International Journal of the History of Sport* 19 (March 2002), 47.
33   Untitled cartoon by W.K. Haselden, *London Daily Mirror,* 20 November 1922, n.p.
34   "Ladies in Sport," 3.
35   "Ladies in Sport, Lawn Tennis and Golf," *London Times,* 1 March 1919, 5.
36   Kathleen E. McCrone, *Playing the Game: Sport and the Physical Emancipation of English Women, 1870-1914* (Lexington: University Press of Kentucky, 1988), 247.
37   Marjory Pollard, *Cricket for Girls and Women* (London: Hutchinson, 1934), 16-17.
38   During the interwar period, the feminist movement was split into two distinct groups – equality feminists and difference feminists. For further discussion, see J. Hannam, "Women and Politics," in *Women's History: Britain 1850-1945,* ed. J. Purvis (London: Routledge, 2000), 235.
39   Hargreaves, *Sporting Females,* 94.
40   Skillen, oral history interviews.

41   See W.K. Haselden, "Will women give up playing football?," *London Daily Mirror,* 9 December 1921, 11; and W.K. Haselden, "The Modern Woman and Sport," *London Daily Mirror,* 6 January 1925, 12, for examples.

42   "Physical Education of Girls," *British Medical Journal* 3216 (19 August 1922): 321.

43   Maill, "Athleticism for Women: Is It Carried Too Far?" 1092-96.

44   Margo McCaig, "Playing the Game 1880-1970" (Master's diss., University of Strathclyde, 1996), 23; Jean Williams, *A Game for Rough Girls: A History of Women's Football in Britain* (London: Routledge, 2003), 26-28.

45   McCaig, "Playing the Game," 23.

46   "Football," *Glasgow Herald,* 6 December 1921, n.p.

47   McCaig, "Playing the Game," 45.

48   Skillen, "'When Women Look Their Worst,'" 56.

49   Ibid., 57.

50   Ibid., 42.

51   Joyce Wethered quoted in J. Wethered and R. Wethered, *Golf from Two Sides* (London: Longman, Green, 1922), 10, 12.

52   B. Burman, "Racing Bodies: Dress and Pioneer Women Aviators and Racing Drivers," *Women's History Review* 9 (2000): 305.

53   Horwood, *Keeping Up Appearances;* Solande, *Becoming Modern.*

54   A survey of a wide range of magazines, such as *Women's Own, Good Housekeeping, Tatler, Eve, Nash's Pall Mall Magazine, Saturday Review of Politics, Literature, Science and Art, Quiver,* and the *Lady* indicates this growing trend. See also Chapter 9 in this volume.

55   "Dear Christine," *Nash's Pall Mall Magazine,* July 1934, 74.

56   See the regular columns Highway of Fashion, *Tatler,* and Dear Christine, *Nash's Pall Mall Magazine,* through the period.

57   The sentiment that every woman who was in "the know" must be a New Woman was echoed in American women's magazines. For details, see Chapter 8 in this volume.

58   Jaeger advertisement, quoted in Horwood, *Keeping Up Appearances,* 7.

59   Horwood, *Keeping Up Appearances,* 7. White has also found similar examples in her study. See Cynthia White, *Women's Magazines 1693-1968* (London: M. Joseph, 1970), 114. For examples of how to update clothing, see *Good Housekeeping* features throughout the period, especially "The Mending Basket," February 1922, 12. Companies also advertised their alteration services, emphasizing their abilities to modernize last season's fashions. See Stevenson's of Dundee, *Tatler* 115 (1925): 96.

60   Although it was most common to find dress patterns in working-class publications, even staunchly middle-class magazines such as the *Lady* began printing them during this period.

61   Ladies Corner, "Tennis Clothes," *Paisley and Renfrewshire Gazette,* 4 July 1928, 3.

62   E. Shanks, "The Revolution in Dress," *Saturday Review of Politics, Literature, Science and Art,* August 1925, 231.

63   Regular feature, The Highway of Fashion, *Tatler,* 1925-39.

64   Ladies Golf Union Minutes 1933, Misc. Files, Ladies Golf Archives, Museum of Scotland, Edinburgh.

65   For related discussion, see Chapter 7 in this volume.

66   Pollard, *Cricket for Women,* 23.

67   This is also explored in Chapter 8 in this volume.

68   White, *Women's Magazines,* 94.

69   Ibid., 94-105.

70   Ibid., 113-15.

71   G. Dyer, *Advertising and Communication* (London: Routledge, 1988), 1; J. Williams, *Decoding Advertisements* (London: Boyars, 1978), 13.

72 Dyer, *Advertising and Communication*, 2.

73 *Tatler* was sampled between 1925 and 1935, and specific focus was placed on campaigns that employed images of sportswomen. Only the years 1925, 1930, and 1935 were analyzed in depth because although the interwar period was a time of economic instability, these particular years were relatively prosperous; thus, advertising should not have been negatively affected by economic slumps. Ads featuring women playing sports were recorded in a database in order to detect patterns or themes.

74 J. Benson, *The Rise of Consumer Society in Britain 1880-1980* (London: Longman, 1994), 111-13.

75 In 1925, an average issue of *Tatler* consisted of eighty-five pages; by 1935, the number had risen to ninety-four.

76 R. Elliot, *Women and Smoking since 1890* (Abingdon: Routledge, 2008), 59.

77 Peter Scott, "Consumption, Consumer Credit and the Diffusion of Consumer Durables," in *20th Century Britain: Economic, Cultural and Social Change,* ed. Francesca Carnevali and Julie-Marie Strange (Harlow: Pearson Education, 2007), 162-80.

7

Aesthetic Athletics: Advertising and Eroticizing Women Swimmers

Marilyn Morgan

On 6 August 1926, Gertrude Ederle became the first woman to complete the harrowing swim across the English Channel, surpassing by nearly two hours the world record previously established by men.[1] The press transformed her into a national hero, and headlines of her triumph dominated the front pages of the *New York Times,* the *Chicago Daily Tribune,* the *Washington Post,* and other major American newspapers for days. After her successful swim, millions clogged city streets to glimpse "Trudy," showering her with over four hundred tons of confetti in New York's (then) largest tickertape parade.[2] When polled by the press in Chicago and Washington, DC, more women aspired to be like Ederle than like Miss America. The *Nation* included her among H.L. Mencken, Henry Ford, and Clarence Darrow as the most important individuals of 1926.[3] In the mid-twenties, major American newspapers devoted more front-page press coverage to women athletes who swam the English Channel than to athletes in other sports, and advertisers used images of powerful female swimmers to successfully endorse products ranging from swimsuits to Rolex waterproof watches.[4] As brand-name businesses used muscular female athletes to promote products, they completely altered American cultural mores: where etiquette once required that women swim in heavy woollen layers to obscure their shape, the tight one-piece suits, modelled after those worn by serious athletes, accentuated their anatomy. Initially, open-water marathon swims were democratizing; despite the scanty suits, the water obscured sexual characteristics and even some physical handicaps. In the water, female swimmers could be regarded as athletes, not beauty queens. The unprecedented athletic accomplishment of women endurance swimmers in the 1920s held the potential to challenge traditional gender stereotypes. Instead, savvy manufacturers and advertisers used the respect and legitimacy that female swimmers gained for the swimsuit to create and completely transform women's fashion, and to establish society's acceptance of the modern woman. Due in part to mass advertising campaigns, the swimsuit, once the hallmark of a serious athlete, became associated more with sexy starlets than with competitive sports. Ederle's example of amazing strength and endurance was all but forgotten within four years.

The history of women's marathon swimming, the widespread media attention that female swimmers received, and the marketing of women's swimsuits have not attracted consistent, in-depth scholarly attention. Those who have examined the distance swimming phenomenon dismiss it as part of the marathon craze and "youth-centred fads" that swept America in the 1920s.[5] On the surface, such an explanation seems plausible, as by 1932, newspaper coverage of women Channel swimmers had decreased. But despite a sharp decline in media reporting of female marathon swimmers, increasing numbers of women participated in marathons; curiously, at the same time, the tone of advertisements and reports on women swimmers and cultural associations with the swimsuit changed drastically. This chapter examines how the modern media and advertisers moulded and eroticized the public perception of the female swimmer.

Popular Images of the Modern Woman

In the 1920s, two images of women dominated newspapers, magazine covers, and popular fiction: the flapper and the athletic girl. The flapper perhaps first captured the public imagination in F. Scott Fitzgerald's fiction and was etched into the national memory by John Held's colourful illustrations.[6] Characterized by youth, dynamism, and rapid movement, the flapper flouted tradition by smoking in public, bobbing her hair, dancing, and often swilling illegal booze. Her brazen disregard for convention and authority made her an emblem of freedom. For the most part, although the flapper embodied rebellion in form, she did not seriously threaten traditional masculine authority. Most young working-class women barely earned a living wage; if they wanted to follow the flapper lifestyle as described in popular magazines – maintaining their bobbed hairstyles, dressing stylishly, and frequenting dance halls and movie theatres – they needed to depend on treats from men.[7] As Joshua Zeitz observes, most flappers aspired not to financial independence, but to marriage.[8] Though many women lacked fiscal independence, whether single or married, advertisers quickly recognized the new modern woman's potential power in influencing the consumer market.[9]

During the interwar years, the modern sportswoman also appeared as a dominant image in American and British advertisements, magazine covers, tabloid photos, and films. As Fiona Skillen observes in Chapter 6 of this volume, the proliferation of women's sports exploded in the interwar era, and the cultural response to the sportswoman was mixed and complicated. Whereas female athletes in sports such as track and field risked being denigrated as muscle molls, their counterparts in "feminine" sports such as ice-skating, golf, and diving became popular and respected.[10] As women's swimming clubs arose in America, England, and France, international marathons were held, and the feats of professional "mermaids" generated widespread media attention. Shunning traditional woollen swimming tights and voluminous dresses, these mermaids (mostly single and working-class women) sported snug, short, modern one-piece swimsuits. In doing so, they began to compete with and outdistance men in open-water marathon swims held in Boston, New York, and Washington, DC. By 1926, the achievements of women endurance swimmers had received unprecedented (and substantive) newspaper coverage.

The most serious swimmers concentrated their efforts on the English Channel, a contest that veteran sportswriters then described as the quintessential challenge to athletic prowess, strength, and endurance.[11] In the wake of the First World War, Western nations cast the swim as an international competition as participants from North and South America, Australia, Egypt, Europe, and Japan entered the unique event. As some adventurous Americans raced to climb mountains, and women exerted their new political rights, the twenty-one-mile expanse of water between England and France symbolized more than just a marathon. Swimming the Channel unaided represented an almost impossible challenge, a new frontier for modern Americans.

Between 1875 and 1926, only five men had completed the swim. In 1922, the *New York Times* remarked, "When a woman swims the English Channel it will have to be acknowledged that there is no physical feat in which she may not compete with man. It is the supreme test."[12] At the time, no American woman had even attempted the feat. Within four years, eight women from Argentina, Austria, England, France, and the United States had embarked on the swim; many tried several times. The press eagerly reported on their endeavours, printing the progress of their training, their strokes per minute, their diets, even their favourite songs. Channel swimming had so completely captivated the American news media in 1926 that even women who started the swim but failed to complete it became minor celebrities.

As Fiona Skillen, Kathleen McCrone, and other scholars have noted, although the women's suffrage moment coincided with women's increased participation in sport, and though both causes furthered women's social emancipation, they seemed to remain puzzlingly separate. Most suffragists prioritized political and economic rights, paying scant attention to women's sports, and at the same time many female athletes failed to connect their participation in sports with women's political rights.[13] However, a minority of women did equate the two causes. English suffragist and swimmer Lillian Smith audaciously declared, "I am going to swim the Channel in order to demonstrate that woman is the physical equal of man. I am going to put a stop forever to all this twaddle about the weaker sex."[14] By the mid-twenties, after American women were enfranchised, first-wave feminists acknowledged that the Channel swim provided a chance to disprove Victorian beliefs of women's innate physical weakness and inferiority. The first woman to cross the Channel promised to bring unprecedented honour to her country and her gender at a time when open-water marathon swimming was considered a gruelling physical challenge best undertaken by men. Prevailing social ideologies held that middle-class women lacked both the physical and mental strength to swim distances; as a result, they were formally discouraged from participating in marathons, and many could not swim at all.

Sink or Swim

At the start of the twentieth century, drowning presented such a serious threat that Learn to Swim campaigns swept America. Initiated by physical educators to prevent death by accidental drowning, these campaigns stressed that women especially should receive swimming instruction to protect themselves and the nation's children.[15] At the time, women's swimsuits consisted of multiple layers of thick, obscuring fabric and voluminous skirts that nearly incapacitated the wearer in the water (Figure 7.1). Women typically sewed their own swimsuits, and popular magazines such as *Godey's* and *Harper's Bazaar* reported on the latest swimwear and published fashionable patterns, recommending dark wools and flannels as the best fabrics. Depending on the type of fabric, seven to ten yards were required to make one woman's bathing suit.[16]

In the early 1900s, Australian swim champion Annette Kellerman revolutionized swimwear for women, inventing the first form-fitting, one-piece swimsuit worn by American and European women. Kellerman attempted to swim the English Channel in 1904 and 1905. Although she failed to complete the crossing, her ability to endure the rough, bitterly cold water for nearly nine hours sparked international media coverage (as did her bold swimsuit), and she was invited to perform a swimming act on stage. Initially, Kellerman wore a dark union suit that exposed her limbs from the thigh down; however, before

Figure 7.1 Sisters Dorothea and Maryal Knox in the surf at Rye, New York, c. 1900.
Source: Photograph of sisters, c. 1900, Maryal Knox Papers, 1880-1856, A-28, folder 2-10, Schlesinger Library, Radcliffe Institute, Harvard University.

performing for a royal audience, she was instructed to cover her bare legs. To retain freedom of movement, she sewed black tights onto the leg openings of her union suit. Because of Kellerman's popularity, manufacturers were quick to replicate this new form-hugging swimwear, and soon women could purchase the "Kellerman suit" in department stores across America.[17] Made of thin black silk, the sleek suit hugged the body and sparked controversy (Figure 7.2). Whereas traditional skirted bathing suits were created to promote modesty, "to

Figure 7.2 Annette Kellerman, modelling the suit she created,
13 March 1919. *Source:* George Grantham Bain Collection,
Library of Congress.

cover, conceal and obscure," the new streamlined suit accentuated women's
anatomy.[18]

Lured by the potential profits to be garnered from the American vaudeville
circuit, Kellerman left England and took her act to Chicago, New York, and
Boston, where she attracted the attention of respected Harvard physical educator
Dudley Sargent, who dubbed her the woman with "the perfect physical form."[19]
Some fans may have flocked to see her fancy dives, but others paid to peer at

her shapely figure, clad in its tight black silk bathing suit. Her manager placed mirrors strategically around the tank so that the audience could see her body underwater from every conceivable angle. Some conservatives found her attire risqué, but Kellerman escaped harsh censure by justifying the swimsuit as neces- sary to her sport. A savvy woman, Kellerman was probably aware that the suit titillated male audiences and boosted her financial success. However, she took great pains to establish her act as an athletic performance and carefully described herself as a serious swimmer; in doing so, she assuaged the fears of conserva- tives by justifying her suit as an essential aspect of professional swimming.

American women wanted to mimic Kellerman and other swimmers, but social propriety prohibited public displays of the body. The American periodical *Life* explained, "The one-piece suits and bare legs are all right in the water for either sex, but they are not suitable in the present state of American sentiment for either sex, for intensive sojournings and meandering in public ashore."[20] Cities across the nation had established local ordinances that prohibited women from wearing one-piece bathing suits on the beach and at poolside.[21] The Playground Commission in Los Angeles petitioned the city council for funds to purchase over six hundred "dull gray" bathing suits with "ample skirts" that women swimmers whose personal suits were deemed immodest could rent for use at municipal pools and beaches.[22] In Pittsburgh, the director of public safety ordered police to arrest women whose bathing costumes did not completely cover them "from neck to knee, at least."[23] Similarly, in Chicago, police forcibly pulled women offenders from the beach and arrested them. Still, the suit marked a symbol of modernity; despite, or perhaps because of, its controversy, women continued to purchase it and to wear it in public.

While Kellerman challenged traditional ideas that associated female beauty with frailty, she simultaneously fused the link between swimming, femininity, and awareness of sexuality. Her vaudeville act became so popular that she was cast in silent films. Her first film, *Neptune's Daughter* (1914), drew record crowds who waited "for hours ... standing in line to see the pictures of Annette Kellerman."[24] Her success earned her the title "Million Dollar Mermaid" and probably encouraged the next generation of modern women swimmers, who made the nation take notice as they surpassed male records in both speed and endurance races during the 1920s.

Images of Athletic Women: Between Fantasy and Reality

Inspired by Kellerman's lucrative career, advertisers and illustrators used images of female swimmers to sell products and to shape standards of beauty in the

1920s. One particular emblem, the Red Diving Girl, was employed as a marketing tool to sell Jantzen swimsuits to women. Embodying youth, independence, physical fitness, and style, the Diving Girl symbolized the radical changes that occurred in attitudes toward women's place in society, athleticism, and fashion during the 1920s. In the late nineteenth century, few women knew how to dive, and those who did were encumbered by traditional swimwear. By the mid-twenties, women had won the battle for political enfranchisement, and physical activity helped many of them shed the corporeal, psychological, and cultural limitations that defined womanhood. The Red Diving Girl became one symbol of women's new-found freedom from corsets and social constraints; however, other more insidious limitations accompanied women's physical, social, and political emancipation. Jantzen used idyllic illustrations of women to promote a new style of swimwear based on the abbreviated suit previously worn exclusively by athletes. Beautiful, young, slim, and posed in mid-dive, the Red Diving Girl was stylishly outfitted in a short red suit, a knitted red cap, and red stockings. Clad in perfectly coordinated swimming ensemble, she represented a fantasized version of the swimmer.

Originally a trademark symbol for swimsuits, the Red Diving Girl appeared first in the Jantzen catalogue, then in advertisements in periodicals such as *Life* and *Vogue*. She quickly became so popular that Jantzen was inundated with requests for her image; the company had over 3 million Red Diving Girl decals created and distributed to car dealers to give to customers. By the mid-twenties, her image adorned windshields, locomotive cars, billboards, dashboards, car bumpers, and windows in America.[25] She was also prominently featured in advertisements in France, though in a slightly modified version.[26] The popularity of the Diving Girl and the stylishly dressed figures Jantzen used in its ads helped create an idealized vision of an athletic woman's form. Such ads cemented the idea of aesthetic athletics, de-emphasizing women's real experience as athletes and also demonstrating how dramatically their swimwear and attitudes about their athleticism had changed in the early twentieth century.

Like other emerging companies of the era, Jantzen utilized creative advertising by linking the imaginary Red Diving Girl to a lifestyle she represented. In the forefront of other swimwear advertisers of the era, Jantzen began associating its suit with happiness and a fulfilled life. Although the ads remained focused on the attractive Jantzen-clad girl, their backgrounds depicted exotic seaside scenes in which smiling, swimsuit-wearing men and women frolicked. In one advertisement (Figure 7.3), a couple stands posed in the background as if flirting (the man holds a cigarette, which carried a glamorous connotation at the time). Ads that appeared in *Life* and *Vogue* promised middle-class consumers a life

Figure 7.3 Illustrated by Ruth Eastman, this ad features a Jantzen girl poised to dive. *Source:* Jantzen Swimming Suits. *Life,* 9 June 1921, 822.

(or at least a summer) of insouciance. The ad in Figure 7.3 asserts, "Those who really enjoy water sports find Jantzen the logical bathing suit. Practical because it permits utmost freedom of action in the water. Beautiful because it fits perfectly and holds its shape permanently." Showing the girl poised to dive, the ad asks, "Isn't it good to be alive?" (and, it implies, wearing a Jantzen).

Jantzen ads from the interwar years show the idyllic lifestyle that the company insinuated could be achieved by buying its suit. C. Coles Phillips, the well-established illustrator known for creating the "fade-away girl," designed a striking image for Jantzen that was featured in *Life* in 1921. Whereas the text in that ad proclaims the suit's functionality, noting "no loose skirts or 'trappings' to impede swimming" and promising "it never binds – never sags," the illustration suggests something more. Facing the viewer, the Diving Girl stands rather seductively in the foreground, the suit hugging her slim but curvaceous figure as she scans the horizon for something (or someone). In the background, amid impressive balustrades and flowing plants that suggest affluence, ease, and the exotic, a swimsuited man lounges, surveying the Diving Girl from behind, hinting at the possibility of romance. The text reads, "the poetry of motion – graceful dives – long, easy strokes – moments of relaxation between swims – yours, if you wear a Jantzen."[27] As several scholars have illustrated, these early marketing campaigns intended to sell not just products, but lifestyles.[28] As a result, Jantzen's sales skyrocketed; whereas in 1917, the company's swimsuit sales totalled just 600, within two years they had hit 4,100, and by 1930, Jantzen had emerged as America's leading swimsuit manufacturer.[29]

Using Swimming to Sell Femininity to American Women

In the burgeoning sportswear industry, Jantzen was among the first manufacturers to use images of attractive and athletic women to appeal to both sexes. Men could admire and ogle the Red Diving Girl's physique, and women could aspire to emulate her freedom. As women became a powerful consumer force, the cosmetics industry also profited by linking feminine beauty to athletics. Some shrewd entrepreneurial women influenced the development of modern consumer culture by underscoring gender differences to appeal to women as consumers.[30] Beauty columnist Antoinette Donnelly used her name to promote soaps, lotions, and creams for sale across the nation, from department stores in major cities to independent shops in rural areas. In her weekly column, "Beauty Hints," which was syndicated throughout the country between 1919 and 1963, Donnelly encouraged readers to swim: "Everybody should learn to swim," she wrote, adding that "for women it is the best sport, because it teaches grace and poise and command."[31]

Donnelly wrote more than eleven thousand columns that covered every imaginable aspect of beauty: breath (bad or good), hygiene, eyes, teeth, posture, corsets, walking, breathing, crow's feet and wrinkles, sagging chins, weight and dieting, skin troubles, hair, and nervousness. Regardless of the affliction, she promised with an air of authority, "I have a tonic, a diet, or a set of exercises for what ails you." She assured readers, "I know of few things that are more healthful than swimming," remarking, "it is a perfect exercise for women, in that it develops where development is needed and reduces all excesses. In order to swim well you must breathe correctly and that in itself is almost an assurance of beauty."[32]

Donnelly commended Annette Kellerman as "just about the best example of the pursuit of beauty and youth," and she encouraged all women to swim.[33] As the emerging health and beauty industry promoted swimming as a beautifier, the sport fulfilled needs in several markets. Historians of advertising, including T.J. Jackson Lears and Daniel Delis Hill, have examined women's new power as consumers that rose as advertising campaigns pervaded the country in the 1920s.[34] As women's homemaking role shifted and women were increasingly valued as powerful consumers, advertisers targeted them, placing ads in popular middle-class periodicals each week and month.[35] By the end of the decade, advertising executives had reshaped American culture and political ideology, selling "lifestyles and values as packaged products."[36] The worship of athletes dovetailed with the rise of mass advertising, and manufacturers realized that selling specialized sporting goods and equipment to the general public marked an important, lucrative new market. In a growing era of celebrity endorsement, athletes were also used to promote a variety of products, from automobiles to wristwatches, which were completely unrelated to sports. In part because of the use of swimmers in advertising, attitudes about the form-fitting, abbreviated swimsuit drastically changed. By the late 1930s, women's bathing suits had become engrained in the landscape of American culture, associated with youth, leisure, and ease.

From Active to Passive: Swimsuits and Beauty

In the 1920s, however, the American middle class displayed conflicting attitudes about the propriety of the swimsuit; on the one hand, it lauded the wholesomeness of female swimmers, but at the same time, many people condemned the immorality of the modern bathing suit worn in public. Middle-class critics especially balked at the use of the suit in beauty pageants. As historian Lois Banner has carefully demonstrated, in the early 1900s, beauty contests were associated with carnivals and working-class burlesque shows.[37] Some contests, week-long affairs that incorporated sporting events and dances, culminated with a Bather's Revue in which women, dressed only in swimsuits, paraded through town. As bathing costumes became more abbreviated, some complained about the increasing sordidness of the parades, and scandals occurred in some contests. The beauty parade provoked criticism from many groups, violating vestiges of Victorian propriety and city ordinances regarding public decency.

The Miss America Pageant, which originated in 1921, was held annually in Atlantic City and featured a regatta, a yacht review, and a boardwalk parade of women in their bathing suits. Over the years, a "nationwide campaign" to end the pageant was launched by several middle-class groups, including the proprietors of boardwalk hotels. Citing the "demoralizing effect" of the Bather's Revue in 1927, business owners protested that the pageant was "unworthy of a great resort like Atlantic City" because it entailed "a method of advertising which involves the exploitation of young women."[38] Women's organizations opposed the pageant "in the interest of public welfare, both from a moral and a financial standpoint."[39] In 1928, the committee of local business owners debated for months regarding how to legitimize the contest and contemplated ending the Bather's Revue. However, faced with a $52,000 deficit, Atlantic City officials cancelled the contest for several years.[40] Although many protested the one-piece swimsuits used in beauty contests and worn by the average woman, the ease and comfort they facilitated made them a permanent feature. To offset criticisms of the shorter suits, advertisers emphasized the wholesomeness of swimming by focusing on the true athleticism exhibited by female Channel swimmers.

Mille Gade Corson, who attained fame as the second woman and first American mother to successfully swim the channel, publicized the fact that she wore a Jantzen during her swim. Clever Jantzen advertising executives did not fail to capitalize on this fact and quickly secured Corson as a spokesmodel, featuring her in prominent ads and in the company's 1927 catalogue. Figure 7.4, a photo spread from the catalogue, shows Corson relaxed and smiling with her children, all proudly sporting Jantzen suits.

Using well-known athletes lent legitimacy to the still controversial bathing suit. In a prominent ad featured in the *New York Times* the day after Corson's welcome parade, Jantzen boasted, "Crowds Cheer Mrs. Corson – Mrs. Corson Praises Jantzen." The ad shows the triumphant Corson surrounded by her family at the city-wide reception held in her honour. It claims that the "vociferous welcome afforded Mrs. Clemington Corson (Mille Gade) yesterday was no whit

Figure 7.4 Jantzen publicity photograph of Mille Gade Corson with daughter Marjorie and son Clemington Jr., all in Jantzen suits. *Source:* Mille Gade Corson Collection, Archives Center, National Museum of American History, Behring Center, Smithsonian Institution.

more sincere and enthusiastic than her praise for the JANTZEN Swimming Suit" that she wore during her victorious swim.[41]

By choosing Corson as its spokesmodel, Jantzen fulfilled two functions. The press lauded her as the first mother to swim the Channel, which meant that her name lent credibility to the new suit. At the same time, her age (twenty-seven) and status as a mother enabled Jantzen to target a far broader audience than if it had chosen a younger and single Channel swimmer such as Ederle. Jantzen arguably led the swimsuit revolution. Other companies, such as A.G. Spalding Brothers and the Ocean Bathing Suit Company, which designed and produced plain professional bathing suits for athletes, began to redesign their ad campaigns. In the mid-twenties, these sports manufacturers started to accentuate the beautifying features built into their suits. As early as 1923, Spalding featured ads that asked the professional distance swimmer, "How well do you look in a Swimming Suit?" An ad touted the practical features of the Spalding suit, such as "no sagging, binding, chafing seams ... no clammy oozing fabric," and highlighted its "new slenderizing bow-shaped seam across the hips."[42] Like Spalding, the Ocean Bathing Suit Company designed suits for the serious professional swimmer. Ads pointed out that the company had produced "swimming suits for experts" since 1883 and that it manufactured the suits for the US Olympic team in 1924.

Ocean targeted the "woman or girl who has mastered the fine points of swimming" by placing ads in every issue of the Women's Swimming Association publication *WSA News*. While the text in Ocean's advertisements underscored the brand's preference among "expert swimmers," by the 1920s, illustrations in ads exaggerated femininity and sexuality (Figure 7.5).[43]

Ironically, by copying and mass producing the suit worn by professional swimmers, Jantzen and other swimsuit companies helped to change conceptions of the competitive and rigorous nature of endurance swimming, which had initially attracted attention and respect from the American media and sports enthusiasts. The sleek, abbreviated racing suit once identified a serious athlete, one who specialized in swimming, and specialization marked an identifying characteristic of sport.[44] In the mid-twenties, the professional-style suit could be obtained by any consumer who could afford it, regardless of skill. Jantzen's advertising campaign proclaimed that its women's swimsuit "changed bathing to swimming." In reality, the widespread availability of the professional suit served to make serious swimming and recreational bathing somewhat interchangeable in the public mind. Anyone could easily purchase a professional suit; it didn't matter if she was swimming the English Channel or sunbathing at her local pool and couldn't swim a stroke.

Jantzen advertisers successfully used professional swimmers to transform public opinion, and over time the company secured acceptance of the new style in women's bathing suits. It was not alone in exploring the use of advertising to persuade. Studies of advertising and marketing flourished at this time; both advertising genius Bruce Barton and Walter Lippmann, co-founder of the *New Republic*, intuited that ideals and "political platforms could be sold as easily as automobiles."[45] Fascinated by studies in social psychology and mass opinion, ad executives began to incorporate emerging business theories such as democratic social engineering in their campaigns.[46] Swimming and swimsuits featured both directly and indirectly in many mid-twentieth-century ad campaigns that had little to do with the sport. As scholar Guy Lewis speculated, the desire for a suntan, which symbolized "the healthy glow of youth," contributed to rapid change in swimming as a popular recreational and sporting activity. When advertisers created ads featuring sunny vacations and real estate in Florida, they used images of women in bathing suits to lure potential buyers. Publicists for beach resorts were among the first advertisers to use the wholesomeness of athletics to effectively promote vacations and real estate. As one journalist noted, "Sunshine and warm climes are luring pleasure-seekers to the lands of palms."[47]

From the late 1920s through the 1930s, advertisers utilized images of female swimmers to promote Miami Beach, Bermuda, and the Mediterranean as top destinations for vacationers.[48] At the same time, several factors, including an increase in the popularity of outdoor sports, helped create a cultural association of tanned skin with youthful exuberance and health. After her triumphant Channel swim, the press described Ederle as fit, happy, and "brown as a berry."[49] As Atchison demonstrates in Chapter 8 of this volume, consumerism promoted the popularity of suntanning among Americans and Europeans during the interwar years. By the 1930s, companies that had previously marketed creams to preserve milky-white skin during exposure to the sun began to sell lotions that promised to turn skin golden brown. Ads used images of attractive bronzed people (not necessarily professional swimmers) in swimsuits to convey ideals of youth, leisure, fitness, and happiness.[50]

Throughout the interwar years, advertisers employed images of svelte swimmers to sell swimsuits, pools, suntans, vacations, and in short, a new American way of life. They embraced traditional gender stereotypes and used clever marketing strategies to effectively manipulate the public's adherence to dominant norms.[51] As advertisers promoted the healthy glow of golden skin, more Americans began to choose vacation destinations that would enable them to sunbathe. Advertisers marketed new skin care products specifically to women. One beauty specialist instructed women that "just as the Channel swimmers [were] covered with grease for protection while staying in the water for a long time," so too must responsible bathers "see to it that every inch of skin appearing outside the swimming suit" is protected.[52]

In 1933, the media continued to promote the activity of swimming as a beautifier, but instead of including detailed instructions on how to swim, or glorifying Channel swimmers, the press focused on keeping women beautiful while swimming. One article instructed, "Protect your hair with a heavy chamois ... Wear a heavy cap or preferably two. Avoid getting salt water into the hair." "Have you protected your skin against sunburn?" the writer queried. "And have you one of the new indelible lipsticks and waterproof rouges and mascaras that promise not to run?"[53]

Hollywood increasingly influenced the physical culture movement and established new standards of beauty that incorporated more traditional concepts of femininity and masculinity.[54] Although women were freed from the physical restraint of corsets, a sleek, slender form, such as that of swimmer Eleanor Holm, represented the ideal of feminine beauty. The press openly admired Holm's figure, which was "curved, without an ounce of extra weight – and certainly not muscular"; she replaced the heavily muscled, stout ideal embodied in the Channel swimmer.[55] Similarly, the media used male athletes, specifically 1924 Olympic swimmer Johnny Weissmuller (who later earned fame on the silver screen as Tarzan), to create representations of ideal masculinity.[56] As abbreviated swimsuits became acceptable in society, bodies were placed on full display. Ironically, advertisers and manufacturers encouraged women who wished to attain the ideal figures of swimmers not to swim, but to purchase dietary aids instead. Despite the shifting attitudes about strenuous distance swimming, bathing suits became firmly entrenched in American culture, and in some ways, the mass appeal of recreational swimming increased.

Physical culture played a significant role in Hollywood, and under that vision swimming took on new meaning. As swimming pools became a symbol of status and "part of the 'signature' of the Hollywood landscape," the sport became associated with passivity and glamour, not endurance contests in rough open waters.[57] As is illustrated by the streamlined physical forms of popular swimmers Weissmuller, Holm, and later Esther Williams (who played the part of Annette Kellerman in films), the youth culture established in the previous decade had rooted and begun to thrive, and advertisers linked a youthful appearance to personal productivity. Manufacturers cautioned that strenuous exercise diminished women's attractiveness, and they touted cosmetics as a better means of achieving a youthful appearance. The expanding beauty industry promised that any woman could be as beautiful as "Nature intended," but unlocking the secrets of "natural" beauty required the regular purchase of face creams, body lotions, makeup, hair dyes, depilatories, and deodorants. By the 1930s, vigorous exercise was no longer equated with feminine beauty. Americans were persuaded, as historian Kathy Peiss notes, that beauty could be purchased in a jar.[58]

The popularity of the large-framed endurance swimmer cooled, and the legitimacy of endurance swimming waned. Though Esther Williams had proven

Figure 7.5 Ocean Bathing Suit Company ad. *Source: WSA News,* June 1926, 8. Women's Swimming Association Archives, International Swimming Hall of Fame Archives, Fort Lauderdale, Florida.

herself as a powerfully strong swimmer, winning three national championships in both the breaststroke and freestyle as well as earning a place on the US Olympic team in 1940 (the Olympics of that year were pre-empted by the Second World War), the media downplayed her strength and emphasized her sleek figure and beauty. Like Kellerman before her, Williams used swimming to catapult into a lucrative career as a movie star. The epitome of glamour, photographs of the swimsuit-clad Williams abounded in the popular press; nearly all of them displayed her posed passively and prettily, not actually swimming (Figure 7.6).

Cosmetics companies launched ad campaigns that preyed on women's insecurities. One claimed that serious competitive athletics created unnatural physical strain and produced ugly, wrinkled women. Max Factor specifically discouraged women from engaging in strenuous distance swims. The company explained that intense physical exertion coupled with salt water damaged the

Figure 7.6 Esther Williams. *Source:* International Swimming Hall of Fame Archives, Fort Lauderdale, Florida.

hair permanently, causing it to thin and possibly fall out. If the threat of baldness were not enough to deter women from competitive sport, Max Factor asserted that "the strain of competitive athletics is too concentrated and prolonged for the feminine sex" and warned women that athletics "tend to disfigure the face in a more or less permanent degree."[59] To underscore the danger of endurance swimming, the article juxtaposed photographs of well-known female swimmers and movie stars. It situated a photograph of an endurance swimmer, Else Jacobsen, gasping for breath while swimming, between photos of glamorous movie stars Marlene Dietrich and Claudette Colbert. The accompanying caption read, "The fact remains that the most beautiful women in pictures take no exercise whatsoever."[60] Manufacturers such as Max Factor and Jantzen advocated recreational "swimming" that resembled the bathing in which women had engaged during the previous century. Modern swimmers wore costumes that made them look like athletes, but, as most did not participate in sport, the suit served mainly to accentuate their form and put their bodies on display.

By the early 1930s, swimsuits had become increasingly associated with a contest of feminine beauty instead of a competitive athletic endeavour historically described as masculine. As the beauty contestants posed before male judges in brief, form-fitting swimsuits, they were perceived by the press and audiences as sexual objects, solidifying a link between "swimming" and feminine beauty. For instance, theatrical producer Florenz Ziegfeld, who interviewed approximately fifty thousand of America's most attractive young women for his Ziegfeld Follies, recommended swimming as the most desirable and effective activity for producing overall beauty.[61] Bernarr Macfadden, creator of *Physical Culture* magazine, advised men to "marry a swimmer." He noted that "a girl who has been swimming regularly for a number of years usually has a strong, splendidly developed beautiful body. She is all woman."[62] Such repeated association feminized the sport of swimming, and over time widespread popularity of distance swimming dropped significantly. The media focused their reporting on male professional sports such as football, baseball, and boxing (accounts of which were more easily broadcast on radio than swimming was).[63] In the late 1920s and early 1930s, the tone, content, extent, and even location of newspaper columns about female swimmers changed drastically. By the end of the decade, the stories of women Channel contestants were all but forgotten by the press.

By the 1930s, protests over the beauty pageants had quieted. By rechristening the Bather's Revue as the "swimsuit competition," promoters of the Miss America pageant successfully downplayed middle-class concerns about the exploitation of contestants and at the same time reinforced the legitimacy of women wearing modern, short, form-fitting swimsuits outside of the water. The swimsuit had become acceptable because of its association with strong female swimmers. Examining erotic images of women athletes in trade cards and cards of the interwar era, Thierry Terret notes, "There are some puzzling absences in the lack of dancers or swimmers."[64] Similarly, T.J. Jackson Lears observes that rather than "introducing sex into advertising," campaigns that emphasized women's athleticism in the early twentieth century preserved "the older prurience in a newer idiom of health."[65] The press so thoroughly associated swimsuits with wholesome athleticism that when swimmer Annette Kellerman appeared completely nude in *Daughter of the Gods,* the film provoked little controversy.[66]

Thus, when officials in Atlantic City revived the Miss America pageant in 1935, the public could endorse all aspects of the contest, and the swimsuit competition became its signature. Paradoxically, Lois Banner observes, as the beauty contestant "shed her clothes, donning a bathing suit so that more of her body can be seen, women also shed their association with morality, masked their professional skills, and became sex objects, competing in an arena where men were the judges and promoters."[67] By the 1930s, the bathing suit had become widely associated with traditional notions of feminine beauty, not accomplishing a physically gruelling athletic feat. Instead of plunging ones' body into sixty-degree water, battling raging tides, and enduring exhausting swims, a woman could aspire to be beautiful. Hollywood began shaping the ideal images of masculinity and femininity, and the powerful physique of women endurance swimmers was denigrated.

Conclusion

At the outset of the 1920s, the mass media presented two images of modernity to women: the flapper and the sportswoman. Although the media often trivialized the frenetic youthful flapper, they marvelled at swimmers such as Mille Gade Corson, who "glides through the water with machine-like precision and with the minimum of effort," and they admired that "she is hard as nails, and the most tireless woman."[68] Reporters also lauded Lillian Cannon, who possessed "24-Karat Grit" and the "spirit which makes athletes in any field."[69] By the mid-thirties, however, images of the flapper and the sportswoman, which signified modernity, had vanished. They were replaced by a more traditional ideal of womanhood, which feminized and eroticized female athletes and suggested that women's virtue lay in their physical beauty.

Epilogue

Just prior to the 2000 Olympic Games, swimmer Jenny Thompson created controversy by posing provocatively for a *Sports Illustrated* photograph. Printed as part of the *Sports Illustrated* article "Unflagging," the photo shows Thompson standing on the beach, legs spread. Wearing only short red boots and boyish Wonder Woman swimming trunks patterned with American stars and stripes (her clenched fists shield her bare breasts), she smiles boldly and confidently into the camera.[70] The controversial image triggered mixed reactions. Some, including the Women's Sports Foundation, criticized Thompson's choice. Donna Lopiano, executive director of that organization, voiced her disappointment, explaining, "It's incongruent to take that body you've worked so hard for and use it for sex."[71] Others, including *Sports Illustrated* and members of the 1999 Australia women's soccer team, championed Thompson's right to display and profit from the body she had worked so hard to attain. As the debates brewed in the papers for two weeks, *Sports Illustrated* reporter Rick Reilly lambasted feminists for their criticism: "Thompson sends young girls a terrific message: Fit is sexy. Muscles are sexy. Sport is sexy. Give it a try sometime."[72] *Sports Illustrated*'s argument that muscular, athletic women are aesthetically pleasing (and that those who opposed displaying the fit female form were out of shape themselves) had surfaced throughout the early twentieth century.

Thompson's decision to be photographed wearing only stars and stripes trunks and boots reminiscent of the Wonder Woman costume unsettled many. Perhaps in part it provoked ambiguous responses because it reinforced the notion that women's power is directly linked to heightened sexuality. Scholars exploring the sociology of sport, media studies, and popular culture, including Patricia Vertinsky, Pamela J. Creedon, Michael Messner, Susan Birrell, Cheryl Cole, and Nancy Theberge, have demonstrated that a fine line snakes between the messages delivered by provocative shots of female athletes.[73] On the one hand, the athletes should be proud of their physicality and should be able to exercise the right to capitalize on their bodies; on the other, depicting out-standing female athletes as sex symbols reinforces the idea that women are judged and valued for emulating traditional standards of beauty in their ap-pearance, not their athletic skill.

Thompson expressed surprise when her photo accompanied "Unflagging"; during an interview with *Sports Illustrated for Women,* she explained that she assumed it would appear in a swimsuit issue that used real athletes, not models. Despite her surprise, she proudly defended her decision, claiming that her pose promoted a new physical standard for women – one of muscular strength. Certainly, neither the idea that "muscles are sexy" nor the muscular standard of beauty that Thompson represents are new. Both mimic the short-lived criteria of strength and beauty set by established physical culturists at the start of the twentieth century, and both reflect the equation of beauty with athletic strength – in the water – established by women swimmers during the 1920s.

The media's fascination with female swimmers declined dramatically, co-inciding with a legitimization of beauty pageants in America. The press coverage of women endurance swimmers and the changes in that coverage reveal a great deal not only about the golden era of sport, but also about current trends in professional athletics, including hero worship and sponsorship, as well as our present standards of physical fitness and beauty and gender roles.

Notes

1 Ederle swam the strait in fourteen hours and thirty-one minutes; the previous record, sixteen hours and twenty-three minutes, was set by Argentine swimmer Enrico Tiraboschi in 1923.

2 "City's Throngs Give Greatest Welcome to Gertrude Ederle," *New York Times,* 28 August 1926, 1.

3 See ibid.; and "Honor Roll for 1926," *Nation,* 5 January 1927, 4.

4 In an incredibly successful advertising campaign, Hans Wilsorf, a co-founder of Rolex, paid 40,000 Swiss francs to purchase the entire front page of the *London Daily Mail,* on which he placed a full-page ad featuring endurance swimmer Mercedes Gleitze endorsing the new Rolex waterproof watch. Rolex ad, *London Daily Mail,* 24 November 1927, 1. Author interview with John E. Brozek, author of *The Rolex Report* and president of QualityTyme.net, 29 July-9 August 2006. Marilyn Morgan, "'The Star-Spangled Channel': Money, the Media, and Gender in Marathon Swimming, 1900-1936" (PhD diss., University of Maine, 2007), 37.

5 Judith Jenkins George studied American women's swimming marathons of the 1920s, including the English Channel swim, and concluded that they were part of a marathon craze, representing little more than one of the "youth-centred fads" that swept America at the time. The dismissal of the event as an isolated American fad overlooks the women from South America, England, Australia, South Africa, Denmark, Germany, and France who not only attempted the English and Catalina Channels and races in the 1920s, but also entered long-distance swims around the world. It also underestimates its cultural significance and other factors that enabled more women to attempt the swim at this time. Judith Jenkins George, "The Fad of American Women's Endurance Swimming during the Post-World War I Era," *Canadian Journal of History of Sport* 26, 1 (May 1995): 52-72.

6 See, for instance, John Held's "The Girl Who Gave Him the Cold Shoulder," *Life,* c. 1925, front cover, "American Beauties: Drawings from the Golden Age of Illustration," Swann Gallery of Caricature and Cartoon at the Library of Congress, 2002, http://www.loc.gov/.

7 Kathy Peiss, *Cheap Amusements: Working Women and Leisure in Turn-of-the-Century New York* (Philadelphia: Temple University Press, 1986).

8 Joshua Zeitz, *Flapper: A Madcap Story of Sex, Style, Celebrity, and the Women Who Made America Modern* (New York: Crown, 2006); Angela J. Latham, *Posing a Threat: Flappers, Chorus Girls and Other Brazen Performers of the American 1920s* (Hanover, NH: Wesleyan University Press, 2000).

9 Penny Tinkler and Cheryl Krasnick Warsh, "Feminine Modernity in Interwar Britain and North America: Corsets, Cars, and Cigarettes," *Journal of Women's History* 20, 3 (Fall 2008): 113-43.

10 See Chapter 6 in this volume; and Susan Cahn, *Coming On Strong: Gender and Sexuality in Twentieth-Century Women's Sport* (Cambridge, MA: Harvard University Press, 1994), 36-51, 209-17.

11 Will Rogers, "And They Call Prize Fighting a Sport!" *Washington Post,* 23 August 1926, SM2; W.O. McGeehan, "Down the Line," *New York Herald,* 7 August 1927, 14.

12 "Topic of the Times," *New York Times,* 4 September 1922, 10.

13 Chapter 6 in this volume; Kathleen E. McCrone, "Class, Gender, and English Women's Sport, c. 1890-1914," *Journal of Sport History* 18 (Spring 1991): 159-82; Kathleen E. McCrone, *Playing the Game: Sport and the Physical Emancipation of English Women, 1870-1914* (Lexington: University Press of Kentucky, 1988); Jennifer Hargreaves, "'Playing like Gentlemen While Behaving like Ladies': Contradictory Features of the Formative Years of Women's Sport," *British Journal of Sports History* 2, 1 (May 1985): 40-52.

14 "'I'll Swim to France to Win Votes for Women!" *Washington Post,* 26 October 1913, MS6.

15 See, for instance, "Importance of Swimming," *Boston Daily Globe,* 9 August 1904, 6; and "Women Drown at Annisquam," *Boston Daily Globe,* 24 June 1910, 9.

16   Claudia B. Kidwell, *Women's Bathing and Swimming Costume in the United States* (Washington, DC: Smithsonian Institution Press, 1968), 1-31.

17   Emily Gibson with Barbara Firth, *The Original Million Dollar Mermaid* (Crows Nest, New South Wales: Allen and Unwin, 2005), 29-30.

18   Kidwell, *Women's Bathing and Swimming Costume*, 28.

19   Sargent's notes describing physical characteristics of swimmers, Dudley Sargent Papers, GV342 Sa 73h, box 6, Harvard University Archives, Cambridge, MA; "Modern Woman Getting Nearer the Perfect Figure," *New York Times*, 4 December 1910, SM4.

20   "Sea Bathing and Land Bathing," *Life*, 28 August 1919, 366.

21   Jeff Wiltse, "Contested Waters: A History of Swimming Pools in America" (PhD diss., Brandeis University, 2003), 30-31.

22   "What Ho! Put Skirts on Bathers," *Los Angeles Times*, 12 July 1920, II5.

23   "Peek-a-Boo Bath Suits Barred," *Chicago Daily Tribune*, 20 July 1908, 1.

24   Percy Hammond, "Annette Kellerman in Pretty Pictures," *Chicago Daily Tribune*, 19 May 1914, 14.

25   Carol Alhadeff, telephone interviews by author, 31 July 2006, 6 September 2006, Jantzen Archives, Portland, Oregon; Lena Lenček and Gideon Bosker, *Making Waves: Swimsuits and the Undressing of America* (San Francisco: Chronicle Books, 1989), 48-49.

26   Olivier Saillard, *Les Maillots de bain: Les Carnets de la mode* (Paris: Éditions du Chêne, 1998), 38.

27   Jantzen advertisement, *Life*, 9 June 1921, 822.

28   Mark Dyreson, "The Emergence of Consumer Culture and the Transformation of Physical Culture: American Sport in the 1920s," *Journal of Sport History* 16, 3 (Winter 1989): 277; Zeitz, *Flapper*, 197-200; T.J. Jackson Lears, *Fables of Abundance: A Cultural History of Advertising in America* (New York: Basic Books, 1994), 188-89.

29   Lenček and Bosker, *Making Waves*, 47.

30   Kathy Peiss, "American Women and the Making of Modern Consumer Culture" (lecture delivered at the University at Albany, State University of New York, 26 March 1998, recorded for the *Journal for MultiMedia History* 1, 1 [Fall 1998], http://www.albany.edu/).

31   "Swimming and Bathing Fine as Beautifiers," *Chicago Daily Tribune*, 13 August 1917, 14. See also the following articles in the *Chicago Daily Tribune*: "Beauty Hints," "Why Make the Waves so Wild Mother?" "Learning to Swim," 25 July 1920, D3; "How to Swim," 1 August 1920, E3; "Why You Should Swim," 17 July 1921, D3; "Take a Swim and Drown That Weary, Worn Out Feeling," 8 June 1925, 19; "Swim, If You Would Keep Your Figure Evenly Proportioned," 18 August 1930, 19; "Now's the Time to Slenderize for Swim Suit," 27 April 1938, 16; and "Swim Away to Shapeliness," 26 June 1960, D2.

32   Antoinette Donnelly, "Double Chins Give Away to Neck Exercises," *Chicago Daily Tribune*, 6 July 1917, 15.

33   Antoinette Donnelly, "Annette Kellerman Is Rich in the Wisdom of Staying Young," *Chicago Daily Tribune*, 28 July 1935, C3.

34   See T.J. Jackson Lears, "American Advertising and the Reconstruction of the Body, 1880-1930," in *Fitness in American Culture: Images of Health, Sport and the Body, 1830-1940*, ed. Kathryn Grover (Amherst: University of Massachusetts Press, 1989), 47-66; Daniel Delis Hill, *Advertising to the American Woman, 1900-1999* (Columbus: Ohio State University Press, 2002); Nancy G. Rosoff, "'Every Muscle Is Absolutely Free': Advertising and Advice about Clothing for Athletic American Women, 1880-1920," *Journal of American Culture* 25, 1-2 (March 2002): 25-31; and Laura L. Behling, "'The Woman at the Wheel': Marketing Ideal Womanhood, 1915-1934," *Journal of American Culture* 20, 3 (Fall 1997): 13-30.

35   Hill, *Advertising to the American Woman*; Martha Banta, *Imaging American Women: Idea and Ideals in Cultural History* (New York: Columbia University Press, 1987), 88.

36 Dyreson, "The Emergence of Consumer Culture," 261-81, 276.

37 Lois Banner, *American Beauty* (New York: Knopf, 1983), 249-70.

38 "Attack Beauty Pageant," *New York Times,* 1 March 1927, 3; "Atlantic City to Hold Fall Beauty Pageant," *New York Times,* 20 February 1928, 23.

39 "Women Open Fight on Beauty Pageant," *New York Times,* 18 November 1927, 12.

40 "To Decide on Beauty Pageant," *New York Times,* 19 February 1928, 14.

41 Jantzen advertisement, "Crowds Cheer Mrs. Corson – Mrs. Corson Praises Jantzen," *New York Times,* 11 September 1926, 3.

42 A.G. Spalding Brothers advertisement, *WSA News* (Women's Swimming Association, New York), September 1925, 7.

43 Ocean Bathing Suit Company advertisement, *WSA News,* June 1926, 8.

44 Allen Guttmann, *From Ritual to Record: The Nature of Modern Sports* (New York: Columbia University Press, 2004), 16, 36-47.

45 Lippmann, interested in the growing field of social psychology and mass opinion, encouraged President Wilson to form an official publicity office, populated with advertising men, editors, and directors. See Dyreson, "The Emergence of Consumer Culture," 277; Zeitz, *Flapper,* 197-200; and Lears, *Fables of Abundance,* 188-89.

46 Zeitz, *Flapper,* 200-8.

47 Guy Lewis, "Sport, Youth Culture and Conventionality 1920-1970," *Journal of Sport History* 4, 20 (1977): 134; Virginia Pope, "All Aboard," *New York Times,* 11 December 1932, X13.

48 Tabloids had been purposefully "using swimmers as circulation pullers," and "the real-estate promoting corporations in Florida, California, and New York" had been employing images of attractive swimmers in bathing suits "for bait for years." Paul Gallico, *Farewell to Sport* (New York: A.A. Knopf, 1938), 246.

49 T.G. Middleton, "Miss Ederle Happy, Won't Try It Again; Is Hailed in France," *New York Times,* 8 August 1926, 1; see Chapter 8 in this volume.

50 Lewis, "Sport, Youth Culture and Conventionality 1920-1970," 129-50.

51 Dyreson, "The Emergence of Consumer Culture," 277; Zeitz, *Flapper,* 197-200; Lears, *Fables of Abundance,* 188-89.

52 Viola Paris, "Beauty and You," *Washington Post,* 24 July 1927, SM8.

53 "Fat or Slim, for the Figure Learn to Swim," *Washington Post,* 19 July 1933, 9.

54 Heather Addison, *Hollywood and the Rise of Physical Culture,* American Popular History and Culture Series, ed. Jerome Nadelhaft (New York: Routledge, 2003).

55 Antoinette Donnelly, "Eleanor Holm, Swim Star, Disproves Old 'Rig Muscle' Bogy That Athletic Training Destroys Feminine Beauty," *Chicago Daily Tribune,* 11 August 1933, 21.

56 Donald J. Mrozek, "Sport in American Life: From National Health to Personal Fulfillment, 1890-1940," in Grover, *Fitness in American Culture,* 18-46.

57 Addison, *Hollywood and the Rise of Physical Culture,* 38.

58 Kathy Peiss, *Hope in a Jar: The Making of America's Beauty Culture* (New York: Henry Holt, 1998).

59 Dorothy Wooldridge, "Do Athletics Destroy Girlish Beauty?" *Los Angeles Times,* 18 December 1932, I5.

60 Ibid.

61 Florenz Ziegfeld Jr., "Behind the Scenes in Beauty Land," *Atlanta Constitution,* 7 August 1921, D1.

62 Bernarr Macfadden, "Marry a Swimmer," *Evening Graphic,* n.d., clipping in *WSA News,* March 1926, 1.

63 Banner, *American Beauty,* 264.

64 Thierry Terret, "Sports and Erotica: Erotic Postcards of Sportswomen during France's Annes Folles," *Journal of Sport History* 29, 2 (Summer 2002): 280.

65 Lears, *Fables of Abundance,* 117.

66 "Director Brenon First to Exhibit Nudity on Screen," *Washington Post,* 2 March 1924, AA3.
67 Banner, *American Beauty,* 264.
68 Clipping from unidentified newspaper, 17 July 1926, scrapbook, William Killingley Collection, Dover Museum, Dover, UK.
69 Milton Bronner, "24-Karat Grit; That's Lillian Cannon Who Will Tackle Channel," *The Bee* (Danville, VA), 26 June 1926, 5; Untitled article, *Coshocton Tribune,* 14 May 1926, 6.
70 Jack McCallum, "Unflagging," *Sports Illustrated,* 14 August 2000, 52.
71 Quoted in Kelli Anderson, "The Other Side of Jenny," *Sports Illustrated for Women,* November-December 2000, 119.
72 Rick Reilly, "Bare in Mind," *Sports Illustrated,* 4 September 2000, 112.
73 For a discussion of the media's role in objectifying women (often without their collusion) and perpetuating gender stereotypes, see Pamela J. Creedon, "Women, the Media and Sport: Creating and Reflecting Gender Values," in *Women, the Media and Sport: Challenging Gender Values,* ed. Pamela J. Creedon (Thousand Oaks, CA: Sage, 1994), 3-27; Mary Jo Kane and Susan Greendorfer, "The Media's Role in Accommodating and Resisting Stereotyped Images of Women in Sport," in Creedon, *Women, the Media and Sport,* 28-44; Pamela J. Creedon, "Women in Toyland: A Look at Women in American Newspaper Sports Journalism," in Creedon, *Women, the Media and Sport,* 67-107; Michael A. Messner, "Sports and Male Domination: The Female Athlete as Contested Ideological Terrain," in *Women, Sport, and Culture,* ed. Susan Birrell and Cheryl Cole (Champlain, IL: Human Kinetics, 1994), 65-80; and Nancy Theberge, "A Content Analysis of Print Media Coverage of Gender, Women, and Physical Activity," *Journal of Applied Sport Psychology* 3 (1991): 36-48.

8

Shades of Change: Suntanning and the Interwar Years

Devon Hansen Atchison

Coco Chanel was one of the most admired and emulated European women of the early twentieth century. Her signature black dress pushed black to the heights of fashion. When she accidentally singed some of her hair while getting ready for a night at the opera, she simply chopped off the dead hair with a pair of household scissors and made her way to the show. Short hair, which had been on the fringes of high fashion for some time, became widely popular after her public appearance with it.

And when Chanel changed her vacation spot and her skin colour in the 1920s, the world paid heed. During that decade, she began holidaying in the south of France, long seen as an undesirable vacation destination, with nothing more to offer than sand and blazing sunshine. Nobody wanted a tan, that emblem of the agrarian, poor, working class; those few poor painters who did venture to the south shielded themselves from exposure to the sun. But when Coco Chanel began frequenting the area, it quickly became a hotspot. Even more notable, according to suntanning lore, Chanel got a tan on the Duke of Westminster's yacht during an early 1920s journey from Paris to Cannes. With that, the suntan, which had once been considered a blemish, rapidly entered into fashion consciousness.[1] As was so often the case with Chanel, she did not actually initiate this trend: rather, when she adopted something, its popularity proliferated.[2]

This rising attractiveness of suntanning was a surprising development – in the early twentieth century, the tan was seen as distasteful and as a marker of working-class social status. Tanning was promoted or expected only among certain groups – namely, sickly children, tubercular patients, and some working-class women who got inadvertent suntans while enjoying precious leisure time at parks, beaches, and outdoor areas.[3] But when Chanel showed off her accidental tan in the early 1920s, tanning left the domain of the marginalized and became mainstream, first in Europe and soon in America.

Though Chanel may have propelled tanning into the American zeitgeist, a number of additional factors converged during the 1920s to allow for its rising popularity and its seeming permanence in American culture. Most important was America's evolution from a producer to a consumer nation in the first three decades of the twentieth century. The growing attention to consumption led fashions to change, new ideals of femininity to emerge, and advertisers to tout identities rather than the actual products they were selling. That suntanning became more than just a passing fad was due to the emphasis that American society placed on female beauty and the use of appearance-altering products such as cosmetics or lotions to heighten it. Advertisements prodded women to embrace European fashion and new visions of femininity, but they simultaneously addressed emerging cultural ideals shaped by American women. In particular, women's growing rejection of Victorian morality and traditional feminine conduct in the 1920s helped pave the way for more risqué behaviour and fashions. Many young Americans embraced a freer lifestyle that upended notions of morality and traditional gender behaviour, while enjoying the new creature comforts made possible by technological advancement.[4] American women increasingly flaunted their new freedom by wearing cosmetics, skimpy bathing costumes, and even skimpier clothing, all of which would help cement suntanning's place in early-twentieth-century consumption and visions of the American dream.

Additionally, in the early part of the twentieth century, Americans saw their work week diminish by almost ten hours, offering them more leisure time.[5] Industries such as film rapidly gained popularity as working-class Americans, who also now had disposable income to go along with their leisure time, flocked to the theatres.[6] And as people began enjoying their newfound leisure moments in public, they also began to spend money on their appearance, purchasing stockings, lipstick, and other consumer goods.[7] By the 1920s, leisure time and leisure spending had become part of American life. This was so much the case that even when the Great Depression struck, Americans still focused on leisure activity; getting a tan cost nothing, which was one reason why it became even more popular during the thirties.

With this novel attention to mass consumption, mass culture, and leisure time, Americans saw a new way of life and a new standard of living emerge;

cultural arbiters referred to these new activities as modern. As a result, sun-tanning became a symbol of America's attention to modernity and an illustration of changing gendered behaviours for women and changing consumer behaviours for all Americans.

The New Consumerism

As Americans of the 1920s focused on the new consumption of the era, adver-tisers and producers tapped into this and began marketing new products directly to women, with an emphasis on the link between their products and modern behaviour. Since tanning was considered a symbol of modernity, skin became the place where the badge of modernity was worn. Accordingly, advertisers addressed the trend, particularly in the interwar years, by concentrating on skin products such as lotions, soaps, and cosmetics, and on skimpier bathing suits. For example, one of the most successful skin care brands of the period, Jergens, dramatically altered its marketing strategy to match the changing times. Earlier ads had depicted Jergens as a lotion for workers and housewives, but by the 1920s, the company began to highlight the attributes of its products for sun-tanned women. One Jergens ad for Woodbury Soap depicted "the Fashionable Summer colonies at Newport and Bar Harbor [where] 169 women tell why they find this soap best for their skin ... Never were the women as beautiful as now – like tropical flowers in their brilliant sports frocks; their cheeks touched to carnation by sun and wind, arms and throats delicately sun-browned."[8] Advertisers underscored the "fashionable" nature of suntanning to encourage American women to buy more.

As a result, tanning – and touting a product's link to it – became increasingly popular. *Advertising and Selling* magazine reported in 1929 that "the vogue for tan is with us, and the wise buyer has availed himself of this trend to increase the sales of his department." The writer went on to lambaste companies that had yet to debut a suntan cosmetic and advertisers who had not yet used tanning as a marketing strategy.[9] As advertisers, producers, and other cultural mediators became aware of the power of suntanning throughout the late 1920s and the 1930s, magazines increased the numbers of both prescriptive articles and ads promoting the pastime. Ads for makeup, lotions, bathing suits, food, and bever-ages were particularly apt to refer to tanning.

This new strategy emerged because advertising studies of skin care products revealed that American notions about suntanning had changed by the interwar years. Gone were the negative associations that had appeared in 1920s surveys, which had depicted tanning as troublesome.[10] By the 1930s, one of the largest advertising agencies of the time, J. Walter Thompson, conducted surveys revealing that women were now using lotions to soften, rather than whiten, their skin.[11]

J. Walter Thompson also undertook studies of the newly emerging market of sun lotion products. In its 1937-38 campaign for Skol, a popular suntan cream, the company examined sales trends for tanning lotions and similar products, and it performed consumer investigations on sunburn preparations. Its first study, conducted in two coastal towns in September 1937, found that "of 229 persons interviewed, 140 – 41.3 percent – have used a sunburn preparation this summer" and that "53.4 percent of those using a sunburn preparation, use it more than 10 times during the summer."[12] By 1938, suntan creams and sunburn preparations were high sellers across the nation.[13] More Americans than ever were going to the beach and wanted tans but hoped to prevent or remedy sunburn. J. Walter Thompson's clients and other producers responded by creating more suncare products to meet consumer demand.

As a complement to these goods, new makeup was produced that reflected the popular trend. In the late 1930s, J. Walter Thompson also conducted a number of studies for the makeup division of Pond's; in particular, it surveyed women regarding shades of face powder, including a suntan shade. Pond's had developed an earlier version of suntan powder, but it wished to stay on top of the bronzed makeup market. As women began "vetoing a pallid white skin or a deeply burned one" for "a nice, moderate biscuit tone," Pond's tested a new, more palatable shade with forty-five women in the South, all of whom were tanned to some degree.[14] The survey concluded that "apparently a slight tan is more popular this season than the dark tan women acquired previously ... The New Sun Tan Powder looked better and appeared more suitable to the sun tanned skins. It seemed to give the 'tan' a glow and blended with the skin tones while the Old Powder appeared heavy and dark."[15] Rather than merely following the trend of tanning as a whole, Pond's followed the desires of its customers in order to find the perfect suntan shade.

Advertisers and consumers alike drove the consumer market during the interwar years; advertisers associated products with modernity and modern behaviour, thus increasing the popularity of both the products and the activities; for their part, American consumers pushed advertisers to respond to the popular trends, such as suntanning, that they were now enjoying. Products directed at women particularly demonstrated this relationship; the ads for these goods consistently used the trends to influence their buyers but also responded to the trends their buyers were participating in. By advertising about and to the new and modern woman of the 1920s, companies drew more women into consumption.

For example, advertisers began underscoring the popularity of European styles and ways of living, closely linking Europe with modernity and class. In particular, Paris and Parisian trendsetters were increasingly presented as authorities on fashion. Coco Chanel was the most obvious example of this, but advertisers drew other connections as well. American monthlies offered Parisian patterns, boasting that "'the line of Paris, the finish of Paris, the charm of Paris, may be had in any home.'"[16] An ad in the *Ladies' Home Journal* claimed,

> "It's Smart to be Sun-Tanned!" The fad has swept the chic resorts of Europe and America. First the Lido, then Cannes, Le Touquet, Palm Beach, Newport, Southampton. Now everyone, everywhere, by lake and sea, in mountains and in country, is seeking her place in the sun, toasting her skin to a delightful brown. The fad began literally out of the clear blue sky. A Parisian elegante was ailing. She was advised to bathe in the summer sun.[17]

Women who wanted to be Parisian-chic knew they needed to do the same.

Mass-produced images similarly affected women's conceptions of beauty in the 1920s as visions of glamorous movie stars, Parisian elegantes, wealthy debutantes, and cutting-edge flappers flooded magazines, ads, and other media. These images, which were intended to influence women's consumer choices, depicted women of differing cultures and ethnicities on the same page for the first time.[18] In addition, advertisers spoke to the new conceptions of gender and beauty that women of the 1920s created for themselves, as they rejected the strictures of Victorian ideology. Their ads seemed to have succeeded, for makeup, fashion, and enhanced beauty were the order of the day. And by the 1930s, suntanning lotions and, more notably, tinted face powder and bronzers had become major staples in the medicine cabinets and makeup drawers of American women.[19]

These powders and bronzers also appealed to the young adult female population of America that, for the first time in the nation's history, embraced cosmetic use. This was a result of the new emphasis on appearance and the rejection of traditional behaviour that was so prevalent among 1920s American youth. Their use of makeup changed long-held beliefs about the immorality of cosmetic use.

Prior to the 1920s, women who wore visible makeup were marked, figuratively and literally, as "painted women"; prevailing views condemned wearing makeup as over-sexualized and improper. Any alteration of the skin was socially and morally suspect. Thus, accidental sunburns or tans invariably led nineteenth-century women to seek quick remedies. One such woman, reddened by the sun during an outdoor charity event, turned to a close friend for a homeopathic treatment that would quickly and discreetly bring her face back to its desired tone of "polished whiteness."[20]

Yet among the working class at the turn of the century, some women were already beginning to paint their faces.[21] Additionally, women in the upper class began wearing makeup during this period, again emulating high-fashion Parisian women. But it was not until suntanning became popular that makeup manufacturers began to advertise their products' ability to improve appearance and skin tone. In 1925, makeup ads in American women's magazines increased dramatically, with a particular focus on the tan. That year, Pert Rouge advised women that their cheeks should be glowing, Bourjois's Manon Lescaut Face Powder claimed that "summer sun is a constant reminder that beauty is at least skin deep," and Tangee Rouge told women, "When you're in the spotlight of the sun, you need color – natural color – color that stays on in spite of wind, sun, [and] waves."[22] The simultaneous popularity of makeup and suntanning was no accident. Makeup use and tanning, both of which altered the skin's colour and appearance, were part of the same trend. Because it created a vast new market, existing products jumped on the bandwagon, new products were developed to meet changing needs and desires, advertisers and magazines promoted and propelled the trend, and American women began purchasing more and more products to change their skin's appearance. A popular advertising trade magazine congratulated Macy's department store, in 1929, for "step[ping] forward and capitaliz[ing] on the sun-tan mode in cosmetics by installing a Sun-Tan Shop in the toilet goods department ... That the consumer is actually fascinated by the becomingness of sunburned skin is shown by the fact that the Sun-Tan Shop at Macy's is besieged by customers."[23] This new market and the infusion of women's dollars into it constituted a major reason why a darkened skin colour was more than a passing fancy in American culture.

By 1929, American cosmetics and perfume manufacturers had proliferated, nearly doubling their numbers since the turn of the century and netting a profit almost ten times as large. Sociologist Robert Lynd wrote that Americans, rich and poor, were hooked on the cosmetics industry, spending an estimated $700 million per year on makeup by 1929.[24] One Princess Pat advertisement went so far as to ask, "Are you one who knows there is a new fashion in use of rouge? And in your estimation is it a fashion to last?"[25] Women were called on to adopt makeup, not as a passing fancy, but as a style to last and a permanent symbol of American beauty and American fashion authority. In this way, advertisers could, in later years, rely less on the authority of Parisian fashion and more on the selling power of American products and styles. And American women listened, purchasing about "26,500 tons of skin lotion ... 8750 tons of tinted foundation ... and 2375 tons of rouge" per year in the 1920s.[26]

This rising popularity of makeup suggested that the most notable changes of the era had to do with appearance, specifically the way in which women presented themselves, or were expected to present themselves, in public. One young women's tome, *Any Girl Can Be Good-Looking,* warned teenage women, "Everybody is thinking more these days about good looks. The bar has been raised for the jump. The passing mark is higher. Being good looking is no longer optional ... There is no place in the world for women who are not." Those less confident would have found little reassurance in the description of the world that awaited them: "Competition is so keen and ... the world moves so fast that we simply can't afford not to sell ourselves on sight. What if we are kind? And quick-witted? And make wonderful biscuits? ... People who pass us on the street can't know that we're clever and charming unless we look it."[27]

Advice such as this and the message of advertisers pressured women to focus on their looks and to follow fashion. Suntanning was one of the most prominent ways that women could look hip, alter their appearance, and enhance their beauty (naturally and almost effortlessly, to boot!).

This is not to say that all Americans accepted the new trend without comment. Cultural arbiters were less accepting, at first, of the tanned woman. Magazines decried the demise of the genteel woman and her Victorian morals. In 1901, as historian Dorothy Brown noted, the refined lady was depicted in *Atlantic Monthly* as "the steel-engraving lady, who ... sat peacefully looking out from the casement window of her apartment. 'Her eyes were dreamy, and her embroidery frame lay idly upon the little stand beside her.' Her sleeve 'fell back, revealing the alabaster whiteness of her hand and wrist.'" This woman was tranquil and happy with her traditional pastimes and appearance. Her opposite, the Gibson Girl, whose image began to grace magazines at the turn of the century, shunned everything that the genteel woman stood for: "Sunburned and fit, the Gibson Girl wore a 'short skirt and heavy square-toed shoes, a mannish collar, cravat and vest, and a broad-brimmed felt hat tipped jauntily on one side.'" She was unafraid of men, concerned only with her own happiness and desires, educated, extroverted, athletic, and confident.[28] The Gibson Girl was not warmly or immediately welcomed by either the *Atlantic Monthly* or the American public; she was too mannish, too independent, and too tanned.

The New Woman of the early 1900s, personified by the Gibson Girl, represented a stereotype of the suffragettes and other non-traditional women who were beginning to gain notice (often not positive) in American culture.[29] In the 1920s, the Gibson Girl was joined by her newer and more controversial sister, the flapper. Though contempt for these new female personas persisted, many women began to embrace the freer, more beautiful version of the independent woman; gone was the "steel-engraving lady" who had been the model of femininity at the turn of the century. As Brown remarked, the flapper of the 1920s was

> breezy, slangy and informal in manner; slim and boyish in form, covered with silk and fur that clung to her as close as onion skin; with carmined lips, plucked eyebrows and close-fitting helmet of hair; gay, plucky and confident ... She cared little for approval or disapproval and went about her 'act,' whether it were a Marathon dancing contest, driving an automobile at seventy miles an hour, a Channel swim, a political campaign or a social-service settlement.[30]

The flapper represented a generation of new, independent women – new compared to her feminist predecessor, who was frequently depicted as rejecting marriage for career, dressing unfashionably, and behaving improperly on issues of decorum. If contemporary magazines are to be believed, the flapper was flirty, fashionable, and free. To be sure, not all women saw themselves as flappers – the embodiment of the New Woman – but a few habits of the flappers became increasingly popular among all women, such as wearing makeup, opting for shorter skirts, and enjoying and participating in various amusements, from movies to bathing beauty contests.[31]

Suntanning quickly became a marker of a woman's new-found sense of rebellion, her rejection of Victorian morality, and her attention to beauty and outward appearance. With this embrace of tanning, coupled with the growing strength of the image of the flapper and the new woman, advertisers began asking women new questions that straddled the divide between propriety and impropriety, old and new, modest and stylish. Pond's Cream asked women the ever-important question:

> What kind of skin will you have at the end of the summer? Burned, coarsened, rough? Or fair, smooth and soft? ... Sunburn has a certain charm – if you can keep it within bounds ... A golden tan is a stunning accompaniment to the sports costume. But all too quickly it thickens your skin, makes it dry and leathery.[32]

Women were urged to tan in moderation, to control their appearance by walking the fine line between the fashionable and the gauche, and a number of lotion makers in the mid-twenties created products that promised to help them achieve that balance. The Pond's advertisement quoted above and many others like it also addressed the New Woman of the 1920s who went outdoors to play sports or for some other liberated reason.[33] Advertising and fashion often dictated women's behaviour and appearance; advertisers had only to offer women the suggestion of power and strength to sell them not only a product, but an image. But, of course, women themselves had embraced power and strength, a development that advertisers exploited when they shaped their campaigns.

Unsurprisingly, as tanned skin became increasingly popular, as suntanning posed greater challenges to tradition, other moral battles broke out. For example, as women began to crave both a tan and the leisure time spent in achieving it, fashion designers presented skimpier bathing suits to expose more skin to the sun. Initially, the modern bathing suit was a fitted tank suit that bared the arms, perhaps a bit of the upper chest, and anywhere from the upper thigh to the knees down; it revealed very little skin. Nevertheless, this practical but form-fitting suit was banned in many parts of the country during the early 1920s.[34] At the end of the decade, designer Elsa Schiaparelli introduced Parisians to a tank suit with a fairly high-cut bottom, but Americans, still struggling with revealing so much skin, resisted going down the same path. Instead, most American bathing suits still resembled a modern-day shorts and tank-top set.[35] And even they were seen as a dramatic departure from the voluminous, all-encompassing costumes that women wore until about 1925.[36]

However, the growing popularity of the flapper's raised hemline, coupled with the new attention to female athleticism and female suntanning, eventually helped make the smaller swimsuit more acceptable, as Marilyn Morgan illustrates in Chapter 7 of this volume. Once again, American women took the necessary steps, in this case trimming swimsuits to meet their athletic and fashion needs, and transforming public opinion in the process. As a result, fashion designers presented increasingly sexy bathing suits to the public, such as Jean Patou's two-piece suit of the late 1920s, which was "'cut down very much at the back for sunbathing.'"[37] This suit and others like it opened the door for greater risks in the following years.

By the 1930s, the transformation of beach wear had become even more marked. Influenced by the knee-length skirts that had enjoyed popularity during the twenties, women became increasingly comfortable baring their legs and parts of their bodies in public. Beach pyjamas, first introduced by Coco Chanel during the 1920s, appeared on American beaches in the 1930s, with their wide, flared-leg pants and sleeveless, often backless tops. Beach dresses showed even more skin, cutting well above the knee and completely revealing shoulders and backs.[38] These 1930s fashions allowed women to take risks, at least in the dress sense, and to be sexually alluring.

One of the most popular bathing suit companies of the time, Jantzen began advertising in magazines and (what better place?) outdoors. Magazine ads for its nearly backless swimsuit suggested that the wearer would be "Strikingly Individual!"[39] And it offered "figure-control in a swimming suit" that would "gently mold the body into graceful lines."[40] Jantzen's magazine ads promoted individuality and healthy activity ("Keep Trim, Keep Fit, Swim" was a popular Jantzen slogan during the 1930s), because, as its Red Diving Girl emblem reminded women, sunbathing and swimsuits revealed a woman's body to all, and her body should look as good as possible.

To make its point even more directly, Jantzen created a series of outdoor advertisements in the 1930s. The most famous of these were light-up billboards on the Atlantic City Boardwalk, featuring Jantzen's trademark outline of a slim woman, diving in a form-fitting bathing suit. Jantzen maintained these prominent signs in popular beach areas well through the 1930s and beyond. The image lent a sense of permanence to skimpy bathing suits and to the activities -- swimming, tanning, and diving – that went with them.[41]

Another series of Jantzen billboard ads from the 1930s illustrates how far bathing suits had come, thanks in no small part to the growing popularity of suntanning. Artist George Petty drew the ads, most of which featured a beautiful woman, looking gorgeous in her fit-like-a-glove Jantzen suit and golden tan. Two of Petty's illustrations also depicted a bronze Adonis, looking equally ravishing in his swim gear and perfect tan. The message was obvious – be athletic, watch your figure, wear Jantzen, and be tanned to enjoy ultimate happiness.[42] Overt female sexuality was no longer banished; rather, by the 1930s, it was celebrated, and wearing a new, sexy bathing suit to get a great tan or to show it off was becoming the order of the day.

Swimsuits were not the only articles of clothing that were affected by the rising popularity of suntanning. Fashion magazines realized that a tan was the equivalent of an article of clothing or at least an accessory to clothing. Accordingly, many advised women on how best to complement their tans. One *Ladies' Home Journal* article from July 1929, titled "Paris Creates a Midsummer Mood," remarked, "Interesting notes from Paris to be considered in selecting colours for Paris designs are the predominance of yellow – a becoming color to almost all sun-tanned skins."[43] Short skirts, sportswear, dresses with plunging necklines, and short-sleeved or sleeveless outfits all seemed to cater to, or require, a tan. The backless evening dress also enjoyed popularity, as women desired to show off the fruits of their suntanning labour. As exposing legs and other body parts became en vogue in the fashion world, getting the perfect tan became a fashion must.[44]

Suntanning constituted one way in which women could continue to reject the authority of Victorian morality, even as many other forms of this attitude would fade during the following decades. In this period, women helped change morality, fashion, and behaviour. Makeup, short skirts, bobbed haircuts, and smoking were all introduced as new ways for women to demonstrate their approval of this change. Suntanning also transformed the way that women behaved as consumers (and were regarded as consumers). It pushed the limits of appropriate dress, makeup, and feminine behaviour. It provided such a useful vehicle for implementing change that its permanence very quickly seemed a foregone conclusion. Even as the 1930s erased some of the gains women had previously made, tanning was one of the few transformations that persisted as America defined and redefined itself, and as American women grappled with who they had been, who they were, and who they wanted to be. In fact, as tanning began to challenge the larger issues of race and ethnicity, as well as class and leisure in the 1930s, it would cease being a trend and would become part of the American ideal.

The Great Depression and Leisure Time

Women dramatically influenced fashion and consumption in the 1920s, and the New Woman significantly altered traditional gender behaviour. But when the Great Depression hit in 1929, the nation hearkened back to traditional gender roles; for women, this often meant that the achievements, the new behaviours, and the attention to consumption of the recent past were put on the backburner.[45] Given this, one would expect that leisure time and the money that leisure required would also revert to older modes. Yet Americans were reluctant to abandon their hard-earned leisure time; as they grappled with the difficult economic realities of the 1930s, they simultaneously searched for new, affordable forms of entertainment. Suntanning, which had long marked wealth despite its democratic nature, grew as an affordable form of leisure and a way to diminish class differences. The bathing beach, a new forum for leisure in the 1930s, helped tanning become more entrenched in American life. Prior to the 1930s, many Americans frequented beaches such as Atlantic City's Boardwalk but did not lie out to get a tan. Beaches were areas for strolling and even for relaxing, but those who used them were expected to stay under the cover of an umbrella or a sunshade and always to be fully clothed.[46] In the 1920s, women's bathing suits were "only somewhat less voluminous than everyday street wear."[47] But by the 1930s, swimsuits had become more wearable and more revealing, and sunbathing on the beach was one of America's favourite pastimes.

Another important development that led to the widespread popularity of the bathing beach was the availability of the automobile in the thirties. Ford's affordable Model A debuted in the 1920s, and by the 1930s, there were over 25 million passenger cars on America's roads.[48] Though it seemed somewhat antithetical that automobile sales continued to be high during the Great Depression, one housewife put it best in 1929: "The car is the only pleasure we have." For many, the car ranked above electricity, a telephone, and even food.[49] Automobiles opened the horizons of leisure: for the price of a tank of gas, a family or a group of friends could head down to the beach, whether it was fifteen minutes or an hour away, and spend the day playing in the ocean or lying on the sand. No longer were they limited to catching a few stolen rays in the back-yard. Now they could emulate their wealthy French counterparts lounging on the shores of the Riviera. It seemed unsurprising, then, that bathing beaches, and suntanning on them, became popular during the Depression era.

Advertisements began selling vacation spots for their sunny beach-side locales, such as one 1931 invitation from Southern California to "Cool Off Beside the Pacific."[50] And many travel brochures urged vacationers to visit New Mexico, Arizona, Colorado, and various other spots for their sunshine.[51] The abundance of these ads and brochures illustrates that tanning had become widespread and was an effective marketing tool. It had become a viable leisure activity and a way for many to enjoy the otherwise unattainable lifestyle of the middle class.[52]

Advertisers capitalized on the growing popularity of beach-going. Cosmetic manufacturer Marie Earle, for example, also tailored its ads and products to the ever-growing popularity of suntanning with the introduction of its Camera Beach Kit. This featured "all the beauty aids you need for civilized sunning," including "a smooth-spreading Lipstick and box of Perfection Powder, both in shades to flatter your summer complexion." The kit provided everything needed to achieve the perfect tan and suggested that women who used it would be spending their time "motoring, week-ending, on all jaunts away from the dress-ing table." Further, it offered all Americans a way to tan in a "civilized" manner – in other words, the kit constituted a way to live the proper, middle-class life for relatively little money.[53]

Leisure time also spoke to Americans' ongoing struggles with issues of class. In the past, leisure had been seen as the domain of the wealthy. But the difficult times of the 1930s, coupled with the growth of consumption in America during the early twentieth century, infused leisure activities into all classes. Most ads and cultural discussions about leisure promoted a middle-class version of it, one that some could enjoy and many more could strive to reach. Prescriptive literature, for example, promoted the now entrenched pastime of sunbathing and gave Americans visual ideas on how to spend their leisure time in an appropriate manner. By discussing tanning in relation to recreation, beauty, and even Hollywood, magazines further embedded it in the lexicon of American feminine culture. *Life* magazine, a general-interest periodical catering to the average middle-class American, ran a number of articles and photo montages about outdoor life. These pieces showed young men and women enjoying a refreshing swim, a "Beach Party at Newport Beach with some of California's handsomest models," and even an Olympic swimmer, Eleanor Holm, in a bathing suit, with the message, "Most girl swimmers make good pictures. Even those who are not especially pretty look attractive in tight bathing suits."[54] In these difficult times, offering Americans not only happiness, but also status and beauty, and all in one affordable package, was powerful. Suntanning did all of this.

Even before the Depression began, the campaigns of many advertisers served to reduce the differences between the wealthy and the less fortunate. J. Walter Thompson took this concept a step further during the Great Depression. Its 1930s surveys revealed that women were still using beauty products, and it hoped that its clients would not lose customers during the tough times. Thus, its ads and those of other companies sought to diminish the gap between the rich and the poor even more. For example, Elizabeth Arden's Sun-Pruf Cream, which promised women "a rich, uniform tan" and the prevention of "a nasty burn," depicted beautiful, wealthy-looking women. This, along with the name "Elizabeth Arden" and the company's Fifth Avenue address, suggested, at the very least, that a tan could help ordinary consumers look like the darlings of Fifth Avenue.[55]

An ad for Dorothy Gray Sunburn Cream made this connection even more explicit in its tagline "Where Fifth Avenue Meets the Sea." The ad stated that "New York's loveliest women dash in for one last luxurious facial before leaving for the seaside" and claimed that their favoured tan was "a cool, even café au lait shade," which could be achieved with "a generous film of Dorothy Gray Sunburn Cream."[56] To the Depression-era woman, the loudest message was that a suntan would allow her to share something with even the wealthiest society women.

Makeup advertising followed a similar pattern. Helena Rubenstein, a glamorous New York cosmetics manufacturer, provided women with their "Cosmetic Portrait for Summer," complete with Sunburn Oil for "a smart golden tan," Sunproof Cream to protect skin from "the actinic rays which burn and age the skin," and "the new dusky Terra Cotta or radiant Mauresque Powder and gorgeous Terra Cotta rouge" to complete the "Cosmetic Portrait of the Dashing Summer-Girl." Helena Rubenstein's suntan products offered women the chance to be on a level with the women who frequented "the gold sands of Malibu ... at Biarritz and Cap d'Antibes."[57] Her salon even featured an early version of the tanning bed, where "clients stretched out on sun-loungers lying on real sand, heated by ultraviolet recessed ceiling lamps which 'bounced' back rays from an aluminum surface"; the bed guaranteed users the exact shade they desired.[58] Helena Rubenstein offered women choice and control – over which shade they desired, over whether to tan or not – and the middle-class appearance of golden skin.

Likewise, a Camay Soap ad from June 1934 told women, "You cannot, of course, change the contour of your chin or the color of your eyes. But you can change – and change very much for the better – the condition of your skin."[59] The changing of one's skin by getting a tan gave women control over their bodies in ways that only fashion had before.

Whatever the marketing strategy, it was obvious by the mid-thirties, particularly as a new, hopeful spirit washed over the Depression-fraught country, that suntanning was finally a permanent part of middle-class American life. Though not all Americans belonged to the middle class in the thirties, middle-class status was equated with the American Dream, and many Americans would strive to attain or maintain middle-class status for the next fifty years. Once suntanning became part of what defined the middle class, it was here to stay.

Journalist Farnsworth Crowder wrote about California in 1936, arguing that its sunny climate led Californians on "an unapologetic pursuit of pleasure." The state had many stories of hard times and people just scraping by – witness the Joad family of John Steinbeck's novel *The Grapes of Wrath* – but upper- and middle-class Californians still managed to enjoy outdoor activities such as swimming, tennis, golf, barbecues, beach days, and backyard parties. California was fast becoming a trend-setting state, and the outdoor activities of middle- and upper-class Californians shaped American notions of the good life.[60] This equation of a suntan with middle-class status, then, ensured that tanning had become a part of the national identity – an identity that would change very little over the following decades.

Discussions about class status and leisure in the 1930s catapulted suntanning from a trend to a national pursuit. The 1930s brought trials and tribulations to many, but the decade was also a unique opportunity to forge new and unconventional paths in certain arenas. In particular, tanning opened up a discussion of race and ethnicity that changed the American ideal for years to come. By the end of the thirties, America had come to accept and celebrate altered skin colour and began to define an American by his or her skin colour. Yet this definition insisted that the authentic American's darkened skin was not permanently dark; African Americans and other dark-skinned people continued to be shunned.

Despite the limitations of this new definition of the American Dream, the permanence of suntanning illustrated the dramatic changes that women and stereotypes about women underwent during the interwar years. American women took advantage of the post–First World War emphasis on modernity and used it to modernize and liberalize images of femininity. No doubt, they were pulled into the consumption of modern products and goods that allowed them to challenge tradition, but more importantly, they themselves pushed advertisers, cultural arbiters, and mainstream Americans to accept a different, independent, freer woman. Suntanning, an obvious symbol of this new, modern woman, became a part of the American Dream, not just because American culture popularized it but, more significantly, because women forced American culture to do so.

Notes

1   Ruth G. Sikes, "The History of Suntanning: A Love/Hate Affair," *Journal of Aesthetic Science* 1, 2 (May 1998): 6-7; Kerry Segrave, *Suntanning in 20th Century America* (Jefferson, NC: McFarland, 2005), 3; Pond's advertisement, *Ladies' Home Journal*, July 1929, 31; Laura Torbet, ed., *Helena Rubenstein's Book of the Sun* (New York: Times Books, 1979), 5.
2   Marcel Haedrich, *Coco Chanel: Her Life, Her Secrets*, trans. Charles Lam Markmann (Boston: Little, Brown, 1972), 118-40; Rhonda K. Garelick, "The Layered Look: Coco Chanel and Contagious Celebrity," in *Dandies: Fashion and Finesse in Art and Culture*, ed. Susan Fillin-Yeh (New York: New York University Press, 2001), 45-46.
3   Kathy Peiss, *Cheap Amusements: Working Women and Leisure in Turn-of-the-Century New York* (Philadelphia: Temple University Press, 1986), 115-23; D. MacDougall King, *The Battle with Tuberculosis and How to Win It; A Book for the Patient and His Friends* (Philadelphia: J.B. Lippincott, 1917), 18.
4   Gary S. Cross, *An All-Consuming Century: Why Commercialism Won in Modern America* (New York: Columbia University Press, 2000), 39-40.
5   Ibid., 18.
6   Steven J. Ross, *Working-Class Hollywood: Silent Film and the Shaping of Class in America* (Princeton: Princeton University Press, 1998), xii-xiii, 4-9; Richard Maltby, "Sticks, Hicks and Flaps: Classical Hollywood's Generic Conception of Its Audiences," in *Identifying Hollywood's*

Audiences: Cultural Identity and the Movies, ed. Richard Maltby and Melvyn Stokes (London: British Film Institute, 1999), 38; Melvyn Stokes, "Female Audiences of the 1920s and Early 1930s," in Maltby and Stokes, *Identifying Hollywood's Audiences,* 43-44.

7   Peiss, *Cheap Amusements.*

8   Woodbury Soap advertisement, *Ladies' Home Journal,* July 1926, 31.

9   Marie DuBois, "What Is Sun-Tan Doing to Cosmetics?" *Advertising and Selling,* 12 June 1929, 64.

10 "Investigations, 1922-1925; Investigation among College Women," December 1922, J. Walter Thompson Company Archives (JWT), 16MM Reel Research Reports, Reel 45, Duke University Archives, Raleigh, North Carolina (DUA).

11 "Investigation of Consumer's Sending for Sample of Jergen's Lotion," May 1934, JWT, 16MM Reel Research Reports, Reel 46, DUA; Jergens advertisement, 1930, JWT, DUA.

12 "Consumer Investigation on Sunburn Preparations," for Skol, September 1937, JWT, 16MM Reel Research Reports, Reel 233, DUA.

13 "Trend in Sales of Sun Tan Lotions ...," for Skol, August 1938, JWT, 16MM Reel Research Reports, Reel 233, DUA.

14 "Half-Baked," *Vogue,* 1 July 1935, 48-49.

15 "Report on Pond's New Sun Tan Powder," for Pond's, March 1935, JWT, 16MM Reel Research Reports, Reel 221, DUA.

16 Angela J. Latham, *Posing a Threat: Flappers, Chorus Girls and Other Brazen Performers of the American 1920s* (Hanover, NH: Wesleyan University Press, 2000), 32-33.

17 Pond's advertisement, *Ladies' Home Journal,* July 1929, 31.

18 Kathy Peiss, *Hope in a Jar: The Making of America's Beauty Culture* (New York: Henry Holt, 1998), 134.

19 "Report on Pond's New Sun Tan Powder," for Pond's, March 1935, JWT, 16MM Reel Research Reports, Reel 221, DUA; various research reports for Skol Suntan Cream, 1937 and 1938, JWT, 16MM Reel Research Reports, Reel 233, DUA.

20 Peiss, *Hope in a Jar,* 26.

21 Ibid., 54.

22 Pert Rouge advertisement, *Cosmopolitan,* July 1925, 197; Manon Lescaut Face Powder advertisement, *Cosmopolitan,* July 1925, 215; Tangee Rouge advertisement, *Cosmopolitan,* August 1925, 174.

23 DuBois, "What Is Sun-Tan Doing to Cosmetics?" 62, 64.

24 Robert S. Lynd, "The People as Consumers," in U.S. President's Committee on Social Trends, *Recent Social Trends in the United States* (New York: McGraw Hill, 1933), 1:889, 1:905. See Peiss, *Hope in a Jar,* 97.

25 Princess Pat advertisement, *Ladies' Home Journal,* June 1928, 181.

26 Lindy Woodhead, *War Paint: Madame Helena Rubenstein and Miss Elizabeth Arden: Their Lives, Their Times, Their Rivalry* (Hoboken, NJ: John Wiley and Sons, 2003), 148.

27 Hazel Rawson Cades, *Any Girl Can Be Good-Looking* (New York: D. Appleton, 1927), n.p. See Elizabeth Haiken, *Venus Envy: A History of Cosmetic Surgery* (Baltimore: Johns Hopkins University Press, 1997), 91.

28 Dorothy Brown, *Setting a Course: American Women in the 1920s* (Boston: Twayne, 1987), 30.

29 Feminist activists successfully gained suffrage with the Nineteenth Amendment in 1920 after a protracted battle for gender equality. Though the women's rights movement ceased to be as powerful or productive after the ratification of the amendment, a freer, more independent and often less feminine depiction of women became commonplace. The characteristics that had once described feminist suffragettes became attached very directly to the modern woman of the 1920s.

30 Brown, *Setting a Course*, 32.

31 Ibid., 183-84.

32 Pond's Cream advertisement, *Ladies' Home Journal*, August 1926, 45.

33 Latham, *Posing a Threat*, 96.

34 Ibid., 65-97.

35 Dilys E. Blum, *Shocking! The Art and Fashion of Elsa Schiaparelli* (New Haven: Yale University Press, 2003), 24; John Peacock, *20th Century Fashion: The Complete Sourcebook* (London: Thames and Hudson, 1993), 67.

36 Peacock, *20th Century Fashion*, 59.

37 Quoted in Linda Watson, *Vogue Twentieth Century Fashion: 100 Years of Style by Decade and Designer* (London: Carlton Books, 1999), 205.

38 Elizabeth Ewing, *History of Twentieth Century Fashion* (Totowa, NJ: Barnes and Noble, 1986), 113-14.

39 Jantzen advertisement, *Cosmopolitan*, July 1931, 117.

40 Jantzen advertisement, *Cosmopolitan*, July 1933, 107. For more on Jantzen swimsuits, see Chapter 7 in this volume.

41 Jantzen outdoor billboard photographs (Atlantic City Boardwalk), 16 July 1933, R.C. Maxwell Outdoor Advertising Collection, DB29, DUA.

42 George Petty Jantzen illustrations, 1937-38, Outdoor Advertising Association of America Archives, PN23, DUA.

43 "Paris Creates a Midsummer Mood," *Ladies' Home Journal*, July 1929, 28.

44 Ewing, *History of Twentieth Century Fashion*, 113-14.

45 Whereas women of the 1920s saw increased opportunities in politics, education, and employment, the financial crisis of the Great Depression reversed many of those gains, particularly in employment. With job opportunities scarce, popular culture pressured women to exit the workforce so that jobs would open up for the traditional breadwinners, men. Women's purchasing power, and thus their power as consumers, diminished because of the Great Depression.

46 Leslie Dorsey and Janice Devine, *Fare Thee Well: A Backward Look at Two Centuries of Historic American Hostelries, Fashion Spas and Seaside Resorts* (New York: Crown, 1964), 295.

47 Latham, *Posing a Threat*, 67.

48 Foster Rhea Dulles, *America Learns to Play: A History of Popular Recreation, 1607-1940* (New York: D. Appleton-Century, 1940), 318.

49 Quoted in ibid., 319.

50 "Cool Off Beside the Pacific," *Ladies' Home Journal*, July 1931, 101.

51 Albuquerque Civic Council, *Sunshine and Health in Albuquerque* (Albuquerque, NM: Albuquerque Civic Council, c. 1937); Tucson Sunshine – Climate Club, *Tucson, Arizona: Man-Building in the Sunshine Climate* (Tucson: Tucson Sunshine – Climate Club, [193-?]); Colorado Springs Chamber of Commerce, *Welcome to Colorado Springs: El Paso County, Colorado: The City of Sunshine* (Denver: The Service, [1925?]); all brochures are in the Denver Public Library Western History and Genealogy Department Collection, C917.8856 W449, Denver, Colorado.

52 Kevin Starr, *The Dream Endures: California Enters the 1940s* (New York: Oxford University Press, 1997), 4.

53 Marie Earle advertisement, *Vogue*, 15 July 1935, 73.

54 "*Life*'s Party," *Life*, 19 July 1937, 84; "*Life* Goes to a Beach Party," *Life*, 21 August 1939, 70-71; "Eleanor Holm Is Photogenic," *Life*, 9 August 1937, 10-11.

55 Sun-Pruf Cream advertisement, *Vogue*, 1 July 1935, 71.

56 Dorothy Gray Sunburn Cream advertisement, *Cosmopolitan*, July 1935, 97.

57   Helena Rubenstein advertisement, *Vogue,* 1 July 1935, 69.
58   Woodhead, *War Paint,* illustration on insert page.
59   Camay Soap advertisement, *Ladies' Home Journal,* June 1934, 43.
60   Starr, *The Dream Endures,* 3-4.

Part 3 MODERN GIRLS

.
.
.

9

Beauty Advice for the Canadian Modern Girl in the 1920s

Jane Nicholas

In the 29 September 1928 issue of the Canadian periodical *Saturday Night,* the resident beauty columnist "Valerie" responded as usual to letters from anxious Canadian women in need of special beauty advice. To "Peggy," Valerie replied, "Thank you for the kind words said about this paper and this column. I have indicated where you may get the cleansing cream – also the nourishing one. The homemade article of this nature is hardly worthwhile. There are ever so many good soaps nowadays of which you may take your choice but most modern women prefer a cleansing cream."[1] Valerie's response to Peggy's unprinted query is indicative of a number of important aspects of feminine modernity in Canada during the 1920s: women seeking advice on how to negotiate the increasingly complicated consumer scene, the position of the beauty expert as a trusted source of information, and the connection between appearing modern and specific mass-produced products. In dispensing advice, Valerie did more than offer beauty tips; she helped Canadian women navigate the modern scene, where new "techniques of appearing – the manner and means of execution of one's visual effects and status" – were intimately interwoven with consumer culture and modern feminine subjectivities.[2] As a "trusted expert" in becoming beautiful, Valerie, and others like her, provided Canadian women with important details on how to create and maintain modern, female bodies and the look of the Modern Girl as they helped to normalize, and at times contest, her appearance. Closely reading these columns along with the advertising and articles in key mass-market commercial Canadian magazines reveals the peculiarly modern mix of women's visibility, mass consumption, and objectification achieved through various techniques of appearing required for the thoroughly modern Canadian Millie.[3]

Bodies did not simply transform into being modern but were carefully produced through a host of techniques intimately connected with the culture of mass consumption. Women's bodies were situated at a critical juncture under modernity, and feminine visibility in public was a key aspect of modern life. As part of being modern, women experienced this intensification of the visual scene in a number of ways, one being new means of producing a modern body and another the intensification of the critical judgment of the performance of their bodies. Techniques of appearing became inherently tied to the consistent use of particular commodities, especially cosmetics, which helped to create a modern female subjectivity exemplified by the Modern Girl. *Chatelaine's* beauty columnist, Mab, summarized the work required when she wrote, "To-day, beauty demands that a woman be slender, graceful, and exceedingly well groomed. This is the age of revelation. We have no billowy skirts, false hair or veils to hide our defects, and eternal youth is the cry of the hour. For the most part beauty is not obtained or retained without a good deal of personal effort."[4] This particular and popular narrative of the 1920s was not the first to structure the critical judgment of women's bodies, but it significantly revealed the new level of intensity of women's appearance on the modern scene and the type of work expected to produce a modern female body.

The Modern Girl was deeply connected to commodity culture, and magazines with beauty culture "experts" played an important role in delineating modern femininities within the new logic of commodity culture, visuality, and display. As Penny Tinkler and Cheryl Krasnick Warsh have recently argued with regard to *Vogue,* magazines encouraged women "to imagine themselves as participants in the modern world and encouraged [them] to remake themselves as modern feminine subjects through their consumption practices."[5] Magazines and other periodicals were diverse in their composition, with editorials, articles, advertisements, and sometimes a number of columnists. As a result, they provide a heterogeneous voice, and although I draw from the multiple parts of the magazines, this chapter focuses on beauty expert columns and ads. If advertisers became modern "experts" on bodily care and techniques of appearing, the message of bodily preparation for women was also supported by magazine columns that usually reinforced advertisers' messages of body maintenance and consumption.[6] Both *Saturday Night* and *Chatelaine* contained regular beauty columns, which are an excellent source to explore how messages of consumption were reinforced and modified for Canadian women. *Saturday Night's* beauty columnist, Valerie, wrote a regular feature titled "The Dressing Table," and

Chatelaine's columnist Mab was the author of "The Promise of Beauty."[7] Columnists cultivated relationships with readers through regular monthly or bi-weekly features that were meant to provide direction and expertise to English-speaking women across the country that seemed more intimate, personal, and direct than advertisements or articles. The columnists followed a typical formula of discussing key issues related to beauty, fashion, and dieting, and also responded to individual letters and queries (either directly or indirectly), often providing glimpses into their own "real-life" experiences, beauty practices, and concerns. As a result, their columns created a sort of intimacy that worked especially well, given the type of personal advice sought by readers. Readers were also encouraged to write to their beauty columnist if they wanted personalized advice on how to improve their appearance. *Chatelaine* readers were told, "It may be that you are dissatisfied with the condition of your skin, your hair or your figure. Mab will be glad to answer your individual questions if you will write her in care of 'The Chatelaine,' enclosing a stamped addressed envelope." In the early 1920s, readers of the *Saturday Night* columnist were informed, "Correspondents throughout the breadth of this Dominion, so greatly blessed with cold cream and hair tonics, are warned that in future, all demands for private replies must be accompanied by a stamped and addressed envelope."[8] Valerie, like cold creams and hair tonics it seemed, was popular.

By critically reading these columns, this chapter explores how expert advice regarding techniques of appearing encouraged the production of modern female bodies in Canada during the 1920s, where women's bodies were embroidered with a sort of modern consumer magic that shored up the idea that goods were a necessary investment and encouraged their use in particular ways. It argues that the advice columns provided critical information to Canadian women on how to negotiate a complicated consumer scene focused on being modern and beautiful. Although I recognize such discourses of beauty as intensely problematic, I also examine the promises of pleasure that made the production of modern beauty potentially appealing. These advice columns, however limited, show the similarity and disjuncture of discourses of modern beauty in the Canadian context – discourses that differ greatly from that of interwar nationalism, which has dominated the historiography. Written by Canadians for Canadians, the columns show how a global (although seemingly American-propelled) discourse was suited to a particular landscape, and they subtly reveal a complicated relationship with the global Modern Girl. The appearance of the global Modern Girl in Canada came at a critical juncture in the wake of the First World War as Canadians were consciously trying to develop a (high) Canadian culture to match the country's more mature status. The anxieties over the Modern Girl's appearance were complicated by existing discourses of interwar nationalism and modernity.[9] What modernity meant to Canadians was dynamic and impermanent, but a few significant issues formed the crux of concern: an increasingly crowded urban environment, perceived changes in gender relations, the co-mingling of classes and races, new heterosocial amusements, mass consumption of goods, and the alleged disjuncture between past and present, which was frequently depicted as a generational clash between mothers and daughters.[10] The Modern Girl's behaviour epitomized the urban, industrial, machine-age modernity, where technology transformed space as well as public and private relations. To some Canadians in the 1920s who valued rural, agricultural society, her appearance marked the dangerous import of American culture and some of the more distasteful compromises of modern life, but to many others she was intimately appealing. Her ambivalent reception in Canada was matched by the conflict regarding her appearance in other locales, as Chapters 10 and 11 in this volume aptly reveal for Mexico City and Argentina.

In exploring this topic, I draw on a rich international literature on femininity, advertising, and the Modern Girl, and I focus on two Canadian publications: *Saturday Night* and *Chatelaine*.[11] Both provide excellent examples of the types of advertising and advice that appeared in commercial mass media magazines. Whereas *Saturday Night* was intended for both men and women, *Chatelaine* was (and still is) a women's magazine. First published in March 1928, *Chatelaine* appeared late in the decade, but it made a significant and immediate impact on the Canadian cultural landscape, selling fifty-seven thousand copies a month by December of 1928.[12] It is difficult to determine who was actually reading and writing to the columnists in the 1920s, but discussions frequently assumed a white, largely middle-class, female readership looking to negotiate the boundaries of feminine modernity. That said, columnists often saw themselves as part of a wider project of public education for working-class, rural, and immigrant women.[13] Given the ubiquitous image of the Modern Girl and her relatively uniform look across race, class, and even national lines, assuming a singularly narrow audience could be problematic. Yet, as we shall see, the discourses of modern female subjectivity in Canada were interlaced with those of age, class, and race.

Do You Believe in Magic?

> *Shopping for beauty makes one realize the staggering number*
> *of things in pots and bottles and sachets that are full of the promise*
> *of beauty ... Women are serious in their desire to improve their*

*appearance and they are succeeding beyond their most sanguine
expectations. Is it any wonder that they believe in magic?*

— Mab, *The Promise of Beauty*

By the 1920s, cosmetics and other beauty aids littered the Canadian cultural landscape, and most promised physical improvement along with other less tangible benefits. Commodity magic did not happen by chance, but if products were used frequently and correctly (Valerie chastised readers for being reckless and failing to follow instructions but expecting results), significant benefits were promised: an attractive mate, popularity, and personal and professional success. Magic imbued goods with a sense of optimism that one could improve with their use, but suspicion of "snake oil salesmen" remained. Columnists traversed the troubled terrain of commodity magic, providing careful recommendations of safe products while intertwining modern science and magic. In the world of modern science's "fairy magic," as *Chatelaine* beauty culture columnist Mab extolled, "The scientist is accomplishing truly magical things."[14] A mythical re-enchantment of goods (magic allegedly made safe by the gloss of science) was part of the essence of modern advertising, and the fact that one could shop for beauty, as opposed to cultivating it from within, revealed some of the challenges consumer culture presented to established standards of beauty. The promise of improvement, however, also introduced the "democratic and anxiety-inducing idea that beauty could be achieved by all women – if only they used the correct products."[15] In advocating for the thoughtful use of makeup, Mab bluntly informed readers, "Anything that a woman can do to improve her appearance is right to do."[16] In displacing homemade beauty treatments and remedies, modern beauty, as one advertisement declared, required "the best," which was often equated with the mass-produced and the store-bought. By the late 1910s, Canadian beauty columnists had stopped hawking specific products but would nonetheless provide their names to readers who wrote for advice.[17] Columnists were keenly aware, however, that modern beauty culture was one of consumption, and regular features from the 1920s typically highlighted some type of commodity and attempted to keep Canadian readers up to date on modern styles of bodily care, fashion, accessories, and diet. For those living on a budget, who may have found the cost of commodity magic prohibitive, columnists provided sly ways to continue to be modern. They also offered recipes so that women could make their own beauty products, but typically only if the alternative were nothing at all. Valerie challenged the argument that "the business woman has not time or money to attend to her beauty." She suggested that businesswomen, who "often have a whole free evening to keep her good looks," should purchase an extensive list of ingredients, including lemon, milk, hydrogen peroxide, white wax, almond oil, elder-flower water, boracic acid, rosewater, olive oil, a cucumber, a strawberry (when in season), and olive oil soap. Used properly, these ingredients were meant to mimic the effect of mass-produced cosmetics (in fact, some were simpler versions of those goods). Although Valerie recognized that time was at a premium for businesswomen, she implied that it was a better sacrifice than beauty, and she subtly reinforced the notion that, in a quickly moving modern world, commercial preparations were simply easier. Valerie's advice was probably mediated by other constraints, such as her editor, who would have been keenly aware of the need to maintain a positive relationship with financially powerful advertisers.[18]

For women, the belief in modern magic was only part of the formula, as the "desire to improve their appearance" and to become modern was ultimately of import. As much as advertisements turned the body into an object for consumption, they also appealed to notions of subjectivity by framing commodity displays as intimately connected with modern female subjectivity.[19] The line between consumer objects and women's subjectivity was complicated, and representations were closely tied with techniques of appearing. Part of the complication was that women were encouraged to carefully examine the body from the outside – taking on a critical, often masculine, gaze – in order to respond to its perceived needs. The idea of the body as visual image, in need of constant attention and improvement, "made the body into a project" and imparted the message that it was no longer enough to experience one's body and respond simply to physical sensations or to be judged on the basis of one's character.[20] Projects were deemed to be constant and specific, and were connected to particular commodities. After a series of instructions on makeup application (in one of her many columns on the subject), Mab told readers to remember a key point: "Be your own most severe critic, and study your face from all angles."[21] Her advice reinforced a popular discourse that encouraged self-scrutiny on an intensely detailed level and reinforced the idea that women were to study their bodies through the lens of a male gaze, thus encouraging the co-opting of a powerfully misogynistic scopic regime in order to promote further corporeal discipline.[22] Popular advertisements encouraged self-scrutiny by including large photographs depicting women looking into mirrors. The techniques of modern filmmaking, with close-ups and the ability to zoom in and slow down, were borrowed for advertising, revealing the intimacies of surveillance. One ad, featuring a seated woman who leans forward and looks intently into a mirror, demands, "Look at Yourself!

Are you satisfied?"[23] An ad for Pompeian Night Cream includes a large photo-graph of a seated woman who holds a hand mirror and studies her reflection. The caption states, "Miss Van Q. regards with critical eye the exquisite beauty of her skin, which she keeps properly cleansed and cared for with Pompeian Night Cream."[24] On crowded urban streets, in seemingly anonymous depart-ment stores or movie theatres, women were judged by passersby, who, according to advertisers, scrutinized their bodies and noticed details such as ragged cuticles and damp underarms. This made the "critical eye" a necessary part of the process of appearing. The critical eye, however, inevitably required consumer goods – a manicure kit or a deodorant – to solve the perceived problem. Not only did they offer magical solutions, they also promised the kind of confidence that enabled one not to worry about ragged cuticles being noticed by strangers. In a depilatory ad, a young woman reclines in her slip and raises one arm above her head, exposing her underarm, which is marked with an "x." The caption reads, "From the man's viewpoint." The text warns that "should he glimpse the slightest trace of unsightly hair – the whole impression is spoiled; he classifies you from then on as a woman lacking in fastidiousness."[25] The pain of chemical hair removal was, of course, not mentioned, as women were encouraged to recall how "he" would see it – a small, rather intimate piece of the body.

The notion of constant surveillance contested the boundaries between public and private displays. In the 1920s, not all body projects were expected to be performed in secret or to look natural, despite some suggestions to the contrary. Rather, they were part of modern techniques of appearing in which women revealed aspects of their work. If the Gibson Girl looked effortlessly and natur-ally beautiful, the Modern Girl flaunted her physical changes, wearing obvious makeup in shades that one beauty columnist described as not "humanly pos-sible."[26] Producing a Modern Girl's body required a tricky sort of cultural nego-tiation, and important advice on how to create it and to deal with the troublesome issue of "touching up" was provided by magazines and ads selling particular commodities. Ads for Gouraud's Oriental Cream declared "Stop 'Touching Up'" and offered a solution to the ongoing problem of maintenance by promising a "24 hour complexion." Columnists and other writers debated the appropriate-ness of the oft-witnessed performances of beauty upkeep on Canadian streets. Valerie reported, "The modern girl, however, has thrown all boudoir reticence to the winds and produces her compact on all occasions – in the street-car, in the theatre – and even in the crowded ball-room. So far, the compact has not been seen in church – but then the modern girl is not often seen at church." Mab argued that makeup could not stay fresh all day if the wearer were in contact with "the busy world." She advised that it was "absolutely necessary to carry restoratives to repair the damage," though she warned that being seen applying lipstick, powder, or rouge in public was "undesirable." Openly and obviously touching up in public may have been seen as crass, but the standards of continuous maintenance often deemed it necessary.[27] Moreover, the requirement of constantly appearing at one's best (even apparently for a twenty-four-hour period) suggested that little time would remain for anything else; letting the performance slip was to risk arousing the critical judgment of others.

Notions of perpetual public surveillance, the endless and time-consuming process of disciplining the body, and the need to be up to date with the latest techniques had their nefarious side. The 1920s were a significant period for Canadian women, who by the early years of the decade had fought for and won the right to vote at the federal and provincial levels, with the exception of Quebec.[28] Increasing access to higher education for the white middle class and the growing presence of women in the public arena helped to spark a reordering of gender relations. However, the idea of female emancipation seems quickly to have been reduced to conspicuous consumption. As Cheryl Krasnick Warsh argues, "The fragile figure of the flapper, the emphasis on short-term gratification, and the espousal of the value of fashion – ephemeral and unproductive – dissipated some of the anxieties caused by increasing public roles for women. Power was now defined as purchasing power, the goal of which was the traditional one of pleasing a man."[29] Bobbed hair, lipstick, a complicated skin care regime, and all the other body projects promoted in advertisements and articles encouraged women to spend their available time in enhancing their appearance and associated their physical improvement with power. Further, increasing feminine visibility added another layer to the physical mastery that women were expected to acquire before entering into the public sphere. Agnes Macphail, Canada's first female member of parliament, was elected on 6 December 1921 and endured bitter attacks for her "mannish" behaviour and her "plain" style.[30] Despite other successes, women were constantly reminded that their bodies were on display and that power was associated with attracting positive attention through the gaze of others. Mothers were warned to train their daughters in the proper regimens of bodily care. One advertisement for Palmolive Soap stated, "When she grows up ... She will be beautiful, of course, in the rosy future pictured by a mother's dreams. But – this future beauty will not be left to chance, for modern mothers know how to make their dreams come true."[31] Consumption of goods to stay new, fresh, and young was allegedly the solution to marital difficulties. Such issues were also addressed in the dialogues between beauty columnists and readers, who wrote in asking for help with specific problems.[32]

As a result, these discussions made both the threat of social and personal failure and the solutions, embedded as they were in consumer culture, seem real.

A single ad often merged many of these diverse themes. For example, Bovril connected its product with modern femininity by appealing to women's "need" to look thin and young. Under the headline "Keep Your Youthful Figure," a woman sits at a table, with her back to the viewer. Two slim, fashionably dressed young women appear at the right, one of whom remarks, "She is a dear old soul but a little Bovril in her daily diet ... would be of great benefit to her figure." In case readers might miss the point, the line "her friends chuckle behind her back when she puts on *excess* weight" runs across the bottom of the ad. The behaviour of the two women suggests a normalization of the cultural policing of the female body through surveillance. Though their friend is "a dear old soul," her appearance is clearly more important than her character. Moreover, she is behind the times, for her clothes date from at least a decade earlier, and she is seated alone in a domestic setting.[33] This image of "sad," outdated tradition is juxtaposed with young, thin, modern women who are out and about having fun in public. In a somewhat paradoxical appeal, given the flapper's figure, the ad also suggests that consuming Bovril gives women the strength to "resist epidemics" and therefore implies some sort of health benefit.

Overall, we are certainly meant to feel sorry for the lonely, old-fashioned, and perhaps unhealthy woman, but the underlying implication is that she has chosen to be old, and with that comes a wide-reaching set of cultural assumptions. In Canadian beauty columns, youth is linked with alertness, elasticity, vitality, energy, and enthusiasm, whereas old age is associated with "fatty degenerations," misshapenness, conceit, laziness, flabbiness, and having "lost the magic of youth."[34] In the Bovril ad, it is difficult to know the age of the seated woman, but perhaps more important is the fact that she is presented as choosing to be old and unstylish because, unlike her supposed friends, she has not updated her clothing or disciplined her body to the thin, elongated, and lissome shape expected of the Modern Girl.

Magazines offered a great deal of advice on how to retain a youthful appearance. Almost every month, the beauty column in *Chatelaine* lauded youth as the main characteristic of beauty and provided tips for women to hold on to it. For example, readers were told that "a tiny fund of youth ... can be tapped by right thinking and right exercise and lotions and by keeping strict account of calories."[35] Women also learned that old age had become optional and that "intelligent care of their bodies every day will postpone old age, indefinitely."[36] Valerie declared, "The woman of today regards her wrinkled cheeks and sagging chin and goes forth to buy a special astringent for which she pays five dollars and a half. Then she applies this tightening preparation, afterwards a vanishing cream, and finally a dash of her favourite powder. Then she throws a kiss to Father Time."[37] Consumption of the right goods would, it seemed, restore one's youthful appearance after the signs of aging had begun to appear, a point at which the beauty expert's advice became so important. Valerie suggested an alternative for older women who had not kept their bloom: they were literally to clear the floor for beautiful young things wishing to dance in public. She suggested, "Why not dance in private?"[38] Women's advice columns, however, also warned of dangerous, desperate, and obvious attempts to remain youthful. Hair dyes as well as facelifts and other types of surgical intervention (including one reported case of the injection of paraffin wax to fix wrinkles) by disreputable and unqualified people (often labelled "American") were said to give bad results that deceived only the purchaser.[39] Staving off aging, then, did not involve purchasing whatever was available in a landscape seemingly bursting with options, but rather a careful and calculated consumption of the correct goods. To this end, Valerie responded to questions about the safety of cosmetics. Magic, even modern, scientific magic, required ongoing management and careful regulation.

The Promise of Beauty

> Carefully chosen aids to beauty as Christmas gifts will be interesting
> and satisfying purchases. Such gifts will help to keep youth in the hearts
> as well as in the bodies of the recipients, because of the promise that
> they suggest.
>
> – Mab, The Promise of Beauty

The promise of beauty was an apt and ambiguous concept, and as much as women were encouraged to take up new ways of seeing, performing, and caring for the body, it challenged, not totally replaced, existing standards for women's appearance in public. Many North American cultural commentators shared concerns over the appearance of the Modern Girl. A stinging critique of modern youth, especially women, appeared in a 1919 issue of *Saturday Night* and questioned the dramatic rise in numbers of painted Canadian faces. Included in a list of problem behaviours such as reading salacious literature, unsupervised dating, and watching questionable films was the use of cosmetics. Famous first-wave feminist Nellie McClung lamented the rise of the young "lip-stick beauty" in an article titled "I'll Never Tell My Age Again!"[40] A *Chatelaine* article described the impact of advertisements and the pressure on young women to conform to particular standards. Writing of the "tremendous outside pressure" exerted on young women and girls, the author pointed out that "the youngsters of to-day are fortified with nothing but a tyrannical code picked up from each other and crammed down their throats by every type of modern publicity."[41] This was one of many ironic statements made regarding women's relationship to consumption during the decade. Even as magazines and newspapers played central roles in delivering the messages, they also found ways to critique them.

Appearing modern in public was discussed as both potentially pleasurable and perilous in Canadian magazines. Whereas ads appealed to notions of pleasure, critics discussed the downside of appearing in public. An ad for Gaytees Shoes, for example, states, "You know those evenings – that leisurely feeling – the pleasure of seeing and being seen."[42] A Harvey Hosiery and Lingerie's advertisement plays on the double meaning of seeing and being seen. In it, a woman poses in her underwear; behind her is a large oval. In the picture, it is unclear whether we are seeing the woman directly or through the back of her mirror as she stares into her own reflection. The caption reads, "To the eye enchantment! To the wearer, contentment because of her knowledge that the finest materials, perfect fit and beautiful lasting shades are what she buys when she insists upon Harvey Hosiery."[43] Although there could be pleasure in knowing that one was being watched, there was also inherent danger, and pleasure in being seen was not limited to the experience of self-surveillance. Underlying this idea was that others would find the appearance agreeable and pleasurable. Yet attracting public attention was still thought to border on the distasteful at best and the dangerous at worst. Magazines warned that women who deliberately sought attention in obvious or dramatic ways were socially offensive and were perhaps even placing themselves in danger. Women who wore suggestive clothing, critics claimed, distracted a man, tempting him by "forcing too much of their physical form upon his gaze."[44] In the pamphlets produced by the Canadian National Council for Combating Venereal Disease, for instance, young women were cautioned to maintain self-control "in order to avoid arousing the sexual desire of men by words or acts or suggestive clothing."[45] In the misogynistic Canadian legal system in the 1920s, women who were sexually assaulted often found their behaviour and dress under scrutiny during their trial.[46] Women were encouraged to emulate a modern look that Mab associated with "the age of revelation," but they potentially risked their reputations and more in doing so. Despite the burgeoning culture of visuality in which popular media promoted modern techniques of appearing, women still paid an incredibly high and universally unfair price for meeting such standards. Modern Girls needed to strike a precarious balance, and in stipulating the correct amounts of rouge and lipstick, columnists attempted to define what that was for readers.[47]

In response to admonishments from various "authorities in the press and the pulpit," Valerie wrote, "It is true that the women of this continent spend many millions on articles that may properly be described as cosmetics. Yet who shall say that the money is wasted? The world needs all of the prettiness that it can beg, borrow or buy. Too much of the artificial is ugly; but a touch of it is really necessary, unless one is very young." She went on to warn women whose husbands disagreed with their use of cosmetics, suggesting that the husbands' eyes would surely turn to the "flapper who has a velvety finish of her favourite powder." Husbands might disagree with its use, but they could not resist the charm of youth and the beauty of women who wore it. Later in the column, Valerie dealt with the inevitable pressure placed on Canadian women by advertising. In an overtly critical moment, she revealed that she "resented the implications of the advertisements," but nonetheless, she followed their advice.[48] A year later, in a decidedly more chipper tone, Valerie's column pointed to a neglected aspect of undertaking various performances and techniques of appearing: pleasure. A letter from "Dolores," which Valerie answered as part of her column rather than in the usual separate section following it, reinforced a popular narrative of pleasure in the care of the body. Valerie wrote,

> Dolores, who is only eighteen years old, declares that she is an ugly duckling with a 'perfectly terrible' complexion. Now, when I awakened this morning, the world seemed cold and drab and I had a complexion to match. So, I hastened to a pretty sea-green jar and took some nice, smooth cream from it, which I applied to my drab-colored face, 'rubbing upward and outward,' and finally wiping off with a cloth dipped in cold water. The drabness vanished as if by magic and the world became rose-colored once more. So, Dolores, begin all over again and become a swan.[49]

After all, magic implied pleasure, and despite the work and the anxiety involved in attaining it, moments of enjoyment were at least promised. Revitalizing a complexion, eliminating the dullness and monotony of life (albeit through a regular routine), and returning to the promise of beauty were to be a pleasurable process. Even a problem that was more difficult than an imperfect complexion, it appeared, could be massaged away with cream from a sea-green jar. This levelling of surfaces – the assumption of similarity, that Valerie's solution could work for Dolores and that they shared the same problem – is troubling. The deeper significance of the promise of beauty is an assumption of a singular standard, and in this regard, columnists were in line with other dominant trends of the period such as international beauty contests that measured "national" beauty against very particular North American standards emerging from the desire of their sponsors (typically film companies) to find a new Hollywood starlet.[50]

Yet even the beauty experts who helped women navigate the increasingly cluttered world of commodities did not entirely embrace the complete look of the Modern Girl. Valerie, seemingly the more conservative of the two columnists, was particularly hesitant to encourage the bob – one of the most dramatic and popular symbols of modern femininity.[51] Although short hair may have had a wide appeal, it was also seen as disconcerting, since it was often depicted in connection with young women who engaged in questionable behaviour such as smoking, drinking, and petting. In Calgary in 1927, the negative associations of the bob meant that four nurses in training were dismissed for bobbing their hair. Newspapers reported that this was the second time nurses had been fired for choosing the popular hairstyle.[52] Decades later, Canadian Jake Foran, who had been a young man in the 1920s, recalled that bobbed hair was so significant and surprising that he took photographs of it: "I have pictures of the first girls I ever saw with bobbed hair. That was considered wicked almost, bobbing one's hair. The older people thought the world was going straight to hell because they bobbed their hair and shortened their skirts."[53] Valerie's concerns, however, ran along different lines. She warned readers about the upkeep of the bob, noted that it did not flatter everyone, and held on to older notions of a woman's hair as her "crowning glory." In many ways, the promise of beauty was not universal despite rhetoric to the contrary.

The promise of beauty located Canadian women within a broader global culture of beauty in the 1920s. As Chapters 10 and 11 of this volume reveal, in the burgeoning global market of interwar commodity culture, the concept of the Modern Girl was layered with particular national ideologies that helped to contextualize her within local boundaries.[54] Many advertisements in Canadian magazines and newspapers were indistinguishable from their American counterparts. Adhering to the burgeoning cultural nationalism of the interwar period, some Canadians found this disconcerting and also objected to the flood of other American cultural goods such as movies, magazines, and dime novels. The Modern Girl was not only potentially a symbol of reckless youth and a new social order, but also of the alleged Americanization of the Canadian popular cultural landscape. Efforts were made to stem the tide – attempts at creating a popular Canadian film industry, the development of a Canadian women's magazine, the support of a self-consciously Canadian artistic movement – but

Canadian companies often used images of the Modern Girl as part of their appeals to Canadian pride. She was not simply at odds with Canadian cultural nationalism. Some companies that produced Canadian-made goods promised to meet or exceed the standards set by the global fashion capitals, especially New York City, and depicted a Canadian modern girl in their ads as evidence. A Penmans Hosiery ad states, "From these famous centres experts send Penmans the latest styles – the newest shades – and Penmans incorporates them into their hosiery so that Canadian women may be 'in the mode' just as soon as fashionable New York." By taking this approach, Penmans suggested that, rather than being left behind, Canadian women could compete with stylish New Yorkers; their distance from the fashion epicentres of Paris, London, and New York did not excuse them. Canadian department stores such as Eaton's and Simpson's advertised that they sold the most up-to-date fashions for Canadian women and offered both in-store and mail service. *Chatelaine* described new Paris fashions in detail and announced, "A fashion expert was saying the other day that Canada is now no farther behind Paris than the length of an ocean voyage." Even American-made goods attempted to appeal to the national pride of Canadians: an ad for Colgate's Talc Powder stated that the powder was "Dear to the Women of Canada."[55] Women could express nationalism by purchasing Canadian goods, and without sacrificing style or fashion. In other ads, the product was merely couched as Canadian, even if the reality was far more complex. Many American companies with Canadian branch plants emphasized a Canadian address and included "Made in Canada" in their ads. Referring to the "Canadian winter," as Pond's and Woodbury's did, was also popular.[56]

Climate was a recurring theme in beauty columns, and certain types of goods were overlain with national sentiments that modified their use for what was seen as a challenging natural environment. Mab's March 1929 column advocated the use of artificial sun-ray lamps for Canadian women suffering the darkness of winter.[57] Not only was tanned skin increasingly fashionable, but "canned sun" also offered the possibility of fortifying the nation's health. Mab reported, "According to one of our Canadian doctors the next generation, by having the right food and the necessary sunlight, will be immune from rickets and other such dwarfing diseases, and will grow up straight and strong. Indeed, he believes that in time, as a result of the wonderful facilities for health that are being constantly discovered, we may have human beings like gods inhabiting the earth!" Nonetheless, Mab argued that since these gods had yet to inhabit the earth, Canadian women still needed to rely on commercial enhancements, especially during the month of March. As she paradoxically pointed out, the "wear and tear of winter" was indiscreetly highlighted by the "merciless" way the sun revealed "defects."[58] The solutions were clear: special cream for the eyes, hot-oil hair and face treatments, vanishing cream, powder, lipstick, and blush. These consumer goods were not only necessary for the modern woman, but also specifically for the modern Canadian woman fighting a harsh climate. The northern-ness and bleakness of the climate formed a significant narrative in the constellation of discourses of Canadian nationalism during the 1920s. Intimately connected to issues of race and gender, the great white north was seen as an escape from the soft, feminized, racialized landscape of the urban environment, and the Canadian climate was often used as a justification to exclude people of colour who, it was argued, could not handle Canada's cold, difficult winters. Given Canada's ongoing project of colonization of Indigenous populations, the privileging of whiteness and the naturalization of the association with beauty were coupled with discourses that connected whiteness, progress, and modernity. If white women could briefly compromise their whiteness with a touch of sun for the health of the nation, this was a sign of their privilege. Women of colour were largely excluded from consumption discourses in Canadian magazines, and mention of "brown" skin in beauty columns was typically followed by a "cure" that would return it to its "natural" white. More often than not, such references were part of a chastisement, especially for women who had let a touch of summer sun stay too far into the fall.

For many Canadian women, commodities could be beyond reach. Economics, geography, and time all hindered access to consumer goods, and promoters were well aware of this.[59] Advertisers and columnists did not, however, allow such limitations to impede the discourse of consumption, and in doing so, they reduced structural inequities to personal care issues. In the world of commodity culture, racism, poverty, distance, and lack of time were no excuse. Nevertheless, Canadian women performed modernity and appeared modern to varying degrees in the 1920s, and this required a constant production and cultural negotiation in a country where modernity was uneven and contested, and where the feminine modernity exemplified in the beauty columns was naturalized as a white project by the frequency and singularity of its representation.

Conclusion

Valerie and Mab frequently challenged critics – both male and female – who dismissed their areas of expertise as frivolous.[60] Beauty, they asserted, mattered, and given the far-reaching web that connects individual bodies and techniques of appearing to issues of feminine subjectivity and modernity, it clearly did.

Although Canadian women faced restrictions in regard to consumption, commodity display advocated techniques of appearing that were expected to be and were employed. For women, being modern meant being a consumer, not only of goods, but also of many of the deeper and perhaps more troubling messages of the culture of consumption that intimately shaped their bodies and lives. Women were encouraged to surveil their own bodies and those of others, acting as unofficial gatekeepers for the performance of modernity. If Victorian notions of being judged by character rather than looks had any resonance in the 1920s, the balance had certainly shifted toward an emphasis on appearance. No modern woman could be without particular commodities, and opting out of the flourishing commodity culture could bring ridicule and scorn. Nor was age an excuse as, in 1928, Valerie revealed herself to be a sixty-one-year-old grandmother who nonetheless found it "so easy to keep young – if you know how."[61] Canadian women were not, however, simply dupes of the media or of advertisers, and beauty columnists served as experts in helping them steer through a complex consumer landscape. Columnists' answers to mostly unprinted letters reveal that women across the country took many of these issues to heart. Changes in techniques of appearing also linked Canadian women to other women influenced by the global Modern Girl. In the manufacturing of surfaces, the Modern Girl's connection to modernity was a complicated mix of power and pleasure but one that placed growing emphasis on how women looked. In many ways, these issues resonate today. Glossy magazines, though increasingly targeted to specialized audiences, dedicate pages (if not entire issues) to selecting the best products, and many still have beauty advice columnists who answer letters from readers. The slew of new products and demands for improvement (high definition skin!) overwhelm even those of us who, despite years of quiet training with our friends in bathrooms and bedrooms and years of careful study of powerful feminist critiques, find ourselves confused, angry, and maybe even still seduced by commodity magic.

Acknowledgments
Thanks to the editors of this collection, especially Cheryl Krasnick Warsh, for their support throughout the gestation of this project, as well as Tracy Penny Light and the anonymous reviewers for their helpful suggestions that improved the chapter.

Notes
1 Valerie, The Dressing Table, *Saturday Night,* 29 September 1928, 16. The title of Valerie's column changed from "My Lady's Dressing Table" to "The Dressing Table" on 10 March 1928.
2 Liz Conor, *The Spectacular Modern Woman: Feminine Visibility in the 1920s* (Bloomington: Indiana University Press, 2004), 2.

3 This phrase is a take on the 1967 musical *Thoroughly Modern Millie*. Set in New York during the 1920s, it plays on the stereotypical narratives of the decade.
4 Mab, The Promise of Beauty, *Chatelaine*, October 1928, 30, and September 1928, 29.
5 Penny Tinkler and Cheryl Krasnick Warsh, "Feminine Modernity in Interwar Britain and North America: Corsets, Cars, and Cigarettes," *Journal of Women's History* 20, 3 (Fall 2008): 113. See also Abigail Solomon-Godeau, "The Other Side of Venus: The Visual Economy of Feminine Display," in *The Sex of Things: Gender and Consumption in Historical Perspective*, ed. Victoria de Grazia with Ellen Furlough (Berkeley: University of California Press, 1996), 113-50; and, for a Canadian perspective, Cynthia Wright, "Feminine Trifles of Vast Importance: Writing Gender into the History of Consumption," in *Gender Conflicts: New Essays in Women's History*, ed. Franca Iacovetta and Mariana Valverde (Toronto: University of Toronto Press, 1992), 229-60. For an overview of the Canadian historiography on consumption, see Donica Belisle, "Toward a Canadian Consumer History," *Labour/Le travail* 52, 2 (Fall 2003): 181-206.
6 Marjory Lang, *Women Who Made the News: Female Journalists in Canada, 1880-1945* (Montreal and Kingston: McGill-Queen's University Press, 1999), 164. On advertising, see the classic works Roland Marchand, *Advertising the American Dream: Making Way for Modernity, 1920-1940* (Berkeley: University of California Press, 1985); and T.J. Jackson Lears, *Fables of Abundance: A Cultural History of Advertising in America* (New York: Basic Books, 1994).
7 There were important differences between the two columns. Valerie dealt with a greater range of topics, including women's behaviour, than did Mab, who was more singularly focused on consumer goods and appearance. Valerie's column also tended to be slightly more critical of recent changes, although this did not temper its overall message during the period under study here.
8 Mab, The Promise of Beauty, *Chatelaine*, September 1929, 32; Valerie, My Lady's Dressing Table, *Saturday Night*, 31 July 1920, 24.
9 On the global Modern Girl, see Alys Eve Weinbaum et al., eds., *The Modern Girl around the World: Consumption, Modernity, and Globalization* (Durham, NC: Duke University Press, 2008); Paul Rutherford, "Made in America: The Problem of Mass Culture in Canada," in *The Beaver Bites Back: American Popular Culture in Canada*, ed. David H. Flaherty and Frank E. Manning (Montreal and Kingston: McGill-Queen's University Press, 1993), 260-80.
10 The 1921 census revealed that, for the first time, almost half of the Canadian population lived in an urban environment. On the cultural import of this and other developments, see Cynthia Comacchio, *The Dominion of Youth: Adolescence and the Making of a Modern Canada, 1920-1950* (Waterloo: Wilfrid Laurier University Press, 2006).
11 The body of literature is too large to list in its entirety. For an excellent introduction, see Weinbaum et al., *The Modern Girl around the World*.
12 Valerie Korinek, *Roughing It in the Suburbs: Reading* Chatelaine *Magazine in the Fifties and Sixties* (Toronto: University of Toronto Press, 2000), 33-35.
13 Lang, *Women Who Made the News*, 2.
14 Valerie, My Lady's Dressing Table, *Saturday Night*, 15 September 1928, 29; Mab, The Promise of Beauty, *Chatelaine*, October 1928, 30. On myth, enchantment, and advertising, see Susan Buck-Morss, *The Dialectics of Seeing: Walter Benjamin and the Arcades Project* (Cambridge, MA: MIT Press, 1989), Chapter 8. On "safe," "modern" cosmetics, see Valerie, My Lady's Dressing Table, *Saturday Night*, 9 July 1927, 28.
15 Kathy Peiss, "Making Up, Making Over: Cosmetics, Consumer Culture, and Women's Identity," in de Grazia and Furlough, *The Sex of Things*, 311. See also her *Hope in a Jar: The Making of America's Beauty Culture* (New York: Henry Holt, 1998).
16 Mab, The Promise of Beauty, *Chatelaine*, April 1928, 34.
17 On the changes in beauty columns, see Lang, *Women Who Made the News*, 177. See, for example, Valerie, My Lady's Dressing Table, *Saturday Night*, 28 January 1928, 32.

18 Valerie, The Dressing Table, *Saturday Night*, 28 January 1928, 32. On columnists' relationships to editors and advertisers, see Lang, *Women Who Made the News*, 172-73.

19 Recent literature that questions the divide between representation and subjectivity includes Conor, *The Spectacular Modern Woman;* Tinkler and Warsh, "Feminine Modernity"; and Katrina Srigley, "Clothing Stories: Consumption, Identity, and Desire in Depression-Era Toronto," *Journal of Women's History* 19, 1 (2007): 82-104.

20 Joan Jacob Brumberg, *The Body Project: An Intimate History of American Girls* (New York: Random House, 1997), 101; Veronica Strong-Boag, *The New Day Recalled: Lives of Girls and Women in English Canada, 1919-1939* (Toronto: Copp Clark Pitman, 1988), 85-86.

21 Mab, The Promise of Beauty, *Chatelaine*, March 1929, 32.

22 Christian Metz coined the term "scopic regime" in the 1970s, applying it to film studies. I'm using it in the broader sense, which is now common in the literature, to refer to culturally defined means of and relations of seeing that are neither natural nor universal. See Martin Jay, "Scopic Regimes of Modernity," in *Vision and Visuality,* ed. Hal Foster (Seattle: Bay Press, 1988), 3-23.

23 Princess Complexion Purifier advertisement, *Saturday Night*, 24 September 1927, 30. The cosmetic industry provided female consumers with the option of purchasing a small handheld mirror. Brumberg argues that these mirrors "allowed women to scrutinize and 'reconstruct' the face almost anywhere, at a moment's notice." Brumberg, *The Body Project*, 70.

24 Pompeian Night Cream advertisement, *Maclean's*, 15 February 1926, 33.

25 X-Bazin advertisement, *Maclean's*, 1 February 1926, 54.

26 Mab, The Promise of Beauty, *Chatelaine*, April 1928, 37.

27 Gouraud's Oriental Cream advertisement, *Saturday Night*, 9 July 1927, 28; Valerie, The Dressing Table, *Saturday Night*, 10 March 1928, 32; Mab, The Promise of Beauty, *Chatelaine*, April 1928, 37.

28 For an overview of these events, see Alison Prentice et al., *Canadian Women: A History*, 2nd ed. (Toronto: Harcourt Brace Canada, 1996), Chapter 8.

29 Cheryl Krasnick Warsh, "Smoke and Mirrors: Gender Representation in North American Tobacco and Alcohol Advertisements before 1950," *Histoire sociale/Social History* 31, 62 (1998): 200.

30 Doris Pennington, *Agnes Macphail: Reformer: Canada's First Female MP* (Toronto: Simon and Pierre, 1989), 41-43; Terry Crowley, *Agnes Macphail and the Politics of Equality* (Toronto: James Lorimer, 1990), 57-60.

31 Valerie, My Lady's Dressing Table, *Saturday Night*, 3 February 1923, 23, and 4 June 1928, 28; Palmolive advertisement, *Saturday Night*, 3 February 1923, 27.

32 See, for example, Mab, The Promise of Beauty, *Chatelaine*, October 1928, 30, 38, and December 1928, 32, 38.

33 Bovril advertisement, *Chatelaine*, October 1929, 70 (emphasis in original).

34 See, for example, Mab, The Promise of Beauty, *Chatelaine*, July 1928, 32, January 1929, 32, and February 1929, 30, 42.

35 Mab, The Promise of Beauty, *Chatelaine*, September 1929, 32.

36 Mab, The Promise of Beauty, *Chatelaine*, February 1929, 30.

37 Valerie, My Lady's Dressing Table, *Saturday Night*, 24 December 1927, 22.

38 Valerie, The Dressing Table, *Saturday Night*, 11 August 1928, 24.

39 See, for example, Valerie, My Lady's Dressing Table, *Saturday Night*, 3 September 1927, 24, and 15 October 1927, 32. A 1928 *Saturday Night* article warned especially of "alleged professional gentry from the United States already discredited in their own country." See "The 'Magic' of Plastic Surgery," *Saturday Night*, 10 March 1928, 2.

40 Beatrice M. Shaw, "The Age of Uninnocence," *Saturday Night*, 24 May 1919, 31; Nellie L. McClung, "I'll Never Tell My Age Again!" *Maclean's*, 15 March 1926, 15.

41 An In-Between [pseud.], "Ready-Made Youngsters: A Plea for the Younger Generation," *Chatelaine*, April 1928, 1, 4.

42 Gaytees Shoes advertisement, *Saturday Night*, 12 November 1927, 35.

43 Harvey Hosiery and Lingerie advertisement, *Chatelaine*, May 1928, 27.

44 "Catholic Girls Promote Modesty in Dress," *Catholic Register*, 23 May 1929, 4.

45 Suzann Buckley and Janice Dickin McGinnis, "Venereal Disease and Public Health Reform in Canada," *Canadian Historical Review* 63, 3 (1982): 348.

46 Karen Dubinsky, *Improper Advances: Rape and Heterosexual Conflict in Ontario, 1880-1929* (Chicago: University of Chicago Press, 1993); Lori Chambers, *Misconceptions: Unmarried Motherhood and the Ontario Children of Unmarried Parents Act, 1921-1969* (Toronto: Osgoode Society for Canadian Legal History/University of Toronto Press, 2007), 72-75.

47 See, for example, Mab, The Promise of Beauty, *Chatelaine*, April 1928, 37, March 1929, 32, 60; and Valerie, My Lady's Dressing Table, *Saturday Night*, 28 February 1920, 26, and 22 October 1927, 29.

48 Valerie, The Dressing Table, *Saturday Night*, 19 November 1927, 32, and 24 September 1927, 29.

49 Valerie, The Dressing Table, *Saturday Night*, 14 January 1928, 28.

50 On Canadian women's participation in international beauty contests during the 1920s, see "Miss Toronto Marries," *New York Times*, 15 October 1922, 30; "Miss Canada Draws Vanderbilt's Praise," *Victoria Times*, 26 May 1927, 9; and "Marriage Proposals Most Exciting of Miss Canada's Trip," *Victoria Times*, 31 May 1927, 5.

51 Valerie, My Lady's Dressing Table, *Saturday Night*, 27 January 1923, 23, 23 July 1927, 24, 30 July 1927, 26, and 6 August 1927, 24.

52 "Dismiss Nurses for Bobbing Hair Again," *Manitoba Free Press* (Winnipeg), May 1927, 1; "Well, Isn't This 'Shear' Nonsense?" *Vancouver Sun*, 4 May 1927, 2.

53 Jake Foran interview in *The Great War and Canadian Society: An Oral History*, ed. D. Read and R. Hann (Toronto: Hogtown Press, 1978), 213.

54 See also Ann Heilmann and Margaret Beetham, eds., *New Woman Hybridities: Femininity, Feminism and International Consumer Culture, 1880-1930* (London: Routledge, 2004); and Weinbaum et al., *The Modern Girl around the World*.

55 Penmans advertisement, *Maclean's*, 1 April 1926, 76; T. Eaton Company advertisement, *Saturday Night*, 18 February 1928, 40; Robert Simpson Company advertisement, *Saturday Night*, 19 January 1929, 19; "Fashion Commentaries on the Canadian Mode," *Chatelaine*, April 1928, 20; Mary Wyndham, "Paris Favors a Feminine Mode," *Chatelaine*, March 1928, 22-23, 65; Colgate's Talc Powder advertisement, *Saturday Night*, 8 July 1922, 3.

56 Pond's advertisement, *Saturday Night*, 27 January 1923, 23; Woodbury's advertisement, *Maclean's*, 15 February 1927, back cover.

57 On the connection between cosmetics and the rising popularity of suntanning during the interwar period, see Chapter 8 in this volume, which correctly notes that moderation in tanning was advised.

58 Mab, The Promise of Beauty, *Chatelaine*, March 1929, 32, 60.

59 For a broader discussion, see Strong-Boag, *The New Day Recalled*, Chapter 1; Carolyn Strange, *Toronto's Girl Problem: The Perils and Pleasures of the City, 1800-1930* (Toronto: University of Toronto Press, 1995); and Comacchio, *The Dominion of Youth*, Chapter 6.

60 See, for example, Valerie, My Lady's Dressing Table, *Saturday Night*, 20 March 1920, 26, and 19 November 1927, 33; and Mab, The Promise of Beauty, *Chatelaine*, August 1928, 32, and March 1929, 32, 60.

61 Valerie, The Dressing Table, *Saturday Night*, 18 August 1928, 28.

10

(En)gendering a Modern Self in Post-Revolutionary Mexico City, 1920-40

Susanne Eineigel

In the 1920s and 1930s, residents of Mexico City, weary from nearly a decade of revolutionary bloodshed and chaos, devoured the latest fads found in magazines and department stores, and flocked to the cheap amusements of theatres, movie houses, and dance halls. The Mexican Revolution (1910-20) had overturned an aging dictatorship, largely dismantled an elite francophile culture, and left nearly a million people dead.[1] Out of its ashes, a generation came of age amid the heady yet tumultuous growing pains of a nascent post-revolutionary state and a vociferous Roman Catholic reaction. Both sides vehemently claimed to represent Mexican society and fought to establish their authority on what constituted modernity and progress. The consumer market also vied for the attention and allegiance of a large young population eager to escape the post-revolutionary period's economic difficulties and continuing political instability. By patronizing nightclubs, cabarets, and movie theatres, and purchasing cheap consumer goods, young *capitalinos* (residents of Mexico City) fashioned identities that challenged previous notions of gender, class, and sexuality. The emergence of a modern subjectivity among the working and middle class of Mexico City formed a new relationship to the body as well as to the psyche.

In Mexico, as elsewhere, young people differentiated themselves from the preceding generation by participating in consumer culture. An attack on prior notions of appropriate gendered behaviour and affect signalled a generational shift of transnational proportions. The *chica moderna* (modern girl) of Mexico City had her equivalent in the *modan gāru* of Tokyo, the *garçonne* of Paris, the *Bubikopf* of Berlin, and the flapper of New York City.[2] Although at times the modern girl appears strikingly similar in studies of regions around the globe, national contexts and local discourses shaped a native modern sensibility. Recent scholarship on the varied local manifestations and experiences of modernity has pluralized the notion of the modern.[3] The following analysis of Mexico adds to studies on "alternative modernities" and joins those scholars who warn against judging these modernities against a supposedly original or authentic one found in Western Europe and the United States.[4]

Recent and exciting scholarship on Mexico City between 1920 and 1940 traces global phenomena and national contexts that informed a modern way of behaviour, thought, and sentiment. Scholars have shown how a combination of transnational trends and post-revolutionary concerns shaped educational reforms and familial law that yielded a new attitude toward the family, childhood, and adolescence. Shifting discourses about criminality reformed legislation around prostitution, and the prostitutes themselves used revolutionary rhetoric to defend their rights.[5] Nascent research on white-collar work in the 1930s has revealed how the large numbers of Mexican women entering office employment threatened middle-class masculinity.[6] The meagre earnings of these *empleadas* (female employees) afforded them cheap luxuries such as modish dresses and tickets to the movies. They fashioned themselves as *pelonas* (flappers), or chicas modernas, and became subject to satire and hostility.[7] Historians of modern Mexico have argued that the female figure came to symbolize the modernizing city and its Art Deco architecture, while simultaneously embodying an imagined rural landscape and Indigenous culture conjured up by artistic nostalgia.[8] This chapter contributes to such scholarship by focusing on how transnational consumer culture helped the residents of Mexico City shape a modern consciousness that required bodily and psychical change. Along with technological innovations, modernity called forth new forms of gendered self-consciousness, bodily self-expression, and interpersonal relations. Indeed, as Harvie Ferguson argues, modernity became meaningful only once individuals embodied new ways of experiencing the world.[9]

In Mexico City, magazines and newspapers, state and church archival material, and personal recollections attest to how the promises and fantasies of the consumer market existed in relation to the demands and hopes of the post-revolutionary state and the Catholic Church. Mexico's federal governments during the 1920s and 1930s sought to rebuild the country through a discourse of hygiene and racial fitness. New consumer products simultaneously bolstered the discourse of state mediators such as teachers, doctors, and reformers, and the principles espoused by the Catholic hierarchy and the church's various lay organizations. Both public and Catholic schools supported children's physical education, as the new athletic ideal became ubiquitous in various forms of popular culture, most notably in advertisements for consumer products. Furthermore, post-revolutionary secular politicians and Catholics agreed on the dangers of modern amusements and entertainment, although each used rhetoric based on differing sets of values. Mediated by their class backgrounds, family life, religious beliefs, and politics, young capitalinos fashioned a modern sense of self amid the intersecting discourses of the post-revolutionary state, the church, and consumer culture.

Cheap Pleasures for the Modern Female Body

In the 1890s, French and German immigrant families opened Mexico City's first department stores, whose ornate window displays enticed consumers into palaces of dreams and desires. These shopping centres represented the capital's transformation under Porfirio Díaz, the Mexican president from 1867 to 1911, who cemented Mexico City's commercial and administrative dominance through expanding the federal government bureaucracy, attracting foreign investment, and completing railway lines. In 1900, with a population of nearly half a million, Mexico City boasted grand boulevards and stately buildings that purported to exemplify the Díaz regime's Positivist motto of order and progress.

The growing middle class, searching for ways to distinguish its status and cosmopolitanism, became an important group of window shoppers. The expansion of white-collar work led a growing number of clerks and office employees to join the ranks of an existing, albeit small, professional middle class. A handful of middle-class women joined this office corps, and many more enrolled as students or worked as teachers at public and private vocational schools. Yet, more than any other public space, the department store helped to legitimize middle-class women's departure from the confines of the domestic sphere. Department store owners wisely created domestic-like settings in order to soothe male and female anxiety over middle-class women's movement into the public sphere.[10] In reaction to the popularity of department stores, critics warned of female consumption as a wasteful and immoral indulgence. Nevertheless, over time, shopping became a legitimate and respectable pleasure in pre-revolutionary Mexico.[11]

Shopping promised access to a social metropolitan culture in which women were not only urban actors, but also bodies to be satisfied, indulged, excited, and improved. Advertisers encouraged female consumers to draw attention to themselves through clothes and cosmetics. Such ideas marked a significant departure from popular etiquette manuals that stressed restrained behaviour and an inconspicuous outward appearance. As a means to mark class membership, Mexico's middle class had prided itself on abiding by the rules of propriety set out in these manuals.[12] The principles of self-regulation and self-discipline, described by Michel Foucault as fundamental to the nineteenth-century emergence of the modern body, came up against an early-twentieth-century consumer culture that legitimized and popularized pleasing the body.[13]

In the early decades of the post-revolutionary period (1920-40), mass marketers found an eager audience of Mexico City residents as they attempted to rebuild, regain, and reinvent their lives. The chaos and violence of the revolution resulted in a flood of rural migrants into the capital and quickly increased the city's population to nearly a million inhabitants by 1920. The economic collapse of many middle-class families as a consequence of the revolution compelled female family members to enter the workforce, particularly within the realm of public administration. Between 1921 and 1930, the number of women employed in Mexico City's government sector grew from under two hundred to almost six thousand.[14] By 1940, the capital's government sector employed over fifteen thousand women.[15] For these women, cheap pleasures bought with their limited salaries offered a refuge from worries about political instability, economic downturns, overcrowded neighbourhoods, and the lack of urban services.[16]

Female consumption of goods such as clothes and cosmetics represented a major shift in attitude toward the female body in Mexico. During the Porfirian period, only stage actresses and prostitutes or other women of questionable moral character wore makeup. Etiquette manuals raised suspicions about what women hid behind their "made up" faces and condemned cosmetics for their ability to falsify a woman's inner spirit. Short stories such as those written by José Thomás de Cuéllar literally exposed women's dark skin behind whitening makeup and gloves.[17] The early-twentieth-century cosmetics industry encouraged women to accentuate or minimize specific facial features.[18] Through movie star endorsements, cosmetics companies promised customers the features of popular actresses. Max Factor, for instance, guaranteed that its product gave women the lips of Clara Bow.[19] An older generation regarded women's use of makeup as tampering with divine providence. In a popular Mexico City newspaper column from 1921, an aged aunt asks her youthful niece why she does not "leave [her eyebrows] the way God gave them to her?" The niece continues to paint her brows and replies, "Because God gave me very few."[20]

Advertising of consumer products not only encouraged women to cultivate a new face and hairstyle, it also promoted an ethic of physical self-improvement and hygiene. As Jane Nicholas finds in her study of Canadian beauty columns

(Chapter 9 of this volume), in Mexico City ads for products such as soap, toothpaste, and mouthwash heightened fears over proper personal hygiene. Both women and men became sensitive to bodily sights and smells that had not bothered a previous generation. In the rapidly expanding capital city, these sensitivities were magnified as newly urbanized individuals became increasingly anonymous, and first impressions mattered. Moreover, physical proximity to the opposite sex increased as women entered the public spaces of trams, offices, classrooms, and movie theatres. Advertisers equated good hygiene not only with beauty and sex appeal, but even with the guarantee of future matrimony. For instance, Colgate Toothpaste alarmed young readers with its story about Irene, whose bad breath threatened to leave her a spinster.[21]

The selling of cleanliness through beauty products intersected with the larger discourses of hygiene and eugenics put forth by educators and reformers. A decade of revolutionary violence and epidemics had depleted the country of 5 percent of its population. In the 1920s, post-revolutionary governmental plans for national progress began to focus on moulding healthy (re)productive citizens.[22] Mexican educators and doctors emphasized self-improvement through physical exercise. Although their message had its roots in the late nineteenth century, the widespread institution of hygiene and physical education classes in public schools did not appear until the 1920s and 1930s.[23] Public school education provided many female students with their first opportunity to become involved in sports. As a student at the National Preparatory School in the 1920s, Guillermina Mostalac played on Mexico's first women's basketball team. Other students experienced the novelty of wearing a bathing suit and bloomers for the first time.[24] On screen and in magazines, young women saw a reflection of this cultural shift toward the glorification of a stronger and more athletic female body. Popular women's magazines presented photographs of movie stars with exercise machines and published articles on at-home exercise regimes. As a result, the young middle-class woman learned to experience her body, not as an ethereal substance, but as a physical entity that exuded strength and vitality.

Whereas exercise machines and beauty products helped regiment the body, the new clothing styles allowed women greater freedom of movement. A market for less confining clothes emerged in Mexico City among the growing number of middle-class women entering office- and service-related professions. The disappearance of the corset and form-conscious shaped dress resulted in a radical change in how middle-class women moved and held their bodies. A 1924 cartoon in the newspaper *El Universal* depicts this dramatic transformation. In the sketch, a woman dressed in nineteenth-century style sits stiffly upright while she sews. In contrast, next to her a New Woman lounges on a couch with a cigarette in one hand and a book in the other.[25] When not sprawled out reading the latest romance novel, the chica moderna danced the shimmy and Charleston at Mexico City's many popular dance halls.

The flapper-style fashions of the 1920s suggested a rejection of the maternal body. Loose-fitting fabric and low waistlines hid hips and breasts, unlike the outdated corset, which accentuated curves. Nonetheless, an older, though re-formulated rhetoric of motherhood appeared alongside consumer culture's celebration of youth and individual pleasure. Politicians placed enormous emphasis on the role of mothers, who, in concert with physicians, eugenicists, and educators, would (re)produce a racially fit Mexico. State-funded radio programs instructed mothers in matters of hygiene and "scientific" childrearing and homemaking. Consumer marketing did not neglect the supposed needs of mothers but pledged to help develop "strong and healthy children," as one advertisement for Quaker Oats claimed.[26] Thus, the marketplace hailed women as consumer-savvy mothers, while at the same time it celebrated the era's new single and working female shoppers.

Muscular Manliness Counters Threats from Modernity

Although many of the manufacturers' consumer goods catered to women, advertisers also encouraged men to develop an ethic of consumption related to their physical appearance. Products pledged to help the middle-class man fashion a respectable look while restoring his masculinity. In the two decades following the revolution, Mexican men faced a myriad of economic and social transformations that undermined traditional notions of manliness. Post-revolutionary reformers urged men to domesticate their energies through evenings at home with the family. At the same time, male supremacy as head of the household came under attack from an increasingly paternalistic state. After the fabled manly heroics of the revolution, modernity and urban living threatened a rough-and-tumble Mexican masculinity.

For middle-class men, the modern office presented challenges to their sense of manliness. Clerical work, particularly within the state bureaucracy, came under considerable attack by critics who considered middle-class men's dependence on public sector employment to be a sign of their meekness and passivity. In addition, the increasing presence of women in the government bureaucracy feminized the office environment. In her work on female office employees in 1930s Mexico City, Susie Porter details how their male counterparts verbally attacked the women's class status as a means to protest their presence

in the office.[27] Part of the backlash presumably stemmed from a national financial crisis that jeopardized men's ability to economically support their families.
Male heads of households, who suffered the humiliation of needing to send
female children out into the paid workforce, could no longer guarantee their
family's honour. Theatre audiences witnessed such a struggle in the play *Cándido
Cordero, Public Employee,* which debuted in Mexico City in 1925. Mr. Cordero,
the protagonist, is a henpecked husband and spineless employee whose meagre
salary and bouts of unemployment endanger his family's middle-class standard
of living. Moreover, a rumour in the office of an affair between the boss and
Cordero's daughter, also a government employee, endangers her honour and
confirms her father's impotence.[28]

Despite Cándido Cordero's sufferings, advertisers portrayed white-collar
work as representative of the ideal modern life. Office positions required certain
standards of hygiene and self-presentation that consumer products promised
to meet. Gillette Razor advertisements depicted potential consumers as men
wearing suits and ties, and working in modern settings. Emphasizing how
personal appearance marked social distinction, the Gillette Company informed
potential buyers that the use of its razor ensured an "air of distinction so ap-
preciated by good society."[29] Touting its product as the most scientific shaving
instrument available, the company promised a "sensation of absolute cleanliness."[30] By the early 1920s, according to one newspaper article, young male
students shaved their faces "a la moderna," with the help of a "gilette" [sic].[31]

At the same time, advertisements heightened anxieties about modern society's debilitating effects on manhood. Numerous products, such as energy
drinks and electricity belts, promised to revitalize male consumers.[32] As the
happy couple in one ad for an electricity belt suggested, the regeneration of men
made their wives content and righted the world to its proper gender hierarchy.
Along with the stress of urban life and office work, the sexualized woman endangered male potency and vigour. A number of ads for a variety of elixirs
depict sexually provocative half-dressed women hovering over men, who presumably lack the ability to perform adequately in the bedroom, and perhaps
outside of it as well.[33]

Popular concerns about the weakening of middle-class men surfaced at a
time when the muscular masculine body became a sought-after ideal. Various
discourses emphasized male athleticism. As part of larger eugenics efforts,
post-revolutionary educators and reformers encouraged both working- and
middle-class young men to funnel their energy into sports and physical exercise.
In public schools and at the Young Men's Christian Association (YMCA), male

youth practised gymnastics and played sports such as soccer and basketball. As a young man in the 1930s, Gregorio Walerstein learned judo at the YMCA, where he and his fellow Jews were accepted. Outside the YMCA, Walerstein played on the student-league basketball team of the National University's School of Commerce.[34] Many Roman Catholic young men also desired to have athletic bodies. Since the church hierarchy prohibited them from joining the Protestant YMCA, Catholic students joined other private organizations. For instance, José de León Toral, a leader of the Young Men's Catholic Association (Asociación Católica Juventud Masculina), joined the Club de Alvardo, where he competed in running and gymnastics and played on the soccer team.[35]

Ads for sport and gymnastic equipment in local newspapers caught the attention of young men who sought to emulate the new muscular ideal. The daily *El Universal* ran ads for sports equipment that called on male readers to "Develop Your Strength."[36] Publications by Catholic groups such as the National Catholic Student League also advertised gym equipment. In one ad, a well-built youth lifts weights in his family's living room.[37] Such ads reflected the enthusiasm of young Catholics for physical exercise and bodybuilding. Family photographs record the gym that José Toral built in the back lot of his parents' house, where he trained on parallel bars and boxed with cousins and friends. In front of the camera, Toral posed shirtless and flexed his muscles. Perhaps his own body served as a model for the muscular male figure he painted in a large mural at art school.[38]

Condemning Consumerism and the Modern Gendered Body

The new consumer market provoked anxiety among critics who feared consumerism's pernicious influence on Mexican youth and gender norms. Female consumption drew the most condemnation, as both liberal and conservative critics denounced it as immoral and suspicious narcissism. Opponents particularly invested the female body with responsibility for maintaining markers not only of gender, but also of race and class. Criticism was also directed at men who put on pretentious airs and overly concerned themselves with their appearance. Thus, the male type known as the *fifí* (dandy) became a standard character of satire in cartoons and theatre during the 1920s.

In a satirical column of 1921 titled "Death of the Boulevard Stroller," Sánchez Filmador described the fifí as the contemporary version of the nineteenth-century *lagartijo* (dandy), or *flâneur*. Whereas the latter used to stroll down the main avenues, the contemporary fifí ogles women while standing in front of the fashionable El Globo café. Filmador likens the fifí to a "great buffoon," who, with his clean fingernails and attenuated eyebrows, "exhibit[s] a figure that thinks of itself as an Adonisian creature."[39] Tidy nails and groomed brows suggest an effeminate man who vainly and foolishly presents himself as a beauty worthy of a Greek god. In the play *Cándido Cordero,* the fifí appears as an "office type" prevalent among the young generation of middle-class employees who worried solely about their appearance, impressing women, and consuming the latest fads. The character Pepito, for example, dresses stylishly, flirts with the typists, and spends his nights teaching girls how to dance.[40] A similarly vain character drives to work in a car, appears in a new suit every month, boasts of having two lovers, and surrounds himself in the office with young women.[41]

Observers directed most of their complaints at women who used the mass market to blur class and racial lines. A growing consumer market dovetailed with post-revolutionary attempts to legitimize working-class, folkloric, and Indigenous cultures as expressions of Mexican identity *(mexicanidad)* and "the people" *(el pueblo).* As in the case of the Argentinian gaucho discussed by Cecilia Tossounian in Chapter 11 of this volume, middle-class public officials, intellectuals, and artists looked to the Indian *(el indio)* as representative of an authentic Mexico that was being lost through modernization. In the process, they began to rehabilitate the image of the Indian in the 1920s. They turned local Indigenous crafts into high art and sponsored beauty pageants to award the "pretty Indian" (India Bonita). In the 1930s, the socialist regime of Mexican president Lázaro Cárdenas intensified the discourse of *indigenismo,* while at the same time glorifying the industrial worker as the ideal Mexican citizen. In tandem with the state's official discourse celebrating dark-skinned lower classes, mass consumer culture further tolerated, even encouraged, the blurring of race and class boundaries. A new social order that elevated the Indian and the manual labourer unsettled many members of the middle class, who desperately sought to clearly demarcate class lines.

The advent of affordable fashions in clothing and accessories allowed an increasingly larger percentage of the population to participate in each commodity's promise of instant gratification and permanent self-transformation. The production of ready-to-wear clothes made cheap versions of high-style fashions accessible to a broader segment of the female population. Mexican women, who learned to sew at vocational schools or at home, stitched together modish dresses with the help of paper patterns found in women's magazines and shared between family members and friends. Popular trends such as the bobbed haircut further undermined class distinctions. Writing about Mexico

City in the 1930s, Salvador Novo noted that the city's barbershops were not prepared for the "invasion" of young women who wanted their hair cut short. The demand came from women of all classes and social standing. According to Novo, the new hairstyle craze prompted the opening of beauty salons in areas ranging from aristocratic elite neighbourhoods to those of the tenement-house poor.[42]

Modern fashion's ability to grant social status through the mere display of material attributes unleashed a furor of physical and discursive harassment. Some residents felt that only women of the upper classes should show off modern styles. For instance, at the height of the pelona (flapper) craze in 1924, a group of young male medical students assaulted a working-class female student who sported a bob.[43] This vicious attack reveals the high level of anxiety around modern forms of self-presentation and the sense of entitlement well-to-do male youths felt in guarding boundaries of class. Others felt that skin colour determined who had the right to wear modern fashions. In a 1929 newspaper article, one writer complained about situations in which "at times the skin is dark [but] the stockings are not black."[44] For the author, supposedly sheer or light-coloured stockings that marked modernity were reserved for women with skin to match. Thus, the dark-skinned women traversed a colour line when they appropriated modern styles. The indiscriminate availability of consumer products challenged Mexico City's long-standing markers of race, class, and gender. Thus, consumer and popular culture offered an exciting, as well as frightening, potential.

The modern girl's androgynous body type and hairstyle became the subject of much derision and criticism. Cartoonists depicted the chica moderna as a mannish woman who, like the fifí whose vanity prompted him to become an effeminate dandy, inverted gender norms.[45] The new fads signified more than a choice in clothing, as fashions rehearsed and re-enacted changing social and sexual boundaries, however exaggerated. The stereotypical chica moderna and the fifí threatened to destabilize gender roles through their exchange of work, marriage, and family for a life of hedonistic pleasures. Conservative Roman Catholics especially perceived new dress styles as an attack on traditional gender mores and church teachings. The fervent young Catholic José de León Toral, who assassinated Mexican president Álvaro Obregón in 1929, conveyed his worries about the immorality of modern times. While awaiting trial in prison, he wrote letters to his family and friends condemning the latest fashions and insisting that Christ's last judgment would occur only when each gender wore the appropriate "pants and petticoats" in Mexico.[46]

Few practising Catholics in Mexico City rejected modernity or modernization outright. Pious Catholic women entered the public world of office work
and even served as employees of Mexico's anti-clerical state bureaucracy. The
church hierarchy supported programs of lay Catholic organizations that used
radio and film to spread religious teachings. However, Catholics premised
femininity and masculinity on a distinct set of values and on a specific understanding of the body. An individual existed in reference to the larger structure
of the family, the church, and the kingdom of God. The monitoring and disciplining of the gaze and speech, combined with controlled and modest movements, expressed and constituted an internal attitude of a pious self. Catholics
eagerly emphasized hygiene because a clean and tidy body mirrored the condition of the soul. At the same time, an emphasis on cleanliness needed to be
balanced against the sins of vanity and pride.

Ardent Roman Catholics responded with alarm to the new styles of clothes
and types of behaviour that turned women's bodies into modern spectacles.
Knee-length skirts, transparent stockings, and bobbed hair revealed legs and
necks, parts of the female body that were previously covered. Although Catholic
women also rid themselves of the corset and wore fashionable flapper-style
dresses, the skirts generally reached the ankles rather than stopping at the knees.
Members of Damas Católicas, a women's Catholic organization, condemned
parents for allowing their daughters "to go naked according to current fashion."[47]
Catholic youth leader José Toral similarly worried about the length of women's
hemlines. In a sketch drawn in prison, he depicted his young aunt Lola with
bobbed hair, dangling earrings, and high heels. Standing in front of Jesus, Lola
attempts to pull her skirt over her knees. Jesus, indicating a few inches with his
finger, tells her, "A little bit longer."[48]

Desire, Affect, and the Experience of Modernity

Along with a new relationship to the body, modern culture simultaneously
ushered in a transformation in personal affect and public intimacy. For the first
time, middle-class Mexican women were encouraged to experience the body
as something enjoyable in itself. In turn, physical feelings of sensuality and
desire became more acknowledged. Mass media pushed sentimentality out of
the private sphere and presented greater and much more public sexual candour
than ever before. With cheers, laughs, tears, and sighs in the city's new public
arenas, patrons were sharing emotions and their bodies in unprecedented intimate ways.

In the late nineteenth century, mass-produced postcards became a popular way for people to express their affection and love. By the 1920s and 1930s, such postcards reflected notions of sentimentality emerging from the new mass media. The tokens of love and friendship, often collected into albums, depicted embracing movie star couples and included lyrics of love songs popularized by the radio. To spare customers the effort of seeking original poetic inspiration, the publishing company Casa Miret printed postcards that bore verses by well-known poets.[49] Other novelties included the Kiss-o-Gram postcard.[50] The cards reveal not so much a change in sentimentality as a shift in the experience of the body as an unashamed site of pleasure and sex appeal. Theatre and film stars portrayed on postcards from the 1920s epitomize the fun and spectacle of the sexualized body. María Conesa, Celia Padilla, Mimi Derba, and Esperanza Iris boldly showed off cropped hair, nail polish, and lipstick while flirting with the camera in revealing outfits.[51]

Emulating their favourite celebrities, young women paraded their fashionable looks in Mexico City's many dance halls. In 1920, only a few years after the revolutionary violence ended, the iconic Salón México opened its doors to a heterogeneous group of capitalinos. Patrons gathered on three different floors separated by social class to dance the foxtrot, the tango, the shimmy, and the Charleston. These modern dances necessitated a new type of physicality between the sexes in public space. Subtle modern dances such as the *danzón* required partners to move in a tight embrace and helped transform notions of public intimacy.[52] In the home, the gramophone and radio transmitted feelings of romantic love and, at times, erotic desire. In the 1920s, young people went wild over the energetic rhythms and syncopated beats of jazz. A decade later, the bolero escaped from the cabarets through the radios that extended its sound to the masses. The crooning voices of Guty Cárdenas and Agustín Lara enticed the imaginations of radio listeners.[53]

At the cinema, Mexicans watched private emotions magnified on the silver screen. In the forty-four cinemas Mexico City boasted in 1924, capitalinos experienced a transformation in gender behaviour and interpersonal relations.[54] Most probably, in Mexico, as in interwar Italy, the movies taught young people new ways of moving the body.[55] Certainly, movie-goers sought to imitate the embraces and kisses they saw on the screen. Guillermo Zendejas remembers that, when he was a boy in the 1930s, a girl asked him to "kiss me, embrace me like they do in the movies."[56] Dimly lit movie theatres gave young sweethearts opportunities to experiment with new types of gendered behaviour and expressions of love and affection beyond the watchful eyes of their parents.

Along with cinemas, other new public spaces such as dance halls and office buildings allowed for occasions to evade familial authority, dodge parental moralizing, and learn how to flirt, date, dance, drink, and smoke. At the same time, a range of professionals began to perceive childhood and adolescence as distinct phases in human development. According to historian Ann Blum, this corresponded with the family becoming increasingly based around a new type of emotional investment and affect.[57] The bourgeoning youth culture stemmed in part from the prolonging of school education and the growing numbers of young women working outside the home. Manufacturers, merchants, and advertisers exploited the new category of youth to sell a wide range of products aimed at students and young working professionals. Consumerism's emphasis on the individual and on the gratification of personal desires celebrated this liminal stage in the life cycle. In the process, notions about the purpose and meaning of life may have shifted. In the play *Cándido Cordero,* the secretary Flora plucks and pencils her eyebrows while sitting sleepily at her desk and recounting her escapades from the night before. Of life, she tells her co-worker Coti, one has "to get the most out of it as possible."[58]

Consumerism, as a means to experiment with fashioning a modern self, signified an investment in modernity. As Wilson Chacko Jacob argues in his work on early-twentieth-century Cairo, the middle-class desire to be modern fuelled an espousal of consumerism.[59] Likewise, in Mexico City, participation in consumer culture presumed an enchantment with the modern itself.[60] The transformative powers of commodities and modernity's liberating promises incited dreams that transcended the boundaries of class and geography. In *Cándido Cordero,* Manuela, one of Mr. Cordero's daughters, insists she will become a Hollywood star. After all, as she proudly tells her father, she has the face of Mary Astor and Pola Negri, the eyes of Norma Talmadge, and the passionate kisses of Bárbara la Mar.[61] Certainly Manuela, and the play's female audience members, had read about the real and exaggerated humble beginnings of Hollywood stars. If a working-class Brooklyn girl such as Clara Bow could find fame, maybe Mexico City's chicas modernas were right to dream big.

Anxious Critics of Modernity's Corrupting Influences

Proposed governmental legislation and hysterical accounts in newspapers and Roman Catholic publications attest to the anxiety generated by modern popular culture. One newspaper article worried that jazz, as a foreign sound, threatened Mexican national and folkloric music. Moreover, the article's author warned that the pulsating jazz rhythms were too much for the already sensitive and fiery blood of the Latin race.[62] Mexican Catholics and conservative observers attacked the popular singer Agustín Lara, whose lyrics evoked a public declaration of erotic desires for women, often prostitutes. Convinced of Lara's transgression of family values and public morality, Catholic clergy and laity condemned both him and his listeners.[63] In 1936, prompted by concerns that Lara's lyrics corrupted children, Mexico's national secretary of public education prohibited his songs in schools.[64]

Politicians and Roman Catholic leaders in Mexico City shared worries that movie-going stimulated dangerous libidinal forces. In 1922, the head of the municipal Department of Entertainment asked the city's municipal president for the right to review American and European films in order to halt the "continuing exhibition of movies denigrating to Mexico." Another municipal councillor agreed that movies were "true examples of criminality" that harmed honourable viewing families and their children.[65] Similarly, Catholic associations organized to ban films considered damaging to the morality of viewers. In 1933, Mexico City's division of the Knights of Columbus (Caballeros de Cólon) created a Mexican Legion of Decency (Legión Mexicana de la Decencia) through which, among other things, films were reviewed for (im)moral content. By 1935, the legion claimed to have "censured" two thousand films whose titles had been published in eighty bulletins.[66]

Other types of popular entertainment and consumerism fomented behaviour and emotions that steered capitalinos away from the bonds of the family. Catholic women denounced certain types of dancing that encouraged close physical contact between the sexes.[67] Municipal councillors spoke out against dance marathons, which they reported as having caused two women to spontaneously abort.[68] Popular diversions such as dancing not only threatened women's reproductive capacities, but also changed ideas about courtship. In 1921, satirical writer Sánchez Filmador described how in the past a suitor went once a week to the home of the woman he was courting. In the presence of the mother, sister, aunt, and dog, he may have passed a note or love letter. A kiss, however, would have garnered a slap. In contrast, the contemporary young man gives so many kisses that his girlfriend cries out, "Ay, don't be so cloying [*ampalagoso,* literally sickly sweet]!"[69] A 1929 newspaper article fretted that parents were allowing their daughters to attend cinemas and theatres, and to stroll "alone and very close to their current male wooer," who was not courting them with matrimony in mind.[70]

Despite the shifting of gender roles and the pushing of boundaries of social convention, Mexican society continued to judge women on older notions of gendered honour. Modesty and moderation in word and deed still defined a woman's moral character, sexuality, and class.[71] For many, vanity lay at the root of immodest behaviour. Hence, prostitutes were often associated with vanity's symbol, the mirror. A collection of pornographic postcards distributed in 1920s Mexico depicts naked women looking at themselves in a mirror or surrounded by mirrors.[72] Contemporary observers claimed that hedonistic consumerism and female narcissism, like prostitution, turned the female body into an object for egotistical self-actualization, rather than an instrument of reproduction.[73] Such sentiments continued into the 1930s. In Chapter 9 of this volume, Jane Nicholas writes of Canadian critics who condemned women's suggestive clothing for inspiring male immorality. Similarly, a Mexico City judge in 1935 made clear that women's public behaviour mattered in arbitrating rape cases: "It follows that a woman, even a virgin, who does not keep composure in her actions and words, who frequents places of corruption or centers of vice, who tolerates bad company is not honest and cannot be a passive subject of rape *[estupro]*." For this judge, honesty implied "composure, decency, moderation in actions and words ... modesty, reserve, courtesy, and decorum."[74]

Conclusion: The Production of the Gendered Modern Subject

In 1920s and 1930s Mexico City, young people came of age as a culture of popular entertainment and cheap consumer goods enabled new ways of experiencing and imagining the exterior body and its psychical interior of affect and desire. Consumer products and consumption practices offered men and women not only a shared "horizon of experience," but also a powerful physical (embodied) and emotional (psychical) investment in modernity.[75] The modern world required a new consciousness and sensibility that celebrated a subjectivity informed not only by temperance, self-control, and constraint, but also by the celebration of pleasure. Gender formed a crucial part of the construction and perception of the modern subject, as well as of modernity itself.

The rupture of the revolution and the advent of a mass consumer market transformed the lives and gender norms of Mexico City's inhabitants. Young women, however, may have experienced the most dramatic change, as they entered educational institutions and the paid workforce in unprecedented numbers. An emphasis on physical activity, along with the jettisoning of the corset and the adoption of short hairstyles, altered not only the appearance of the female body, but also how women moved through an enlarged public sphere of work and leisure. Discourses of woman-as-consumer and fears of unleashed desires produced a gendered vision of transgression and deviance. For pious

Roman Catholics, government officials, and urban critics alike, modernity constituted a threatening aberration of Mexican femininity and masculinity.

In a period of political and economic instability, with competing discourses from the post-revolutionary state bureaucracy, the church, and the mass marketers, the people of Mexico City inhabited and traversed the inherent tensions. Labour, hygiene, and exercise required a body of discipline, whereas popular diversions and consumer goods catered to a body of pleasure. The middle-class male, the ideal employee and domesticated family man, faced emasculation from the drain of modern urban life and vain consumerism. Shopping legitimized a new public role for the middle-class woman, but the display of her body and the expression of her desires threatened her sense of morality and class status. Catholics insisted on the need to preserve a Mexican femininity and masculinity based on religious values. Alongside Catholics, municipal councillors and urban reformers agreed on the need to constrain modernity's rapid changes, particularly those related to popular diversions, consumer spending, and gender behaviour. In the midst of contentious debates, a modern Mexican identity emerged as capitalinos watched movies, bought the latest fashions, and danced in each other's arms.

Notes

1 The Mexican Revolution was a major armed struggle that began in 1910 with an uprising led by Francisco I. Madero against President Porfirio Díaz. Over time the revolution became a multi-sided civil war. See Thomas Benjamin, *Mexico's Great Revolution as Memory, Myth, and History* (Austin: University of Texas Press, 2000); Michael J. Gonzalez, *The Mexican Revolution, 1910-1940* (Albuquerque: University of New Mexico Press, 2002); and Alan Knight, *The Mexican Revolution* (New York: Cambridge University Press, 1986).

2 See Susan K. Besse, *Restructuring Patriarchy: The Modernization of Gender Inequality in Brazil, 1914-1940* (Chapel Hill: University of North Carolina Press, 1996); Harry Harootunian, *History's Disquiet: Modernity, Cultural Practice, and the Question of Everyday Life* (New York: Columbia University Press, 2000); Katharina von Ankum, ed., *Women in the Metropolis: Gender and Modernity in Weimar Culture* (Berkeley: University of California Press, 1997); Alys Eve Weinbaum et al., eds., *The Modern Girl around the World: Consumption, Modernity, and Globalization* (Durham, NC: Duke University Press, 2008); and Joshua Zeitz, *Flapper: A Madcap Story of Sex, Style, Celebrity, and the Women Who Made America Modern* (New York: Three Rivers Press/Crown Press, 2006).

3 See Dilip Parameshwar Gaonkar, ed., *Alternative Modernities* (Durham, NC: Duke University Press, 2001); and Bruce M. Knauft, ed., *Critically Modern: Alternatives, Alterities, Anthropologies* (Bloomington: Indiana University Press, 2002).

4 Harry Harootunian argues against the use of adjectives such as "alternative" or "divergent" to describe the modernities of countries outside of Western Europe and the United States. He correctly points out that such modifiers imply a supposed original modernity based elsewhere. See Harootunian, *History's Disquiet,* 163.

5   See Katherine Bliss, *Prostitution, Public Health, and Gender Politics in Revolutionary Mexico City* (University Park: University of Pennsylvania Press, 2001); and Ann S. Blum, "Breaking and Making Families: Adoption and Public Welfare, Mexico City, 1938-1942," in *Sex in Revolution: Gender, Politics, and Power in Modern Mexico,* ed. Jocelyn Olcott, Mary Kay Vaughan, and Gabriela Cano (Durham, NC: Duke University Press, 2006), 127-44.

6   See Susie S. Porter, *Working Women in Mexico City: Public Discourses and Material Conditions, 1879-1931* (Tucson: University of Arizona Press, 2003); and Patience A. Schell, *Church and State Education in Revolutionary Mexico City* (Tucson: University of Arizona Press, 2003).

7   See Joanne Hershfield, *Imagining la Chica Moderna: Women, Nation, and Visual Culture in Mexico, 1917-1936* (Durham, NC: Duke University Press, 2008); and Anne Rubenstein, *Bad Language, Naked Ladies, and Other Threats to the Nation: A Political History of Comic Books in Mexico* (Durham, NC: Duke University Press, 1998).

8   See Rick A. López, "The India Bonita Contest of 1921 and the Ethnicization of Mexican National Culture," *Hispanic American Historical Review* 82, 2 (2002): 291-328; Ageeth Sluis, "City of Spectacles: Gender Performance, Revolutionary Reform, and the Creation of Public Space in Mexico City, 1915-1939" (PhD diss., University of Arizona, 2006); and Adriana Zavala, "De Santa a la India Bonita. Género, raza y modernidad en la Ciudad de México, 1921," in *Historia de mujeres y hombres en perspectiva de género, México siglos XIX y XX,* ed. María Teresa Fernández Aceves, Susie Porter, and Carmen Ramos Escandón (Mexico City: CIESAS, 2006), 149-87.

9   Harvie Ferguson, *Modernity and Subjectivity: Body, Soul, Spirit* (Charlottesville: University Press of Virginia, 2000), 20.

10 See Steven B. Bunker, "'Consumers of Good Taste': Marketing Modernity in Northern Mexico, 1890-1910," *Mexican Studies/Estudios Mexicanos* 13 (Summer 1997): 227-96.

11 See Erika D. Rappaport, "'A New Era of Shopping': The Promotion of Women's Pleasure in London's West End, 1909-1914," in *The Gender and Consumer Culture Reader,* ed. Jennifer Scanlon (New York: New York University Press, 2000), 30-48.

12 See Susanne Eineigel, "Visualizing the Self: Modernity, Identity, and the *Gente Decente* in Porfirian Mexico" (Master's thesis, University of British Columbia, 2003).

13 Michel Foucault, *History of Sexuality,* trans. Robert Hurley (New York: Pantheon Books, 1978), 1:126.

14 The number of female public employees increased from 171 in 1921 to 5,967 in 1930. *Quinto censo de población, 1930.* Dirección General de Estadística, México, DF. See also Susie S. Porter, "Empleadas públicas: normas de feminidad, espacios burocráticos e identidad de la clase media en México durante la década de 1930," in Aceves, Porter, and Ramos Escandón, *Historia de mujeres y hombres,* 189-213.

15 *Sexto censo de población 1940.* Dirección General de Estadística, México, DF. The censuses from 1930 and 1940 show a discrepancy for the year 1930. According to the 1940 census, female public employees increased from 5,701 in 1930 to 15,342 in 1940.

16 On the importance of consumer culture for single working-class women in the United States, see Nan Enstad, *Ladies of Labor, Girls of Adventure: Working Women, Popular Culture, and Labor Politics at the Turn of the Twentieth Century* (New York: Columbia University Press, 1999); and Kathy Peiss, *Cheap Amusements: Working Women and Leisure in Turn-of-the-Century New York* (Philadelphia: Temple University Press, 1986).

17 For example, see José Thomás de Cuéllar, "Having a Ball," in *The Magic Lantern: Having a Ball and Christmas Eve,* ed. Margo Glantz, trans. Margaret Carson (New York: Oxford University Press, 2000), 5-118.

18 On the debates about makeup in the twentieth century, see Sabine Hake, "In the Mirror of Fashion," in von Ankum, *Women in the Metropolis,* 185-201; and Kathy Peiss, "Making Up, Making Over: Cosmetics, Consumer Culture, and Women's Identity," in *The Sex of Things:*

Gender and Consumption in Historical Perspective, ed. Victoria de Grazia with Ellen Furlough (Berkeley: University of California Press, 1996), 311-36.

19   Max Factor advertisement, *Nuestra Ciudad*, April 1930, 32.

20   The old aunt also criticizes her niece for going to the cinema with a man during Lent. Denying that she is going to the cinema or to see her sweetheart, the niece explains that she "saw him [already] this afternoon after exercising." Sánchez Filmador, "Sermón de Cuaresma," *Zig Zag*, 17 March 1921, 43.

21   Colgate Toothpaste advertisement, "¿Irene, vas a ser una solterona?" *La Familia*, May 1937, n.p.

22   See Alexandra Minna Stern, "Responsible Mothers and Normal Children: Eugenics, Nationalism, and Welfare in Post-Revolutionary Mexico, 1920-1940," *Journal of Historical Sociology* 12 (December 1999): 369-97.

23   Previous prevailing medical views considered physical activity debilitating for middle- and upper-class women. These ideas shifted in the late nineteenth century when doctors and educators encouraged women to engage in recreational activity. See Schell, *Church and State Education*.

24   See the video-recording Mariana Romo Patiño, director, *Las Modernas: Preparatorias de la Generación de los viente* (Mexico City: UNAM, 1996).

25   *Lo Que Va de Ayer a Hoy, El Universal*, 3 August 1924, sec. 3, 7.

26   Quaker Oats advertisement, "Niños Fuertes y Saludables," *Excelsior*, 24 January 1923, sec. 1, 4.

27   See Porter, "Empleadas públicas."

28   Julio Jiménez Rueda, *Cándido Cordero, empleado público; farsa en tres actos* (Mexico City: Tallers gráficos de la nación, 1928). Even before watching the play, the audience would have grasped the meek character of the protagonist. The word *cordero* means weak and docile. The play appeared at the height of a debate about the state of Mexican literature and the masculinity of its prose, content, and authors. In February 1925, the playwright Julio Jiménez Rueda contributed to the debate with an article titled "The Misery of the Man of Letters," in which he described how "bureaucratic life kills all virility in intellectuals [and] that's why eunuchs crowd the offices." Quoted in Víctor Díaz Arciniega, *Querella por la cultura "revolucionaria"* (Mexico City: Fondo de Cultura Económica, 1989), 115. On masculinity in this period, see also Héctor Domínguez-Ruvalcaba, *Modernity and Nation in Mexican Representations of Masculinity: From Sensuality to Bloodshed* (New York: Palgrave Macmillan, 2007); and Ilene V. O'Malley, *The Myth of the Revolution: Hero Cults and the Institutionalization of the Mexican State, 1920-1940* (Westport, CT: Greenwood Press, 1986).

29   Gillette Razor advertisement, *Excelsior*, 12 January 1923, sec. 1, 7.

30   Gillette Razor advertisement, *El Universal*, 3 August 1927, sec. 1, 10.

31   "¿Travesuras de 'Muchachos'?" *Omega*, 17 April 1924, 1 and 3. The Gillette Company also urged women to use razors to shave the nape of their necks, newly exposed by the bob cut. See Gillette Razor advertisement, *El Universal*, 7 August 1927, sec. 3, 6.

32   Ovomaltina advertisement, *El Universal*, 26 October 1923, sec. 1, 9; Electricity Belt advertisement, *El Universal*, 23 November 1922, sec. 1, 12.

33   Mastin's Vitamin Tablets advertisement, *El Universal*, 11 June 1922, sec. 2, 3. The city itself became associated with the feminine and therefore dangerous for modern men. In his 1932 novel *La luciérnaga* (The firefly), Mariano Azuela laments the transformation of the capital into "that noisy feminine world that imposes its atmosphere on trains, automobiles, buses, converging and diverging pedestrians in the central square." Mariano Azuela, *La luciérnaga*, in *3 Novelas de Mariano Azuela* (Mexico City: Fondo de Cultura Económica, 1995), 104. Ageeth Sluis similarly argues that architects and artists in the 1920s and 1930s attempted to "feminize" the spaces of Mexico City. See Sluis, "City of Spectacles."

34   Gregorio Walerstein, interview by María Alba Pastor, 17 June 1975, PHO/2/25, Instituto Mora, Archivo de la Palabra, Mexico City.

35 Esperanza de León (daughter of José de León Toral), author interview, 12 March 2007.
36 Palacio de Hierro advertisement, *El Universal,* 10 July 1922, sec. 1, 8.
37 Other products advertised in Roman Catholic publications include calculating machines, Oliver Typewriters, and Kodak Cameras. *Estatutos o Bases Generales de la Liga Nacional de Estudiantes Católicos,* 1912, Fondo CLXXXII, Caja 1, Legado 05, Centro de Estudios de Historia de México (CONDUMEX), Mexico City.
38 Private collection of Esperanza de León, Mexico City.
39 Sánchez Filmador, "Murió el Boulevardeo," *Zig Zag,* 24 February 1921, 43.
40 Jiménez Rueda, *Cándido Cordero,* 63.
41 Ibid., 14.
42 Salvador Novo, *Nueva grandeza mexicana* (Mexico City: Conculta, 1946), 57.
43 See Anne Rubenstein, "'The War on *Las Pelonas:* Modern Women and Their Enemies, Mexico City, 1924," in Olcott, Vaughan, and Cano, *Sex in Revolution: Gender, Politics, and Power in Modern Mexico,* 57-80.
44 "La Moda Agente de Prostitución," *El Hombre Libre,* 2 October 1929, 4.
45 For example, see untitled cartoon, *Revista de Revista,* 26 August 1926, 28.
46 José de León Toral personal papers, private collection of Esperanza de León, Mexico City.
47 "La Moda Agente de Prostitución," 1.
48 Private collection of Esperanza de León, Mexico City.
49 Postales poéticas, 1924, Fondo Fototeca, G3-E4, Archivo General de la Nación (AGN) Mexico City. See also Isabel Fernández Tejedo, *Recuerdo de México: La Tarjeta Postal Mexicana, 1882-1930* (Mexico City: BANOBRAS, 1994), 124-25.
50 Gloria Fraser Gifords, ed., *La Tarjeta Postal* (Mexico City: Artes de México, n.d.), 72.
51 Fotos de Mujeres, 1925, Fondo Instrucción Pública y Bellas Artes, Propiedad Artistica y Literatura (IPBA. PAL), Caja 451, Exp. 3766, AGN.
52 See Robert Buffington, "'La Dancing' Mexicana: Danzón and the Transformation of Intimacy in Post-Revolutionary Mexico City," *Journal of Latin American Cultural Studies* 14 (March 2005): 87-108. See also Alberto Dallal, *El "dancing" mexicano* (Mexico City: SEP/Lecturas Mexicanas, 1987); and Marco Velázquez and Mary Kay Vaughan, "Mestizaje and Musical Nationalism in Mexico," in *The Eagle and the Virgin: Nation and Cultural Revolution in Mexico, 1920-1940,* ed. Mary Kay Vaughan and Steve Lewis (Durham, NC: Duke University Press, 2006), 95-118.
53 Mexico City boasted nineteen radio stations by 1929. See Joy Hayes, *Radio Nation: Communication, Popular Culture, and Nationalism in Mexico, 1920-1950* (Tucson: University of Arizona Press, 2000), 30. See also Pablo Dueñas and Jesús Flores y Escalante, *XEW: 65 Aniversario* (Mexico City: Sistema Radiópolis, 1995). On the bolero, see Carlos Monsiváis, *Mexican Postcards,* trans. John Kraniauskas (London: Verso, 1997), 180; and Mark Pedelty, "The Bolero: The Birth, Life, and Decline of Mexican Modernity," *Latin American Music Review* 20 (Spring-Summer 1999): 30-58.
54 Aurelio de los Reyes, *Cine y Sociedad en México, 1896-1930,* vol. 2, *Bajo el Cielo de México, 1920-1924* (Mexico City: UNAM, 1993).
55 Victoria de Grazia, *How Fascism Ruled Women, Italy 1922-1945* (Berkeley: University of California Press, 1992), 211.
56 Guillermo Zendejas, author interview, 16 March 2007.
57 Blum, "Breaking and Making Families," in Olcott, Vaughan, and Cano, *Sex in Revolution,* 127-44.
58 Jiménez Rueda, *Cándido Cordero,* 56.
59 Wilson Chacko Jacob, "Working Out Egypt: Masculinity and Subject Formation between Colonial Modernity and Nationalism, 1870-1940" (PhD diss., New York University, 2005).

60 Rita Felski, *The Gender of Modernity* (Cambridge, MA: Harvard University Press, 1995), 144.
61 Jiménez Rueda, *Cándido Cordero*, 34.
62 "Esta el 'Jazz' Condenado a Desaparecer?" *Cronos,* 18 June 1922, sec. 2, 2.
63 See Monsiváis, *Mexican Postcards,* 179.
64 See Mark Couture, "The Importance of Being Agustín Lara: Cursilería, Machismo, and Modernity," *Studies in Latin American Popular Culture* 20 (2001): 69-80.
65 "Censura para las películas de los cines," *Cronos,* 18 September 1922, sec. 1, 1.
66 "Legión Mexicana de la Decencia," 29 July 1935, Base de Pascual Díaz Barreto, Caja 41, Exp. 14, Archivo Histórico del Arzobispado de México, Mexico City.
67 "Moda y Bailes," *Omega,* 1922, sec. 1, 1 and 4, Caja 18, Exp. 12, Archivo Unión Femenina Católica Mexicana (UFCM), Mexico City. See also "Los Bailes Modernos, Las Modas Imperantes y la Trata de Blancas," *El Universal,* 1922, Caja 18, Exp. 13, UFCM.
68 *Actas y Versiones del Consejo Consultivo,* Tomo 21-2-T. 22 1, 23 February 1933, Archivo Histórico de Distrito Federal, Mexico City.
69 Sánchez Filmador, "Cosas de Viejos," *Zig Zag,* 13 January 1921, 22.
70 "La Moda Agente de Prostitución," 4.
71 See Katherine Elaine Bliss and Ann S. Blum, "Dangerous Driving: Adolescence, Sex, and the Gendered Experience of Public Space in Early-Twentieth-Century Mexico City," in *Gender, Sexuality, and Power in Latin America since Independence,* ed. William E. French and Katherine Elaine Bliss (Lanham, MD: Rowman and Littlefield, 2007), 163-86.
72 Desnudos, 1924, IPBA. PAL, G3-E3, AGN.
73 William E. French, "Prostitutes and Guardian Angels: Women, Work, and the Family in Porfirian Mexico," *Hispanic American Historical Review* 72, 4 (1992): 529-53.
74 Felipe Contla, "El delito de estupro," *Criminalia* 2 (April 1935): 111, quoted in Ira Beltrán-Garibay, "A State of Danger: Sexuality in Criminological and Judicial Discourse in Mexico, 1900-1940" (unpublished manuscript in author's possession), 21.
75 Miriam Hansen, *Babel and Babylon: Spectatorship in American Silent Film* (Cambridge, MA: Harvard University Press, 1991).

11

The Argentine Modern Girl and National Identity, Buenos Aires, 1920-40

Cecilia Tossounian

In Argentina, as was the case in countries around the world, new images of young womanhood flourished in the mass media during the 1920s and 1930s. Trend-conscious upper-class young women, wearing the latest imported fashions and pictured walking down Florida Street or racing around the city in top-down cars, were a common feature in newspapers and magazines of the interwar period. In sharp contrast to the traditional depiction of women as homemakers and caregivers, these stylish young women rapidly became the symbol of the modern city of Buenos Aires. And these trend-setting images were only the tip of the iceberg: relations between the sexes were also undergoing far-reaching transformations in Buenos Aires, part of the new gender practices and ideologies being disseminated by means of the global circuits comprising films, advertisements, and commodities.

During the interwar period, there was a growing sense of class and gender tumult and transformation. Rapid urbanization, the emergence of a consumer society, upward social mobility, the advent of mass politics, and the resulting political polarization all questioned past securities.[1] Concomitantly, traditional gender identities were being reconfigured by the rise in consumerism among middle- and upper-class women, the growing number of working-class women in the workforce, and the political challenges posed by feminists. Also worthy of note was the plethora of foreign images and styles in the mass media, where the fear that women were being masculinized and men feminized became a topic of debate. These processes, combined with a decrease in the fertility rate and a parallel decline in immigration following the First World War, prompted concern about the future of Argentina as a nation.[2]

Around 1910, the sense that Argentina was in the throes of a "moral crisis" was being discussed in the mass media, where concerned elitist intellectuals, journalists, and writers formulated their version of the clash between Argentine nationhood and modernity. The conclusion was that the excessive cosmopolitanism caused by foreign influences was threatening authentic Argentine cultural traditions and customs. Cultural nationalists gave voice to a nostalgic discourse that vilified the imported innovations they saw as irremediably destroying the past. In this context, "moral regeneration and the restoration of the national spirit appeared as two sides of the same movement."[3] Tradition was seen as the only force capable of counteracting the spread of moral and national dissolution. One outcome was the elevation of the mestizo gaucho, the cowboy of the Pampas, who embodied the virile, "atavistic" values of strength, honesty, and pride firmly rooted in the Argentine past, to combat the Europeanized elites residing in the morally corrupt city of Buenos Aires. Thus, the rural masses became the bearers of authentic Argentine nationhood. During the 1930s, Argentine identity acquired a populist, anti-elitist, and anti-imperialist undercurrent.[4] Among the gender images configuring the discourse on the risk that Argentina might lose its very soul in the course of becoming civilized and the anxiety this caused, the figure of the modern girl played a stellar role, as was the case in Canada and Mexico.[5]

According to recent historiography, the modern girl made her appearance on the world stage during the first half of the twentieth century.[6] Indeed, she was the creation of the set of global transformations occurring in the wake of the First World War. As Carolyn Kitch has shown, two factors were particularly important in this regard. On the one hand, a new morality became linked with an emergent youth culture, and on the other, there was a boom in leisure activities and products.[7] By the 1920s, the spread of multinational corporations and expanded mass media readership afforded this dual process a transnational dimension. Nevertheless, within each country, the transnational archetype of the modern girl was reshaped by the traditions and values inherent in the individual national context. My aim in this chapter is to analyze how the modern girl was defined in terms of gender relations and national identity in Buenos Aires during the 1920s and 1930s. To this end I will explore the uses to which her image was put in the mass media, specifically in general interest and women's magazines, folletines (serialized stories), and films. In the first section, I analyze the debate on gender role redefinition permeating the mass media of the period. In the second and third, I reconstruct the figure of the modern girl as young, upper-class woman, examining the diverse values she embodied as her image altered over time between 1920 and 1930. Viewing the modern young *porteña* (female resident of Buenos Aires) from different perspectives makes it possible to understand the paradoxes entailed in her evolution.

Gender Troubles: The Masculinization of Women and the Feminization of Men

A wide-ranging debate on gender role transformations took place in Argentina between the mid-1910s and the 1930s. During this period the behaviour of the modern girl, as well as the much-feared blurring of gender distinctions, was a frequent topic of discussion in the mass media. Cartoons were a favourite form of expression for gender reversal. In the late 1910s, the newspaper *Crítica* printed a series of cartoons under the title *Mujer Moderna* (Modern Woman) in which women toyed with men's sentiments whereas, unable to react, men were portrayed as too weak to confront the new situation. Two examples of cartoon dialogue are as follows:

> He (overjoyed) – So, are you going to be mine?
> She (aggressively) – No, that is not going to happen.
> He (surprised) – But you have just said that you are going to marry me.
> She (dogmatic) – That is different.[8]

> She – Am I the first woman you ever loved?
> He – Yes! And am I the first man who ever loved you?
> She (irritated) – Sir, you are insulting me.[9]

In another series of cartoons, the modern girl is depicted as a confident subject who merely flirts with men without taking them seriously. Titled *Mecha y su sombra* (Mecha and her shadow), it appeared in the women's magazine *Para Ti* between 1925 and 1931. Mecha, a young upper-class woman who spends her time going to parties with friends, is chased by Rino Pegotti, an unconditionally devoted suitor who never stops pursuing her, even though she constantly takes advantage of him. Bored with the adoration of this short, unattractive man who willingly submits to her humiliations, she prefers to go out with tall, handsome men far richer than he is.[10] Another example, titled *Exceso*, shows a modern girl and a man chatting in a bar. She announces, "I would be the happiest woman in the world if I had a boyfriend." The man exclaims, "How is it possible that you don't have one?" She responds, "The problem is that I have nine."[11] And in 1929, *Atlántida* published a cartoon in which a modern girl's mother says, "Dora, your behaviour is inappropriate. You are going out with a different man every day!" Her daughter responds, "You are right, mother. But find me one man who can afford to play tennis, golf, go for a drive and go out dancing during the week."[12]

Cartoonists tended to ironically and humorously portray men as victims of confident, often selfish modern girls who merely dallied with them. A far louder alarm was sounded by journalists such as Alberto Casal Castel at the social consequences of this gender role reversal. In a 1937 article published in *El Hogar*, he affirmed that the decline in the Argentine fertility rate was due to a "modern and new" concept of life lacking in moral fibre. Preferring to go out and have fun instead of bearing children, upper-class women in particular were pointed to as primarily responsible for the decline in the Argentine birth rate.[13] A related topic in vogue among cartoonists at the time was the risk run by a country with a population of masculinized women and feminized men. One cartoon, titled *Ante la duda* (When in doubt), shows a boy looking curiously at a masculinely dressed woman, who, when asked why he doesn't answer her, responds, "Because I don't know whether to call you Mr. or Miss."[14] In a second cartoon, *Cuestión peliaguda* (A tricky question), a woman looking at an ad for facial wax says to the pharmacist, "I'm not interested in waxing products. Would you have something that will make my moustache grow?"[15] And in a third, titled *Evas modernas* (Modern Eves), a woman states, "Why waste time arguing with my husband? Everybody knows men don't know anything about politics. Let's just chat while he serves us some tea."[16]

The problem of altered gender roles was taken up in 1930 by the well-known Argentine writer Horacio Quiroga. In an article titled "Las Amazonas" (The Amazons) that appeared in the magazine *El Hogar*, he described the "flapper" as someone who subjugated men by usurping their traditional spaces at the cost of her own femininity. He argued that contemporary women were fond of practising masculine sports and driving a car, whereas men were becoming feminized, and he cited two advertisements that exemplified the transformation. In the first, a woman embodying masculine values such as bravery is depicted next to a car, and in the second, a man representing the "delights of toiletries" is shown smelling perfume. For Quiroga these images were proof of the "subversion of sexual roles," a violation of the rules of nature. By permitting the masculinization of women, men were emasculating themselves.[17]

The figure of the morally emancipated, masculinized modern young woman also captured the attention of the feminist movement. Alicia Moreau de Justo, a socialist and one of the most prominent feminists in Argentina during the interwar period, protested against the widespread association of female emancipation with loose morals. She argued that copying men's vices would never liberate the modern woman. Only through work, not a "liberalization of her morals," could a woman gain her independence. "The fact that a woman smokes, drinks or has her own 'garçonnière' [woman's apartment] will never be taken as proof of independence," she stated. "Vice reduces the freedom of both women and men, and for many women who carry a packet of cigarettes next to their lipstick in their purse, this is their only modern trait."[18] In the view of feminists and left-wing women, the modern girl was sorely mistaken when she saw emancipation as synonymous with new habits such as smoking, drinking, and having a more open sexual life. This masculine behaviour was reprehensible not only because it masculinized women, but also because it represented the decadent morality of the upper class, especially its female members. In contrast, the New Woman feminists envisioned her emancipation as based on work, through which she would gain equal status with men without losing her femininity in the process.

There was considerable debate concerning the gender transformations under way, most notably in Buenos Aires. The sense that gender reversal had turned the world upside down provoked much anxiety. On the one hand, women were adopting what formerly had been considered men's prerogatives such as smoking, drinking, and dating more than one person at a time, and this masculinized them. On the other, by allowing women to get away with this, men were becoming feminized. The apparent cause of these gender role reversals was the new fashions and modern concept of life, as one author put it, that placed modern women in the spotlight. But just who was this modern woman, and why did she arouse such anxiety?

The Rise of the Upper-Class Modern Girl: Denationalizing the Nation

The modern woman in Argentina is best represented by the figure of the upper-class porteña modern girl. The class status of the Argentine *joven moderna,* as she was then called, dramatically differentiated her from the modern girl figure in the USA, where, as suggested by Kathy Peiss, young urban working-class women "pioneered many of the elements that constitute the modern girl" by embracing new fashions and undertaking daring excursions to dance halls and amusement parks. By contrast, in countries such as South Africa, China, India, Mexico, and Argentina, the modern girl was identified with an upper- or middle-class origin.[19]

Complementing journalists' articles and commentaries on the modern girl is "La Beba: Historia de una vida inútil" (La Beba: The story of a futile life), a weekly moral and satirical tale that appeared under the pseudonym Roxana in the magazine *Caras y Caretas* from June 1927 to March 1928. The protagonist, Beba, a seventeen-year-old upper-class modern girl, is portrayed in the first episode as frivolous, fanciful, and conceited, the symbol of an entire generation of young porteños, both female and male, who enjoy a "frenetic," "agitated," modern way of life "without caring about its consequences."[20]

Beba is pictured as thin and lithe, wearing abundant makeup and short skirts, and having bobbed hair. Her foil is her sister Martha, described as intelligent, quiet, somewhat old-fashioned, and always worrying about Beba's improper, impulsive behaviour. As the author noted, the sisters belong to two very different generations. Where Martha is reflexive and calm, Beba is flighty and frivolous – someone who "embodies all the manifestations of modern lightness." Together, the sisters represent the "past and the present" of Argentine society.[21]

In the following thirty-five episodes, Beba appears in various scenarios, carrying out diverse activities. She goes to theatres and the cinema, and to cafés and dance halls. She assiduously does the Charleston and dances the tango. She also smokes, drinks, sings tangos, drives her own car, and dresses up as a theatre actress for Carnival. Indeed, perpetual motion appears to be her defining characteristic. In every chapter, Beba goes to a different place to do something different.

Beba is first depicted as almost "innocent," someone who wants to experience life and comes progressively in contact with the customs of the modern city that corrupt her spirit. From the beginning, the author leads the reader to understand that challenges to morality originate outside traditional Argentine values in the form of a materialistic lifestyle imported from the USA. Various examples of this contamination process are offered. On the one hand, Beba is determined to see an allegedly "immoral" Hollywood film that provokes licentious desires in her.[22] On the other hand, the aspiration to trendiness of porteña modern girls like Beba induces them to adopt the fashions and customs of US and Argentine actresses – miniscule bathing suits and low-cut dresses, dancing the Charleston and the tango – that make them look cheap, like the lower-class actresses and singers of dubious morals who populate porteño cabarets (known as *bataclanas*).[23] Beba's interest in the "morbid" contents of foreign novels by "modern writers" shrivels her innocent soul.[24] And finally, the fact that Beba likes modern dances such as the Charleston and the tango, which require close physical contact and intimate postures, is considered scandalous because of the sexual connotations.[25] These influences serve to pervert an old type of "native" morality embodied in Martha and depicted nostalgically. By satirizing Beba and elevating Martha, the author was denouncing the penetration of foreign values and practices.

From the above, one would conclude that being modern clearly signified a wholehearted embrace of American manners and fashions. However, Beba's story makes equally clear references to certain national popular traditions such as the tango and the plebeian way of dressing and customs of actresses that Beba also adopted. The contamination of upper-class modern girls came not solely from American culture, but also from the Argentine national popular cultural tradition. These two cultural currents were presented as alien in a dual sense: they lay outside the traditions of the nation and of its upper classes.

From one standpoint, Beba likes modern dances such as "the Charleston, shimmy and black-bottom," which had been imported from the USA and, even worse, were "exotic," "savage," "uncivilized," and "inspired by the dances of African black people."[26] The author argued that modern/African dances were copied by Hollywood film stars and then adopted by Argentine girls in hopes that their enjoyment of these savage, exotic dances would mark them as different and modern.

From another standpoint, Beba is fond of the tango. In this story the tango retains its popular connotations, and dancing it implies downward mobility on the social scale. In addition, not only do modern girls like Beba dance the tango; they sing it as well. The lyrics, based on a popular jargon called *lunfardo*, were characterized by sexual references.[27] The author considered it indecent for upper-class girls to employ this popular argot.[28] Indeed, Beba embraces the tango and lunfardo slang to differentiate herself from her parents and sister, and to assume the role of an "ultra-chic" rebellious modern girl. An interesting aspect of this situation is that, in a sort of mirror gaze game, young women in Europe and the USA often danced the tango and dressed tango style in order to appear different, exotic, and modern themselves. Furthermore, these girls were often criticized for being "lascivious and decadent," and for "encouraging encounters between young ladies and men who might be of American and South American Negroid origin."[29]

Beba is also described as incapable of emotional commitment. She has several "modern" boyfriends who endorse the same values as she does. They flirt with her but, just like Beba, do not want to commit to a serious relationship.[30] In terms of morality, the contrast with Martha is apparent, for Martha desires sentimental romantic love and is an embodiment of the old morals.[31] In the last chapter of the story, the reader gets a glimpse of Beba, who, though now married, will eventually revert to the habits of her single life. Her new husband is an older man whom she hardly knows and with whom she is not in love. Beba chose the match because it will give her more freedom, but according to the author, this will eventually lead to the "crumbling of her future home," a dismal forecast of the consequences in store for national life.[32]

To sum up, Beba's modernity is cumulatively constructed in the course of the serialization of her story in a popular magazine. The initial prerequisites are physical: a short skirt on a slim body, bobbed hair, and heavy makeup. There is also a prescribed series of activities that include flirting and dancing the tango, watching Hollywood films, reading risqué novels, and speaking the Argentine thieves' argot called lunfardo. Always on the move, the joven moderna speeds from one cultural site to another in her own car, and her consumption habits include smoking and drinking in public. Seen as exemplifying the rapid pace of modern life, her body in perpetual motion signifies ongoing social change.[33] Beba is eloquent in this regard. Adopting foreign fashions and manners cost money, which meant that only those of upper- or at least comfortable middle-class status could afford them. However, Argentines who disdained the cosmopolitanism of the Europeanized elite did approve of one sector of well-off young women, who were seen as the repository of traditional aristocratic values. A case in point is Beba's sister Martha, who is depicted as the ultimate safeguard of the authentic femininity that constitutes the cornerstone of Argentine nationhood.

During the 1920s, a new approach to Beba's somewhat superficial modernity made its appearance. The female protagonist of writer and journalist Josué Quesada's short stories was sexually dangerous. This liberated variant of the modern porteña girl had an independent temperament that contravened traditional morality and socially accepted behaviour. The main character in a short story titled "La casa de soltera" (The single girl's apartment), written by Quesada but signed with the pseudonym Elsa Norton and published in *La Novela Semanal* in 1922, is a fearless young upper-class woman named Elsa who has her own car, is a jockey, can fly a plane, and has lived in Europe following a failed affair with an older man. On her return to Buenos Aires, she shares an apartment with her Russian lesbian lover. However, this bisexual love story is open-ended: unable to forget her former male lover, Elsa fires a shot from her gun when he proposes a ménage à trois.[34] Thus, the lesbianism Elsa acquired in Europe under the influence of a foreigner serves the author to denounce the extreme consequences that practitioners of modernity can suffer.

Another example of the dangers of modernity is found in a short story titled "La patotera" (A rowdy girl), written by Luis Cané and published in *La Mejor*

Novela in 1928. The protagonist, Clara, is a young married woman who hates her husband and has several lovers. Despite her wealth, Clara is snubbed by upper-class porteña women because of her provincial background. Her reaction is to seek out the company of men, and over time, she begins organizing "immoral parties" and snorting cocaine. The story ends with her death from an overdose. According to the author, this is yet another of "the consequence of the social disequilibrium" that Argentina is suffering from. He adds that modern girls like Clara emerge because of "our deficient education, our neglected culture, our exaggerated tolerance of some sorts of things and our national patience towards some social ills." They are the "rubbish of a noble and healthy community, where ... a sterile race of foolish women and effeminate men are being forged."[35]

Inexpensive editions of salacious stories portraying the vice-ridden porteña as rich women, typically from the upper classes, enjoyed a certain vogue in the 1920s; a number of them were published under the pseudonym Elsa Norton. The sexually dangerous joven moderna was sister to the figure of the vamp, or femme fatale, who threatened men with her audacious sexuality.[36] "Infidelity, adultery, drug abuse, lesbianism, the defence of divorce and disdain of arranged marriages" were common themes.[37] The storyline generally took the form of a cautionary tale forewarning middle- and working-class readers against the dire consequences awaiting female porteña elite members who indulged in morally aberrant behaviour. The constant punishment of the protagonist's assertive sexuality warned the target audience against any deviation from propriety and decorum.[38] Spiritual redemption came with death, either in the form of suicide or induced by disease or drug addiction. In any case, moral transgressions involving violations of accepted female behaviour inevitably resulted in tragedy. The manners and moral laxity of these upper-class modern girls were constantly wielded as the source of the urban malaise that was responsible for the degeneration of Argentine society.

In short, a graspable image of the modern porteña girl took shape in the mass media during the 1920s, its popularity peaking between 1925 and 1930. Although for all practical purposes their age, social class, appearance, and activities were constant, protagonists tended to be divided into two categories: the modern girl was either shallow and insensitive or dangerous and decadent. However, both variants were described as confident, selfish, and often masculinized subjects who imitated foreign fashions and toyed with men's sentiments. Male writers and journalists made use of the modern girl to address the negative effects of modern life on Argentine women.

The Feminization of the Upper-Class Modern Girl: Domesticating the Nation

In the course of the 1930s, the modern girl's inherent traditionally feminine and maternal attributes came into play. In two films shot during this period, the upper-class modern girl was conceived of in a new way. Both were directed by Manuel Romero (1891-1954), who worked for Lumiton studios and was one of the most prolific and popular Argentine filmmakers in the 1930s. This film director, journalist, producer of musical variety shows, and tango lyric writer knew how to construct recognizable archetypes that "symbolize the popular imagery of Buenos Aires" for filmgoers.[39] One such character was the upper-class modern girl. Following the Hollywood model of the 1930s, especially the sophisticated comedy genre, Romero directed *La rubia del camino* (The blond on the road), a 1938 film whose narrative structure was moulded on the model of the Frank Capra film *It Happened One Night* (1934).[40] Both this film and the subsequent *Isabelita* (1940) employ the same formula: a rich modern girl – independent, liberated, fanciful, and snobbish – is domesticated by the love of a man of humble origin, who redeems her from her frivolous existence by introducing her to the values of the working-class world. Both films end happily when love and marriage triumph over class prejudice. Framed as melodramas, these comedies portray the upper class as snobbish, egocentric, and sometimes evil, in sharp contrast to the generous, noble characters of humble origin.[41] I will focus on *La rubia del camino*, a box office success revived on several occasions, because it exemplifies the basic model of this variant of the modern girl that was employed in subsequent films.

In the opening scenes of *La rubia del camino*, the main character, Betty (played by Paulina Singerman), is shown in an expensive hotel in the south of Argentina (the Llao Llao in Bariloche), where she is spending her holidays with her family, her womanizing boyfriend, and a gold-digging Italian count. The film opens with Betty being rude to servants and making snobbish remarks about the "*chusma*" and "*gentusa*" (rabble) invading the hotel. She is portrayed as a glamorous, fashionably attired blond – as noted in the title – who likes to smoke. Feeling trapped by the hounding of her boyfriend and the Italian count, and by her father's attempt to control her choice of a spouse, she runs away from her engagement party and persuades a truck driver, Julián (Fernando Borel), to drive her to Buenos Aires. Before fleeing, she asks her grandfather what life is all about. He answers, "Life is struggle, grief, work and suffering." She protests, "But I am rich! There's no reason why I have to work, struggle, or suffer." Her grandfather replies, "Some day you'll understand me." In a previous scene, faced with Betty's childish whims, her grandfather complains, "She is what we all have made of her, a modern girl [chica moderna] ... spoilt and arrogant."

During their one-week trip to Buenos Aires, Betty and the truck driver experience a series of adventures and ultimately fall in love. The most interesting part of the film concerns Betty's transformation from frivolous upper-class modern girl to a woman worthy of becoming Julián's wife. Described in different ways in the film, the relation between modernity and national identity is resolved in the end when Betty – the protagonist's foreign nickname – becomes Isabel, an authentic female Argentine.

Julián and Betty represent the classic noble, generous poor versus the arrogant, fanciful rich. At first, they feel uncomfortable with each other. Julián rejects Betty's caprices, and she, in turn, is disgusted by his working-class behaviour, scorning the cheap cigarettes he smokes, his dull taste in music, and the food he eats. Yet Betty's stubbornness and arrogance make her determined to complete the trip. Soon she begins to feel attracted to Julián, especially after a fight in which he saves both of them from being robbed by a gang. Admiring his courage, an attribute utterly lacking in her urban suitors, Betty finds herself falling in love with a man who can defend her. Following this scene, she agrees to sleep on the ground and even to drink mate, the green tea favoured by the Argentine working class for breakfast. Mate is brewed in a gourd, but she does not know how to prepare it because, as she explains to Julián, she was educated in Europe. She confesses that she had tried it once and found it repugnant. Looking at her with a mixture of surprise, disdain, and paternalism, Julián teaches her how to make a good mate, which she enjoys drinking. The symbolic role of mate, the national beverage associated with the gaucho and his traditional rural lifestyle, which Julián embodies, is significant. Julián also insists on calling Betty by her real name, Isabel, and not her foreign nickname. For her part, she exchanges her expensive, glamorous attire for the plain garments she is offered by a female friend of Julián's. Betty's increasingly close contact with the Argentine working-class world represented by Julián and his friends leads her to rethink her own lifestyle and attitude toward the characters of humble origin in the film who, supportive and noble, offer her food, shelter, clothes, and the possibility of returning to Buenos Aires, without asking anything in return.

The turning point of *La rubia del camino* comes when Betty helps deliver the baby of the wife of an Italian friend of Julián's who lives on a hardscrabble farm in the country without access to medical care. At this point, the roles are reversed. The hopelessly impractical, inept Betty takes charge, whereas Julián, who until this time has patronized her, is completely at sea. Now Betty teaches

Julián a lesson in life. From then on, her condescending attitude disappears, and she unreservedly embraces the values of the popular version of Argentine nationhood by eating *salamines y pan* (sausage and bread), the typical working-class fare she formerly disdained, listening to popular music, and even singing popular songs along with Julián in the truck. Moreover, seeing her through different eyes, Julián remarks on her transformation: "What a change! You don't seem like the same woman I found on the road yesterday ... A modern, useless, frivolous girl like you turned out to be a fairy godmother to those poor people." Matthew Karush has accurately pointed out the importance of the birth scene.[42] Betty discovers her femininity by letting her maternal instinct emerge, despite her shallow, immature past. She is transformed during the scene, becoming not only a grown woman, but also an authentic Argentine capable of loving Julián for what he is. The modern, rich, Europeanized Betty has given birth to Isabel.

When they reach Buenos Aires, however, the couple's relationship is threatened by the class differences that arise as an obstacle to their happiness. Isabel introduces Julián to her parents, and, faced with their reproving gaze, exclaims, "Don't think I'm the same person. This trip has transformed me. I have become a woman." But once Isabel is back in Buenos Aires, her recently acquired traditional Argentine womanhood becomes blurred. She begins giving orders to the servants again; she takes Julián shopping with her and tries to dress him up like a millionaire in expensive clothes. In other words, the upper-class modern Betty reappears. Her modern friends call Julián "Tarzan," suggesting he change his name to something more French and consequently, more chic. In Buenos Aires, it is Julián who must adapt to a new environment. But the director does not advance this storyline. Instead, he paints cosmopolitan upper-class porteño society as too snobbish, frivolous, and decadent to accept Julián for what he is, a truck driver. Concomitantly, Julián will never abandon his authentic popular Argentine identity in order to be accepted by a phoney Europeanized elite. At a party celebrating Betty's engagement to Julián, her old boyfriend shows up and tries to convince her that marrying a truck driver is a mistake. Feeling humiliated and betrayed, Julián decides to go back to driving a truck, leaving both Buenos Aires and Betty. However, she soon realizes that she was wrong in forcing Julián to become something that he was not. Understanding that she herself must change, she returns to the poor Italian's farm in the country. In the final scene, she appears holding the baby she helped bring into the world, exclaiming to the surprised Julián, "I am not Betty, I am Isabel." Interclass love as a symbol of national reconciliation triumphs in the end when Betty definitively assumes the role of Isabel.

Various values, some contradictory, are attached to the characters of this film. Betty is not only rich and fond of foreign fashions and customs, she is also modern and lives in Buenos Aires. By contrast, though poor, Julián is an "authentic" Argentine, with a traditional understanding of life, who lives in the countryside. Betty's modernity is the driving force in the film. Her independent, capricious nature is what induces her to defy her father and flee the hotel, embarking on the adventure that leads her to Julián. Nevertheless, this same modernity must be sacrificed so that she can become a noble Argentine woman. In order to have a future, the modern girl is obliged to abandon her elite, Europeanized milieu in Buenos Aires and become a domesticated housewife living in the country, where the true values of Argentine nationhood reside.

The preponderant role played by the figure of the modern girl in the formation of Argentine nationhood is clearly delineated in *La rubia del camino;* her transformation from modern girl to traditional Argentine wife and mother is the precondition for national reconciliation. This requires a coherent reformulation of national identity, based on the pre-existing authentic Argentine values embodied in the male protagonist Julián. The result is a conservative vision of Argentine nationhood constructed around the pillars of tradition and male chauvinism.

Final Remarks

A change in gender relations took place in the city of Buenos Aires during the interwar period. A decline in the fertility rate and the blurring of gender distinctions prompted concerns about both the behaviour of porteño women and men, and the future of the Argentine nation. The consequences of these modifications in gender roles were the subject of intense debate in the mass media of the period. At the core of the ongoing controversy was the figure of the modern girl; the debate centred on who she was and what she represented. She owed this privileged position to the fact that her image conveyed the idea of modernity and its tensions more effectively than the figure of the modern guy.

The image was not uniformly expressed. It was variously portrayed as a masculinized, frivolous, fanciful, conceited, and egocentric subject that was sexually adventurous at times and liked to imitate foreign fashions and manners; the sole constant among the variants was the overstepping of the conventional boundaries delimiting the roles of devoted daughter and wife.

Above all, the modern girl embodied the values associated with the innovations in lifestyle experienced during the 1920s and 1930s; more than anything else, she was a male construction. Modernity was perceived by male intellectuals, writers, and essayists as an invasive, foreign-inspired process that threatened to destroy Argentina's unique, authentic character. In their view, the menace of moral and national dissolution should be countered by an interlinked process that would bring about moral regeneration and the restoration of the Argentine national spirit; the modern girl was seen as the personification of both dangers. By defying gender norms and integrating a transnational commodity culture, she threatened national identity. She was attacked as an agent of the denationalization and emasculation of Argentine identity. To counteract this dual peril, critics proposed a categorical return to traditional values and notions of femininity. Most of the sources analyzed for this chapter voiced a straightforward critique of the Europeanized, cosmopolitan lifestyle of the porteño elite, which was blamed for Argentina's loss of its authentic soul. The implement for making this point was the figure of the upper-class modern girl. However, more than one argument was made to reach this conclusion.

From one perspective, the much-feared merging of gender distinctions was seen primarily as the consequence of the masculinization of mainly upper-class women. The inability of men to impede it elicited gender role reversal, turning males into feminized members of the weaker sex. The blame was pinned on the modern girl, who was held responsible for emasculating the nation and the national identity. The remedy was to elevate the virile figure of the gaucho.

Another approach was to mount a defence of the traditional concept of womanhood by contrasting it with the modern girl's penchant for adopting foreign values and customs, especially those imported from the USA. A prime example is the serialized story of Beba, whose calm, modest sister Martha maintains her affinity for the old lifestyle and morality. It was equally important for upper-class women to preserve the traditional boundary between elite and popular cultures, as certain intellectuals and journalists viewed the merging of the two with a jaundiced eye. By dancing and singing the tango, Beba was clearly guilty of crossing the line. Thus it was that conservative upper-class girls became the ultimate bearers of the traditional notion of Argentine nationhood that rested on a glorified past and an idealized interregnum, during which uncontaminated female elites behaved properly.

The decadent modern girl portrayed in inexpensive short-story collections was a variation on the same theme. The unhappy fate of their upper-class protagonists with lax morals served to warn a working- and middle-class audience about the consequences of embracing modernity, which brought pain and death to the female protagonists. It could also be concluded that these corrupt rich girls could in no way be taken as moral models for the Argentine nation. But because there was no tradition to revert to, no alternative solution could be offered in this case: confident sexual femininity was transgressive and had to be punished with death – end of story.

For the modern girl, the final turn of the screw was her depiction as the antagonist of *el pueblo* (the people) and its values that circulated during the 1930s. *La rubia del camino* is a prime example of this variant. In it, the Argentine upper class enthusiastically endorses the decadent cosmopolitan values that are the enemy of the ideals of the poor, honest, unselfish, hard-working women and men who are genuine Argentines. The viewpoint taken by modern girl critics now assumes a populist stance: the traditional uncorrupted sector of the porteña upper-class women represented by Martha in the battle against Beba's modernity has been replaced by el pueblo, comprising the working class and its traditions. In the end, the repository of authentic values underlying the Argentine nationhood that was being sullied by the figure of the joven moderna shifted from the traditional sector of the female porteña elite to the working-class world and its values.

Notes

1 By the 1930s, Buenos Aires had become a large cosmopolitan metropolis, with 2,300,000 inhabitants. José Luis Romero, "La ciudad burguesa," in *Buenos Aires: Historia de Cuatro Siglos,* ed. José Luis Romero and Luis Alberto Romero (Buenos Aires: Abril, 1983), 2:9. For the emergence of a consumer society, see, among others, Fernando Rocchi, "La Americanización del Consumo: Las Batallas por el Mercado Argentino, (1920-1945)," in *Americanización: Estados Unidos y América Latina en el siglo XX,* ed. María Barbero and Andrés Regalsky (Buenos Aires: EDUNTREF, 2003), 131-89.

2 By 1947, female labour represented 28 percent of the economically active population. Zulma Recchini de Lattes and Catalina Wainerman, "Empleo femenino y desarrollo económico: algunas evidencias," *Desarrollo Económico* 17, 66 (1977): 301-17. By the beginning of the 1930s, the birth rate had fallen to under thirty per thousand, a tendency that continued for the entire period (1914, thirty-six per thousand; 1947, twenty-one per thousand). The average number of children per woman in Buenos Aires fell from 3.38 in 1914 to 1.34 in 1936. Susana Torrado, *Historia de la familia en la Argentina moderna 1870-2000* (Buenos Aires: De la Flor, 2003), 84-87, 240-54, 323-41; Victoria Mazzeo, ed., Situación Demográfica de la Capital Federal, *Serie Análisis Demográfico* 10 (Buenos Aires: INDEC, 1997), 12.

3 Carlos Altamirano, "La fundación de la literatura argentina," in *Ensayos Argentinos: De Sarmiento a la Vanguardia,* ed. Carlos Altamirano and Beatriz Sarlo (1983; repr., Buenos Aires: Ariel, 1997), 207.

4 Jean Delaney, "Imagining El Ser Argentino: Cultural Nationalism and Romantic Concepts of Nationhood in Early Twentieth-Century Argentina," *Journal of Latin American Studies* 34, 3 (2002): 625-58.

5 See Chapters 9 and 10 in this volume.

6 See, among others, Alys Eve Weinbaum et al., eds., *The Modern Girl around the World: Consumption, Modernity, and Globalization* (Durham, NC: Duke University Press, 2008); and Ann Heilmann and Margaret Beetham, eds., *New Woman Hybridities: Femininity, Feminism and International Consumer Culture, 1880-1930* (London: Routledge, 2004).

7   Carolyn Kitch, *The Girl on the Magazine Cover: The Origins of Visual Stereotypes in American Mass Media* (Chapel Hill, NC: University of Chapel Hill Press, 2001), 121.

8   Mujer Moderna, *Crítica*, 13 December 1919, 2.

9   Mujer Moderna, *Crítica*, 15 December 1919, 5.

10   *Para Ti*, several issues.

11   Exceso, *Caras y Caretas*, 8 January 1927, n.p.

12   Untitled cartoon, *Atlántida*, 12 September 1929, 19.

13   Alberto Casal Castel, "Neomalthusianismo," *El Hogar*, 5 November 1937, 3.

14   Ante la duda, *Caras y Caretas*, 1 January 1927, n.p.

15   Cuestión peliaguda, *Caras y Caretas*, 8 January 1927, n.p.

16   Evas Modernas, *Crítica*, 3 July 1919, 3.

17   Horacio Quiroga, "Las Amazonas," *El Hogar*, 17 January 1930, 8.

18   Alicia Moreau de Justo, *La mujer en la democracia* (Buenos Aires: El Ateneo, 1945), 110.

19   Kathy Peiss, "Girls Lean Back Everywhere," in Weinbaum et al., *The Modern Girl around the World*, 352; Joanne Hershfield, *Imagining la Chica Moderna: Women, Nation, and Visual Culture in Mexico, 1917-1936* (Durham, NC: Duke University Press, 2008), 5; see also Chapter 10 of this volume.

20   "La Beba: Historia de una vida inútil," *Caras y Caretas*, 11 June 1927, n.p. Consuelo Moreno de Dupuy de Lôme wrote for several magazines under the pseudonym of Roxana. One of Argentina's first female journalists, she also worked as a high school inspector and in the Consejo Nacional de Mujeres, doing charity work. Lily Sosa de Newton, *Diccionario Biográfico de Mujeres Argentinas*, 3rd ed. (Buenos Aires: Plus Ultra, 1986), 427. I would like to thank Julia Ariza for sharing this information.

21   "La Beba ya está en sociedad," *Caras y Caretas*, 2 July 1927, n.p.

22   "Beba va al cine por la tarde," *Caras y Caretas*, 30 July 1927, n.p.

23   "Beba se baña en el mar," *Caras y Caretas*, 26 January 1928, n.p.; "Beba aprende a bailar el Charleston," *Caras y Caretas*, 10 September 1927, n.p.

24   "Beba va a comprar libros," *Caras y Caretas*, 5 November 1927, n.p.

25   "La Beba se presenta en sociedad," *Caras y Caretas*, 25 June 1927, n.p.

26   "Beba asiste a lecciones de baile," *Caras y Caretas*, 29 October 1927, n.p.; "Beba aprende a bailar el Charleston," n.p.

27   Lunfardo is understood as a collection of words brought by the immigration process of the turn of the century and used by the working classes of Buenos Aires. Originally, it was a slang used by criminals. José Gobello, Nuevo Diccionario Lunfardo (Buenos Aires: Corregidor, 2008), 9.

28   "Beba canta tangos," *Caras y Caretas*, 3 December 1927, n.p.

29   Mica Nava, "The Cosmopolitanism of Commerce and the Allure of Difference: Selfridges, the Russian Ballet and the Tango, 1911-1914," *International Journal of Cultural Studies* 1, 2 (1998): 179.

30   "Beba regresa del crucero," *Caras y Caretas*, 22 October 1927, n.p.

31   "Beba se tutea con sus amigos," *Caras y Caretas*, 10 December 1927, n.p.

32   "Beba es ahora una señora casada," *Caras y Caretas*, 24 March 1928, n.p.

33   Vicky Unruh, *Performing Women and Modern Literary Culture in Latin America: Intervening Acts* (Austin: University of Texas Press, 2006), 15.

34   Elsa Norton, "La casa de soltera," *La Novela Semanal* 222 (1922): n.p. For an analysis of this short story, see Francine Masiello, *Between Civilization and Barbarism: Women, Nation and Literary Culture in Modern Argentina* (Lincoln: University of Nebraska Press, 1992), 170-71.

35   Luis Cané, "La patotera," *La Mejor Novela* 7 (1928): n.p. "Patotera" is a lunfardo word that denotes membership in a gang composed of wealthy young men who generally meet in the

streets and attack or mug peaceful people for fun or out of sheer boredom. Gobello, *Nuevo Diccionario Lunfardo*, 195.

36 The vamp was characterized as a dark sexual subject who sought revenge by destroying men and who lived outside the sphere of home and family. She was usually categorized with the prostitute. Kitch, *The Girl on the Magazine Cover*, 60-61.

37 Under the pseudonym of Elsa Norton, Enrique García Velloso published "Un casamiento en el gran mundo," *La Novela Semanal* 15 (1918): n.p. Also under the same pseudonym, Josué Quesada published "El escándalo de la avenida Alvear," *La Novela Semanal* 178 (1921): n.p. See also Margarita Pierini, ed., *La Novela Semanal. Buenos Aires 1917-1927: Un proyecto editorial para una ciudad moderna* (Madrid: Consejo Superior de Investigaciones Científicas, 2004), 104-5.

38 Masiello, *Between Civilization and Barbarism*, 168.

39 Ricardo Manetti, "Manuel Romero," in *Cine Argentino: Industria y Clasisismo, 1933-1956*, ed. Claudio España (Buenos Aires: Fondo Nacional de las Artes, 2000), 1:80-81.

40 Domingo De Núbila, *La Época de Oro: Historia del Cine Argentino* (1960; repr., Buenos Aires: El Jilguero, 1998), 1:81.

41 In *Isabelita*, the modern girl (played by Paulina Singerman, who also starred in *La rubia del camino*) falls in love with a working-class tango singer.

42 Matthew B. Karush, "The Melodramatic Nation: Integration and Polarization in the Argentine Cinema of the 1930s," *Hispanic American Historical Review* 87, 2 (2007): 323.

Part 4   TEXTS AND IDEOLOGIES
         OF MODERNITY AND
         CONSUMERISM

⋮

12

Protecting Gender Norms at the Local Movie Theatre: The Heidelberg Committee, 1919-33

Kara Ritzheimer

Defeat in the First World War did little to dampen Germans' enthusiasm for the movies, perhaps because cinema enabled them to buy a momentary escape from the trials and tribulations of daily post-war life and enter into a dream world where their favourite movie stars acted out thrilling melodramas. This was, after all, the cinematic era in which Fritz Lang's futuristic *Metropolis* (1927) wowed audiences, Peter Lorre delivered a chilling portrayal of a child murderer in *M* (1931), and Marlene Dietrich gave a memorable performance as Lola Lola in *The Blue Angel* (1930).

Film's widespread popularity in the 1920s signalled not only a general enthusiasm for cinema but also the arrival of a modern consumer culture that had been maturing since the late nineteenth century. The twin processes of industrialization and urbanization helped to produce consumers who shopped in large department stores, read advertisements, and spent their free time and disposable income in restaurants, dance halls, and cabarets. By the early 1900s, these new consumers could read cheap novels and pamphlet stories, join sports clubs, or visit amusement parks. Rationing, censorship, and stringent military restrictions during the First World War temporarily suppressed this consumer culture, but by the 1920s, it was in full swing. Advertisements encouraged Germans to buy, among other things, floor polish, shoe polish, electric stoves, vacuum cleaners, refrigerators, baby cereal, body creams, makeup, toothpaste, automobiles, cameras, mass-produced clothing, and vacations. Relatively cheap and readily available, cinema soon became a widely consumed and highly visual commodity in the interwar period. In 1925, the number of cinemas in Germany peaked at 3,878.[1]

The medium's popularity and visual nature made it both attractive and suspect. Its ability to captivate viewers and transport them to another place and time undoubtedly contributed to its popularity in a Germany that had endured defeat, loss, revolution, hyperinflation, and even foreign occupation during the years immediately following the First World War. Yet from the perspective of many critics, film was a potentially destabilizing force. It projected onto screens new definitions of femininity and masculinity, such as the vamp and the playboy, that might undermine the nation's recovery by discouraging women and men from assuming traditional gender roles and practising sexual mores that would generate more marriages, produce higher birth rates, and heal the physical and spiritual damage inflicted by war. Measured in bodies, the war had killed over 2 million soldiers and left another 4 million wounded. Measured in terms of family structure, the damage was clear; marriage rates had dropped markedly, fertility rates had declined, and the number of illegitimate births had increased.[2]

This chapter argues that in interwar Germany, men and women who were unnerved by perceived shifts in gender ideals sought to use film censorship as a means of shoring up traditional definitions of masculinity and femininity. It does so by studying a film-monitoring committee that operated in Heidelberg, a university town located in the southwestern state of Baden, during the Weimar era. This committee emerged during an eighteen-month period in which there was no legal basis for censorship at either the regional or national level (November 1918 to May 1920). It initially operated as a local censor before becoming an enforcer of the 1920 National Motion Picture Law. As such, it submitted several proposals asking that federal authorities reconsider the permissibility status of a specific scene or an entire film. Its members, this chapter argues, used their authority to request censorship for scenes or films in which characters contravened traditional gender norms and sexual mores. In doing so, they used the state's power to regulate consumer culture and suppress new and troubling definitions of femininity and masculinity.

Censorship Laws and "Enlightenment Films"

In July 1919, a commentator in the southwestern city of Freiburg asserted that movies were functioning as an "uninterrupted stream of poison" invading the population and endangering the nation's future.[3] In the same month, a state legislator in Baden argued that whereas the war had killed eight thousand soldiers daily during the last weeks of fighting, cinema was claiming more than three thousand souls a day.[4] These complaints about film must be placed in the context of Germany's defeat in the First World War.

War's end had an immediate impact on Germany's political system that in turn affected censorship laws. Cognizant of their loss, by October 1918 military commanders began to transfer power back to civilian authorities, who initiated a democratization of government in hopes of securing a more tolerable peace from the Entente powers. To this end, they persuaded Kaiser Wilhelm II to abdicate on 9 November. An interim government called the Council of People's Representatives (Rat der Volksbeauftragten) replaced him until new elections could be held for a constituent assembly that would solidify Germany's transformation from a constitutional monarchy to a parliamentary democracy. In an effort to eradicate the authoritarian vestiges of the prior regime, this interim government repealed all forms of censorship on 12 November 1918.[5] This action invalidated both pre-war state laws and the strict regulations that military commanders had imposed on cinema between 1914 and 1918.[6] In August 1919, article 118 of the new constitution codified this repeal by decreeing, "Within the limits of the general laws, every German has the right to express his opinion freely in words, writing, print, pictures, or in other ways." But the article also contained a proviso that read, "There is to be no censorship, but the law may provide otherwise for motion pictures." Such language was intended to provide future lawmakers with the jurisdiction they needed to craft a national film law.[7]

The initial regulatory vacuum created by these changes fuelled the production of so-called enlightenment, or *Aufklärung*, films. This genre of movies built on a tradition first laid down by individuals such as Richard Oswald and Magnus Hirschfeld, two sex reformers who had produced films during the First World War that sought to provide movie-goers with valuable information about sexuality and disease prevention.[8] After the war, film producers exploited the suspension of censorship laws to create titillating films that would draw audiences into theatres and generate profits. Between November 1918 and May 1920, approximately 150 such movies were produced in Germany, finding their way into small and large towns alike.[9] In Freiburg, for example, local observers complained in 1919 that theatres were showing movies with titles such as Hyenas of Lust, The Troubled Wedding Night, Forlorn Daughter, The Soul Seller, Dirty Gold, and The Diary of a Lost One.[10]

This genre of films motivated many organizations to lobby local officials to take action in the absence of national censorship. They justified their demands by underscoring the harmful impact that enlightenment films could have on traditional gender norms. In November 1919, several Freiburg women's associations urged municipal authorities to impose local controls on the grounds that these films frequently depicted women as prostitutes and pleasure objects, thereby degrading them and undermining "a healthy sentiment for family and marriage."[11] In the same month, forty-eight women's groups in Heidelberg complained that enlightenment films emitted a poison capable of undermining the "moral health of the population" and were therefore destroying the nation's future.[12]

Censorship returned to Germany on 12 May 1920 when the Reichstag approved the National Motion Picture Law (Reichslichtspielgesetz). Under this legislation, filmmakers were required to submit their movies to federal censors for approval before releasing them to theatres throughout the nation.[13] The law effectively reintroduced censorship, yet not before enlightenment films had heightened concerns about how men and women were behaving, both in public spaces and in their bedrooms.

The Post-War Challenge to Traditional Gender Norms

Germany's effort to fight a total war was responsible for much of this post-war anxiety about gender. Over the course of four years, the government had mobilized 13.2 million men, an astounding 41 percent of the male population. In their absence, women lived alone with greater frequency, shifted into industrial jobs, and learned how to function as single parents. While men found themselves confined physically and emotionally in the cramped trenches of the frontlines, women seemingly experienced greater freedoms at home and in the workplace.[14] War's end did little to restore traditional gender norms. Many soldiers returned home physically and psychologically wounded, and the new republican government sealed women's liberation by granting them full legal and political equality. From the perspective of contemporaries, war and defeat had weakened established definitions of femininity and masculinity. As evidence, they pointed to new and destabilizing gender "types."

One type frequently used to characterize many young women's rejection of traditional roles was that of the New Woman. She was identifiable, the stereotype proclaimed, by her bobbed haircut, her un-corseted body, her short hemline, and her newly acquired penchant for smoking. Such visual markers became the trademark of the modern woman, a type who supposedly "took the principle of equality in the Weimar Constitution seriously, and played her part at work and in public life with confidence."[15] This New Woman supposedly spent her days working as a typist or retail clerk and her evenings watching films and reading magazines and romance novels. She was also thought to be more sexually aggressive than her female predecessors, who had not enjoyed such political or economic freedoms.[16]

Research indicates that the New Woman was both myth and reality. According to the stereotype, the emergence of financially independent and sexually aggressive women resulted from their increasing representation in Germany's labour markets. In fact, the number of German women employed after the war remained rather static, and their employment increased by only 0.7 percent between 1907 and 1925; yet a clear shift had taken place in the kinds of jobs that women held. The number of women working in white-collar positions rose 200 percent in the same time period.[17] Yet, as Katharina von Ankum argues, the New Woman "was perceived as a threat to social stability and an impediment to Germany's political and economic reconstruction."[18] Furthermore, contemporary research revealed that young middle-class women did seem inclined to look on pre-marital sexuality as acceptable and even favourable.[19]

Such behaviour clearly transgressed nineteenth-century gender norms that tended to depict women as modest, protective, loving, sympathetic, intuitive, emotional creatures who were best suited for the domestic sphere and for issues related to the family.[20] Traditional definitions of femininity were imbued with notions of domesticity that urged women to be hard-working caretakers of the home and family by practising "snow white cleanliness, relentless thrift, and the maintenance of good household order."[21] The new women, who rejected family, marriage, domesticity, and motherhood, therefore embodied the extreme denial of these values. Whereas she may have typified youth and freedom in Britain, and, as the American flapper, may have personified a form of rebellion that "posed no serious threat to traditional masculine authority," in Germany, as Adam Stanley argues, she was "a cultural construct encompassing everything that society found dangerous or threatening about women's expanded roles and visibility in the public sphere."[22]

On the male side of the equation, the stereotype of the damaged soldier served as evidence that the masculine ideal was under assault. The damaged soldier had several permutations. The first type, the soldier suffering from psychological trauma, confronted wartime doctors with a disorder for which they initially had no name. In the course of the war, German doctors encountered men who displayed "shaking, shuttering, tremors and tics, muteness, deafness, and paralysis." Lacking a uniform diagnosis that could be applied to such a diverse collection of symptoms, doctors eventually settled on the term "war hysteria." This descriptor revealed a prejudicial approach to the affliction and categorized men who exhibited such symptoms as seeking to shirk their duty and secure a government pension.[23]

German doctors dealt with about 600,000 men who suffered from psychological trauma, but a much more pervasive and worrying development was a supposed increase in homosexuality among frontline soldiers and a disturbing rise in physical violence and sexual violence inflicted by demobilized soldiers on their partners and spouses at home. Both types, the homosexual soldier and the abusive veteran, Jason Crouthamel argues, had sacrificed that part of their sexuality that had enabled them to embody the masculine ideal: their control over their bodies and their sexual impulses.[24] Magnus Hirschfeld described the latter as the "bestialized" man, one made primitive by fighting, killing, living in trenches, and constantly confronting death.[25]

These post-war types, men who suffered from war hysteria or whose sexuality and self-control were now in question, undermined a bourgeois ideal of masculinity that had been refined during the nineteenth century. This ideal demanded that men maintain their moral composure and use their bodies to exhibit "virility, strength, and courage." According to these prescriptions, a "real" man was "in control of his passions ... [and] devoted to harmony of the body and mind." The truly masculine man exhibited chivalry, honour, strength, and courage, was willing to sacrifice all for the nation, and demonstrated purity rather than lustfulness. This ideal, George Mosse asserts, "corresponded to modern society's need for order and progress." Men who embodied such characteristics, he continues, reflected "the image society liked to have of itself."[26]

Both stereotypes, the damaged soldier and the New Woman, served as easily visualized examples of the forces eroding traditional gender values and long-existing family norms in post-war Germany. Nineteenth-century ideals of masculinity and femininity had proffered marriage as the best means of ensuring appropriate gender behaviour for both sexes.[27] Yet in the years following the First World War, marriage seemed to be under constant assault from these new types, the New Woman and the damaged soldier. Many contemporaries identified film as a disruptive force because it depicted men and women choosing alternatives to marriage and sometimes behaving badly. Contemporaries who hoped to battle these subversive developments focused their attention on one point of origin for new gender behaviours: film.

Local Censorship in Baden and National Film Law

Post-war concerns about uncensored cinema motivated state authorities to consider various forms of self-help. To this end, on 31 July 1919, the Badish legislature unanimously voted in favour of a proposal calling for public ownership of all movie theatres.[28] Although Baden did not ultimately adopt communalization, the legislature's flirtation with this policy encouraged the National Federation of German Movie Theatre Owners (Reichsverband deutscher Lichtspiel Theaterbesitzer) to state its opposition to such plans and endorse the "speedy introduction of a federal censor."[29] This declaration enabled states such as Baden to enact a preventative censor. Many communities throughout the state quickly took advantage of this opportunity. The industrial city of Pforzheim, for example, established several four-member censor committees in the summer of 1919.[30] By February 1920, the newly created Youth Office (Jugendamt) in Heidelberg had erected a local film watch committee that included four women, four men, and a local movie theatre owner.[31]

The passage of the National Motion Picture Law in May 1920 standardized censorship at the federal level and subjected all new films to federal control prior to their national release. The law's first section stipulated the grounds on which films could be partially or completely censored; federal authorities could censor specific scenes or entire films that had the capacity to endanger public order, injure religious feelings, harm Germany's relations to other nations, or have a brutalizing or depraving impact on audiences. The law's second section explained the creation and composition of two federal review boards, one in Berlin and another in Munich, which were responsible for reviewing all films. This section also covered the establishment of an appellate board in Berlin that would oversee the process and address complaints about the review boards' decisions. The legislation's third section specified the appeals process by which local and state officials could seek the reconsideration of a film's acceptability. The final section dealt with the review of films already in circulation and disciplinary action for individuals who violated the new law.[32]

Although the film law diminished the autonomy of local committees, it did not render them unimportant or impotent. First and foremost, federal censors relied on local and state officials to help enforce their decisions. Furthermore, the law provided municipal and state authorities with a means by which they could remain relevant in the censorship process; article 4 of the law permitted state authorities to submit a proposal to the appellate board, asking that a movie be reviewed once again.[33] In January 1922, the Badish Interior Ministry called on municipalities throughout the state to assist Badish authorities in fulfilling this role. The ministry directed all communities of fifteen thousand or more to establish Local Committees for Monitoring Movie Theatres (Ortsausschuss für Lichtspielpflege), which in turn would support local police in monitoring screens.[34] Members of these committees visited movie theatres, observed their programming, and drafted requests for federal reconsideration when they encountered an offensive film. These appeals were then delivered to district authorities who passed them on to state authorities. If an appeal was deemed viable, it was advanced to the appellate board.

In Heidelberg, the initial watch committee created by the Youth Office in February 1920 became the Local Committee for Monitoring Movie Theatres in 1922. It operated throughout the Weimar era under the direction of Dr. Karl F. Ammann, who was also director of the Youth Office.[35] By May 1921, it possessed a chairman, two honorary members, and twelve participants who helped to monitor local theatres.[36] And by April 1925, it had grown to twenty-one members, eight of whom were charged with actively observing local screens, whereas the other thirteen were tasked with occasionally visiting theatres and reviewing their programming.[37] The committee used a rotating six-week schedule, in which, committee members would systematically visit, each week, one of Heidelberg's five movie theatres. Committee members had the sixth week free.[38]

Heidelberg's committee became a leading national participant in the appeals process. As of 31 March 1926, it had submitted twenty-two successful proposals convincing the appellate board to alter a film's acceptability status. As a comparison, during the same time period, only sixty-four successful proposals were submitted nationally, including those from authorities in Heidelberg.[39]

The men and women who helped police Heidelberg's movie screens were among its notable citizens and had come of age during the late nineteenth century. Director Karl Ammann, born in 1883, had worked as an administrator for the railroad system in Baden. After the war, he used his legal training to help found Heidelberg's Youth Office in December 1919.[40] Member Georg Zink, born in 1879, began his employ with the City of Heidelberg in 1906 when he helped to establish its municipal library and public reading hall.[41] Martin Dibelius, born in 1883, had been a theology professor at the University of Heidelberg since 1915.[42] Camilla Jellinek, born in 1860, was the widow of a renowned constitutional theorist (Georg Jellinek). In the winter of 1900-1, she had co-founded (along with Marianne Weber) a local agency that provided free legal aid to poor women. She also became a national advocate for women's legal equality and the decriminalization of abortion in Imperial Germany.[43] Rupert Rohrhurst, born in 1860, had been a theology professor at the University of Heidelberg and a state legislator.[44] All of these individuals ranged in age from forty to sixty when they joined Heidelberg's film committee. Although not inherently conservative, they had grown up in an era in which the masculine and feminine ideals were, by most historical accounts, reaching their apogee in bourgeois Europe.

Gender Norms and Censorship: Prohibitions against Men and Women Behaving Badly

Members of the Heidelberg watch committee used the appeals process provided to them by section 4 of the 1920 film law to register their objections to movies already reviewed by one of two federal review boards and approved for national distribution. They produced a significant number of proposals asking federal authorities to reconsider particular scenes or entire films whose portrayals of women, men, and their interactions were – and here they used the language in article 1 of the 1920 film law – "depraving" and "brutalizing." In doing so, they invoked the state's regulatory power for the purpose of protecting traditional gender norms.

Their objections implicitly outlined the ideal gender types they were attempting to defend. Female types included the virtuous woman, the submissive lover, the faithful wife, and the dutiful mother. Male types comprised the honourable citizen and the rational man able to control his emotions and physical urges. These figures may have had their origins in an earlier era, but in post-war Germany, many people linked them with the nation's ability to heal itself and produce a new generation. As an alliance of women's groups in Freiburg asserted in November 1919, "Our people's recovery will be unattainable unless a new sanctification of gender relations and marriage itself takes place."[45] Key to this sanctification and rebirth was the defence of traditional ideal types.

Of immediate concern was the way in which post-war films belittled female virtue. In arguing that enlightenment films objectified women and reduced them to "pleasure objects" meant to titillate men, Freiburg women's groups contended that these movies denigrated women and harmed gender relations.[46] To shore up the ideal of the virtuous woman, film monitors in Heidelberg invited federal censors to target particular scenes and films that seemed to present women as objects meant for consumption. Two films in particular, The Queen of the Review (Die Königin der Revue) and *The Joyless Street* (Die Freundlose Gasse), raised alarm in Heidelberg because of the way in which they commodified women's bodies. The first, a French film produced in 1927, told the story of a young seamstress who hoped to build a career as a revue star. Interwoven into the film were two segments in which Josephine Baker performed her trademark dances, including her banana dance, at the Folies-Bergere in Paris. The second film was directed by G.W. Pabst in 1925, starred Asta Nielsen and Greta Garbo, and was set in Vienna during the era of post-war inflation; it focused on two young women who must decide whether to sell their virtue in order to preserve themselves and their families. Their story depicted the rise of sexual profiteering and the moral decline of the middle class in post-war Vienna.[47]

Heidelberg's film committee took issue with the way in which the films depicted women, or portions of their bodies, as pleasure objects rendered visible and touchable to strange men. In the autumn of 1928, it lodged complaints against The Queen of the Review, calling for partial censorship and focusing on the scenes that afforded audiences a glimpse of Baker's characteristic moves. The committee justified its stance on the grounds that Baker was dressed only in "white scraps of cloth" *(Fetzen)* and was dancing in a "shameless and immoral way." Especially corrupting, the committee's petition contended, was her belly dancing, the "quite excessive" way in which she surrendered her body to the rapacious eyes of the men seated around her, and the "servile sensuousness" *(gemein-sinnlich)* of her own expression as she danced.[48] Pabst's film, *The Joyless Street,* elicited a request for federal reconsideration that was signed by four members of the monitoring committee, who asked that the film be banned in its entirety on the grounds that its intent was to depict how "Viennese girls were compelled by the need and misery of the inflationary time to sell their moral honour and earn their bread in bordellos." One particular aspect of the film's plot was found particularly offensive, a scene in which a butcher gives extra and illegal rations of meat to young women who are willing to exchange their bodies for beef. The butcher is able to consume these girls both visually and physically. His shop is located under street level, and as the young women descend the stairs one by one, portions of their bodies are revealed to him, and to the audience – first their legs, then their skirts, and then their torsos. Once the girls are in his shop, he takes them into his larder, where, the film implies, he seduces them. The attention that the four petitioners drew to the details and nuances of this scene suggests their own sensitivity to the way in which the girls' bodies were visually parcelled into pieces and savoured by both the butcher and movie audiences.[49] Furthermore, the film's suggestion that women were easily enticed into selling their virtue deeply contradicted the ideal of the chaste woman who preserves her virginity at all costs for marriage.

Just as dangerous to harmonious gender relations was the vamp, a sexually assertive man-eater who used her powers of seduction to attain material reward. The vamp was not only the antithesis of the virtuous woman, she was also a socially destabilizing force whose sexual aggressiveness disturbed the sexual balance between men and women and thereby threatened the institution of marriage. In the words of Crouthamel, such women prevented men damaged by the war from normalizing their sexual behaviour; only if women played the part of submissive wife and nurturer could men play the role of normal hetero-sexual male.[50]

Although the state's regulatory power could not be used to place limitations on women's sexual behaviour, it could suppress cinematic representations of women who used their sexuality for personal gain. Committee members targeted the vamp in their petitions for federal reconsideration. Films that contained such femme fatale characters included *Asphalt,* directed in 1929 by Joe May, and Carl Boese's 1931 My Cousin from Warsaw (Meine Cousine aus Warschau). *Asphalt* tells the story of a police sergeant who arrests a female jewel thief. She convinces him to accompany her to her apartment so that she can retrieve her identification papers. While there, she employs her powers of seduction and successfully persuades him to set her free. When he later returns to her apartment, he encounters the thief with her lover. A fight ensues, during which the officer kills the lover. He is subsequently indicted for the murder and released only when the thief testifies that her lover was a wanted criminal and that the sergeant was simply defending himself.[51] My Cousin from Warsaw focuses on a married woman, Frau Lucienne, who has been unfaithful to her husband, Adolphe, and who must choose between him and her lover, Fred. Deciding to test their fidelity, she asks a friend, the vampish Sonja, to attempt to seduce them both.[52]

Members of Heidelberg's film committee found both films offensive because they depicted women seducing men, thereby assuming the dominant sexual role and completely impeding men's ability to take on normal sexual and gender roles. In 1930, for example, committee leader Ammann asked federal authorities to selectively censor *Asphalt,* specifically those scenes in which the female thief, whom he described as a "harlot" *(Dirne),* springs from her bed and, dressed only in skimpy underclothes, wraps her legs around the young officer's waist while she passionately kisses him. Ammann asserted that "the almost violent seduction of a man by a woman" was likely to be morally corrupting "to a high degree."[53] Two years later, members of the committee in neighbouring Pforzheim registered their opposition to the cinematic release of My Cousin from Warsaw. They suggested that the film should be censored in its entirety because its format and content could damage the "moral feelings and thoughts of a normal, average person" and might serve as a teaching tool in the art of seduction. Particularly objectionable were Sonja's efforts to seduce the husband and the lover; in testing Adolphe's fidelity, complainants noted, she passionately grabbed him and pressed herself against him in a "revolting manner" before slowly rubbing her body against his, going so far as to brush her breasts against his lower body.[54]

Although this complaint focused largely on Sonja's behaviour, it also criticized Frau Lucienne's casual attitude regarding her marriage vows, and the
petition disparaged the film's "flippant" treatment of her marriage. Similarly,
two female members of Heidelberg's watch committee, Camilla Jellinek and
Theodora Aberle, objected to the glib depiction of marriage in the 1931 film
The Men around Lucy (Die Männer um Lucy). The movie follows the romantic
adventures of a young woman named Lucy, who falls in love with a composer
called Robert but marries Prunier, a rich man. As the plot progresses, Lucy
realizes that she is unhappy in her marriage. She and Robert end up at a hotel,
where the owners mistake them for newlyweds. On arriving to retrieve his wife,
Prunier overhears her quarrelling with Robert and decides to leave, seemingly
renouncing his claim on her.[55] Jellinek and Aberle requested that the film be
banned because of its poor quality, suggestive kissing scenes, lengthy nude
scenes, and the husband's blasé attitude regarding his wife's flirtations with
other men.[56] If, as Freiburg women claimed in 1919, the country's renewal relied
on the re-sanctification of marriage, an unfaithful and flirtatious wife not only
betrayed her husband, but also deceived the nation that counted on her to
perform traditional gender roles.

Just as treacherous as the deceitful wife was the bad mother who failed to
nurture her children and shield them from harm. One movie that elicited criticism for its portrayal of a bad mother was the 1925 film The Humble One and
the Singer (Der Demütige und die Sängerin). It recounts the story of Liesegang,
a "playboy" who is intent on bedding a young woman named Toni Seidewitz.
The petitioner, Ammann, devoted a significant portion of his appeal for selective
censorship to detailing scenes in which Toni's moral downfall is facilitated by
her own mother, Frau Bülow. Enticed by Liesegang's promise of financial support, Frau Bülow initially encourages Toni to become a kept woman. When
Toni refuses, Bülow secretly barters her away for cash and abandons her, after
which Toni soon falls victim to Liesegang's lust.[57] Ammann's overwhelming
focus on the mother's treachery reveals his rejection of female characters that
contravened the ideal of the nurturing, protective mother.

Harlots, vamps, unfaithful wives, and bad mothers endangered the post-war
nation by discouraging women from engaging in the institutions and rituals
that were crucial to its metaphorical and physical rebirth. Men behaved badly
when they failed to live morally, proved unable to control their passions or their
violence, and became tormentors of the weak and vulnerable. Whereas the
feminine ideal was tacitly linked to the country's ability to reproduce itself
physically, its masculine counterpart was associated with Germany's ability to
rehabilitate social relations and its international reputation. As Mosse asserts,

men who were "loose-living [and] without the proper moral standards, cut at the roots of society, threatening to destroy its tender fabric."[58] In post-war Germany, the tender fabric seemed to be rendered even more vulnerable by an assault on the values crucial to immediate reconstruction and long-term redemption: honour, strength, decorum, and chivalry. Men who failed to display such virtues not only disrupted social relations but also endangered the nation's reputation in the world.

In post-war Germany, a decline in honour among men seemed readily apparent in the behaviour of profiteers, individuals who took advantage of inflation, political transformations, and the misery of others to increase their wealth and satisfy their appetites regardless of the cost to society. During the eighteen months in which censorship was discontinued, profiteering seemed rampant within the film industry itself. A Freiburg newspaper journalist asserted in October 1919 that theatre owners were so "capitalistically oriented" they were willing to earn their "Judas wages" by offering enlightenment films to their fellow citizens.[59] Repeatedly, movie theatres and filmmakers were accused of betraying their country for a quick profit. Whereas Badish and national legislators had sought to counteract such greediness with proposals for communalization and socialization, members of Heidelberg's watch committee used the appeals process to target films containing male characters that seemed to revel in bad behaviour.

Two films in particular embodied an assault on the masculine ideal of men acting honourably. These were the 1923 The Sins of Youth (Jugendsünden) and the 1926 The Young Man from the Confection (der Jüngling aus der Konfektion). The first tells the story of Rolf Schmette, the ne'er-do-well son of a public prosecutor who falls into a life of crime that eventually leads to his imprisonment on murder charges. In the second film, protagonist Moritz Spiegel is an apprentice in a fashion house of which he eventually becomes part owner. Along the way, Moritz falls in love with a female apprentice who works for the same firm.[60]

Both movies captured the attention of film monitors because of the dishonourable way in which male characters behaved. Dr. Schumacher, a member of the Badish Youth Office, called for partial censorship of The Sins of Youth, noting the several incidents in which Rolf's behaviour contradicted the male ideal. Rolf leads a frivolous life among women. He pays for his pleasures with money that his mother has given him, and when he finds himself hard up for cash, he forges his father's signature. After this crime is uncovered, he permits his friend Hugo, the son of a porter, to take the fall for it. While Hugo endures an unjust punishment, Rolf seduces Hugo's sister. And when the two lovers swear to engage in a suicide pact, Rolf is too cowardly to shoot himself, even though he has already shot his lover. Although she is not mortally wounded, he is tried on murder charges. In jail, he finally accepts responsibility for all his crimes before committing suicide.[61] Two months after the Badish Youth Office objected to The Sins of Youth, a member of the Heidelberg watch committee followed suit, similarly focusing on Rolf's dishonourable behaviour in requesting complete censorship of the film. The petitioner described Rolf as a "vain, morally degenerate person."[62]

Whereas Rolf typifies the dishonourable and cowardly male, a character in The Young Man from the Confection epitomizes a man who rejects the virtues of chivalry and plays the part of the lecher. Committee members Ammann and Jellinek requested censorship of scenes in which one of the fashion house's favoured customers, Rolf Schwarzschild, seeks to seduce Moritz's love interest, Karoline Schuster. The seduction begins with Schwarzschild's request that Karoline deliver several dresses to his hotel room, and it continues when he asks her to model the clothes for him. To try on the dresses, Karoline must change behind a cloth screen, and since Schwarzschild has ensured that the screen is backlit, both he and the audience are able to enjoy her naked form.[63] The planned nature of the seduction is revealed by a table set for two in anticipation of Karoline's pliability. Ammann and Jellinek justified their appeal on the grounds that such scenes were immoral, but their emphasis on Schwarzschild's orchestrated seduction reveals their rejection of men who exploited their wealth and influence to become sexual profiteers.

Films that encouraged men to indulge their sexual urges, even if they were violent, also captured the attention of Heidelberg's monitors. In 1927, for example, they drafted a proposal calling for selective censorship of the 1921 film The Prince of the Mountains (Der Fürst der Berge). The movie follows the exploits of an adventurer named Unus who joins a band of robbers and eventually becomes a hero, for he helps save two girls kidnapped by his fellow criminals. The petitioner, Ammann, focused on two scenes that violated the male ideal that a man must control his physical and sexual passions: a brutal fight between two men, and a scene in which the robber captain attempts to rape one of the kidnapped girls.[64] Committee members also objected to scenes in the 1926 film Maciste among the Lions (Maciste unter der Löwen), in which a male antagonist twice uses violence in his attempts to rape a young woman.[65]

Even more disturbing were films that implied a rape had actually taken place and revealed the pleasure of the attackers in terrorizing their victims, for such depictions completely contravened the ideal of the man who exerts self-control over his urges and disciplines his strength. One movie in particular embodied this negative portrayal, the 1923 City in Sight (Stadt in Sicht), which centres on a married couple, Anna and Fritz, who live with their seventeen-year-old foster-son on a boat. One night they rescue an escaped murderer from the water, unaware of the man's past. He soon terrorizes the family and drugs them into unconsciousness. Petitioners requested that the film be partially censored, particularly its depictions of the stranger's assaults on Anna. In one scene, he hugs and kisses her despite her "sharp resistance," and later, as she climbs the stairs, he grabs her leg and strokes it. In another scene, he approaches her while she sleeps, drugs her, and carries her to his bed, whereon he flings his own body on hers. When Anna tries to fend him off, he strangles her until she is unconscious. He then goes looking for her husband in order to rob him.[66] The film concludes with a fight between the husband and the murderer that leaves both men in the water, where they drown.

When movies portrayed men engaging in such bestial violence, many critics feared, they perpetuated negative stereotypes of Germany. As Anna v. Gierke, a member of the German National People's Party, asserted in the context of national discussions regarding renewed censorship in early 1920, post-war films tended to depict German men as "perpetually assaulting, abusing, and drugging women" in order to satisfy their sexual desires. These cinematic portrayals seemed too reminiscent of wartime enemy propaganda posters that depicted German soldiers as brutal apes wearing Prussian helmets.[67] Such movies interfered with Germany's rehabilitation, both internationally and domestically.

Conclusion

Censorship was a means by which federal and local officials confronted the realities of an emerging and powerful consumer culture capable of challenging traditional gender norms. Their emphasis on film was logical; movie-going was an extremely popular pastime in the post-war years and film was an enormously visual commodity. When men and women went to the movies, they not only purchased entertainment and a brief respite from reality, they also bought ready-made images. Contemporaries feared that these images might penetrate the psyches of audiences and cause irreparable harm. As one critic warned in 1919, "These images, which are viewed in a dark room, can pass into the subconscious and reappear in dreams."[68] What if they encouraged impressionable movie-goers to forgo life choices that would have an immediate impact on society, such as marriage and parenthood – institutions critical to the nation's physical recovery? What if they encouraged viewers to give free rein to their rage, take advantage of another's misfortune, or sell their virtue for a fancy dress or a nice cut of steak – decisions that might imperil the nation's moral renewal? Other consumer goods, such as cosmetics or cars, may have enabled men and women to act out new gender roles, but film was unique in its supposed ability to encourage new behaviours.

The men and women who comprised Heidelberg's film watch committee employed the power of the 1920 national film law and its appeals process to censor entire films and specific scenes that, in their opinion, disseminated images of men and women behaving badly. They asked federal authorities to censor films that showed women as tramps, vamps, and neglectful mothers, and that depicted men as lechers and rapists. In doing so, they revealed their own sensitivity to shifting gender norms. Their objections also suggest that instead of interpreting new gender behaviours as progressive, they saw them as destabilizing forces that endangered Germany's post-war recovery.

Germans' responses to films, and the gender shifts they might be encouraging, must be read in light of the nation's First World War defeat. Traditional definitions of masculinity and femininity offered stability to a nation eager to rehabilitate itself and a society beset by crisis. Perhaps novel gender types, such as the New Woman, reminded many Germans of everything they had lost in the war and of their nation's tenuous grip on the future.

Notes

1 Lynn Abrams, "From Control to Commercialization: The Triumph of Mass Entertainment in Germany 1900-1925?" *German History* 8 (1990): 280-82; Warren G. Breckman, "Disciplining Consumption: The Debate about Luxury in Wilhelmine Germany, 1890-1914," *Journal of Social History* 24 (1991): 485. For a thorough discussion of how advertisers marketed these goods to German consumers, see Adam C. Stanley, *Modernizing Tradition: Gender and Consumerism in Interwar France and Germany* (Baton Rouge: Louisiana State University Press, 2008). For an analysis of how American producers tried to capture European markets, see Victoria de Grazia, "Big-Brand Goods: How Marketing Outmaneuvered the Marketplace," in *Irresistible Empire: America's Advance through 20th-Century Europe* (Cambridge, MA: Belknap Press, 2005), 184-225.
2 Ute Daniel, *The War from Within: German Working-Class Women in the First World War* (New York: Berg, 1997), 129-35.
3 Dr. E. Krebs, "Die Totengräberarbeit unserer Kino-Bühnen," 11 July 1919, clippings, C4/XII/30/6, Stadtarchiv Freiburg (StF), Freiburg.
4 *Öffentliche Sitzung der Badishen Landtag*, 31 July 1919, 1627-30, Abg. Karl, 42, C4/XII/30/6, StF.
5 James D. Steakley, "Cinema and Censorship in the Weimar Republic: The Case of Anders als die Andern," *Film History* 11 (1999): 189.
6 Gary D. Stark, "All Quiet on the Home Front: Popular Entertainments, Censorship, and Civilian Morale in Germany, 1914-1918," in *Authority, Identity and the Social History of the Great War*, ed. Frans Coetzee and Marilyn Shevin-Coetzee (Providence: Berghahn Books, 1995), 65.

7   Quoted in Frederick F. Blachly and Miriam E. Oatman, *The Government and Administration of Germany* (Baltimore: Johns Hopkins Press, 1928), 665-66.

8   Steakley, "Cinema and Censorship," 181, 189-90.

9   Ibid., 190.

10 Krebs, "Die Totengräberarbeit unserer Kino-Bühnen"; Zentrums-Stadt Verordneten, "Selbstschutz der Stadtgemeinde gegenüber der sittlichen Gefahren der Freiburger Kinovorführungen betreffend," 20 October 1919, C4/XII/30/6, StF.

11 "Betr. Vorgehen gegen das Kinounwesen, to the Stadtrat der Hauptstadt Freiburg zur gefl. Weitergabe an den Bürgerausschuss," November 1919, C4/XII/30/6, StF.

12 Frau Dekan Odenwald, "Zur Kino-Reform," *Heidelberger Tageblatt,* 9 November 1919, clippings, Sozialamt 1791, Stadtarchiv Heidelberg (StH), Heidelberg.

13 "Lichtspielgesetz. Vom 12. Mai 1920," *Reichs-Gesetzblatt, Year 20,* no. 107, 953-58.

14 Roger Chickering, *Imperial Germany and the Great War, 1914-1918* (Cambridge: Cambridge University Press, 2004), 192; Daniel, *The War from Within,* 37, 45; Stanley, *Modernizing Tradition,* 2-3.

15 Ute Frevert, *Women in German History: From Bourgeois Emancipation to Sexual Liberation,* trans. Stuart McKinnon-Evans (New York: Berg, 1997), 176.

16 Cornelia Usborne, "The New Woman and Generation Conflict: Perceptions of Young Women's Sexual Mores in the Weimar Republic," in *Generations in Conflict: Youth Revolt and Generation Formation in Germany 1770-1968,* ed. Mark Roseman (Cambridge: Cambridge University Press, 1995), 142-43.

17 Katharina von Ankum, "Introduction," in *Women in the Metropolis: Gender and Modernity in Weimar Culture,* ed. Katharina von Ankum (Berkeley: University of California Press, 1997), 4.

18 Ibid.

19 Usborne, "The New Woman and Generation Conflict," 162.

20 Karin Hausen, "Family and Role-Division: The Polarization of Sexual Stereotypes in the Nineteenth Century – an Aspect of the Dissociation of Work and Family Life," in *The German Family: Essays on the Social History of the Family in Nineteenth- and Twentieth-Century Germany,* ed. Richard J. Evans and W.R. Lee (Totowa, NJ: Barnes and Noble, 1981), 55-56.

21 Nancy R. Reagin, *Sweeping the German Nation: Domesticity and National Identity in Germany, 1870-1945* (Cambridge: Cambridge University Press, 2007), 42-43.

22 For Britain, see Chapter 6 in this volume; for the flapper as no serious threat to male authority, see Chapter 7 (137) in this volume. Stanley, *Modernizing Tradition,* 3-4.

23 Paul F. Lerner, *Hysterical Men: War, Psychiatry, and the Politics of Trauma in Germany, 1890-1930* (Ithaca: Cornell University Press, 2003), 61, see also 62, 64, 71.

24 Jason Crouthamel, "Male Sexuality and Psychological Trauma: Soldiers and Sexual Disorder in World War I and Weimar Germany," *Journal of History of Sexuality* 17 (January 2008): 63-64, 68-69, 73.

25 Magnus Hirschfeld, *The Sexual History of the World War* (New York: Cadillac, 1941), 284-90.

26 George Mosse, *The Image of Man: The Creation of Modern Masculinity* (New York: Oxford University Press, 1996), 77, 79, see also 22-23, 59, 75, 144.

27 Ibid., 101.

28 *Öffentliche Sitzung der Badischen Landtag,* 1627-42.

29 Kongress Büro des Reichsverbandes deutscher Lichtspiel-Theater-Besitzer e.V., Resolution sent to the Badischen Landtag, 11 August 1919, Generallandesarchiv Karlsruhe (GLA) 237/27001, Karlsruhe.

30 Bezirksamt Pforzheim, "Überwachung der Lichtspieltheater betr.," 16 December 1919, Stadtarchiv Karlsruhe, Bezirksamt Karlsruhe, Karlsruhe.

31 "Die Einrichtung einer Kinozensur betr.," 5 February 1920, Sozialamt 1791, StH.

32 "Lichtspielgesetz. Vom 12. Mai 1920," 953-58; Peter Jelavich, *Berlin Alexanderplatz: Radio, Film, and the Death of Weimar Culture* (Berkeley: University of California Press, 2006), 128-29.

33 "Lichtspielgesetz. Vom 12. Mai 1920," 953-58.

34 "Staatsanzeiger. Den Vollzug des Lichtspielgesetzes," *Karlsruhe Zeitung*, 23 January 1922, 4.

35 Jo-Hannes Bauer, "'Es wird zu leicht zur Sucht': Kino und Zensur in Heidelberg in den zwanziger Jahren," *Heidelberg. Jahrbuch zur Geschichte der Stadt* 4 (1999): 102.

36 Städtisches Jugendamt Heidelberg, listing of committee members belonging to the Ortsausschuss für Lichtspielpflege, 7 May 1921, Sozialamt 1791, StH.

37 "Auf eine Eingabe der Frau Schulten über die Ausübung der Kinoüberwachung," 8 April 1925, Sozialamt 1791, StH.

38 "Kinoaufsicht vom 1. August bis 31. Dezember 1920," Sozialamt 1791, StH.

39 "Geschäftsbericht des Stadtjugendamts Heidelberg für die Zeit vom 1. April 1929 bis 31. März 1930," Sozialamt 1810, StH.

40 Dr. Karl Friedrich Ammann, 47.74.30 Ammann/we, StH.

41 Joachim Heimann, "Georg Zink und die HeidelbergVolksbibliothek und Volkslesehalle," *Heidelberg. Jahrbuch zur Geschichte der Stadt* 11 (2006-7): 96-97, 120.

42 Karl-Heinz Fix, "Martin Dibelius, die Politik seiner Zeit und zwei Theologenberufungen 1930/1931 und 1946," *Zeitschrift für die Geschichte des Oberrheins* 138 (1990): 496-99, C20, StH.

43 Klaus Kempter, *Die Jellineks 1820-1955: Eine familienbiographische Studie zum deutschjüdischen Bildungsbürgertum* (Düsseldorf: Droste Verlag, 1998), 364-65, 368-69, 396-99, 402-9.

44 "Rupert Rohrhurst: dem Schulmann und Politiker zum 70. Geburtstag," *Heidelberg Tageblatt*, 13 February 1930, 5, StH; "Rupert Rohrhurst," *Rhein-Neckar Zeitung*, 10 October 1952, 3; "Rohrhurst, Rupert," *Das 'Goldene Buch' des KFG: Autobiographien Heidelberger Pädagogen (1812-1939)*, schriftenreihe des Stadtarchivs Heidelberg Heft 5 (Heidelberg: Verlag Brigitte Guderjahn, 1994), 106.

45 "Betr. Vorgehen gegen das Kinounwesen," 3 November 1919, C4/XII/30/6, StF.

46 Ibid.

47 Patrice Petro, *Joyless Streets: Women and Melodramatic Representation in Weimar Germany* (Princeton: Princeton University Press, 1989), 199, 204-11; Siegfried Kracauer, *From Caligari to Hitler: A Psychological History of the German Film* (Princeton: Princeton University Press, 1974), 167-69.

48 "Widerruf von Bildstreifen Betr.," proposal written by members of the Ortsausschuss für Lichtspielpflege in Heidelberg, sent to district authorities in Heidelberg, 21 November 1928, Sozialamt 1796, StH.

49 "Lichtspielwesen, hier Widerruf eines Bildstreifens betr.," proposal written by members of the Ortsausschuss für Lichtspielpflege in Heidelberg, 11 December 1925, and "Antrag auf Widerruf Bildstreifens 'Die freudlose Gasse,'" 16 December 1925, Heidelberg, Sozialamt 1796, StH.

50 Crouthamel, "Male Sexuality and Psychological Trauma," 78-79.

51 Kracauer, *From Caligari to Hitler*, 158; "Asphalt," in *Der Film der Weimarer Republik 1929: Ein Handbuch der zeitgenössischen Kritik*, ed. Gero Gandert (Berlin: Walter de Gruyter, 1997), 168-69.

52 "Widerrufsantrag gegen den Film 'Meine Cousine aus Waschau,' betreffend," proposal written by members of the Ortsausschuss für Lichtspielpflege in Pforzheim, 23 February 1932, Sozialamt 1797, StH.

53 24 May 1930, Sozialamt 1797, StH.

54 "Widerrufsantrag gegen den Film 'Meine Cousine aus Warschau' betreffend," 23 February 1932, Sozialamt 1797, StH.

55 Film-Oberprüfstelle, 9 September 1932, Sozialamt 1797, StH.

56 4 July 1932, Sozialamt 1797, StH.

57 25 May 1925, Sozialamt 1795, StH.

58 Mosse, *The Image of Man,* 79-80.

59 "Gegen Schmutz und Schund," *Freiburger Bote,* 24 October 1919, clippings, C4/XII/30/6, StF.

60 "Widerrufsantrag betr.," initiated by Ammann and Jellinek of the Ortsausschuss für Lichtspielpflege, 29 March 1927, Sozialamt 1796, StH.

61 Sitzung des Arbeitsausschusses des Landesjugendamts in Baden, 15 November 1929, 235/37.487, GLA.

62 19 January 1930, Sozialamt 1797, StH.

63 "Widerrufsantrag," 29 March 1927, Sozialamt 1797, StH.

64 14 June 1922, Sozialamt 1795, StH.

65 27 June 1927, Sozialamt 1796, StH.

66 14 March 1924, Sozialamt 1795, StH.

67 Nationalversammlung, 162. Sitzung, 15 April 1920, 5173, http://www.reichstagsprotokolle. de/.

68 *Öffentliche Sitzung der Badishen Landtag,* 1628.

13

Guilty Pleasures: Consumer Culture in the Fiction of Mary Quayle Innis

Donica Belisle

Between 1922 and 1947, Toronto historian and writer Mary Quayle Innis published over eighty short stories and one novel. Accomplished literary works in their own right, they are especially valuable for their treatment of consumer culture. In story after story, Innis explores consumer longing, conspicuous consumption, material disparity, and spousal conflict over purchases. For Innis, fiction was an outlet for investigating the personal and moral meanings of consumer capitalism, especially as they pertained to women.

One of the first things that students of fiction learn is that authors exist separately from narrators and characters. How narrators recount tales and how characters experience events are products of the author's craft. Nevertheless, a study of an author's fictional œuvre, especially one as substantial as that of Innis, makes it possible to pinpoint a writer's major preoccupations. The experiences of contemporary homemakers comprise the bulk of Innis's 1930s and 1940s tales, and the author pays special attention to wives and mothers of bourgeois, working-class, and destitute statuses. Innis's stories also reveal an interest in how economic power creates enjoyment for the privileged and marginalization for the non-privileged. Her fiction is thus rooted in prevailing social conditions and represents an attempt to work through issues she believed to be of pressing concern. Her interest in homemakers' lives and her explorations of power and marginality offer important insights into how English-speaking, middle-class women experienced the emergence of consumer capitalism in Canada during the first half of the twentieth century.

Born Mary Quayle in Ohio in 1899 and raised in the southern United States, Mary Quayle Innis obtained a bachelor's degree in English from the University of Chicago in 1919. She married Ontario-born Harold Innis, her former economics instructor, who had been working on his doctorate. Harold accepted a position in political economy at the University of Toronto, and in 1921, the couple moved to Canada. They raised four children between 1923 and the 1950s; and while Harold became a renowned scholar and built his academic career, Mary looked after their children and home, helped Harold with his research and writing, entertained academic guests, attended faculty functions, and embarked on a remarkable lifetime of writing.[1]

Innis began publishing during the early years of her marriage. In the 1920s, she focused on fiction, but in the 1930s, she began authoring historical and non-fiction works. In 1935, drawing from her husband's and her own research, she published *An Economic History of Canada*. So well received was this book that it remained the standard Canadian economic history undergraduate text until the late 1950s. In 1936 and 1937, Innis published three articles on economic history, one of which was so highly regarded that it was republished "nearly 40 years later in a collection of classic historical essays on Upper Canada." In the early 1940s, Innis began publishing historical and travel sketches. Most of these appeared in *Saturday Night, Maclean's*, and the *Dalhousie Review*, of which the former two targeted popular readers, whereas the latter aimed at intellectuals.[2]

Given Innis's strong research background, one might see her decision to use fiction to study contemporary homemakers' experiences as curious. It was a logical choice, however. Few academics of this period conducted sustained or sensitive inquiries into domesticity, gender, or consumerism. Especially in the field of Canadian history, with which Innis was most familiar, scholars focused on politics, wars, trade, and exploration. The economy was a major interest as well, but Canadian economic theorists, including Harold Innis, believed consumption to be secondary to exports and trade. Economic historians and political economists of this period paid little attention to consumer motivation.[3]

A distaste among intellectuals regarding domestic issues, especially consumption, probably compounded Innis's fictional turn. Many English Canadian critics of the thirties and forties were appalled at the seemingly passive and conformist tendencies of mass culture, particularly movies, radio, and shopping. Into the 1950s, they portrayed mass culture as inimical to human creativity, community participation, and civic engagement. Appearing after Innis stopped publishing fiction, but nonetheless illustrative of this view, was the well-received *Crestwood Heights* (1956), a sociological study by J.R. Seeley, R.A. Sim, and E.W. Loosley of a Toronto suburb. As Veronica Strong-Boag notes, this book portrays suburbia as all that is wrong with modern life. Suburban fathers were career-obsessed, mothers were narcissistic, and "both sexes were overly materialistic."[4]

Innis's position as a full-time mother and homemaker was another factor behind her use of fiction. It is significant that after her four children were grown, she concentrated again on historical research. She updated four of her husband's major books, wrote history texts for schoolchildren, authored a history of the Young Women's Christian Association, and edited Lady Simcoe's diaries as well as collections on women in Canada's past and on nursing education. When Innis's children were young and her husband busy, she would have had little time to conduct the research that these projects required. She thus turned to creative writing, a craft that did not demand prolonged research and in which she was gifted. Yet rather than being a stopgap in her career, her fictional record is both valuable and significant. Apart from being a formidable literary achievement, it gave Innis the intellectual freedom and space required to explore homemakers' lives, a decidedly unscholarly topic during her time. Indeed, it was perhaps the feminist conclusions she reached through her fiction that encouraged her later interest in women's history.[5]

With the exception of "Quarrel" (1922), Innis's five published stories from the 1920s are set in frontier and pioneer times. With "Recital" in 1930, she shifted to more contemporary settings. Between 1930 and 1935, she published ten stories in the *Canadian Forum,* a monthly Toronto-based periodical with a leftist view and a predominantly intellectual readership. In 1936, Innis published one story each in *Midland, the Publication of the Toronto Writers' Club,* and *New Frontier.* She found a new home in 1937 at the Toronto-based *Saturday Night,* in which she published approximately sixty-five stories over the next decade. With a circulation of approximately thirty thousand during this period, *Saturday Night* was a weekly magazine with a primarily liberal outlook; it printed political and economic commentary, arts and letters coverage, poetry, and fiction. Edited by former Queen's University English professor and well-known public intellectual B.K. Sandwell, it enjoyed, as Robert Fulford writes, "a position of eminence" that it "never reached ... since."[6] In 1943, Innis also published one novel, *Stand on a Rainbow,* with Collins in Toronto.

Though never fully autobiographical, Innis's fiction drew from personal experience. According to her daughter Anne Innis Dagg, Innis's interwar stories were "largely based on her life in Toronto," and her 1940s stories drew from "events recalled in Mrs. Innis's youth." During an interview with J. David Black, Dagg further indicated that *Stand on a Rainbow* was "drawn almost entirely from incidents in Mary's domestic life." It is impossible to pinpoint which stories borrow most heavily from experience and which ones are purely fictive, and the exercise would be fruitless anyway because all fiction is to some extent invented. Yet Innis's sensitivity and talent enabled her to create characters and situations that are believable. She writes with such veracity that it is probable her insights into consumerism were based on personal experience and careful social observation.[7]

Exploring Consumers' Subjectivities

Perhaps in an effort to understand women's motivations for consuming, Innis made the attractions of consumption central to her exploration. Several pieces examine reasons compelling characters to go shopping, as well as the fun they have while in stores. In "Day to Keep Always" (1942), main character Leslie asks her three children about their favourite Christmas traditions. To her surprise, they all state that their annual trip to Woolworth's is their favourite. Leslie is disappointed, for it "seemed depressingly secular and material," and she always experienced it as a "nightmare." When she and her children visit Woolworth's that year, however, she changes her mind: "Inside the [store] door they stood together for a moment looking exultingly into the tangle of lights and garlands, the press of people." Thinks Leslie, "The movement and stabbing colour, the light, the clatter of talk made one dizzy and at the same time happy." She finally understands why the children get "intensely excited" about the trip. It "was a mixed spice of intrigue, curiosity, and speculation." And unlike other shopping expeditions, it is completely selfless. "It touched her to see so many people," including her own children, "preparing pleasure for other people."[8]

Not only does "Day to Keep Always" demonstrate that shopping need not be about buying things for oneself, so does it show that shopping can be sensual. The "bright crowded order of merchandise" and the "cheerful noise" are stimulating and comforting.[9] It was not only Christmas when Innis's characters experienced shopping as congenial. In "Holiday" (1932), wife and mother Nettie Samchuk visits a department store to take a break from her domestic routine. Although her family is "on the charities" and she is penniless, she enjoys admiring the giant retailer's perfume, dresses, garden furniture, children's clothing, and cakes. She finds it stimulating to smell and see these items, and to imagine what it would be like to own them. "Her favourite game," relates the narrator, is "to dress her children." By looking in the showcases, she "could choose outfits for all of them."[10] To explain Nettie's rationale for visiting a particular department store, the narrator states that she "had earned a holiday." She worked hard at home, and now that "she was out she meant to stay a while."[11] Innis here suggests that homemakers treated shopping as a cost-free social outing that allowed them to escape their primary workplace.

Innis may have used some of her stories to convey the joys that homemakers took in shopping, but she was also aware that consumerism was multi-layered. One of the most interesting themes in her writing is that of consumption as antidote. Several of her works suggest that homemakers turned to shopping to alleviate feelings of inadequacy and loneliness. Her novel, *Stand on a Rainbow,* includes a scene in which main character Leslie pauses in front of a dress shop window. She reflects that whenever she thinks about "new clothes," she becomes "susceptible to a kind of seizure." When she tries on a new dress, she always thinks, "I never knew I could wear a dress like this and it's very becoming. I've been wearing stodgy old things that were too old for me." She would look "into the long mirror and [see] a young and lovely Leslie; it was incredible that a dress could make such a difference." She would think about "how surprised the children would be" and how "pleased" her husband. Soon "she could scarcely wait to put the dress on at home" and would buy the garment.[12] For Leslie, fashion is a way of feeling younger and prettier; it is also a way of gaining attention from her children and husband.

Lonely females' use of fashion to attain attention recurs throughout Innis's fiction. Frustrated by her husband's inattentiveness, and lonely for her children who had all moved "far away," Mrs. Archer of "The Wave" (1939) decides to perm her hair. "What would it be like to have [her husband] look at her with interest?" this homemaker wonders. It would be like the days when, after they were first married, he would say, "'Well, who've we got here?'" whenever she put on a new dress.[13] In "Staver" (1936), a bourgeois wife hopes to attain not her husband's attention through beauty, but that of an indigent man named Staver. He performs odd jobs such as grass cutting for her, and she reciprocates by paying him. She is lonely and begins looking forward to his visits, but he feels neither gratitude nor concern for her. One day she wears a "new blue dress and hat" and walks in "shining white shoes" over the grass he has just cut. She wishes "childishly that Staver would notice her." But instead of complimenting her, he asks for more money. Afterward, he stops visiting her. She thinks of him often and months later, believes she sees him downtown, wearing a suit. Assuming he has gotten work, "she felt her world go black." Exposing the loneliness that motivates some women to "do good," as well as the absurdity of the hope that destitute men might give middle-class women the comfort they desire, "Staver" is an ironic portrayal of women's use of fashion. Though its protagonist is aware of the class gulf that separates her from Staver, she still hopes that her expensive clothes will attract him.[14]

These stories indicate that Innis believed some women turned to fashion and beauty to help them feel younger, happier, and more attractive. This connection between appearance, youth, satisfaction, and desirability is apparent not only in Innis's fiction, but in advertising geared toward women during this period. As Strong-Boag notes, the "overwhelming message ... was that women should devote additional time to the maintenance of looks that were on the downhill slope."[15] When combined with "Staver," *Stand on a Rainbow* and "The Wave" also suggest that women who felt lonely and drab resorted to fashion and beauty products. At times they relied solely on men, including their husbands and otherwise, for approval and love.

Innis's characters also employ consumption to attain status. In "The Party" (1931), Innis explores a working-class homemaker's use of home decor to elevate her standing. In preparation for a dinner party, main character Ethel purchases new objects for her home. For years her invited guests have looked down on her husband because they have "prophesied that he would never be able to support Ethel." This party is her chance to prove that she and her husband are "really wonderfully well off." Ethel's pursuit of status, however, goes deeper than proving herself to her guests. She also wants to prove her worth to herself. "Every day," she thinks, "she was buying round steak and looking for a really good dollar cleaner. Just this once she wanted to have the kind of bedspread and lamp shade you saw in the movies, the kind of refreshments they probably served at the government house."[16] In Ethel's view, it is unfair that she should have to budget, when other women do not. Indeed, the "society women in the picture section of the newspaper" daily experience "perfection." By splurging on new decor, Ethel attempts to realize the comfort and beauty she believes others enjoy.

Through Ethel, Innis examines the long-held theory, popularized by Thorstein Veblen in 1899, that consumer display is indicative of an attempt to climb the social ladder.[17] Innis recognizes that some women used consumer goods to reflect their desired social position, but she also suggests that their yearning for status-laden goods went beyond a simple wish for social advancement. Hopes for attractive homes arose not only from wishes to impress others, but from a desire to experience the consumerist ideal presented in newspapers, magazines, and movies. According to these media, a well-outfitted home was aesthetically pleasing, comfortable, and relaxing. Given that many homemakers spent their days working hard within their houses, it was logical that many would want attractive and comfortable furnishings. "The Party" further suggests that preparing a beautiful home offered enjoyment to home-makers. Ethel is excited about her new bedspread and lampshade; she derives pleasure both from purchasing them and from displaying them.

In 1944, Innis put decorators' advice to homemakers under the microscope. "Lived-in Look; or Quaint Gourds and Pottery Figures" tells the tale of Mrs. Andrews, who reads a magazine that advises women to put "between meals a bowl of quaint gourds or a group of pottery figures" on the dining table, to "furnish your desk with a massive desk set of leather and brass or a handmade one of chintz," and to keep the home neatly organized. Mrs. Andrews reads the piece "wistfully," thinking that "probably no decorators had children." Every surface in her home is covered with the children's projects and toys; and the children are always misplacing things. She is thus surprised when the article advises that "the room must not appear too studied or immaculate. Leave an open book or a piece of needlework on the table to give the room a lived-in look." This suggestion is so ridiculous that she "threw down the magazine and began to laugh." "Lived-in Look" exposes the absurdity of trying to live up to the standards of decorators. Instead of attempting to match the ideals of maga-zines, Innis suggests, homemakers should simply relax.[18]

"Lived-in Look" reveals Innis's belief that homemakers felt pressured to live up to decorating ideals. Since decorators and magazines pushed the idea that furnishings were "an index" to a woman's character, homemakers felt that if they failed to decorate according to the norm, they would also fail to prove their femininity.[19] One cannot know whether Innis herself experienced this pres-sure, but as a middle-class homemaker who entertained frequently, she was surely aware that standards existed. "Lived-in Look" suggests that homemakers were influenced by advice on consumption. Cultural studies scholar Mica Nava rightly points out that advertising is a flawed historical source in the sense that researchers cannot ascertain whether consumers agreed with or even paid attention to its promises.[20] Yet "Lived-in Look" indicates that at least one per-ceptive and articulate midcentury writer believed the media influenced home-makers' thoughts and actions.

Innis's fiction also investigates another area of homemaking in which experts felt compelled to give advice: grocery buying. Since the early 1920s, home economists had been urging North American women to prepare detailed grocery lists. These would enable them to choose healthy items and avoid impulse buys, and aid them in their menus. As Innis's "Opportunists' Day" (1943) indicates, though, wartime shortages made it impossible to shop according to plan. On her way to the store, main character Leslie meets her neighbour, Mrs. Barker, who shows her a shopping list, a "neatly typed sheet of seven menus." Mrs. Barker says she follows a "businesslike" and "simple" method, easy to produce for "anyone" who "puts her mind to it." For years, Leslie has "been overawed by the systematic shopping of women like Mrs. Barker but overwhelmed by the variety of foodstuffs before her." Thanks to the current shortages, though, "bewildering variety" is a thing of the past. Leslie simply purchases whatever is available. In the store she sees Mrs. Barker leaning on the cheese counter to "make a pencil notation; already the list looked like a hotly contested battleground." Frustrated, Mrs. Barker tells Leslie that due to all the shortages, she cannot follow her menus. Leslie feels "positively smug," for her "simple-minded openness to suggestion had become a virtue." As in "Lived-in Look," "Opportunists' Day" offers a humorous but pointed criticism of experts' advice to homemakers. Demonstrating the pressure that women feel to live up to standards, as well as the effort required to do so, it proposes that women should ease up in their quests for perfection.[21]

Innis also recognized that consumption could be arduous. Foreshadowing by almost thirty years the second-wave feminist argument that consumerism is first and foremost domestic labour, her writings probe the difficulties of homemakers' consumer chores.[22] After spending her summer at a cottage, Leslie of *Stand on a Rainbow* dreads returning to the city. She thinks of "the instant necessity for haircuts, new shoes and trips to the dentist ... the binding autumn routine of music lessons, library books, birthday parties, errands and allowances, winter clothes, longer skis, larger skates, rubber boots, more new shoes and more haircuts." For her, shopping for children's goods is a tiresome component of her endless workload.[23] Ethel of "The Party" also experiences consumption as work. She rents an electric polisher and uses it to clean her floors. It makes her muscles stiff, and "she felt depressingly certain that the society hostesses in the paper didn't have backs that ached the way hers did."[24]

Disappointment pervades the consumer experiences of Innis's characters. Believing that women sometimes buy fashion and decor to assuage loneliness or desires for social prestige, Innis implies that those who transfer their hopes onto material goods will become frustrated. Such is the case in *Stand on a Rainbow*, when Leslie wears new clothes at home. The children are indeed "surprised" and her husband "pleased," but "their emotion" would never be "as keen as she had thought it would be." In "front of the mirror," she will see "defects": one dress will be "too full," another "too narrow" or "too blue." Even though the same process occurs with every new purchase, her "disappointment" is never "lessened" and she repeats the procedure "every season."[25]

Through *Stand on a Rainbow*, Innis suggests that women's vague frustrations with homemaking could not be solved by consumption. In contrast to Keynesian wartime theorists who proposed that consumption was the key to post-war reconstruction, she demonstrates that consumerism was at best an ambiguous activity. Preceding Betty Friedan's famous 1963 assertion that domesticity and consumerism could cause depression and frustration among women, *Stand on a Rainbow* indicates that at least one middle-class midcentury Toronto homemaker questioned the ability of goods to create happiness.[26]

Consumption and Inequality

Innis also investigated the social dynamics of consumption. Spousal economic inequality was a particular concern. In "Somebody from Home" (1937), a woman named Dora who has moved with her husband to Florida because his health is too fragile for Ontario's weather is homesick. Prior to moving, they sold all their possessions, against Dora's will, because her husband did not want to pay for their transport. Dora now misses "the furniture that had been her mother's" and the "gold band china" that had been in her family for a hundred years.[27] Showing that women's stereotypical love of goods arose not only from superficiality but from memories of family and stability, Innis here depicts the hardship that male authority can inflict on women. She also provides further evidence for Joy Parr's argument, which was based on interviews conducted with Canadian women who furnished their homes during the 1940s and 1950s, that some women prized certain goods not because they were status-laden, but because they reminded the interviewees of their parents and grandparents.[28]

Ethel of "The Party" similarly chafes against male authority. In this instance, the focus is the inability of Ethel's husband, Todd, to understand her consumer desires. She hides her new dress from him and hopes he does not notice their new bedspread, lampshade, and ornament. She has long desired these items but could never "explain to Todd" the rationale behind her craving. To her dismay he notices the new purchases as soon as he arrives home from work. As Ethel predicts, he becomes angry. When he learns that supper is not yet ready, and when, simultaneously, their toddler begins crying, his anger deepens. In his view, Ethel's new acquisitions and neglect of household responsibilities represent her wifely failings. Readers, however, are meant to sympathize not with Todd, but with Ethel. Having performed her domestic tasks without complaint, the upcoming dinner party represents for her a moment of esteem and relaxation. In "The Party," Innis resists the easy characterization of male breadwinner as proletarian hero, a trope common among leftists of this period, and delves into material conflict between spouses in the upper tier of the working class.[29]

In Innis's fiction, consumption exacerbates broader social oppression. In "Brotherhood" (1935), the author attempts to understand what it is like for a working-class woman of a minority ethnic group to attend an "All Nations Banquet." Anna, the story's heroine, goes to the banquet with her husband. They have been invited as representatives of the country Natovia. Her husband enjoys the evening, especially the free dinner, but Anna feels like an oversized object on display for the amusement of the dainty "ladies," whose "powdered and cool" faces contrast with her hot and sweating body. She cannot eat, for the ladies are "watching," and she is nervous "about which spoon was the one to use." When her husband gives a speech about brotherhood, his face is "hot and shiny," and "she felt sure ... they were laughing at him." She becomes embarrassed by his "brown suit and red tie" because "the other men had on white and black," and she cannot wait to go home. The ironically titled "Brotherhood" thus portrays affluent Toronto society from the perspective of an ethnic and financial outsider, and suggests that what appears respectable to middle-class Torontonians can cause anguish for those who exist outside this circle. Perhaps influenced by Innis's own encounters with staid Toronto society, "Brotherhood" exemplifies her interest in the way that financial clout, social difference, and commodity display contribute to social alienation. The affluent men and women at the function do not intend to estrange Anna, but their garments and customs make her feel like a laughable outsider.[30]

Innis often used the possessions and consumerism of affluent characters to throw destitute characters' poverty into high relief. One of the most poignant if simplistic of these scenarios occurs in "Two Ears" (1933), in which the narrator recounts a streetcar encounter. Sitting on a bench in the back, she is privy to two conversations. On her left two "well-dressed" women complain about their gardeners and chauffeurs; they also chat about which clothes and hairstyles they intend to purchase. On her right a young "poorly dressed" married couple discuss their options. Having lost their home, they have decided to live separately. The wife, crying, is taking her baby to her father's place in the country; the husband will live homeless in the city and look for work. An unbiased observer, the narrator does not profess outrage at the social gulf between the two parties. Instead, Innis uses their conversations to incite the reader's anger. As the young wife and her baby disembark at the train station, the affluent women talk loudly and unselfconsciously about their expensive wardrobes. The story ends with the destitute husband staring "out of the window long after the [train] station had been passed" and finally looking "silently down at his hands spread open on his threadbare knees."[31]

"Two Ears" offers an excellent example of Innis's belief that the affluent choose to be oblivious of the destitute. "News from Abroad" (1940), a more sophisticated story, reiterates this theme. Told from the point of view of a young woman named Eloise, who has just returned from Europe and is visiting her teacher, Miss Gilder, the piece implies that women who place adventure and fashion above all else marginalize others. Eloise had dreaded the visit because she views Miss Gilder as a drab soul who "wore hard, plain tweedy things which showed her unmerciful angles and her short, straight hair was gray over her ears." After she arrives, she is delighted to learn that Miss Gilder lives with her mother, who is "stout and handsome with beautifully waved mauve-tinged hair and tinted nails." Miss Gilder's eagerness to hear about Eloise's cultural experiences in Europe annoys Eloise, who prefers chatting with Mrs. Gilder about shopping, fashion, and beauty. The elder woman's stylishness and frivolity encourage Eloise to "feel sorry for her for having such a plain, mannish daughter." Fed up with her daughter's questions about Europe, Mrs. Gilder finally asks her why she herself does not visit it. Yet Eloise already knows the answer, for "no teacher in the school could live in a lovely apartment like this and support such a smart-looking mother and have a cent left over." Despite her recognition of Miss Gilder's selfless support of her mother, however, she still prefers Mrs. Gilder. A subtle morality tale, "News from Abroad" conveys Innis's message that privileged people choose to ignore the suffering of the marginalized.[32]

The Morality of Consumption

Of all the characters who recur in different guises in Innis's fiction, that of the superficial woman is especially significant. Not only in "Two Ears" and "News from Abroad," but in the above-mentioned "Holiday" as well as in "Donna, You're the Oldest" (1945), self-centred and materialistic women oppress less privileged females.[33] In "Holiday," Nettie wants to enjoy the department store's displays, but her shabby attire causes so many saleswomen and customers to treat her rudely that her visit is almost ruined.[34] In "Donna," the six-year-old title character is taking a train trip with her family. Her harried mother expects her to entertain her three younger siblings. Two affluent women sit in the seat across from Donna. Bored, they decide to play with her. They wash her tear-stained face, comb her hair, give her chocolates, entreat her to sing, and let her play with their makeup and jewellery. They then go to dinner; after their meal, they are tired and ignore the child. In hopes of regaining their attention, Donna attempts to act cute, but the women brush her off, leaving her devastated.[35]

When considered in tandem with Innis's position as a middle-class home-maker, these portrayals of superficial women indicate that the author felt guilty about her own affluence. At the same time, her frequent depictions of home-makers as women without financial power suggest that she herself was frustrated at her own lack of income. These twin themes come together powerfully in "The Gift" (1934), which focuses on a bourgeois housewife named Judith who receives a note from the mother of her first husband, asking that she attend his funeral. Prior to receiving the letter, Judith had been thinking that she needed a new fur coat and that her present husband had refused to give her the $100 for its pur-chase. After receiving the note, she decides to abandon her plans for shopping, lunch, tea, and bridge, and to attend her first husband's funeral. When she ar-rives, she is reminded of his family's poverty. The gathered women "looked disapprovingly from her smart to their own scrubby black." After the service, her ex-mother-in-law, who has treated her kindly throughout, gives her a sealed envelope, saying that her ex-father-in-law had saved it for her. Judith finally extricates herself and takes the train home. She "relaxed in the comfort of the club car and looked at the bored, well-dressed people around her." She is glad to be "getting home again to her own world"; it is "comforting to feel the dark dream" of her previous "helpless and vulnerable" life "abate." At that point, she opens the envelope. It contains $100.[36]

"The Gift" illuminates what it may have been like for a woman of this period to experience upward mobility. Judith is aware of the difficulties of the poor; she herself had once "worried so ... over food bills and had made soups and stews without end."[37] The narrator does not state that Judith feels guilty about climbing the social ladder, but her thoughts do hint at her discomfort. Sitting in her bright home, she thinks of her dead husband, "who had worshipped the sun." He "would have loved this house." She also thinks it "queer" that "a second fur coat should be as necessary to her now as one decent pair of stockings had been then." Innis intends the story to make middle-class readers uncomfortable. While Judith obsessed about getting a "white fur" bunny coat, so as to camou-flage her "matronly" figure and help her look "girlish," her destitute ex-father-in-law had saved $100 for her. Despite Innis's characterization of Judith as superficial, however, she is also aware of bourgeois housewives' own struggles. Judith's husband keeps her on an "allowance," and she feels pressure to maintain a stylish and youthful appearance so as to please him and keep her affluent friends. "The Gift" is thus a sensitive study of middle-class female consumerism, one that portrays both the self-centredness of bourgeois homemakers and their lack of control over their own financial situation.

Into the late 1940s, Innis remained suspicious of consumerism's broader social consequences. One of the last stories she published, "Hair Ribbon" (1947), shows how affluent consumerism marginalizes less privileged people. In this story, which no doubt draws on Innis's childhood experience of moving with her family from the northern USA to Georgia, a young girl named Erie moves to a small southern town. Against her mother's wishes, she makes friends with a girl named Sadie. Sadie's braids are "twisted round with rubber bands" and are crooked and fuzzy as though they have not been combed out for a long time. When Erie looks at them, she thinks "comfortably of the fresh ribbon above her own shining braids." One day, her mother notices that her ribbon, the "good pink one with the corded edge," is missing. They look for it in the field where Erie and Sadie had been playing but cannot find it. Following her mother's instructions, Erie asks Sadie where it is. In response, Sadie says that she will be right back; when she returns, she is "red and breathless," and she states that they should look for the ribbon in the field. Sure enough, Erie finds it there. Her mother again forbids her to play with Sadie, but her father winks at her, saying that Erie is "broadening."[38]

Erie is oblivious to the class difference between herself and Sadie, and she does not realize that Sadie stole her ribbon. Yet the careful description of the girls' braids, the mother's dislike of Sadie, and the father's comment about the friendship as a "broadening" experience indicate that the reader is meant to recognize that Sadie stole the ribbon due to envy over Erie's comfortable home life. "Hair Ribbon" is thus intended to create reader guilt. Readers are expected to feel embarrassed by the mother's maintenance of class distance and ashamed that Sadie does not have shining braids or pretty ribbons.[39]

Conclusion

"Hair Ribbon" contains many of the themes to which Innis repeatedly returned during the thirties and forties: power, oppression, inequality, femininity, and consumerism. A mother of four, a published and talented historian, a loving wife, a gifted writer, and a brilliant observer of human relations, Mary Quayle Innis was in a unique position to explore these issues with sensitivity and depth. References to them in her fictional oeuvre enable one to reach some conclusions about what it was like to be an English-speaking, middle-class homemaker during the thirties and forties in Toronto.

Innis's fiction explored both the positive and the negative sides of consumption. She recognized that shopping, dresses, and beauty treatments could offer pleasure, status, and fulfillment. At the same time, she was uncomfortable with the motivations compelling women to seek these products. Loneliness, isolation, and a feeling of inadequacy spurred many of her female characters to look for solace in the consumer marketplace. Innis was also uneasy with the consequences of consumption. Superficial female characters obsessed with their own images and possessions appear again and again in her tales. In such stories as "Donna," "The Gift," "Two Ears," and "Brotherhood," their words and actions work to further marginalize those who are already economically and socially disadvantaged.

Taken as a whole, Innis's fiction indicates that this scholar, writer, and homemaker was deeply troubled by the social and economic positions in which many English Canadian women found themselves during the 1930s and 1940s. Showing many to be lonely and dependent on their husbands for approval and financial support, she suggests that motherhood and wifehood offered limited fulfillment. She also implies that women's attempts to remedy their dissatisfactions through consumer goods were themselves dissatisfying. Not only did new purchases fail to fulfill buyers' expectations, so did their display contribute to social alienation and inequality. Even those women who sought to remedy such inequality, such as the philanthropists in "Brotherhood" and the charitable woman in "Staver," were hampered in their efforts to relieve oppression by their own inabilities to reach beyond their affluence and displays of privilege.

Ultimately, Innis's fiction suggests that the socially acceptable avenues of fulfillment open to middle-class women in Toronto during this period were untenable. Motherhood, marriage, consumption, and philanthropy, though offering certain rewards, did not deliver their promised ideals. It is therefore significant that after her children left home, and after her husband's death in 1952, Innis decided to enter a "more public life," as Barbara Pell puts it. In 1955, at the age of fifty-six, she became dean of women at University College, at the University of Toronto, a position she held for nine years. She also served in 1959 as a "Canadian delegate to the Commonwealth Conference on Education held in Oxford"; other positions included being vice chairperson of the Committee on Religious Education in Ontario's public schools.[40]

Innis's fiction is significant on another level as well. Touching on many of the constraining attributes of middle-class womanhood in the thirties and forties, it deepens historical understandings of 1960s feminism. As Innis's fiction reveals, calls for more equality between spouses, better integration of women into public life, and some feminists' rejection of materialism had their roots in the experiences of women in preceding decades. At the same time, the coming of second-wave feminism does not mean that Innis's stories are now irrelevant. Such post-war movements as feminism may have remedied some of North America's ills, but gender inequality, social alienation, economic marginalization, and rampant consumer culture are still major features of contemporary life. Today more than ever, it seems, such trenchant and sensitive explorations of consumerism as those offered by Mary Quayle Innis are necessary.

Notes

1 Barbara Pell, "Innis, Mary Quayle," *Dictionary of Literary Biography*, vol. 88, *Canadian Writers, 1920-1959*, 2nd ser., ed. W.H. New (Detroit: Gale Group, 1989), 132-34.

2 Anne Innis Dagg, "Mary Quayle Innis (1899-1972)," *A Biographical Dictionary of Women Economists*, ed. Robert W. Dimand, Mary Ann Dimand, and Evelyn L. Forget (Cheltenham, UK: Edward Elgar, 2000), 224; Mary Quayle Innis, *An Economic History of Canada* (Toronto: Ryerson, 1935); Mary Quayle Innis, "The Record of an Epidemic," *Dalhousie Review* 16 (1936): 55-60; Mary Quayle Innis, "Philip Henry Gosse in Canada," *Dalhousie Review* 17 (1937): 55-60; Mary Quayle Innis, "The Industrial Development of Ontario, 1783-1820," *Ontario Historical Society* 32 (1937): 104-13, republished in *Historical Essays on Upper Canada*, ed. J.K. Johnson (Toronto: McClelland and Stewart, 1975), 140-52.

3 Bettina Liverant, "Buying Happiness: English Canadian Intellectuals and the Development of Canadian Consumer Culture" (PhD thesis, University of Alberta, 2008), 214-16; see also Chapter 1 in this volume.

4 Veronica Strong-Boag, "Home Dreams: Women and the Suburban Experiment in Canada, 1945-1960," in *Rethinking Canada: The Promise of Women's History*, 3rd ed., ed. Veronica Strong-Boag and Anita Clair Fellman (Toronto: Oxford University Press, 1997), 391; Len Kuffert, *A Great Duty: Canadian Responses to Modern Life and Mass Culture, 1939-1967* (Montreal and Kingston: McGill-Queen's University Press, 2003).

5 Mary Quayle Innis, *Unfold the Years: A History of the Young Women's Christian Association in Canada* (Toronto: McClelland and Stewart, 1949); Mary Quayle Innis, *Changing Canada*, 2 vols. (Toronto: Clarke Irwin, 1951); Mary Quayle Innis, *Living in Canada* (Toronto: Clarke Irwin, 1954); Mary Quayle Innis, *Travellers West* (Toronto: Clarke Irwin, 1956); Mary Quayle Innis, ed., *Mrs. Simcoe's Diary* (Toronto: Macmillan, 1965); Mary Quayle Innis, ed., *The Clear Spirit: Twenty Canadian Women and Their Times* (Toronto: University of Toronto Press, 1966); Mary Quayle Innis, ed., *Nursing Education in a Changing Society* (Toronto: University of Toronto Press, 1970).

6 Robert Fulford, "Introduction," in *Saturday Night Scrapbook*, ed. Morris Wolfe (Toronto: New Press, 1973), xii.

7 Anne Innis Dagg, "Preface," in "Selected Short Works of Mary Quayle Innis" (unpublished monograph, GA 127-11a, University of Waterloo Library, Waterloo), n.p.; J. David Black, "'Both of Us Can Move Mountains': Mary Quayle Innis and Her Relationship to Harold Innis' Legacy," *Canadian Journal of Communications* 28, 4 (2003): para. 11.

8 Mary Quayle Innis, "Day to Keep Always," *Saturday Night*, 12 December 1942, 48, 49.

9 Ibid., 48.

10 Mary Quayle Innis, "Holiday," *Canadian Forum*, June 1932, 141.

11 Ibid., 140.

12 Mary Quayle Innis, *Stand on a Rainbow* (Toronto: Collins, 1943), 162, 163.

13   Mary Quayle Innis, "The Wave," *Saturday Night,* 23 December 1939, 20.

14   Mary Quayle Innis, "Staver," in *Voices of Discord: Canadian Short Stories from the 1930s,* ed. Donna Phillips (Toronto: New Hogtown Press, 1979), 177, 181.

15   Veronica Strong-Boag, *The New Day Recalled: Lives of Girls and Women in English Canada, 1919-1939* (Toronto: Copp Clark Pitman, 1988), 181-82.

16   Mary Quayle Innis, "The Party," in Phillips, *Voices of Discord,* 152, 154.

17   Thorstein Veblen, *The Theory of the Leisure Class: An Economic Study in the Evolution of Institutions* (New York: Macmillan, 1899).

18   Mary Quayle Innis, "Lived-in Look; or Quaint Gourds and Pottery Figures," *Saturday Night,* 2 December 1944, 36, 37.

19   Ibid., 37.

20   Mica Nava, "Framing Advertising: Cultural Analysis and the Incrimination of Visual Texts," in *Buy This Book: Studies in Advertising and Consumption,* ed. Mica Nava et al. (New York: Routledge, 1997), 35-50.

21   Mary Quayle Innis, "Opportunists' Day," *Saturday Night,* 20 November 1943, 33.

22   Ellen Willis, "'Consumerism' and Women," in *Voices from Women's Liberation,* ed. Leslie B. Tanner (New York: New American Library, 1971), 307-13.

23   Innis, *Stand on a Rainbow,* 9.

24   Innis, "The Party," 153-54.

25   Innis, *Stand on a Rainbow,* 162, 163.

26   Betty Friedan, *The Feminine Mystique* (1963; repr., New York: Norton, 2001).

27   Mary Quayle Innis, "Somebody from Home," *Saturday Night,* 1 May 1937, 9.

28   Joy Parr, *Domestic Goods: The Material, the Moral, and the Economic in the Postwar Years* (Toronto: University of Toronto Press, 1999), 185-86. Parr also notes, however, that many Canadian women decorated in a modern style, so as to differentiate their homes from those of their parents.

29   Innis, "The Party," 151-57.

30   Mary Quayle Innis, "Brotherhood," *Canadian Forum,* February 1935, 188, 189.

31   Mary Quayle Innis, "Two Ears," *Canadian Forum,* August 1933, 420, 421.

32   Mary Quayle Innis, "News from Abroad," *Saturday Night,* 13 January 1940, 20.

33   Mary Quayle Innis, "Donna, You're the Oldest, Come Here, Donna, Sing, Donna," *Saturday Night,* 29 September 1945, 32-33.

34   Innis, "Holiday," 140-42.

35   Innis, "Donna, You're the Oldest," 32-33.

36   Mary Quayle Innis, "The Gift," *Canadian Forum,* June 1934, 349, 350, 351.

37   Ibid., 350.

38   Mary Quayle Innis, "Hair Ribbon," *Saturday Night,* 1 March 1947, 25.

39   Ibid.

40   Pell, "Innis, Mary Quayle," 132, 134.

Selected Readings

•
•
•

Aberhart, William, and David Elliott. *Aberhart: Outpourings and Replies.* Calgary: Alberta Records Publication Board, Historical Society of Alberta, 1991.

Abrams, Lynn. "From Control to Commercialization: The Triumph of Mass Entertainment in Germany 1900-1925?" *German History* 8 (1990): 278-93.

Al-Khalidi, Alia. "'The Greatest Invention of the Century': Menstruation in Visual and Material Culture." In Andrews and Talbot, *All the World and Her Husband,* 65-81.

Alexander, S. "Becoming a Woman in London in the 1920s and 1930s." In *Becoming a Woman and Other Essays in 19th and 20th Century Feminist History,* 203-25. New York: New York University Press, 1995.

Andrews, Maggie, and Mary M. Talbot, eds. *All the World and Her Husband: Women in Twentieth-Century Consumer Culture.* London: Cassell, 2000.

Apple, Rima D. "Constructing Mothers: Scientific Motherhood in the Nineteenth and Twentieth Century." In *Mothers and Motherhood: Readings in American History,* ed. Rima D. Apple and Janet Golden, 90-111. Columbus: Ohio State University Press, 1997.

Arnup, Katherine. *Education for Motherhood: Advice for Mothers in Twentieth-Century Canada.* Toronto: University of Toronto Press, 1994.

Bacchi, Carol Lee. *Liberation Deferred? The Ideas of the English-Canadian Suffragists, 1877-1918.* Toronto: University of Toronto Press, 1983.

Baillargeon, Denyse. *Making Do: Women, Family and Home in Montreal during the Great Depression.* Waterloo: Wilfrid Laurier University Press, 1999.

Banner, Lois. *American Beauty.* New York: Knopf, 1983.

Banta, Martha. *Imaging American Women: Idea and Ideals in Cultural History.* New York: Columbia University Press, 1987.

Barlow, Tani E., Madeleine Yue Dong, Uta G. Poiger, Priti Ramamurthy, Lynn M. Thomas, and Alys Eve Weinbaum. "The Modern Girl around the World: A Research Agenda and Preliminary Findings." *Gender and History* 17, 2 (August 2005): 245-94.

Bartky, Sandra Lee. "Foucault, Femininity, and the Modernization of Patriarchal Power." In *Feminism and Foucault: Reflections on Resistance,* ed. Irene Diamond and Lee Quimby, 61-86. Boston: Northeastern University Press, 1988.

Beddoe, D. *Back to Home and Duty: Women between the Wars 1918-1939.* London: Pandora, 1989.

Behling, Laura L. "'The Woman at the Wheel': Marketing Ideal Womanhood, 1915-1934." *Journal of American Culture* 20, 3 (1997): 13-30.

Belisle, Donica. *Retail Nation: Department Stores and the Making of Modern Canada.* Vancouver: UBC Press, 2011.

–. "Toward a Canadian Consumer History." *Labour/Le travail* 52, 2 (Fall 2003): 181-206.

Besse, Susan K. *Restructuring Patriarchy: The Modernization of Gender Inequality in Brazil, 1914-1940.* Chapel Hill: University of North Carolina Press, 1996.

Bingham, A. "'An Era of Domesticity'? Histories of Women and Gender in Interwar Britain." *Cultural and Social History* 1 (2004): 225-33.

Blackwelder, Julia Kirk. *Styling Jim Crow: African American Beauty Training during Segregation.* College Station: Texas A & M University Press, 2003.

Bliss, Katherine. *Prostitution, Public Health, and Gender Politics in Revolutionary Mexico City.* University Park: University of Pennsylvania Press, 2001.

Bliss, Katherine Elaine, and Ann S. Blum. "Dangerous Driving: Adolescence, Sex, and the Gendered Experience of Public Space in Early-Twentieth-Century Mexico City." In *Gender, Sexuality, and Power in Latin America since Independence,* ed. William E. French and Katherine Elaine Bliss, 163-86. Lanham, MD: Rowman and Littlefield, 2007.

Blum, Ann S. "Breaking and Making Families: Adoption and Public Welfare, Mexico City, 1938-1942." In *Sex in Revolution: Gender, Politics, and Power in Modern Mexico,* ed. Jocelyn Olcott, Mary Kay Vaughan, and Gabriela Cano, 127-44. Durham, NC: Duke University Press, 2006.

Blum, Dilys E. *Shocking! The Art and Fashion of Elsa Schiaparelli.* New Haven: Yale University Press, 2003.

Boyer, Kate. "Re-Working Respectability: The Feminization of Clerical Work and the Politics of Public Virtue in Early Twentieth-Century Montreal." In *Power, Place and Identity: Historical Studies of Social and Legal Regulation in Quebec,* ed. Tamara Myers, Kate Boyer, Mary Anne Poutanen, and Steven Watt, 151-69. Montreal: Montreal History Group, 1998.

Breckman, Warren G. "Disciplining Consumption: The Debate about Luxury in Wilhelmine Germany, 1890-1914." *Journal of Social History* 24 (1991): 485-505.

Brodie, Janet Farell. *Contraception and Abortion in 19th Century America.* Ithaca: Cornell University Press, 1994.

Brown, Dorothy. *Setting a Course: American Women in the 1920s.* Boston: Twayne, 1987.

Brumberg, Joan Jacob. *The Body Project: An Intimate History of American Girls.* New York: Random House, 1997.

Buck-Morss, Susan. *The Dialectics of Seeing: Walter Benjamin and the Arcades Project.* Cambridge, MA: MIT Press, 1989.

Buckley, Suzann, and Janice Dickin McGinnis. "Venereal Disease and Public Health Reform in Canada." *Canadian Historical Review* 63, 3 (1982): 337-54.

Buffington, Robert. "'La Dancing' Mexicana: Danzón and the Transformation of Intimacy in Post-Revolutionary Mexico City." *Journal of Latin American Cultural Studies* 14 (March 2005): 87-108.

Bundles, A'Lelia Perry. *On Her Own Ground: The Life and Times of Madam C.J. Walker.* New York: Scribner, 2001.

Bunker, Steven B. "'Consumers of Good Taste': Marketing Modernity in Northern Mexico, 1890-1910." *Mexican Studies/Estudios Mexicanos* 13 (Summer 1997): 227-96.

Butler, Judith. *Gender Trouble: Feminism and the Subversion of Identity.* New York: Routledge, 1990.

Byrd, Ayana D., and Lori L. Tharps. *Hair Story: Untangling the Roots of Black Hair in America.* New York: St. Martin's Griffin, 2001.

Cahn, Susan. *Coming on Strong: Gender and Sexuality in Twentieth-Century Women's Sport.* Cambridge, MA: Harvard University Press, 1994.

Chambers, Lori. *Misconceptions: Unmarried Motherhood and the Ontario Children of Unmarried Parents Act, 1921-1969.* Toronto: Osgoode Society for Canadian Legal History/University of Toronto Press, 2007.

Chuppa-Cornell, Kim. "Filling a Vacuum: Women's Health Information in *Good Housekeeping*'s Articles and Advertisements, 1920-1965." *Historian* 67, 3 (2005): 454-73.

Cleverdon, Catherine. *The Women Suffrage Movement in Canada.* 1947. Reprint, Toronto: University of Toronto Press, 1974.

Clio Collective. *Quebec Women: A History.* Toronto: Canadian Scholars' Press, 1990.

Cohen, Lizabeth. *A Consumers' Republic: The Politics of Mass Consumption in Postwar America.* New York: Alfred A. Knopf, 2003.

Comacchio, Cynthia. *The Dominion of Youth: Adolescence and the Making of a Modern Canada, 1920-1950.* Waterloo: Wilfrid Laurier University Press, 2006.

–. *The Infinite Bonds of Family: Domesticity in Canada, 1850-1940.* Toronto: University of Toronto Press, 1999.

–. *Nations Are Built of Babies: Saving Ontario's Mothers and Children, 1900-1940.* Montreal and Kingston: McGill-Queen's University Press, 1993.

Conor, Liz. *The Spectacular Modern Woman: Feminine Visibility in the 1920s.* Bloomington: Indiana University Press, 2004.

Constanzo, M. "Images of Gender in *Punch* 1901-10." *International Journal of the History of Sport* 19 (March 2002): 31-56.

Cowan, Ruth Schwartz. *More Work for Mother: The Ironies of Household Technology from the Open Hearth to the Microwave.* New York: Basic Books, 1983.

Craig, Maxine Leeds. *Ain't I a Beauty Queen? Black Women, Beauty and the Politics of Race.* New York: Oxford University Press, 2002.

Creedon, Pamela J., ed. *Women, the Media and Sport: Challenging Gender Values.* Thousand Oaks, CA: Sage, 1994.

Cross, Gary S. *An All-Consuming Century: Why Commercialism Won in Modern America.* New York: Columbia University Press, 2000.

–. *Time and Money: The Making of Consumer Culture.* New York: Routledge, 1993.

Crouthamel, Jason. "Male Sexuality and Psychological Trauma: Soldiers and Sexual Disorder in World War I and Weimar Germany." *Journal of History of Sexuality* 17 (January 2008): 60-84.

Crowley, Terry. *Agnes Macphail and the Politics of Equality.* Toronto: James Lorimer, 1990.

Daniel, Ute. *The War from Within: German Working-Class Women in the First World War.* New York: Berg, 1997.

Davies, Andrew. "Broadcasting and Cinema." In *Twentieth Century Britain: Economic, Social, and Cultural Change,* ed. Paul Johnson, 263-81. London: Longman, 1994.

De Grazia, Victoria. *How Fascism Ruled Women, Italy 1922-1945.* Berkeley: University of California Press, 1992.

De Grazia, Victoria, with Ellen Furlough, eds. *The Sex of Things: Gender and Consumption in Historical Perspective.* Berkeley: University of California Press, 1996.

Dehli, Kari. "Fictions of the Scientific Imagination: Researching the Dionne Quintuplets." *Journal of Canadian Studies* 29 (1994): 85-110.

Dodd, Dianne. "Advice to Parents: The Blue Books, Helen MacMurchy, M.D., and the Federal Department of Health, 1920-34." *Canadian Bulletin of Medical History* 8 (1991): 203-30.

Domínguez-Ruvalcaba, Héctor. *Modernity and Nation in Mexican Representations of Masculinity: From Sensuality to Bloodshed.* New York: Palgrave Macmillan, 2007.

Dorsey, Leslie, and Janice Devine. *Fare Thee Well: A Backward Look at Two Centuries of Historic American Hostelries, Fashion Spas and Seaside Resorts.* New York: Crown, 1964.

Dubinsky, Karen. *Improper Advances: Rape and Heterosexual Conflict in Ontario, 1880-1929.* Chicago: University of Chicago Press, 1993.

Duffin, Jacalyn. *History of Medicine: A Scandalously Short Introduction.* Toronto: University of Toronto Press, 1999.

Dulles, Foster Rhea. *America Learns to Play: A History of Popular Recreation, 1607-1940.* New York: D. Appleton-Century, 1940.

Dyreson, Mark. "The Emergence of Consumer Culture and the Transformation of Physical Culture: American Sport in the 1920s." *Journal of Sport History* 16, 3 (Winter 1989): 261-81.

Ehrenreich, Barbara, and Deirdre English. *For Her Own Good: 150 Years of the Experts' Advice to Women.* Garden City, NY: Anchor Press, 1978.

Eineigel, Susanne. "Visualizing the Self: Modernity, Identity, and the *Gente Decente* in Porfirian Mexico." Master's thesis, University of British Columbia, 2003.

Elliot, R. *Women and Smoking since 1890.* Abingdon: Routledge, 2008.

Enstad, Nan. *Ladies of Labor, Girls of Adventure: Working Women, Popular Culture, and Labor Politics at the Turn of the Twentieth Century.* New York: Columbia University Press, 1999.

Ewen, Stuart. *Captains of Consciousness: Advertising and the Social Roots of the Consumer Culture.* New York: McGraw-Hill, 1976.

Ewing, Elizabeth. *History of Twentieth Century Fashion.* Totowa, NJ: Barnes and Noble, 1986.

Felski, Rita. *The Gender of Modernity.* Cambridge, MA: Harvard University Press, 1995.

Ferguson, Harvie. *Modernity and Subjectivity: Body, Soul, Spirit.* Charlottesville: University Press of Virginia, 2000.

Flamming, Douglas. *Bound for Freedom: Black Los Angeles in Jim Crow America.* Berkeley: University of California Press, 2005.

Foucault, Michel. *History of Sexuality.* Vol. 1, translated by Robert Hurley. New York: Pantheon Books, 1978.

Fowler, D. "Teenage Consumers? Young Wage-Earners and Leisure in Manchester, 1919-1939." In *Workers' Worlds*, ed. A. Davies and S. Fielding, 133-54. Manchester: Manchester University Press, 1992.

Fox, Bonnie. "Selling the Mechanized Household: 70 Years of Ads in the *Ladies' Home Journal.*" *Gender and Society* 4 (1990): 25-40.

Fox, Stephen. *The Mirror Makers: A History of American Advertising and Its Creators.* New York: William Marrow, 1984.

French, William E. "Prostitutes and Guardian Angels: Women, Work, and the Family in Porfirian Mexico." *Hispanic American Historical Review* 72, 4 (1992): 529-53.

Frevert, Ute. *Women in German History: From Bourgeois Emancipation to Sexual Liberation.* Translated by Stuart McKinnon-Evans. New York: Berg, 1997.

Friedan, Betty. *The Feminine Mystique.* 1963. Reprint, New York: Norton, 2001.

Gaonkar, Dilip Parameshwar, ed. *Alternative Modernities.* Durham, NC: Duke University Press, 2001.

Garelick, Rhonda K. "The Layered Look: Coco Chanel and Contagious Celebrity." In *Dandies: Fashion and Finesse in Art and Culture*, ed. Susan Fillin-Yeh, 35-58. New York: New York University Press, 2001.

George, Judith Jenkins. "The Fad of American Women's Endurance Swimming during the Post-World War I Era." *Canadian Journal of History of Sport* 26, 1 (May 1995): 52-72.

Gibson, Emily, with Barbara Firth. *The Original Million Dollar Mermaid.* Crows Nest, New South Wales: Allen and Unwin, 2005.

Gidney, R.D., and W.P.J. Millar. "The Origins of Organized Medicine in Ontario, 1850-1869." In *Health, Disease and Medicine: Essays in Canadian History,* ed. Charles G. Roland, 64-95. Toronto: Hannah Institute for the History of Medicine, 1984.

Ginsburg, Rebecca. "'Don't Tell, Dear': The Material Culture of Tampons and Napkins." *Journal of Material Culture* 1, 3 (1996): 365-75.

Glassford, Larry. *Reaction and Reform: The Politics of the Conservative Party under R.B. Bennett, 1927-1938.* Toronto: University of Toronto Press, 1992.

Granatstein, Jack. *The Politics of Survival: The Conservative Party of Canada, 1939-1945.* Toronto: University of Toronto Press, 1967.

Haedrich, Marcel. *Coco Chanel: Her Life, Her Secrets.* Translated by Charles Lam Markmann. Boston: Little, Brown, 1972.

Haiken, Elizabeth. *Venus Envy: A History of Cosmetic Surgery.* Baltimore: Johns Hopkins University Press, 1997.

Hake, Sabine. "In the Mirror of Fashion." In von Ankum, *Women in the Metropolis,* 185-201.

Hall, Kristin. "Prescriptions for Modern Womanhood: Advertising Lysol in Interwar North America." Master's thesis, Laurentian University, 2008.

Hall, Margaret Ann. *The Girl and the Game: The History of Women's Sport in Canada.* Peterborough: Broadview Press, 2002.

Hannam, J. "Women and Politics." In *Women's History: Britain 1850-1945,* ed. J. Purvis, 184-210. London: Routledge, 2000.

Hansen, Miriam. *Babel and Babylon: Spectatorship in American Silent Film.* Cambridge, MA: Harvard University Press, 1991.

Hargreaves, Jennifer. "'Playing like Gentlemen While Behaving like Ladies': Contradictory Features of the Formative Years of Women's Sport." *British Journal of Sports History* 2, 1 (May 1985): 40-52.

-. *Sporting Females: Critical Issues in the History and Sociology of Women's Sport.* London: Routledge, 1994.

Harootunian, Harry. *History's Disquiet: Modernity, Cultural Practice, and the Question of Everyday Life.* New York: Columbia University Press, 2000.

Hausen, Karin. "Family and Role-Division: The Polarization of Sexual Stereotypes in the Nineteenth Century – an Aspect of the Dissociation of Work and Family Life." In *The German Family: Essays on the Social History of the Family in Nineteenth- and Twentieth-Century Germany,* ed. Richard J. Evans and W.R. Lee, 51-83. Totowa, NJ: Barnes and Noble, 1981.

Hayes, Joy. *Radio Nation: Communication, Popular Culture, and Nationalism in Mexico, 1920-1950.* Tucson: University of Arizona Press, 2000.

Heilmann, Ann, and Margaret Beetham, eds. *New Woman Hybridities: Femininity, Feminism and International Consumer Culture, 1880-1930.* London: Routledge, 2004.

Hershfield, Joanne. *Imagining la Chica Moderna: Women, Nation, and Visual Culture in Mexico, 1917-1936.* Durham, NC: Duke University Press, 2008.

Hill, Daniel Delis. *Advertising to the American Woman, 1900-1999.* Columbus: Ohio State University Press, 2002.

Horowitz, Daniel. *The Morality of Spending: Attitudes toward the Consumer Society in America, 1875-1940.* Baltimore: Johns Hopkins University Press, 1985.

Horwood, Catherine. *Keeping Up Appearances.* London: Sutton, 2005.

Howkins, Alun, and John Lowerson. *Trends in Leisure 1919-1939*. London: Sports Council and Social Science Research Council, 1979.

Hoy, Suellen. *Chasing Dirt: The American Pursuit of Cleanliness*. New York: Oxford University Press, 1995.

Huggins, M. "'And Now, Something for the Ladies': Representations of Women's Sport in Cinema Newsreels 1918-1939." *Women's History Review* 16 (2007): 681-700.

Jacob, Wilson Chacko. "Working Out Egypt: Masculinity and Subject Formation between Colonial Modernity and Nationalism, 1870-1940." PhD diss., New York University, 2005.

Jay, Martin. "Scopic Regimes of Modernity." In *Vision and Visuality*, ed. Hal Foster, 3-23. Seattle: Bay Press, 1988.

Jones, Esyllt W. "'Co-operation in All Human Endeavour': Disease Vectors in the 1918-1919 Influenza Pandemic in Winnipeg." *Canadian Bulletin of Medical History* 22, 1 (2005): 57-82.

Karush, Matthew B. "The Melodramatic Nation: Integration and Polarization in the Argentine Cinema of the 1930s." *Hispanic American Historical Review* 87, 2 (2007): 293-326.

Kelley, Thomas P. Jr. *The Fabulous Kelley: Canada's King of the Medicine Men*. Don Mills: General Publishers, 1974.

Kent, S. Kingsley. *Making Peace: The Reconstruction of Gender in Interwar Britain*. Princeton: Princeton University Press, 1993.

Kidwell, Claudia B. *Women's Bathing and Swimming Costume in the United States*. Washington, DC: Smithsonian Institution Press, 1968.

Kitch, Carolyn. *The Girl on the Magazine Cover: The Origins of Visual Stereotypes in American Mass Media*. Chapel Hill, NC: University of Chapel Hill Press, 2001.

Korinek, Valerie. *Roughing It in the Suburbs: Reading* Chatelaine *Magazine in the Fifties and Sixties*. Toronto: University of Toronto Press, 2000.

Kracauer, Siegfried. *From Caligari to Hitler: A Psychological History of the German Film*. Princeton: Princeton University Press, 1974.

Kuffert, Len. *A Great Duty: Canadian Responses to Modern Life and Mass Culture, 1939-1967*. Montreal and Kingston: McGill-Queen's University Press, 2003.

Kunzel, Regina. *Fallen Women, Problem Girls: Unmarried Mothers and the Professionalization of Social Work, 1890-1945*. New Haven, CT: Yale University Press, 1993.

Ladd-Taylor, Molly. *Raising a Baby the Government Way: Mothers' Letters to the Children's Bureau, 1915-1932*. New Brunswick, NJ: Rutgers University Press, 1986.

Lang, Marjory. *Women Who Made the News: Female Journalists in Canada, 1880-1945*. Montreal and Kingston: McGill-Queen's University Press, 1999.

Langhamer, C. *Women's Leisure in England 1920-1960*. Manchester: Manchester University Press, 2000.

Latham, Angela J. *Posing a Threat: Flappers, Chorus Girls and Other Brazen Performers of the American 1920s*. Hanover, NH: Wesleyan University Press, 2000.

Laycock, David. *Populism and Democratic Thought in the Canadian Prairies, 1910-1940*. Toronto: University of Toronto Press, 1990.

Leach, William R. "Transformations in a Culture of Consumption: Women and Department Stores, 1890-1925." *Journal of American History* 71, 2 (September 1984): 319-42.

Lears, T.J. Jackson. "American Advertising and the Reconstruction of the Body, 1880-1930." In *Fitness in American Culture: Images of Health, Sport and the Body, 1830-1940*, ed. Kathryn Grover, 47-66. Amherst: University of Massachusetts Press, 1989.

–. *Fables of Abundance: A Cultural History of Advertising in America*. New York: Basic Books, 1994.

Leavitt, Sarah A. *From Catherine Beecher to Martha Stewart: A Cultural History of Domestic Advice.* Chapel Hill: University of North Carolina Press, 2002.

Lenček, Lena, and Gideon Bosker. *Making Waves: Swimsuits and the Undressing of America.* San Francisco: Chronicle Books, 1989.

Lerner, Paul F. *Hysterical Men: War, Psychiatry, and the Politics of Trauma in Germany, 1890-1930.* Ithaca: Cornell University Press, 2003.

Liverant, Bettina. "Buying Happiness: English Canadian Intellectuals and the Development of Canadian Consumer Culture, 1895-1965." PhD diss., University of Alberta, 2008.

Loeb, Lori. "Doctors and Patent Medicines in Modern Britain: Professionalism and Consumerism." *Albion: A Quarterly Journal Concerned with British Studies* 33, 3 (Autumn 2001): 404-25.

López, Rick A. "The India Bonita Contest of 1921 and the Ethnicization of Mexican National Culture." *Hispanic American Historical Review* 82, 2 (2002): 291-328.

MacDougall, Heather. *Activists and Advocates: Toronto's Health Department, 1883-1983.* Toronto: Dundurn Press, 1990.

Maclachlan, Patricia, and Frank Trentmann. "Civilizing Markets: Traditions of Consumer Politics in Twentieth-Century Britain, Japan and the United States." In *Markets in Historical Contexts: Ideas and Politics in the Modern World,* ed. Mark Bevir and Frank Trentmann, 170-201. Cambridge: Cambridge University Press, 2004.

Maltby, Richard, and Melvyn Stokes, eds. *Identifying Hollywood's Audiences: Cultural Identity and the Movies.* London: British Film Institute, 1999.

Marchand, Roland. *Advertising the American Dream: Making Way for Modernity, 1920-1940.* Berkeley: University of California Press, 1985 and 1986.

Masiello, Francine. *Between Civilization and Barbarism: Women, Nation and Literary Culture in Modern Argentina.* Lincoln: University of Nebraska Press, 1992.

McCaig, Margo. "Playing the Game 1880-1970." Master's diss., University of Strathclyde, 1996.

McClintock, Anne. *Imperial Leather: Race, Gender and Sexuality in the Colonial Contest.* New York: Routledge, 1995.

McCrone, Kathleen E. "Class, Gender, and English Women's Sport, c. 1890-1914." *Journal of Sport History* 18 (Spring 1991): 159-82.

–. *Playing the Game: Sport and the Physical Emancipation of English Women, 1870-1914.* Lexington: University Press of Kentucky, 1988.

McLaren, Angus. *Our Own Master Race: Eugenics in Canada, 1885-1945.* Toronto: Oxford University Press, 1990.

McLaren, Angus, and Arlene Tigar McLaren. *The Bedroom and the State: The Changing Practices and Politics of Contraception and Abortion in Canada, 1880-1980.* 1st ed. Toronto: McClelland and Stewart, 1986.

–. *The Bedroom and the State: The Changing Practices and Politics of Contraception and Abortion in Canada, 1880-1996.* 2nd ed. Toronto: Oxford University Press, 1996.

–. "Discoveries and Dissimulations: The Impact of Abortion Deaths on Maternal Mortality in British Columbia." *BC Studies* 64 (Winter 1984-85): 3-26.

McTavish, Jan R. "What's in a Name? Aspirin and the American Medical Association." *Bulletin of the History of Medicine* 61 (1987): 343-66.

Meckel, Richard A. *Save the Babies: American Public Health Reform and the Prevention of Infant Mortality, 1850-1929.* Baltimore: Johns Hopkins University Press, 1990.

Melman, B. *Women and the Popular Imagination in the Twenties: Flappers and Nymphs.* Basingstoke: Macmillan, 1988.

Messner, Michael A. "Sports and Male Domination: The Female Athlete as Contested Ideological Terrain." In *Women, Sport, and Culture,* ed. Susan Birrell and Cheryl Cole, 65-80. Champlain, IL: Human Kinetics, 1994.

Mintz, Steven, and Susan Kellogg. *Domestic Revolutions: A Social History of American Family Life*. New York: Free Press, 1988.

Mitchinson, Wendy. *The Nature of Their Bodies: Women and Their Doctors in Victorian Canada*. Toronto: University of Toronto Press, 1991.

Molyneaux, Heather. "In Sickness and in Health: Representations of Women in Pharmaceutical Advertisements in the *Canadian Medical Association Journal*, 1950-1970." PhD diss., University of New Brunswick, 2009.

Moore, Shirley Ann Wilson. "'Your Life Is Really Not Just Your Own': African American Women in Twentieth Century California." In *Seeking El Dorado: African Americans in California*, ed. Lawrence B. De Graaf, Kevin Mulroy, and Quintard Taylor, 210-46. Los Angeles: Autry Museum of Western Heritage, 2001.

Morgan, Marilyn. "'The Star-Spangled Channel': Money, the Media, and Gender in Marathon Swimming, 1900-1936." PhD diss., University of Maine, 2007.

Mosse, George. *The Image of Man: The Creation of Modern Masculinity*. New York: Oxford University Press, 1996.

Mrozek, Donald J. "Sport in American Life: From National Health to Personal Fulfillment, 1890-1940." In *Fitness in American Culture: Images of Health, Sport and the Body, 1830-1940*, ed. Kathryn Grover, 18-46. Amherst: University of Massachusetts Press, 1989.

Nava, Mica. "The Cosmopolitanism of Commerce and the Allure of Difference: Selfridges, the Russian Ballet and the Tango, 1911-1914." *International Journal of Cultural Studies* 1, 2 (1998): 163-96.

–. "Framing Advertising: Cultural Analysis and the Incrimination of Visual Texts." In *Buy This Book: Studies in Advertising and Consumption*, ed. Mica Nava, Andrew Blake, Iain MacRury, and Barry Richards, 34-50. New York: Routledge, 1997.

Neatby, H. Blair. *William Lyon Mackenzie King, 1932-1939: The Prism of Unity*. Toronto: University of Toronto Press, 1976.

O'Malley, Ilene V. *The Myth of the Revolution: Hero Cults and the Institutionalization of the Mexican State, 1920-1940*. Westport, CT: Greenwood Press, 1986.

Ogden, Anngret S. *The Great American Housewife: From Helpmate to Wage Earner, 1776-1986*. Westport, CT: Greenwood Press, 1986.

Papazian, Gretchen. "'Feed My Poor Famished Heart': Constructing Womanhood through Consumer Practices." *American Transcendental Quarterly* 21, 2 (June 2007): 127-45.

Park, Shelley M. "From Sanitation to Liberation? The Modern and Postmodern Marketing of Menstrual Products." *Journal of Popular Culture* 30, 2 (Fall 1996): 149-68.

Peacock, John. *20th Century Fashion: The Complete Sourcebook*. London: Thames and Hudson, 1993.

Pedelty, Mark. "The Bolero: The Birth, Life, and Decline of Mexican Modernity." *Latin American Music Review* 20 (Spring-Summer 1999): 30-58.

Peiss, Kathy. "American Women and the Making of Modern Consumer Culture." *Journal for MultiMedia History* 1, 1 (Fall 1998). http://www.albany/edu/.

–. *Cheap Amusements: Working Women and Leisure in Turn-of-the-Century New York*. Philadelphia: Temple University Press, 1986.

–. *Hope in a Jar: The Making of America's Beauty Culture*. New York: Henry Holt, 1998.

Pennington, Doris. *Agnes Macphail: Reformer: Canada's First Female MP*. Toronto: Simon and Pierre, 1989.

Penny, Tracy. "'Getting Rid of My Trouble': A Social History of Abortion in Ontario, 1880-1929." Master's thesis, Laurentian University, 1995.

Penny Light, Tracy. "Shifting Interests: The Medical Discourse on Abortion in English Canada, 1850-1969." PhD diss., University of Waterloo, 2003.

Petro, Patrice. *Joyless Streets: Women and Melodramatic Representation in Weimar Germany.* Princeton: Princeton University Press, 1989.

Phillips, Evelyn Newman. "Ms. Annie Malone's Poro: Addressing Whiteness and Dressing Black-Bodied Women." *Transforming Anthropology* 11, 2 (2004): 4-17.

Porter, Susie S. *Working Women in Mexico City: Public Discourses and Material Conditions, 1879-1931.* Tucson: University of Arizona Press, 2003.

Prentice, Alison, Paula Bourne, Gail Cuthbert Brandt, and Beth Light. *Canadian Women: A History.* 2nd ed. Toronto: Harcourt Brace Canada, 1996.

Pugh, M. *Women and the Women's Movement in Britain, 1914-1959.* Basingstoke: Macmillan Education, 1992.

Reagin, Nancy R. *Sweeping the German Nation: Domesticity and National Identity in Germany, 1870-1945.* Cambridge: Cambridge University Press, 2007.

Rooks, Noliwe M. *Hair Raising: Beauty, Culture, and African American Women.* New Brunswick, NJ: Rutgers University Press, 1996.

Rosenberg, Emily S. "Consuming Women: Images of Americanization in the 'American Century.'" *Diplomatic History* 23 (1999): 479-97.

Rosoff, Nancy G. "'Every Muscle Is Absolutely Free': Advertising and Advice about Clothing for Athletic American Women, 1880-1920." *Journal of American Culture* 25, 1-2 (March 2002): 25-31.

Ross, Steven J. *Working-Class Hollywood: Silent Film and the Shaping of Class in America.* Princeton: Princeton University Press, 1998.

Rubenstein, Anne. *Bad Language, Naked Ladies, and Other Threats to the Nation: A Political History of Comic Books in Mexico.* Durham, NC: Duke University Press, 1998.

–. "The War on *Las Pelonas*: Modern Women and Their Enemies, Mexico City, 1924." In *Sex in Revolution: Gender, Politics, and Power in Modern Mexico,* ed. Jocelyn Olcott, Mary Kay Vaughan, and Gabriela Cano, 57-80. Durham, NC: Duke University Press, 2006.

Rutherford, Janice Williams. *Selling Mrs. Consumer: Christine Frederick and the Rise of Household Efficiency.* Athens: University of Georgia Press, 2003.

Rutherford, Paul. "Made in America: The Problem of Mass Culture in Canada." In *The Beaver Bites Back: American Popular Culture in Canada,* ed. David H. Flaherty and Frank E. Manning, 260-80. Montreal and Kingston: McGill-Queen's University Press, 1993.

Schell, Patience A. *Church and State Education in Revolutionary Mexico City.* Tucson: University of Arizona Press, 2003.

Segrave, Kerry. *Suntanning in 20th Century America.* Jefferson, NC: McFarland, 2005.

Shortt, S.E.D. "Physicians, Science, and Status: Issues in the Professionalization of Anglo-American Medicine in the Nineteenth Century." *Medical History* 27 (1983): 51-68.

Sides, Josh. *L.A. City Limits: African American Los Angeles from the Great Depression to the Present.* Berkeley: University of California Press, 2003.

Sikes, Ruth G. "The History of Suntanning: A Love/Hate Affair." *Journal of Aesthetic Science* 1, 2 (May 1998): 1-7.

Skillen, Fiona. "'When Women Look Their Worst': Women and Sports Participation in Interwar Scotland." PhD diss., University of Glasgow, 2008.

Sluis, Ageeth. "City of Spectacles: Gender Performance, Revolutionary Reform, and the Creation of Public Space in Mexico City, 1915-1939." PhD diss., University of Arizona, 2006.

Smith, F.B. *The People's Health, 1830-1910.* London: Croom Helm, 1979.

Solande, B. *Becoming Modern: Young Women and the Reconstruction of Womanhood in the 1920s.* Princeton: Princeton University Press, 2000.

Srigley, Katrina. "Clothing Stories: Consumption, Identity, and Desire in Depression-Era Toronto." *Journal of Women's History* 19, 1 (2007): 82-104.

Stage, Sarah. *Female Complaints: Lydia Pinkham and the Business of Women's Medicine*. New York: W.W. Norton, 1979.

Stanley, Adam C. *Modernizing Tradition: Gender and Consumerism in Interwar France and Germany*. Baton Rouge: Louisiana State University Press, 2008.

Stark, Gary D. "All Quiet on the Home Front: Popular Entertainments, Censorship, and Civilian Morale in Germany, 1914-1918." In *Authority, Identity and the Social History of the Great War*, ed. Frans Coetzee and Marilyn Shevin-Coetzee, 57-80. Providence: Berghahn Books, 1995.

Starr, Kevin. *The Dream Endures: California Enters the 1940s*. New York: Oxford University Press, 1997.

Staudenmaier, John, and Pamela Walker Lurito Laird. "Advertising History." *Technology and Culture* 30, 4 (1989): 1031-36.

Steakley, James D. "Cinema and Censorship in the Weimar Republic: The Case of Anders als die Andern." *Film History* 11 (1999): 181-203.

Stephenson, H.E., and Carlton McNaught. *The Story of Advertising in Canada: A Chronicle of Fifty Years*. Toronto: Ryerson Press, 1950.

Stern, Alexandra Minna. "Responsible Mothers and Normal Children: Eugenics, Nationalism, and Welfare in Post-Revolutionary Mexico, 1920-1940." *Journal of Historical Sociology* 12 (December 1999): 369-97.

Stewart, Mary Lynn. *For Health and Beauty: Physical Culture for Frenchwomen, 1880s-1930s*. Baltimore: Johns Hopkins University Press, 2001.

Strange, Carolyn. *Toronto's Girl Problem: The Perils and Pleasures of the City, 1800-1930*. Toronto: University of Toronto Press, 1995.

Strong-Boag, Veronica. "Home Dreams: Women and the Suburban Experiment in Canada, 1945-1960." In *Rethinking Canada: The Promise of Women's History*, 3rd ed., ed. Veronica Strong-Boag and Anita Clair Fellman, 375-401. Toronto: Oxford University Press, 1997.

–. *The New Day Recalled: Lives of Girls and Women in English Canada, 1919-1939*. Toronto: Copp Clark Pitman, 1988 and 1993.

Theberge, Nancy. "A Content Analysis of Print Media Coverage of Gender, Women, and Physical Activity." *Journal of Applied Sport Psychology* 3 (1991): 36-48.

Thompson, John Herd, and Allen Seager. *Canada, 1922-1939: Decades of Discord*. Toronto: McClelland and Stewart, 1985.

Tinkler, Penny. *Constructing Girlhood: Popular Magazines for Girls Growing Up in England, 1920-1950*. London: Taylor and Francis, 1995.

–. "Red Tips for Hot Lips; Advertising Cigarettes for Young Women in Britain, 1920-1970." *Women's History Review* 10 (2001): 249-72.

–. "Refinement and Respectable Consumption: The Acceptable Face of Women's Smoking in Britain, 1918-1970." *Gender and History* 15 (2003): 342-60.

–. *Smoke Signals: Women, Smoking and Visual Culture in Britain*. Oxford: Berg, 2006.

Tinkler, Penny, and Cheryl Krasnick Warsh. "Feminine Modernity in Interwar Britain and North America: Corsets, Cars, and Cigarettes." *Journal of Women's History* 20, 3 (Fall 2008): 113-43.

Todd, S. *Young Women, Work and Family in England 1918-1950*. Oxford: Oxford University Press, 2005.

Tomes, Nancy. *The Gospel of Germs: Men, Women, and the Microbe in American Life*. Cambridge, MA: Harvard University Press, 1998.

–. "The Great American Medicine Show Revisited." *Bulletin of the History of Medicine* 79 (2005): 627-63.

–. "Merchants of Health: Medicine and Consumer Culture in the United States, 1900-1940." *Journal of American History* 88, 2 (September 2001): 519-47.

Tone, Andrea. "Contraceptive Consumers: Gender and the Political Economy of Birth Control in the 1930s." *Journal of Social History* 29, 3 (Spring 1996): 485-506.

Trentmann, Frank. "Citizenship and Consumption." *Journal of Consumer Culture* 7, 2 (2007): 147-58.

Tygiel, Jules. "Metropolis in the Making: Los Angeles in the 1920s." In *Metropolis in the Making: Los Angeles in the 1920s,* ed. Tom Sitton and William Deverell, 1-10. Berkeley: University of California Press, 2001.

Unruh, Vicky. *Performing Women and Modern Literary Culture in Latin America: Intervening Acts.* Austin: University of Texas Press, 2006.

Usborne, Cornelia. "The New Woman and Generation Conflict: Perceptions of Young Women's Sexual Mores in the Weimar Republic." In *Generations in Conflict: Youth Revolt and Generation Formation in Germany 1770-1968,* ed. Mark Roseman, 137-63. Cambridge: Cambridge University Press, 1995.

Valverde, Mariana. *The Age of Light, Soap and Water: Moral Reform in English Canada, 1885-1925.* Toronto: University of Toronto Press, 2008.

Velázquez, Marco, and Mary Kay Vaughan. "Mestizaje and Musical Nationalism in Mexico." In *The Eagle and the Virgin: Nation and Cultural Revolution in Mexico, 1920-1940,* ed. Mary Kay Vaughan and Steve Lewis, 95-118. Durham, NC: Duke University Press, 2006.

Vipond, Mary. "Canadian Nationalism and the Plight of Canadian Magazines in the 1920s." *Canadian Historical Review* 58 (1977): 43-65.

von Ankum, Katharina, ed. *Women in the Metropolis: Gender and Modernity in Weimar Culture.* Berkeley: University of California Press, 1997.

Walker, Susannah. *Style and Status: Selling Beauty to African American Women, 1920-1975.* Lexington: University Press of Kentucky, 2007.

Warsh, Cheryl Krasnick, ed. *Gender, Health and Popular Culture: Historical Perspectives.* Waterloo: Wilfrid Laurier University Press, 2011.

–. *Prescribed Norms: Women and Health in Canada and the United States since 1800.* Toronto: University of Toronto Press, 2010.

–. "Smoke and Mirrors: Gender Representation in North American Tobacco and Alcohol Advertisements before 1950." *Histoire sociale/Social History* 31, 62 (1998): 183-222.

–. "Vim, Vigour and Vitality: 'Power Foods' for Kids in Canadian Popular Magazines, 1914-1954." In *Edible Histories/Cultural Politics: Towards a Canadian Food History,* ed. Franca Iacovetta, Valerie J. Korinek, and Marlene Epp, 387-408. Toronto: University of Toronto Press, 2012.

Warsh, Cheryl Krasnick, and Penny Tinkler. "In Vogue: North American and British Representations of Women Smokers in *Vogue,* 1920s-1960s." *Canadian Bulletin of Medical History/Bulletin canadien d'histoire de la médecine* 24, 1 (2007): 9-47.

Watson, Linda. Vogue *Twentieth Century Fashion: 100 Years of Style by Decade and Designer.* London: Carlton Books, 1999.

Weinbaum, Alys Eve, Lynn M. Thomas, Priti Ramamurthy, Uta G. Poiger, Madeleine Yue Dong, and Tani E. Barlow, eds. *The Modern Girl around the World: Consumption, Modernity, and Globalization.* Durham, NC: Duke University Press, 2008.

Whitaker, Reginald. *The Government Party: Organizing and Financing the Liberal Party of Canada, 1930-58.* Toronto: University of Toronto Press, 1977.

Wilder, Joseph E. *Lotions, Potions, and Liniments Cure: A Look at the Drug Trade in Winnipeg in the 1900s.* Winnipeg: Prairie Publishing, 1992.

Williams, Jean. *A Rough Game for Girls: A History of Women's Football in Britain.* London: Routledge, 2003.

Wiltse, Jeff. "Contested Waters: A History of Swimming Pools in America." PhD diss., Brandeis University, 2003.

Woodhead, Lindy. *War Paint: Madame Helena Rubenstein and Miss Elizabeth Arden: Their Lives, Their Times, Their Rivalry.* Hoboken, NJ: John Wiley and Sons, 2003.

Wright, Cynthia. "Feminine Trifles of Vast Importance: Writing Gender into the History of Consumption." In *Gender Conflicts: New Essays in Women's History,* ed. Franca Iacovetta and Mariana Valverde, 229-60. Toronto: University of Toronto Press, 1992.

Young, James Harvey. *The Medical Messiahs: A Social History of Health Quackery in Twentieth-Century America.* Princeton: Princeton University Press, 1967.

–. *The Toadstool Millionaires: A Social History of Patent Medicines in America before Federal Regulation.* Princeton: Princeton University Press, 1961.

Zeitz, Joshua. *Flapper: A Madcap Story of Sex, Style, Celebrity, and the Women Who Made America Modern.* New York: Three Rivers Press/Crown, 2006.

Contributors

•
•
•

Devon Hansen Atchison is an associate professor of American history at Grossmont College, in El Cajon, California. Her research examines gender and the family in American history.

Denyse Baillargeon is a professor of history at the Université de Montréal. She is the author of *Ménagères au temps de la Crise* (1991), published in English as *Making Do: Women, Family and Home in Montréal during the Great Depression* (1999); Un Québec en mal d'enfants: La médicalisation de la maternité, 1910-1970 (2004), published in English as *Babies for the Nation: The Medicalization of Motherhood in Québec, 1910-1970* (2009); and *Naître, vivre, grandir: Sainte-Justine 1907-2007* (2007).

Donica Belisle is an assistant professor of women's and gender studies at Athabasca University. She is the author of several works in Canadian consumer history, including *Retail Nation: Department Stores and the Making of Modern Canada* (2011). She is currently writing the book *Contesting Consumption: Women and the Rise of Canadian Consumer Modernity* and developing a public history website about Canadian consumer society at www.consumingcanada.ca.

Susanne Eineigel received her PhD in history from the University of Maryland, College Park, in 2011. Her dissertation is entitled "Distinction, Culture, and Politics in Mexico City's Middle Class, 1890-1940." She has taught at Brooklyn College, Drew University, Montclair State University, and New York University.

Kristin Hall is a doctoral candidate in history at the University of Waterloo and a sessional instructor at Laurentian University. Her research examines Canadian gender, media, and business during the first half of the twentieth century.

Bettina Liverant is an adjunct assistant professor in history at the University of Calgary. She is completing a book entitled *Buying Happiness: The Complicated Emergence of Consumer Society in Canada, 1890-1960*. Her current research examines the development of corporate philanthropy in Canada.

Dan Malleck is an associate professor of community health sciences at Brock University and the editor-in-chief of *The Social History of Alcohol and Drugs: An Interdisciplinary Journal*. His research is on bureaucracy and government regulation, and his book on liquor control in Ontario, *Try to Control Yourself: Regulating Public Drinking in Post-Prohibition Ontario,* is forthcoming from UBC Press.

Marilyn Morgan is a manuscript processing archivist at the Schlesinger Library on the History of Women in America, and a lecturer in the Women, Gender, and Sexuality program at Harvard University. Her research explores women, gender, and popular culture, and she is completing a book entitled *Forming Figures: A Cultural History of the Swimsuit in America.*

Jane Nicholas is an associate professor of women's studies at Lakehead University. Her research focuses on feminine modernities, the modern body, and extraordinary bodies. With Patrizia Gentile, she is co-editing *Contesting Bodies and Nation in Canadian History* (forthcoming).

Tracy Penny Light is an associate professor in sexuality, marriage, and family studies at St. Jerome's University in Waterloo, Ontario. Her research examines gender, medicine, and consumer culture in Canada and the United States in the nineteenth and twentieth centuries.

De Anna J. Reese is an assistant professor of history and the Africana Studies Program at California State University, Fresno. She earned a PhD in US history from the University of Missouri-Columbia. Her current research explores the relationship between black beauty culture, black female entrepreneurship, and the career of African American beauty pioneer and philanthropist Annie Turnbo Malone.

Kara Ritzheimer is an assistant professor of modern European history at Oregon State University. Her current research examines gender, censorship, and commercial culture in Imperial and Weimar Germany. She is completing a book entitled *Battling Buffalo Bill: Regionalism, Gender, and Censorship in Early 20th-Century Germany.*

Fiona Skillen is a lecturer in the Glasgow School for Business and Society, Glasgow Caledonian University. She obtained her PhD from the University of Glasgow. Her research focuses on discourses concerning gender, modernity, and women's popular culture. Her work includes *Women, Sport and Modernity in Interwar Britain* (forthcoming).

Cecilia Tossounian is a post-doctoral fellow at the Institute for Latin American Studies, Free University of Berlin, researching gender, modernity, and national identity in interwar Argentina.

Cheryl Krasnick Warsh is a professor of history at Vancouver Island University, Nanaimo, British Columbia, and past editor-in-chief of *The Canadian Bulletin of Medical History.* Her books include *Moments of Unreason: The Practice of Canadian Psychiatry and the Homewood Retreat, 1883-1923* (1989), *Prescribed Norms: Women and Health in Canada and the United States since 1800* (2010), and *Gender, Health and Popular Culture: Historical Perspectives* (2011).

Index

• • •